Origin and Evolution of Languages

Origin and Evolution of Languages
Approaches, Models, Paradigms

Edited by Bernard Laks

With Serge Cleuziou, Jean-Paul Demoule and Pierre Encrevé

LONDON OAKVILLE

Published by
UK: Equinox Publishing Ltd., Unit 6, The Village, 101 Amies St., London SW11 2JW
USA: DBBC, 28 Main Street, Oakville, CT 06779
www.equinoxpub.com

First published 2008
Reprinted 2009

British Library Cataloguing-in-Publication Data
A catalogue record for this book is available from the British Library.

ISBN-13	9781845532048	(hardback)
	9781845535537	(paperback)

Library of Congress Cataloging-in-Publication Data

Origin and evolution of languages : approaches, models, paradigms / edited by Bernard Laks ... [et al.].
p. cm.
Includes bibliographical references and index.
ISBN-13: 978-1-84553-204-8 (hb)
1. Language and languages--Origin. 2. Genetics. I. Laks, Bernard.
P116.O74 2007
401--dc22
2007019382

Typeset by Catchline, Milton Keynes (www.catchline.com)
Printed and bound in Great Britain and the USA

Contents

1 Origins and evolution of languages: retrospectives and perspectives

Jean-Paul Demoule
University of Paris I

Bernard Laks
University of Paris X

Serge Cleuziou
University of Paris I

Pierre Encrevé
EHESS

1 Retrospectives and perspectives

The reappearance of modern research on the origins of languages and their evolution is a quite recent phenomenon in the history of contemporary science. One could situate its origins in the typological work of Greenberg and its continuation in that of Ruhlen (Greenberg 1963, 1966, 1971, 1986, 2002; Greenberg & Ruhlen 1992), as well as in the intersection of these linguistic taxonomies with the work on genetic classifications and population genetics initiated at the beginning of the 20th century by Dobzhansky (1937), and more recently by Cavalli-Sforza et al. (1992, 1994). This is quite clearly a revival, because it is known that this research framework was dominant throughout the 19th century, and offered to the *Jungrammatikers* their most solid scientific results. At the end of the 19th century, Historical and Comparative Grammar — and more generally, diachronic linguistics — were nevertheless destined to crumble rapidly into ruins as dominant scientific paradigms, under the combined blows of internal criticisms and emerging synchronic structuralist tendencies, that proposed to surpass their principal internal contradictions.

It is thus significant that the reappearance of this research framework took place at the very end of the 20th century, on epistemological grounds that were really not very different (population genetics and rather classical linguistic Darwinism), but without any critical appraisal (either positive or negative) being proposed for what had been one of the major intellectual enterprises of the preceding century, and which remains, given its main results, at the heart of our understanding of linguistic dynamics. This comes down to underlining the methodological and conceptual immaturity of this new anthropo-linguistic paradigm, that willingly sees itself as marked by the pure outburst of an interdisciplinary line of questioning, and which aims to be 'with neither bonds nor roots', in the manner of the uniquely speculative intellectuals criticised by Mannheim (1929).

One can find one of the signs of this methodological and historical weakness in the ritual that consists in beginning any recent publication devoted to the origin of languages with a reminder of the famous prohibition of debating this question that appeared in the initial statutes of the *Société de Linguistique de Paris* in 1864. Little does it appear to matter that much research in the history and philosophy of language sciences might have shown for a long time what was at stake during this period, on political and ideological levels, in learned societies that were in competition with each other (Bergounioux 1994, 1996, 2002). The ritual remains, like a painful staging of this new interdisciplinary research current. Nevertheless, this famous prohibition, far from being an obscurantist obstacle to the free exercise of scientific thinking, as is often understood today, was in fact directed against the creationist movement of thought, which, in catholic movements, subscribed to a divine origin of language. Being an essentially politically motivated prohibition, it was repealed. And although the question of the origin of languages was in fact little discussed during the meetings and publications of the honourable Society, this is undoubtedly because there were other reasons for it. Historical and Comparative Grammar, being originally a German science, was little by little gaining ground in France. Comparativism fashioned itself within a rigorous linguistic methodology that considered as pure speculation any attempt to go beyond the historical horizon of written attestations, in other words, further back than the barrier of –5,000 years B.C. In his preface of his translation of Bopp (1889), Michel Bréal thus fustigated these useless speculations on the origin of languages and of language, as having neither method nor basis in fact, opposing them to the rigour of the German savant. Soon after, Saussure (1916, 1995) took over from him, and the primacy of the synchronic over the diachronic reigned henceforth for a long time over the young science of linguistics, that would also have, from 1922 onwards, its own international association for which the origin of language was no longer a well-formed scientific question[1]. Nevertheless, one can not deny that in general, the question of origins was one of the grand questions of the 19th century, and so it is important, in order to shed light on its reappearance in the contemporary intellectual arena, to bring to light its phylum.

2 The fascination of origins: the great foundation stories

Up to the fringe of the following century, all of the 19th century was that of the fascination with origins and of the fabrication of the great foundation stories. Whilst the discoveries of prehistory, palæontology, ethnology, and also of the emerging sciences of psychology and biology grew little by little, and whilst on the other hand, the literal interpretation of the Bible lost progressively its authority, the question of the origins of Man established itself firmly on the intellectual scene. Thus, finding his inspiration in the *Lumières* and the speculations of Rousseau (1755) or Condorcet (1793) on the origin of societies, or indeed of languages, Morgan assembled from 1877 onwards the testimonies of explorers, soldiers and missionaries on hundreds of so-called 'savage' societies, constructing the first classification of kinship systems, and thus founding ethnological evolutionism. Marx and Engels were directly inspired by this (Engels 1884). The rapid progress of prehistorical studies enabled Lubbock, being close to Darwin, to establish a quite general description (Lubbock 1871), whereas Tylor published his vast panorama on the history of humanity and of primitive cultures (Tylor 1865, 1871). With the new century, speculative evolutionism developed strongly, being marked by the important work of Westermarck (1906) or that of Atkinson (Lang & Atkinson 1903), that inspired Freud directly once he took on the task of elaborating his own story of foundations (Freud 1913, 1939)[2]. Thus, against the background of a powerful fascination for the question of origins, all the 19th century and the beginning of the 20th century could not avoid being influenced by the stories of origins that were successively proposed. It is not at all neutral to underline the fact that contemporary human and social sciences found their original inspirations and origins in this background. In the final analysis, it is Darwin (cf. in particular, Darwin 1859, 1871) and Darwinism that structured this powerful field of thought and which constituted its fundamental paradigm[3].

At the same time, the Historical and Comparative Grammar of indo-European languages continued to elaborate its rigorous methods that would culminate with the neo-Grammarian school of the *Jungrammatikers* and their concept of phonetic laws[4]. This approach again rejected (and in an explicit way) any speculation on the possible historical reality of what was then being attempted to be reconstructed as proto-indo-European. As Meillet (1926) forcefully insisted, within a structuralist logic, proto-indo-European is nothing other than a 'system of correspondences'[5]. The question of the origins and of the historical incarnation of these languages was nevertheless long lasting, notably in the work of Rask, the co-founder, with Bopp, of Historical and Comparative Grammar. Inspiring himself from botany and the work of Linnaeus, he proposed a classification of languages that raised the question of the coincidence between races and languages. A deep convergence between a theory of races, and then of racism, and linguistics thus came to be born and was unfolded up to Nazism and the Second World War[6]. Following Rask, the enterprise of naturalisation of linguistic taxonomies was taken up by Schleicher who, being himself a botanist, finally formalised the *Stammbaum* and interpreted the simple 'system of correspondences' as henceforth a purely genealogical tree, in the way in which Darwin transformed, at the same period, the simple botanical and zoological tree of Linnaeus into a genealogical taxonomy that allowed time and genetic drift to be theorised. In these approaches, historical time was from then onwards conceived as genealogical time, and socio-cultural dynamics disappeared from the scientific horizon, concealed by the transmission of genes, lineages, blood relations and ethnic identities.

The enterprise of the naturalisation of languages, and thus of linguistics, as it had been opened up by Romanticism, thus found its culmination. The theoretician of the *Stammbaum* (Schleicher 1861), who proclaimed that he had been Darwinian well before Darwin, was particularly explicit with respect to what was at stake in this naturalisation of linguistics. In his open letter to Ernst Häckel, a zoologist who had introduced and diffused Darwin in Germany, he wrote the following: 'Languages are natural organisms that appear without having been determined by human will, grow and develop according to precise laws, then grow old and die; for them also applies that series of manifestations that one usually comprehends under the name of 'life'. Glottism, as a language science, is thus a natural science; its method is globally and generally that of the other natural sciences' (Schleicher 1863, 7).

In passing from taxonomy to genealogy, of languages and of races, this naturalisation of linguistics necessarily had to pass via archæology and its reconstructions, once they themselves had been conceived of in a realist framework. We shall consider the single example of the famous dictionary of indo-European antiquities, in which Otto Schrader, in his capacity as a linguist, takes pains to state with precision that the notion of indo-European (e.g. 'Indo-Germanisch') is in itself 'a notion that is above all linguistic', but continues his text by a detailed reconstruction of the material and spiritual civilisation of primitive Indo-Europeans (Schrader 1901). He already situates its original birthplace in the pontic steppes[7].

There is thus a paradox in 19th century linguistics. The question of origins, as it was theoretically and methodologically deconstructed, was rejected within it, or was at least pushed beyond the field of science by the most rigorous comparativists. Nevertheless, Darwinian naturalism and the ensemble of metaphors to which it gave rise never ceased to return. In the heritage of Romanticism, a kind of spontaneous realism, basing itself on an ideology of scientific genetics, never ceased to theorise, throughout the 19th century, peoples and languages, race and dialect, biological inheritance and linguistic heritage, history and blood. That century was thus that of the construction of the grand stories of origins, that were unceasingly reactivated — even though the question was excluded from science — that of the obsessive question of origins.

3 Races and languages

The year 1859, when Charles Darwin published his *Origin of Species* was also that of the foundation of the *Société d'Anthropologie de Paris*. Created by Paul Broca, it assembled numerous positivist doctors, and was concerned — in its meetings as well as in its bulletin — with questions of physical anthropology, ethnology and prehistory. These three disciplines would only become genuinely autonomous at the end of the 19th century[8], and their conflation or confusion can be seen in all the learned societies in Europe during this period. As was defined in its statutes, the central question with which this society was concerned was therefore 'the scientific study of human races'. Such an object of study logically implied that of the origin and the mode of diffusion of languages, especially Indo-European ones. Two tendencies were opposed to one another. The French tendency, lead by Broca himself, was hostile to the thesis defended by certain German savants of that period. It fought against the primary idea of an Indo-European invasion by a blond dolichocephal 'race'. For French savants, the original French were manifestly brachycephal and dark haired. They were supposed to have been speakers of a variety of original Indo-European or else would have adopted this language by diffusion during contact with diverse peoples. In order to study human races scientifically and to establish a taxonomy of them, during this period anthropology disposed of a measuring instrument and a classificatory theory: craniology.

The second half of the 19th century was in effect the Golden Age of this science of skulls, which founded a science of races[9]. Since the Enlightenment, the question of races had imposed itself. Taking up the method of Linneaus, in his doctoral thesis of 1775, Blumenbach proposed a first classification of races that was to become world famous (Blumenbach 1781). Petrus Camper completed this with a 'facial index' that has also remained famous (cf. Meijer 1999). In 1842, Anders Retzius added a 'cephalic index' that led to opposing brachy- and dolicho-cephales[10], that has remained for posterity. Thus, throughout the 19th century, craniology never ceased to gain in complexity, and the number of races never ceased to diversify, up to the extensive classifications of Ripley (1899) or Deniker (1900)[11].

Nevertheless, as an anticlerical reaction, and against the biblical story of origins, the freethinking doctors of this period, who constituted the principal troops of physical anthropology, still defended the polygenesis of human races, which implied the polygenesis of languages. This virulent opposition to Catholicism was also expressed, as we have already said, by the famous interdiction of the *Société Linguistique de Paris*.

It is in the context of this ideological cleavage that the Italian linguist Alfredo Trombetti undertook the task of making races and languages coincide on the basis of a monogenetic model (Trombetti 1905). This time, he situated the origin of the totality of humanity in the Himalayas and, with the aid of coloured maps, retraced the set of human migrations that would have allowed the simultaneous dispersion of languages and races across the whole of the planet. Despite the considerable scale of the information brought into play, Trombetti's synthesis, that combined the grand evolutionist stories, hypotheses concerning the origins of languages and craniometrics, received little echo. From this period onwards, each of these scientific perspectives would in effect come to know the beginnings of the sterility that would ultimately lead to their being abandoned.

This was how it turned out for craniometrics, which, by dint of multiplying indices and classes, saw its very object of study disintegrate. In proposing up to 5,000 different measures on a single skull, the notion of type passed into oblivion. The more the number of measures augmented, the more the racial typology tottered. Boas had already shown that the shape of skulls was not stable from generation to generation, and that with the help of alimentary practices, one could go from one craniological type to another (cf. note 10, *supra*). At the beginning of the 20th century, craniology and racial linguistics were severely losing ground, at first in the English-speaking world, and then in Germany, where Felix von Luschan[12], for example, definitively decided the issue in stating that 'All the attempts to cut up humanity into artificial groups by basing oneself on skin colour, the length or breadth of the skull or the hair type, etc., are totally misguided' (Luschan 1922). For all that, craniometry did not completely disappear. Although marginalised, it survived, for example, in France in the work of Henri Vallois and his students, up to the 1970s[13]. But it was no longer the scientific theory and taxonomical method that it had been in the 19th century. For the great liberal savants that were Broca in France or Virchow in Germany, it was the scientific weapon for fighting against clerical obscurantism. From the end of the 19th century and onwards, it marginalised itself in becoming one of the main arguments of the principal racist and anti-Semitic ideologies that flourished in the compost of nationalism. Its having been recycled by Nazism ended up in its becoming discredited, along with all supposedly scientific racially oriented work.

4 From diachrony to synchrony

The turn of the 20th century was marked by a fundamental rupture: the evolutionary models and historical dynamics that had been comprehended as explanatory frameworks effaced themselves in favour of a synthetic and synchronic vision. The notion of a structured and organised system, whose fertility had been illustrated by Mendeleyev, in his periodic table of elements in 1869 (cf. Kolodkine 1963), proposed a new paradigm that was applied in all knowledge domains. This manner of thinking of 'the totality seen in synchrony' gave rise to the concept of structure, which Sériot (1999) has shown to be at the heart of *avant-garde* thinking, in its Russian variant in particular. The rupture that took place in favour of synchronic description and analysis brought the notions of system and structural cohesion to the fore. Human sciences in general, and social sciences in particular, found the explanatory model that they required in order to replace that of historical causality, in the concept of a system conceived as a 'structured structure predisposed to function as a structuring structure' (to paraphrase Bourdieu 1972). In such an updating of social sciences as sciences of systems and of structures, in this reconstruction of humanities in a structuralist framework, linguistics played a central role.

It is well known that Saussure attributed the reorientation from which modern linguistics has issued to Whitney. In strongly insisting on the fact that language is a social institution, Whitney (1867) firmly linked the analysis of languages to that of social and cultural systems. The Saussurian conceptions of the social contract and of semiolinguistic consensus thus directly echoes Durkheimian sociology; and his definition of the New Linguistics as 'the science that studies the life of signs within social life' (Saussure 1922: 34) reconnects the science of language definitively to anthropological and social sciences.

This abandonment of the evolutionist and historical paradigm was made possible by the new explanatory value that systemics took on from there on, once it had leant itself on the notion of structure. From the beginning of his research, Saussure (1878) had illustrated the explanatory and even heuristic value of the notion of a system and of abstract relational structure with exceptional *brio*. It is known that structuralism, at first phonological and then linguistic, sprang precisely from a *post mortem* reading of this work and the vulgate of it that Saussure's students gave in 1916. In the 1920s and 1930s, the Prague Linguistic Circle was thus to contribute to the construction and diffusion of a structuralist way of thinking that little by little gained ground in all of the social sciences. The numerous intellectual relations that Jakobson maintained with young thinkers from almost all areas of human sciences constituted their crucible; and the linguists' synchronic approach spread out little by little to other sciences. Thus, ethnologists and anthropologists abandoned the grand evolutionary frescos, written on the basis of written first hand accounts, to the profit of precise descriptions produced on the basis of fieldwork (cf. for example Boas & Stocking 1974; Haddon & Hingston 1934; Radcliffe-Brown 1958). And it was henceforth on the basis of concrete functional descriptions that models were elaborated[14]. In the years just after the war, it was finally Lévi-Strauss who marked with *éclat* the advent of anthropological structuralism (Lévi-Strauss 1947), whilst at the same time signifying that the initial linguistic structuralist paradigm had quite well become the explanatory protocol of the whole intellectual movement, and having organised international research in human sciences from 1950 to 1970 at least[15].

The Saussurian rupture, from which structuralism, and along with it, modern linguistics are descended, is therefore a rupture with a whole way of thinking that was preoccupied with evolution and lineage. Saussure explicitly broke with a particular form of linguistic Darwinism, illustrated by the organicism of Schleicher[16]. He replies to him indirectly in his notes: 'No, language is not an organism, it is not a type of vegetation that exists independently of Man, it does not have its own life implying a birth and a death. Everything is false in the sentence that I have read; language is not an organised being, it does not die in virtue of itself, it does not wither from itself, it does not grow, in the sense that it has no more a childhood than a mature age or an old age, and finally it is not born. […] Never on the whole globe has the birth of a new language been announced. […]. One might say that denying in this sense that no language has been born is just playing with words, and that it suffices to define what one means by birth in order to no longer deny the birth or the progressive development of languages like German or French. I reply that in that case, one is playing on the meaning of another word, that of *language*; in reality, language is not a being that is defined and delimited in time; one can distinguish the French language and the language of Latin, modern German and the German of Arminius […]. All these languages that are being spoken during the same period have the same age; in the sense that they go back to an equal past. […], if one likes, to the origin of language.' (Saussure 2001: 120–121). Certainly, the Saussurian rupture and structuralism did not carry everything away with them, and comparative grammar subsisted, although emptied of theoretical substance and substantial models. It thus became practically intellectually invisible, and one forgot who knows how much, for example, that Meillet was the originator, at the end of the 1930s, of the nostratic hypothesis that would be seen to rise up again with *éclat* around thirty years later[17].

5 Prehistory and migrations

At the beginning of the 20th century, prehistorical archæology followed a direction comparable to that of linguistics and social sciences. The second half of the 19th century was, with the discoveries of Boucher de Perthes (1860), the period during which the major periodisations and grand civilisations were established. These definite frameworks, together with methods for archæological excavations and analyses, were refined. Prehistorians, having positivistic and naturalistic training, took care of interpreting concrete findings. Whilst the question of Indo-European origins had occupied many meetings of the *Société d'Anthropologie de Paris*, the new *Société Préhistorique Française* devoted none to this question. In his preface, Déchelette (1910), who proposed one of the first world syntheses, thus contented himself with dismissing in a footnote 'the Aryan controversy, being essentially a linguistic problem and of which the solution appears to have been somewhat obscured rather than enlightened by the competition between anthropology and archæology. Given that the unity of language does not necessarily imply a community of origins, the peoples of the Aryan language could have belonged to diverse races. [...] This problem occupies one of those crossroads of sciences that, at the present day, easily become crossroads of errors'. Whilst Childe, undoubtedly the most prominent archæologist of the first half of the 20th century, devoted his first book to this problem (Childe 1926), he was soon to regret it, and confessed with a certain panache in his intellectual testament, published in 1958: 'This was childish, not Childeish'.

At the beginning of the 20th century, Germany remained the only country where prehistorical archæology maintained open the question of Indo-European origins. Gustav Kossinna, a professor of prehistory at the University of Berlin, defended the view that Indo-Europeans (e.g. Indo-Germans) had appeared in Scandinavia during recent millennia and from there, had spread themselves out through all Europe and part of Asia in fourteen successive warrior raids. He also defended the view, in a formula amongst the most famous of the history of archæology, that 'cultural provinces that are sharply defined in archæological terms coincide at all epochs with quite precise peoples or tribes'. Finally, he asserted that there was after all correspondence between original Indo-Europeans and a blond race of dolichocephals. This race was said to have been progressively debased in contact with conquered meridional and oriental populations. This correlation between archæological culture (defined as material civilisation), people and race clearly reposed on a biological model. It was also allowed by the concept of the Nation-State that, since the French Revolution and romanticisms, had little by little imposed itself as the only veritable subject of history.

Kossinna was certainly not a marginal archæologist, and Déchelette, as well as Childe, paid homage to his scientific competence, including with respect to the Indo-European question, without nevertheless agreeing with his conclusions. Having died in 1931, he had not been directly compromised with the Nazi regime, which was not the case with certain of his students. But one can consider that he was *de facto* one of its theoreticians. It is this heavy historical responsibility that led to his elimination from the academic history of archæology, at the time when the scientific legitimacy of his hypotheses definitively foundered. This is also what cast suspicion on migrationist or diffusionist theories, particularly in Anglo-Saxon countries. During a major part of the second half of the 20th century, from an archæological point of view, the Indo-European question was thus strongly marginalised. On the other hand, the archæological data that continued to accumulate formally contradicted the idea of a Scandinavian homeland, since no migratory movement from this region had been attested during pre- and proto-historic periods.

Given that the Soviet Union and countries within its orbit felt less ideologically guilty, research on migrations and ethnogenesis continued in this part of the world after the Second World War. A powerful driving force for such research was provided by theories that fixed the possible origins of primitive Indo-Europeans in the Russo-Ukranian pontic steppes (Schrader 1886, 1901). At the moment where Indo-European studies found an echo, Gimbutas (1991, 1992) reformulated this hypothesis under the name of the Kurgan Theory[18].

6 Towards a new synthesis

From the 1980s onwards, the situation of research concerning the origin of Man and of languages witnessed a considerable renewal. The famous question that had been ostracised by the *Société Linguistique de Paris* seemed to be again at the order of the day. In fact, the contemporary scientific horizon has been considerably enlarged. A harvest of new data, the appearance of much more precise and rigorous techniques and methods, and new theoretical interdisciplinary cross-fertilisations have produced an original way of conceiving of the problem that arrogates the label 'the New Synthesis'. It would be out of the question here to analyse all the data, the methods or the interdisciplinary links that have accompanied the emergence of what presents itself immediately as a unifying paradigm allowing a radically new way of thought concerning the question of origins. We shall only point out some of the most salient data.

From the 1950s onwards, our knowledge of human antiquity has considerably increased. In Europe and in Asia, but above all in Africa, a very large number of discoveries have shed light on this period. In particular, they allow a much more detailed description of the genealogical tree of humanity, and the possibility of tracing part of its most ancient migrations. This new data has nevertheless not allowed the debate concerning the emergence of modern Man (*Homo sapiens sapiens*) to be settled. The dominant monolocalist model still defends the hypothesis of an unique African appearance. It thus continues to oppose a multi-regional model that admits, at each stage, local crossings between the new form *sapiens sapiens* and regional evolution of the previously present form, *Homo erectus*.

Palæontological discoveries have also shed light on the morphology of ancient humans. Cranial anatomy has notably allowed hypotheses to be advanced concerning their cognitive capacities and their possible aptitude for articulated language. Even if this palæo-anatomic approach is not without relation to the old craniology and phrenology[19], it has been considerably rejuvenated by state-of-the-art techniques in cerebral imagery and by reconstruction by calculation of forms. Finally, for certain ore deposits that are unfortunately still too rare, the possibility of extracting and studying fossil ADN has considerably enriched the genealogical debate, notably concerning the relations between, *sapiens sapiens* and *sapiens neanderthalensis*.

More recently, research on the ADN of present day populations, and the analysis of the human genome, has opened up a new approach. The revival of interest in the genetic drift model, proposed from the 1930s onwards (Dobzhansky 1937), and the recent bringing to light of new markers, have allowed ancient mutations to be dated. The automatic classification of sampled populations in a genetic tree and the cartographic projection of certain markers have thus induced a spectacular development in population genetics (Cavalli-Sforza et al. 1994). This new disciplinary field, that sometimes receives a high degree of media coverage[20], has opened new avenues to reflexion. Its reliability, being assumed to be stronger than the random collection of real yet rare and fragmented fossil bones, is not for nothing in its international success. The impossibility of producing watertight human classes and the reassertion of the unity of Man in his African origin, popularised by population genetics, has continued to make regress the purportedly scientific racism inherited from the 19th century, and has contributed to the marginalisation of classical physical anthropology. Today, the debate no longer occurs on the basis of visible physical traits, but rather on genes and genetic heritage, which nevertheless leaves open questions concerning the geographical distribution and the historical interpretation of these traits.

In addition to palæontological discoveries, prehistorical and protohistorical research has also strongly progressed in the recent period. Several thousand archæological excavations have been opened up throughout the whole world. They have led to refining our understanding of the evolution of human cultures, migrations and major (pre)historical ruptures (Neolithic, urban revolutions, etc.), just as much as that of the invention and diffusion of techniques. Nonetheless, on the matter of primitive Indo-Europeans, this important progress has not led to the emergence of even a minimal consensus on the choice between the localist Kurgan hypothesis and that of Neolithic colonisation. At the very least, the migrations linked to the diffusion of agriculture are better and better understood and documented, even if the respective contributions of indigenous populations of hunter-gatherers and colonising farmers are still a subject of debate. This is the case with the populating of Europe; and also with Japan, where the role of a massive migration in the establishment and development of the wet culture of rice (e.g. the Yayoi culture) is currently being strongly re-evaluated. In total, the number of known and recorded societies is said to be estimated at 10,000 in number, and that of documented languages at 6,000. The rapid disappearance of these cultures and languages, at the rhythm of several hundreds per year, dramatically marks the contemporary ethnological and ethnolinguistic situation[21].

Finally, the contemporary scientific situation of approaches to studying the origins of Man and of languages is profoundly marked by the evolution of information processing and modelling techniques, as well as by the evolution of computational techniques of representation and simulation. Complex models, such as those of cladistics or simulations involving a very large number of parameters, can now be mastered, thanks to the evolution of computational techniques. Illustrations of these modelling approaches can be found in the present volume.

7 The new paradigms

In the human and social sciences that had been so profoundly marked by the structuralist perspective, the end of the 20th and the beginning of the 21st centuries are marked by deep paradigmatic re-orientations. The language sciences, that had carried and given shape to the structuralist paradigm, almost totally abandoned it. From the 1970s onwards, language sciences were positioned at the avant-garde of the movement towards the cognitive sciences that would lastingly mark the period (Gardner 1985). Generative Grammar, as well as its mutually antagonistic offshoots, reoriented itself in giving precedence to the analysis of the faculty of language as well as that of the cognitive preconditions for spontaneous learning of natural languages (Chomsky 1968). This return to a Cartesian form of linguistics (Chomsky 1966), integrated with a theory of mind (Fodor 1975), is marked by a type of cognitive universalism. In effect, Generative Grammar aims to bring to light the general cognitive mechanisms underlying the language faculty that is specific to the human species. It postulates that these cognitive mechanisms, just as with the necessary preconditions for language learning, are genetically encoded and are part of the human genome. In proposing to characterise the Universal Grammar conceived explicitly as the set of cognitive, formal and substantial functionalities underlying the set of human languages, Generative Grammar confers upon itself a clearly universalist and mentalist research programme (Chomsky 1995). Moreover, whatever may be the divergences of viewpoints and the bitterness of debates concerning the modularity of the human mind, and the strict separation of cognitive linguistic modules postulated by the Chomskyan Generative Grammar[22], this cognitive turn in language sciences is very widely shared. The recent debate between classical symbolic and dynamic sub-symbolic connexionist approaches (Laks 1996) does not lead to a modification of this diagnostic.

The cognitivism and universalism shared by the most recent linguistic theories induces a renewal of certain comparative and contrastive studies. In effect, it is by comparing the structures and functionalities of very diverse languages that one can bring out linguistic universals, whose cognitive and mental foundations one can possibly subsequently question. In this contrastive perspective, linguistic typology and the construction of vast taxonomies have witnessed a spectacular restart, principally initiated by the work of Greenberg (1963). These taxonomies have quickly encountered linguistic genealogy. The reconstruction of vast families of historically related languages has thus been rendered more dynamic by this encounter (Greenberg 1971, 1987, 2002), offering in return a new framework for research on the diversity of languages, linguistic universals and typology (Comrie 1981; Comrie et al. 2003). This work on genealogies has certainly found an interdisciplinary echo, and it is from its intersection with population genetics (Cavalli-Sforza et al. 1994) that the question of the origin and the evolution of languages has found itself renewed, paving the way for the New Synthesis (Cavalli-Sforza 2000)[23]. The same is the case with the Indo-European question, that has for a long time been left fallow, and which has also been taken up again in the framework of the genealogical reconstruction of super-families of languages (Greenberg 2002).

Whilst most work on taxonomies in linguistic genealogy has spontaneously taken up Schleicher's *Stammbaum* model, doubts have recently been raised concerning the imperviousness of the families postulated and the rigidity of hierarchies and filiations that the tree-like model proposes. In effect, independently of taxonomical and genealogical work, 20th century linguistics has paid a great deal of attention to relations between languages, cultures and societies. Having stemmed from dialectology, sociolinguistics has put the question of linguistic change at the heart of its investigations (Labov 1994, 2001), which appears to be intimately linked to that of variation, structural heterogeneity of linguistic mechanisms (Labov 1972) and the relation between linguistic and social differentiation (Laks 1983). The analysis of the contacts between languages (Weinreich 1953) as with that of the emergence of pidgins and creoles (Mufwene 2001) delivers numerous results which all lead to raising doubts concerning the category of a stable, homogenous and invariant language on which the construction of the *Stammbaum* reposes. As Schuchardt had already intuited in the 19th century (Schuchardt 1922, 1979), languages do not appear as separated by barriers of species — which does not invalidate the importation of the Darwinian zoological model — but are to the contrary, objects of mixtures, hybridisations, overlaps, partial importations, reciprocal influences, ecologically conditioned mutations, and continuous and gradual changes. In opposition to the genealogies of the *Stammbaum*, much more complex, dynamic and plastic models appear, that are directly inspired from botany and the ecology of living systems. Backed up by powerful mathematical models, cladistics thus tends to noticeably modify the contemporary genealogical and taxonomical landscape (Nakleh et al. 2005).

In the most recent period, one can also note a parallel evolution in the ensemble of social sciences, where the abandonment of structuralism and the 'cognitive turn' open up in the same way to modelling of anthropological complexity that very carefully takes account of cultural and social dynamics. In contact with prehistoric archæology, ethnology and social anthropology have returned to a type of evolutionism that was for a long time discredited (Sahlins et al. 1960). The progressive change towards more and more complexity and inequality in social organisations (Service 1971b) has thus been rethought out in the framework of a type of cultural evolutionism (Service 1971b). Questions of kinship, gifts, the division of labour and more generally of social complexity have also recently been renewed by an interdisciplinary cross-fertilisation of ethnology, prehistorical archæology, ethology and cognitive science (Godelier 1986, 1999; Testart 1982). In these disciplinary fields, the cognitive turn and the new interdisciplinarities that it has permitted between cultural sciences, behavioural sciences, social sciences and neurosciences has reactivated questions linked to the origin of Man. Even if the precise question of the origin of cognitive and linguistic capacities that are specific to the species continues to oppose Cartesians who defend a fundamental rupture in continuity of a catastrophic kind, and constructivists who defend phylogenetic continuity (Piaget et al. 1980), the great stories of origins are again at the order of the day. The concept of 'exaptation' (Gould & Vrba 1982), for example, thus allows the cognitive specificities of *sapiens sapiens* to be rethought in a Darwinian evolutionist framework (Gould 2002), whereas the intersection of primatology, ethology, ethnology, sociology and neurosciences allows Dunbar to formulate a new evolutive scenario (Dunbar 1997)[24]. Even more recently, the analysis of the human genome and of certain cognitive and linguistic pathologies linked to a deficiency in the foxp2 gene, have led anthropologists to see in the mutation that introduced the modern form of this gene in the heritage of *sapiens sapiens*, the moment of the initial genetic rupture that conditioned the appearance of this species (Klein & Blake 2002).

8 Origins and evolution of languages: retrospectives and perspectives

It is therefore in the context of a profoundly renewed debate concerning the origin and the evolution of languages that the present work has been conceived[25]. Contrary to many publications in the domain that present and defend a single school of thought, or even a single hypothesis, we have attempted to echo the sometimes lively debates and confrontations that structure our field of research. One will thus find herein presentations and defenses of contradictory hypotheses, polemical arguments or incompatible proposals. In a field that is marked by a strong interdisciplinarity, where researchers are thus inclined to take results that are not within their fields of competence as unquestionable givens, and with respect to which they do not master the critical counterarguments, it has seemed particularly important to us to restore the methodological and theoretical oppositions that are internal to each discipline. As all researchers know for their own disciplines, these internal discussions often lead to relativising results that may be presented to the exterior as being beyond doubt. Such a presentation from a critical perspective has seemed to us to constitute one of the major epistemological conditions for the maturation of the field of research with which we are concerned.

Thus, Merritt Ruhlen presents here arguments and methods of reconstitution of an original proto-language, as well as the results he has obtained, whereas Lyle Campbell proposes to demonstrate the numerous methodological and conceptual weaknesses that burden this research perspective. On another plane, Domenico Parisi and his colleagues present a simple tree-like organisation of the diffusion of Indo-European languages in Europe, whereas Don Ringe and Tandy Warnow argue for much more complex models of the evolution of languages in a network. Even further, Luigi Lucas Cavalli-Sforza presents here the main results of the crossing between the classification of languages and the classification of genes, as seen by the New Synthesis, whereas Bernard Comrie points out that recently, two different teams of geneticians have produced diametrically opposed results with respect to the respective parts of the indigenous Palæolithic population and Neolithic Asian colonisers in the populating of Europe.

The second condition for the maturation of the field of research concerning the origin and the evolution of languages bears on the history and the epistemology of these research approaches. As we have attempted to show in this presentation, these questions, however new and renewed they may appear to be, are historically constituted and have given rise to numerous hypotheses and to a large amount of research that are often forgotten today. Certainly, the new actuality of these research approaches owes much to the recent availability of sophisticated techniques and interdisciplinary cross-fertilisations that would previously have been impossible or unrealistic; but one should not forget the considerable mass of studies to which they have given rise. In effect, the history and the epistemology of these research approaches sheds light on the ideological, political and conceptual horizon against which they are unfolded, *nolens volens*. The very high degree of stability, over two centuries of research and polemical debates, of certain fundamental hypotheses and cardinal theoretical choices brings to light perfectly this ideological dimension and its political background. Being convinced that the history and philosophy of a science form integral parts of it, and constitute one of its major conditions for development as a science[26], we have thus also integrated in this volume certain retrospective or critical epistemological contributions.

This volume is organised in two distinct parts. Even if this distinction is sometimes arbitrary, as one may be convinced by reading the different chapters, we have nevertheless grouped them together into two sections. The first part deals with approaches that we are concerned with from an *ab origine* point of view. The second part adopts a *post originem* point of view. This distinction has no utility other than that of organising a debate that, whatever may be the logical or conceptual anteriority with which one approaches it, always bears simultaneously on both aspects. The origin of languages sheds light on their evolution and *vice versa*. Nevertheless, from an argumentative point of view, each author deals with these questions from one or other point of view. This is why we have chosen to group together the chapters in this volume in two large sections.

Luigi Lucas Cavalli-Sforza opens the first part with a presentation of the most important results of the New Synthesis. According to the localist hypothesis, modern humans are the descendants of a small group of individuals, undoubtedly a single tribe, whose presence is located in East Africa around 50,000 years ago. It is the considerable demographic expansion of this group, without doubt linked to a determining selective advantage, the mastery of articulated language, that led to the peopling of the whole of the planet by the descendents of this group, around 15,000 years ago. According to this hypothesis, the original group of *sapiens sapiens* possessed an unique language, from which derived all the languages spoken by the first human peopling and, by extension, all modern languages. The genetics of current populations and the large amount of information that we dispose of concerning the geographical and ethnic distribution of genes, as well as the cartography of different genetic markers, confirm this hypothesis. In effect, as Cavalli-Sforza shows, if one takes into consideration the results of linguistic taxonomy, and notably the families and sub-families that it brings forth, there is a strong correlation between the genetic tree of the human species and its linguistic family tree.

It is also a reconstructivist perspective that is adopted by Bernard Comrie. He shows how a properly interdisciplinary line of argumentation can allow difficult problems of protohistorical reconstruction to be resolved. In combining methods, forms of reasoning and linguistic, anthropological, archæological and genetic results, he sheds light in a new way on three questions concerning the populating of prehistoric Europe: the relation between Azerbaidjanese, belonging to the Turkish family, and Caucasian languages spoken by proximal ethnic groups, the considerable differences in calendar between the expansion of agriculture in Europe and the linguistic coverage of the continent by Indo-European languages, and finally, the Anglicisation of roman Great-Britain. Testing his interdisciplinary method also on the terrain of Malagasy and a Papouese language, he shows how human populations can change their language and completely or partly adopt languages that are foreign to their original linguistic family, thus irremediably breaking the parallelism between languages and genes. Beyond the resolution of complex protohistorical problems, Bernard Comrie's demonstration thus leads to raising critical questions with respect to the Darwinian correlation between languages and genes, which is a fundamental premise of the demonstrations of the New Synthesis.

Andrew Carstairs-McCarthy also adopts an evolutionist perspective. Considering that the characteristics of the languages that we know can have three difference sources, the result of adaptative pressure, the expression of general universal principles that are exterior to evolution itself or the unmotivated result of historical accidents, Carstairs-McCarthy deals principally with the third category of factors. The analysis of phenomena that are generally taken to be synchronically arbitrary, non-functional or non-motivated allows him to construct hypotheses on the prehistory of languages in the manner in which the current survival of these accidental phenomena allows them to be reconstructed.

As for Lylle Campbell, he raises questions with respect to the reconstructivist method that is at the heart of work in linguistic genealogy and on taxonomies of families of languages. His methodological critique, drawing on numerous factual analyses, contests that it might be possible to begin from current day languages in order to reconstruct step by step the languages from which they issued, up to the original source language. Defending the accidental character of numerous similarities between forms, he considers that processes of change and historical differentiations have a power such that no reconstruction can be held to be valid. In thus defending the view that practically nothing of the mother language or of the source languages survives in current day languages, Campbell presents a fundamental critical argument against the approach of drawing parallels between super-families of the *Stammbaum* and groups of genetic markers, in other words, definitively against the methodology of the New Synthesis.

Frederick J. Newmeyer questions the relation between conceptual structures of languages and the way in which they respond to communicative pressures, regarding which it is know that they express pressure towards concision and rapidity of transmission, possibly at the price of ambiguity and imprecision. The relation between conceptual representations and communicative transmission of these representations allows Newmeyer to raise questions concerning the very concept of grammar, on the necessary preconditions for the emergence of this object and on the modalities of its evolution. Newmeyer concludes on the historical priority of conceptual representations over the communication of these representations themselves. The origin of grammars must thus be looked for in the intersubjective communication of rich conceptual structures that pre-existed in the minds of primitive humans. If communicative pressures contributed to the shaping of grammars, it is pre-existing mental representations that conditioned them. It is thus in the new cognitive capacity of elaborating conceptual representations that the origin of language should be looked for.

Gilles Fauconier and Mark Turner pursue a similar line of questioning. As they show, the archæological record shows that during the Upper Palaeolithic, humans developed an unprecedented ability to innovate. They acquired a modern human imagination, which gave them the ability to invent new concepts and to assemble new and dynamic mental patterns. The results of this change were awesome: human beings developed art, science, religion, culture, refined tool use, and language. Fauconnier and Turner offer evidence that this seemingly abrupt and radical change was the product of a standard continuous evolutionary process: the evolution of the basic mental operation known as 'conceptual blending' to its strongest form, 'double-scope' blending.

The second part of this volume is devoted to research that is more directly *post originen*.

Bernard Laks opens this part with an historical and epistemological analysis of concepts and methods that are used in research on the origin and the evolution of languages. Recalling what had been the results and the failures of Historical and Comparative Grammar, he questions the link that connected it to modern studies concerning the history of languages. From genealogy to genetics, he brings to light the conceptual and methodological similarities that bring together the two approaches. Against genealogical trees of the *Stammbaum* type, he shows in what respect cladistics constitutes a serious alternative that allows a certain number of conceptual difficulties that are encountered to be resolved.

Domenico Parisi takes as his starting point an hypothesis recently proposed by Colin Renfrew according to which the peopling of Europe might be due to the diffusion of agricultural techniques and to the migration of the first Indo-European farmers from an original homeland situated in Anatolia. Parisi proposed an extremely detailed and precise computer simulation of this process of progressive diffusion of speakers, their language and techniques. The quantitative and qualitative precision of the simulation allows responding to certain particularly arduous questions concerning this diffusion: what were the respective roles of demographic diffusion and cultural diffusion in this expansion of agriculture? How did the second peopling interact with the initial peoples? Finally, how did the progressive differentiation of languages operate?

In contrast to the simulation of Renfrew's hypothesis proposed by Parisi, Jean-Paul Demoule offers a critical, historical and epistemological analysis of this proposal. He shows in what respect Renfrew's hypothesis corresponds quite precisely to the classical proposal of localisation defended by the German school of archæology. In order to be validated, the hypothesis of the Indo-European diffusion by diffusion of agriculture supposes that the same questions be decided upon as with the classical Indo-Europeanist hypothesis. It encounters the same archæological and linguistic difficulties (absence of material vestiges, strong divergences in linguistic typology, etc.).

In his chapter, Merrit Ruhlen illustrates, with the aid of numerous examples, the comparative and reconstructive method that is the basis of the New Synthesis. Showing how one can become independent from the –5,000 years barrier, generally thought to be unsurpassable, he argues in favour of an exhaustive classification of families and super-families of languages, and refines the family tree proposed in the work of Greenberg. This opens a retrospective pathway for sketching out the contours of an original language, which was that of the first modern humans at the time of the first migration from the initial African homeland.

It is radically a different point of view, methodology and model that are adopted by Don Ringe and Tandy Warnow. They present taxonomical results obtained in the framework of a cladistic computational model. In order to construct this dynamic model, that is much more complex than classical tree-structures, they integrate results of linguistic research on the acquisition of natural languages in linguistic communities, as well as results of work on the divergence of dialects, contacts between languages, creolisation, phenomena of borrowing and linguistic change itself. This leads to a cladistic network model that aims to represent the multifactorial complexity of problems posed by linguistic genealogy.

Salikoko S. Mufwene analyses the question of the origin of language, the preconditions for its appearance and its evolution in different languages, from the point of view of the processes of creolisation and pidginisation, that have often been thought of as modern reflections of prehistoric mechanisms. Mufwene shows that the development of creoles does not replicate the initial conditions of the emergence of language and that the parallel with proto-languages is largely unfounded. By contrast, creolist studies are extremely informative on processes of variation, gradual change and acquisition of languages in natural contexts. From the point of view of the ecology of linguistic practices, creolisation is thus extremely precious for understanding the progressive evolution and differentiation of linguistic systems.

Finally, from an archæologist's standpoint, Serge Cleuziou raises questions concerning the cultural and linguistic context that prevailed at Sumer, at the moment of the articulation between prehistory and history. He shows how, from the dual point of view of languages and cultures (symbolic and material), the –5,000 year barrier remains scientifically insurmountable. In grouping together archæological data and known linguistic traces, he shows how the situation at Sumer, as well as that of the whole region, was much more complex than is generally recognised. The categories and abstract labels with which archæologists and linguists work do not take into account the intricateness of speakers, cultural practices and material productions. This leads to calling into doubt too rigid taxonomies and too unilateral archæological reconstructions.

Notes

1 Saussure thus wrote that: 'the question of the origin of languages has not the importance that has been accorded to it. This question does not even exist. (The question of the source of the Rhône: puérile!)'. Cf. the manuscript sources published by Bouquet and Engler: Saussure (2001).

2 The direct influences of this work on the emerging discipline of sociology, and singularly on Durkheim, are also important, as is shown by the synthesis that Durkheim provides of the work of Atkinson (Durkheim 1903).

3 On this point, cf. the monumental dictionary of Darwinism of Tort (1996).

4 For a synthesis, cf. for example Vendryes (1921).

5 'Since they also operate in general only on common languages that are hypothetically reconstructed, the linguists that reconstruct Indo-European find themselves condemned at a higher level to a purely formal type of work. The Indo-European of linguists has no concrete reality; it is only, as we have already said, a 'system of correspondences'. It follows from this that the most savant *connoisseur* of Indo-European would be incapable of expressing in this language a sentence as simple as 'horse runs' or 'the house is big'. (Vendryes 1921: 330).

6 In this context, the work of one of the founders of phonetics, Van Ginneken, comes to mind, whose involvement in militant Nazism has only just been brought to light (Bonnot & Boë 2001). On phonetic racism, cf. for example Van Ginneken (1932, 1935).

7 This work was to remain undoubtedly incomparable in its ambition during a whole century, up to the work of Mallory & Adams (1997) who besides also situated the birthplace of original Indo-European in the pontic steppes.

8 An example is provided by the creation of the *Société Préhistorique Française* in 1903.

9 For a recent historical study, cf. Eigen & Larrimore (2006).

10 In passing, we note that one of the most well known contestations of the relevance of this cephalic index is precisely due to Franz Boas, an anthropologist and linguist, who founded American linguistics. His study of the craniology of generations of immigrants into the USA (1912–1913) is taken up again in Boas (1940). It was the same Boas who denounced Nazi Aryanism from 1934 onwards (cf. Boas et al. 1934).

11 For a socio-historical study of the science of races, cf. Mucchielli (1997).

12 Felix von Luschan was one of the leaders of the discipline at this period, as an ex-student of Broca and Professor of anthropology at the University of Berlin.

13 One may recall that Fodor (1983) begins his Chomskian analysis of the modularity of mind with a presentation of Gall's theory of faculties, pushed up against a quite moderate variety of craniology.

14 Here one recalls Malinowski's (1922) functionalism.

15 For a history of structuralism, cf. for example Dosse (1991, 1993).

16 It is well known that the *Cours de Linguistique Générale*, as it was assembled by Bally and Séchehaye ends precisely with an explicit critique of Schleicher: 'Whilst at the same time recognising that Scheicher did violence to reality in seeing in language an organic thing that bore within itself its own law of evolution, we continue, without calling ourselves into question, to want to make

an organic thing in another sense, in supposing that the 'genius' of a race or ethnic group tends to unceasingly bring back language into certain determined directions' (Saussure 1916: 305).

17 Being interested in the possibility of constructing broader genealogical groupings than the sole Indo-European family of languages, he thus wrote in the 1937 edition of Meillet (1903): 'one can only glimpse the fact that all the languages of the 'white' races are interrelated'. Pedersen (1938) replied to this suggestion in stating the hypothesis of nostratic in order to group Indo-European languages with Chamo-Semitic, Finno-Ougrian and Caucasian languages.

18 Research on nostratic was pursued in the Soviet Union in the tradition of Russian encyclopædism, around the linguist Vladimir Illic-Svityc, who died in 1966 at 32 years old, whose work in Russian is principally posthumous. This research was conducted, up to the fall of the Berlin Wall, in an undeniable international isolation.

19 For a critical analysis of the relations between cerebral anatomy and classical phrenology, cf. Terrazas & McNaughton (2000).

20 Consider, for example, the media coverage and the number of works aiming at popularising the hypothesis of the African Eve: Science Magazine N° 8, October 1999, 'The southern African Eve'.

21 Cf. Hagège (2000), Nettle & Romaine (2000).

22 Cf. Tomasello (1995) or Jackendoff (2002) for recent critical approaches to these questions.

23 As we have already remarked concerning research on the origin of modern Man (cf. note 18), the popularisation of work in linguistic genealogy on the origin of languages has had a considerable success in the media, cf. for example Ruhlen (1994).

24 One knows that Dunbar rendered himself famous by establishing a relevant numerical correlation: Dunbar's number (Dunbar 1993). It corresponds to 'the cognitive limit to the number of individuals with whom any one person can maintain stable relationships [...] this limit is a direct function of relative neocortex size and that this in turn limits group size'.

25 Under the title '*Origine et évolution des langages: approches, modèles, paradigmes*', we organised an international conference at the *Collège de France* in Paris during September 2002. Most of the chapters in this volume originate from communications made on that occasion. We have added to them a certain number of colleagues who had not been able to participate in the conference in Paris.

26 Here we make an implicit reference to Bourdieu (2001).

References

Bergounioux Gabriel. 1994. Aux origines de la linguistique française. Paris: Pocket.

Bergounioux Gabriel. 1996. Aux origines de la Société de Linguistique de Paris (1864–1876). Bulletin de la Société de Linguistique de Paris, XCI, 1.1–36.

Bergounioux Gabriel. 2002. La sélection des langues: darwinisme et linguistique. Langages, 146.7–19.

Blumenbach Johann Friedrich. 1781. De generis humani varietate nativa liber. Goettingae: Apud viduam Abr. Vandenhoek.

Boas Franz. 1940. Race, language and culture. New York: The Free Press.

Boas Franz, Fishberg Maurice, Huntington Ellsworth and Kohler Max J. 1934. Aryan and Semite; with particular reference to Nazi racial dogmas. Addresses delivered before the Judaeans and the Jewish academy of arts and sciences, March 4th, 1934, in New York City. Cincinnati: Pub. B'nai B'rith.

Boas Franz and Stocking George W. 1974. The shaping of American anthropology, 1883–1911; a Franz Boas reader. New York: Basic Books.

Bonnot Jean-François P. and Boë Louis-Jean. 2001. Stéréotypes et théorie phonétique dans l'entre-deux guerres: le poids des dominantes idéologiques sur les champs disciplinaires. Marges Linguistiques (Online Journal), 6.

Bopp Franz. 1865–1872 [1833-1852]. Grammaire comparée des langues indo-européennes- comprenant le sanscrit, le zend, l'arménien. Introduction de Michel Bréal. Paris: Bibliothèque Nationale.

Boucher de Perthes Jacques Crèvecoeur de. 1860. De l'homme antédiluvien et de ses œuvres. Paris: Jung-Treuttel.

Bourdieu Pierre. 1972. Esquisse d'une théorie de la pratique. Précédé de trois études d'ethnologie Kabyle. Genève: Droz.

Bourdieu Pierre. 2001. Science de la science et réflexivité. Paris: Raisons d'agir.

Cavalli-Sforza Luigi Lucas. 1997. Genes, peoples and languages. Proceedings of the National Academy of Science, 94, 7719–24.

Cavalli-Sforza Luigi Lucas. 2000. Genes, peoples, and languages. New York: North Point Press.

Cavalli-Sforza Luigi Lucas, Minch Eric and Moutain Joanna. 1992. Coevolution of genes and languages revisited. Proceedings of the National Academy of Science, 89, 5620–24.

Cavalli-Sforza Luigi Lucas, Menozzi Paolo and Piazza Alberto. 1994. The History and Geography of Human Genes. Princeton: Princeton University Press.

Childe G. V. 1926. The Aryans: a study of Indo-European origins. New York: Knopf.

Chomsky Noam. 1966. Cartesian linguistics: a chapter in the history of rationalist thought. New York: Harper & Row.

Chomsky Noam. 1968. Language and mind. New York: Harcourt Brace & World.

Chomsky Noam. 1995. The minimalist program. Cambridge, Mass.: The MIT Press.
Comrie Bernard. 1981. Language universals and linguistic typology: syntax and morphology. Chicago: University of Chicago Press.
Comrie Bernard, Matthews Stephen and Polinsky Maria. 2003. The atlas of languages: the origin and development of languages throughout the world. New York: Facts On File.
Condorcet, Jean-Antoine-Nicolas de Caritat marquis de. 1793. Esquisse d'un tableau historique des progrès de l'esprit humain. Paris.
Darwin Charles. 1859. On the origin of species by means of natural selection, or the preservation of favoured races in the struggle for life. London: John Murray.
Darwin Charles. 1871. The descent of man, and selection in relation to sex. London, John Murray.
Déchelette Joseph. 1908–1914. Manuel d'archéologie préhistorique, celtique et gallo-romaine. Paris: A. Picard et fils.
Deniker Jean. 1900. Les races et les peuples de la Terre. Paris: Reinwald.
Dobzhansky Theodosius. 1937. Genetics and the origin of species. New York: Columbia University Press.
Dosse François. 1991. Histoire du structuralisme: le champ du signe. Paris: La découverte.
Dunbar Robin M. 1993. Coevolution of neocortical size, group size and language in humans. Behavioral and Brain Sciences, 16, 681–735.
Dunbar Robin M. 1997. Grooming, gossip, and the evolution of language. Cambridge Mass.: Harvard University Press.
Durkheim Emile. 1903. Compte rendu de Lang et Atkinson 1903. Folklore, 14, 421–25.
Eigen Sara and Larrimore Mark J. 2006. The German invention of race. Albany: State University of New York Press.
Engels Friedrich. 1884. L'origine de la propriété privée de la famille et de l'Etat. Paris Editions Sociales 1948.
Fodor J. 1975. The language of thought. Cambridge: Harvard University Press.
Fodor J. 1983. The modularity of mind: an essay on faculty psychology. Cambridge: MIT press.
Freud Sigmund. 1913. Totem et Tabou. Paris: Payot.
Freud Sigmund. 1939. Moïse et le monothéisme. Paris: Gallimard.
Gardner Howard 1985. The mind's new science: a history of the cognitive revolution. New York: Basic Books.
Gimbutas Maria Alseikaitė. 1992. Die Ethnogenese der europäischen Indogermanen. Innsbruck: Institut für Sprachwissenschaft der Universität Innsbruck.
Gimbutas Marija Alseikaitė. 1991. The civilization of the goddess: the world of Old Europe. San Francisco: Harper.

Ginneken Jacob, Van. 1932. La tendance labiale de la race méditerranéenne et la tendance laryngale de la race alpine. Paper presented at 1st International Congres of Phonetic Sciences, Amsterdam.
Ginneken Jacob, Van. 1935. Ras en taal: Verhandelingen der Koninklijke Akademie van Wetenschappen te Amsterdam, afd. letterkunde. Amsterdam: Noord-Hollandsche uitgevers maatschappij.
Godelier Maurice. 1984. L'idéel et le materiel, pensée, économie, sociétés, Paris, Fayard.
Godelier Maurice. 1996. L'énigme du don, Paris, Fayard.
Gould Stephen Jay. 2002. The structure of evolutionary theory. Cambridge, Mass.: Belknap Press of Harvard University Press.
Gould Stephen Jay and Vrba Elizabeth. 1982. Exaptation: a missing term in the science of form. Paleobiology, VIII.4–15.
Greenberg Joseph H. (ed.) 1963. Universals of Language. Cambridge Mass.: MIT Press.
Greenberg Joseph H. 1966. Language universals, with special references to feature hierarchies: Janua Linguarum Series Minor n°59. La Haye: Mouton.
Greenberg Joseph H. 1971. The Indo-Pacific hypothesis. Current Trends in Linguistics, ed. by Thomas F. Sebeok. La haye: Mouton.
Greenberg Joseph H. 1987. Language in the Americas. Stanford: Stanford University Press.
Greenberg Joseph H. 2002. Indo-European and its closest relatives: the Eurasiatic language family. Stanford: Stanford University Press.
Greenberg Joseph H. and Ruhlen Merrit. 1992. Linguistic origins of Native Americans. Scientific American. 94–99.
Haddon Alfred C. and Hingston Quiggin. 1934. History of anthropology. London: Watts & Co.
Hagège Claude. 2000. Halte à la mort des langues. Paris: Editions Odile Jacob.
Jackendoff Ray. 2002. Foundation of language: brain, meaning, grammar, evolution. Oxford: Oxford University Press.
Klein Richard G. and Blake Edgar. 2002. The dawn of human culture. New York: Wiley.
Kolodkine Paul. 1963. Mendéléiev et la loi périodique. Paris: Éditions Seghers.
Labov William. 1972. Sociolinguistic patterns. Philadelphia: University of Pennsylvania Press.
Labov William. 1994. Principles of linguistic change: internal factors. vol. 1. Oxford: Blackwell.
Labov William. 2001. Principles of linguistic change: social factors. vol. 2. Oxford: Blackwell.
Laks Bernard. 1983. Langage et pratiques sociales: étude sociolinguistique d'un groupe d'adolescents. Actes de la recherche en sciences sociales, 46, 73–97.
Laks Bernard. 1996. Langage et cognition: l'approche connexionniste. Paris: Hermès.

Lang Andrew and Atkinson John J. 1903. Social Origins. Primal Law. London: Longman.
Levi-Strauss Claude. 1947. Structures élémentaires de la parenté. New York: Mouton.
Lubbock Sir John. 1871. The Origin of Civilisation and the primitive Condition of Man. New York: Appleton and Co.
Luschan Felix von. 1922. Völker, Rassen, Sprachen. Berlin: Welt-verlag.
Malinowski Bronislaw. 1922. Argonauts of the western Pacific; an account of native enterprise and adventure in the archipelagoes of Melanesian New Guinea. London: G. Routledge & Sons.
Mallory James and Adams Douglas. 1997. The Encyclopedia of Indo-European Culture. London: Chicago Fitzroy Dearborn.
Mannheim Karl. 1929. Idéologie et utopie: une introduction à la sociologie de la connaissance Paris: Marcel Rivière.
Meijer Miriam Claude. 1999. Race and aesthetics in the anthropology of Petrus Camper (1722–1789). Amsterdam: Rodopi.
Meillet Antoine. 1903. Introduction à l'étude comparative des langues indo-européennes. 8ème édition 1953. Paris: Hachette.
Morgan Lewis H. 1877. Ancient society, or researches in the lines of human progress from savagery through barbarism to civilization. London: MacMillan & Company.
Mucchielli Laurent. 1997. Sociologie versus anthropologie raciale. L'engagement des sociologues durkheimiens dans le contexte «fin de siècle» (1885–1914). Gradhiva. Revue d'histoire et d'archives de l'anthropologie, 21, 77–95.
Mufwene Salikoko S. 2001. The ecology of language evolution. Cambridge: Cambridge University Press.
Nakleh, Ringe Donald and Warnow Tandy. 2005. Perfect Phylogenetic Network: a new methodology for reconstructing the evolutionary history of languages. Language 81, 382–420.
Nettle Daniel and Romaine Suzanne. 2000. Vanishing voices: the extinction of the world's languages. New York: Oxford University Press.
Pedersen Holger. 1938. Hittitisch und die anderen indoeuropäischen Sprachen. København: Levin & Munksgaard.
Piaget Jean, Chomsky Noam and Piattelli-Palmarini Massimo. 1980. Language and learning: the debate between Jean Piaget and Noam Chomsky. Cambridge, Mass.: Harvard University Press.
Radcliffe-Brown A.R. 1958. Method in social anthropology; selected essays. Chicago: University of Chicago Press.
Ripley William Z. 1899. The races of Europe: a sociological study. New York: D. Appleton and Co.
Rousseau Jean-Jacques. 1755. Discours sur l'origine et les fondements de l'inégalité parmi les hommes. Genève.

Ruhlen Merrit. 1994. The origin of language: tracing the evolution of the mother tongue. New York: Wiley.
Sahlins Marshall David, Service Elman Rogers and Harding Thomas G. 1960. Evolution and culture. Ann Arbor: University of Michigan Press.
Saussure Ferdinand de. 1878. Mémoire sur le système primitif des voyelles dans les langues indo-européennes. Leipzig: B.G. Teubner.
Saussure Ferdinand de. 1916. Cours de linguistique générale. Paris: Payot
Saussure Ferdinand de. 1995. Phonétique: Il manoscritto di Harvard (Houghton Library bMS Fr 266(8): Edité par Maria Pia Marchese. Universita degli studi di Firenze. Quaterni del dipartimento di linguistica, studi 3. Florence: Unipress.
Saussure Ferdinand de. 2001. Ecrits de linguistique générale. Paris: Gallimard.
Saussure Ferdinand de. 2002. Théorie des sonantes. Il manoscritto di Genevra (BPU Ms fr 3955). Florence: Universita degli studi di firenze. UNIPRESS.
Schleicher August. 1861/1862. Compendium der vergleichenden Grammatik der indogermanischen Sprachen. Weimar: Böhlau.
Schleicher August. 1863. Die darwinsche Theorie und die Sprachwissenschaft. Offenes Sendschreiben an Herrn Dr. Ernst Haeckel Weimar: Böhlau.
Schrader Otto. 1886. Linguistisch-historische Forschungen zur Handelsgeschichte und Warenkunde. Jena.
Schrader Otto. 1901. Reallexikon der indogermanischen Altertumskunde. Gundzüge einer Kultur- und Völkergeschichte Alteuropas.vol. Edition revue en 1917 et 1929 avec l'aide d'Alfons Nehring. Berlin, Leipzig: W. de Gruyter.
Schuchardt Hugo. 1922. Hugo Schuchardt-Brevier. Ein vademekum der allgemeinen Sprachwissenschaft. Halle: Max Niemeyer.
Schuchardt Hugo. 1979. The Ethnography of variation. Selected writings on Pidgins and Creoles. Ann Arbor, Karoma.
Sériot Patrick. 1999. Structure et totalité. Paris: PUF.
Service Elman Rogers. 1971a. Primitive social organization: an evolutionary perspective. New York: Random House.
Service Elman Rogers. 1971b. Cultural evolutionism: theory in practice. New York: Holt, Rinehart and Winston.
Testart Alain. 1982. Les chasseurs-cueilleurs, ou l'origine des inégalités. Paris: Société d'ethnographie.
Terrazas Alejandro et McNaughton Bruce L. 2000. Brain growth and the cognitive map. Proceedings of the National Academy of Science, 97, 4414–16.
Tomasello Michael. 1995. Language is not an instinct (Review of Pinker 1994). Cognitive Development 131–56.
Tort Patrick. 1996. Dictionnaire du darwinisme et de l'évolution. 3 vol. Paris: PUF.
Trombetti Alfredo. 1905. L'unità d'origine del linguaggio. Bologne: Facsimile Bologne 1966 A. Forni.

Tylor Edward B. 1865. Researches into the early history of mankind and the development of civilization. London.

Tylor Edward B. 1871. Primitive Culture. New York.

Vendryes Joseph. 1921. Le Langage: introduction linguistique à l'histoire. Paris: La renaissance du livre.

Weinreich Uriel. 1953. Languages in contact: findings and problems. La Haye: Mouton.

Westermarck Edvard (Alexander). 1906. The origin and development of the moral ideas. London: MacMillan.

Whitney William Dwight. 1867. Language and the study of language. New York: Scribner.

2 Genetic evolution and the evolution of languages

Luigi Lucas Cavalli-Sforza
Stanford University

1 The expansion of modern humans and the standard model of human evolution

The study of human evolution has made recent advances, and we now have a reasonable model of how modern humans spread around the globe populating it with *Homo sapiens sapiens*. I will summarize in the following the views that are today accepted by an increasing number of scholars and go under the name of standard model of the evolution of modern humans. A recent article with Feldman recently published on Nature Genetics gives some more detailed information. The model is supported by genetic data with many independent markers, in particular from the Y chromosome, and mitochondrial DNA, which are transmitted by only one parent (fathers in the first case, mothers in the second) and are for this reason much more informative especially on the most recent times of modern human evolution than the other genes, which are inherited from both parents and generate therefore more complex genealogies. There is, however, no disagreement with data obtained with uniparentally and biparentally transmitted genes. The basic finding is that modern humans descend from a small group, perhaps a single tribe, which most probably lived in East Africa and spread slowly from there to the rest of Africa beginning around 100,000 years ago. About 50,000 years ago growth became more rapid, generating a fast demographic and geographic expansion that populated all the continents by 15,000 years ago or earlier. The Old World (Africa and Eurasia) was at the time of the modern human expansion inhabited by other earlier humans, who had previously spread from Africa around 1.7 million years ago. The most notable of these earlier, archaic humans were Neandertals. At the time of the expansion of modern humans out of Africa they lived in Europe and West Asia, but disappeared fairly rapidly when modern humans first arrived to Europe, around 40,000 years ago. If there was genetic exchange with modern humans it must have been rare, because no genetic traces of it have yet been detected, and archeological claims of it seem uncertain.

The settlement of the world by modern humans must have started first from East Africa to the nearest parts of Asia. It seems likely that an early branch proceeded along the coast of South Asia to S.E. Asia, from there turning south towards Oceania, settling in Australia and New Guinea 40,000 years ago or even earlier. It also continued north, probably along the coast of East Asia settling in Japan, and later gave rise to a migration to America via the Bering strait, probably the second linguistic migration suggested by Greenberg. It is possible that this expansion initiated via South Asia and kept, initially at least, along the coast, using perhaps rafts or boats. Their use seemed in any case necessary at least for reaching Oceania. Another expansion, probably from the same origin in East Africa, was perhaps slightly later, but was more successful in demographic terms (as is evident in the Y chromosome genealogy) and was directed towards the center of Asia, from where it continued in all directions west to Europe, north to Siberia, and north-east, from where it reached the Americas, and to East Asia where it mixed with the south Asian expansion. The first entry to America was at least 15,000 years ago, although there probably were earlier arrivals, and proceeded rapidly all the way down to Tierra del Fuego, where first human finds are as old as 11,500 years ago.

The stimuli to growth and expansion were very often technological innovations. 10,000 years ago, after the last glaciation the human species had multiplied already perhaps a 1,000 fold or even more, from the few thousands original modern humans to a few millions. In the best areas population had probably reached a relatively high population density and had reached saturation for the foraging economy then available (hunting, gathering vegetables and fishing). The impasse was solved apparently independently in many world areas, all with temperate or subtropical climate, by developing agriculture of the local graminaceae, roots, tubers and fruits which formed the regular food, and by breeding the few local species that were more easily domesticated. This allowed greater further population growth, and the number of humans was multiplied by another factor of a 1,000 in the last 10,000 years.

2 The importance of language in promoting the expansion of modern humans

Perhaps the most important technological innovation that promoted the expansion of modern humans from East Africa was human language. Every human individual, with few exceptions, can learn any language in existence, and all living languages show basically the same degree of sophistication. It is unlikely that language developed suddenly, but it is more likely that there were several stages of improvement, and the current degree of development was reached only in the last phase, before the beginning of the spread of modern humans. Undoubtedly the most important difference between humans and other animals is the ability to speak a language which has so dramatically increased our capacity to communicate. Communication is the source of culture, intended as the capacity of learning from the experience of others and thus accumulating knowledge over generations. Communication and cultural phenomena have been observed in many other animals, but the degree of communication and the cultural accumulation possible in humans is certainly orders of magnitude greater than in any other species.

The standard model gives much importance to language as the property which was common to the group that multiplied and rapidly settled the whole Earth. It seems almost unavoidable to conclude, from a genetic point of view, that this original African tribe that populated the Earth spoke initially a single language, from which most if not all modern languages derived. This does not exclude that there were other languages spoken at the time in other parts of the world, which did not survive.

The rate of linguistic differentiation is so high that most linguists find it very difficult to answer the problem if modern languages had single or multiple origins. Recent pioneering, independent investigations of general linguistic taxonomy are, however, in agreement with the expectation, based on the genetic and demographic analysis of modern humans, that human languages have a single origin. The basic linguistic finding is that a list of words, now nearing a hundred, are found in at least some languages of all or almost all linguistic families (Ruhlen). They are all basic parts of speech, like body parts, numbers one two and three, some pronouns and others (e.g. words like 'louse' are not surprisingly part of the list). They are frequently words learnt early in life, and this fact alone seems to decrease the likelihood of the usual objection that they are borrowings. Inevitably they have undergone substantial phonologic change, as can be expected given the long evolutionary time, but the residual similarity seems to be too close for being coincidental. There has been also substantial semantic change, but this seems perfectly reasonable. As an example, the first universal root, originally described by Greenberg, 'tik', means both finger and number one. This change is easily explained by the common gesture of indicating number one with the index finger. There are other semantic extensions of the root, for instance to hand or even arm, in some languages.

The advantages offered by modern speech, allowing improved communication at critical times like those of exploration and settlement in new country are likely to have been critical during the major world expansion of the last fifty thousand years.

3 The correlation of the tree of genes and that of languages

It is therefore not surprising to find that there is a substantial correlation between the genetic tree of human living beings, and linguistic families. This correlation was pointed out in a 1988 PNAS paper by L. Cavalli-Sforza, A. Piazza, P. Menozzi and J. Mountain, showing that the major linguistic families and superfamilies are largely superimposable with the branches of the genetic tree. The latter has been now confirmed with many different sets of markers, ranging from proteins (blood groups, blood proteins, enzymes etc.) (Cavalli-Sforza, Menozzi and Piazza 1994), Y chromosome DNA markers (Underhill et al. 2000, 2001), mitochondrial DNA (Wallace et al. 2002). The genes-languages correlation is not due to direct causation of gene differentiation on linguistic differentiation. As is well known, what is inherited is the capacity of acquiring a language, but the actual language depends on place and culture of birth. Although the correlation is strong enough that it is easy to appreciate without direct testing, it is difficult to measure with the usual correlation coefficients because of the nature of the quantities being correlated. A criticism that the correlation is not statistically significant (Bateson et al.1991) was answered by showing with two entirely different methods (Cavalli-Sforza et al. 1993, Penny et al. 1993) that the probability that it is due to chance is of the order of 2–4 in 10,000. The common causes responsible for the correlation are the similarity of genetic and cultural transmission, and the common history of spread from a single geographic origin to all parts of Earth. Genetic transmission is well understood and almost without exception causes transfer of the hereditary material from parents to offspring. Cultural transmission, of which that of languages is a major example, has very different patterns depending on whether it takes place from parents to children (vertical transmission) or between unrelated people (horizontal transmission). As shown by the mathematical theory of cultural transmission and evolution by Cavalli-Sforza and Feldman (1981), vertical transmission is much more conservative and cultural evolution is slower than when transmission is horizontal. Language is transmitted both vertically and horizontally, but, as well known, mother tongue can be learnt only in the first four or five years of life, during which there is a powerful drive to learn a language, that can be acquired perfectly only in that short period. The mere common expression ‘mother tongue’ shows that vertical inheritance is very important for language. But if one has acquired a mother tongue in the first years of life, there are many later opportunities for further learning and change, due to action of peers and schools. Moreover, certain political social and economic changes may cause a whole population to switch to a completely different language in few generations. There is no indication of genes favoring the learning of one language over the other. In general, therefore, most of the genes-languages correlation must be understood in terms of similar mechanisms of transmission, and not of direct causation in one direction or the other. If anything, there may be some direct causation in the opposite direction, in the sense that linguistic differentiation may sharpen local genetic differentiation across minor geographic, social or political boundaries by increasing local endogamy on one side of the boundaries. This seems a reasonable explanation of the correlation between linguistic and genetic boundaries shown by Barbujani and Sokal. Both these boundaries are also correlated with physical, ecological (and, in some cases, social –e.g. religious or economic) barriers, which are probably the primary determining factors affecting migration and, with it, the geography of marriage patterns.

The observed genetic differentiation between human groups is certainly the consequence of separation of migrants, colonists etc. who settled in new, often remote places during the great initial expansions, and the many others that followed local agricultural and other economic expansions. Separation of groups who were originally one tend to break or reduce the continuity of genetic exchange existing within local, endogamous communities. Geographic fragmentation causes also linguistic differentiation, and the process that leads to linguistic and to genetic differentiation tends to be the same: the history of fissions of groups, and their later reunions and exchanges.

There are however social, economic, political and military events that have caused imposition of external languages, or interest in acquiring a new language, perhaps eventually losing the original one. These phenomena have created exceptions to the correlation of genes and languages, which were noted in the 1988 paper. Often, however, new languages that take over come from neighbors, who may speak languages belonging to the same linguistic family or subfamily, and therefore the language switch is not necessarily noted when, as in our study, linguistic similarities are established by sharing languages of the same family.

4 Examples of language replacements

There are well known historical examples of language replacements in Europe, as the switch in Britain from earlier languages (spoken by the Picts?) to new ones, of the Celtic subfamily of the Indo-European family, followed by the relatively short and incomplete domination after the Roman conquest of the Latin language, belonging to another Indo-European subfamily. At the end of the Roman empire an Anglo-Saxon language of another Indo-European subfamily, the Germanic one, took over in not entirely understood circumstances. The Norman conquest in 1066, and later the Renaissance introduced many words of Latin origin into the English language, but the structure and perhaps 50% of the vocabulary remained Germanic. In peripheral areas of the British Isles Celtic languages lasted longer, and they are still spoken in Wales and Ireland. A Celtic language was imported to Brittany, France, when Celtic speakers left Cornwall and other Celtic speaking parts of West Britain, following the Anglo Saxon invasion.

Celtic languages were spoken in most of France at the time of the conquest of Gaul by Julius Caesar, except the southwest where a much older language, Basque, was dominant. It is still spoken by perhaps 25,000 individuals who have resisted the imposition of the French language until today. South of the Pyrenees Basque is still spoken by more than a million people. Caesar's conquest brought about a complete replacement of Celtic with Latin, which then transformed slowly into the modern French language(s). The Franks, a Germanic tribe settled in northeastern France after the fall of the Roman empire, and imposed their political rule over all of France but not their language. A similar phenomenon happened with the conquest of most Italy by other Germanic tribes: first the Goths, and later the Longobards (probably originally from Sweden), but modern Italian is derived from Latin, with very few injections of Longobard words. At present Hungary speaks a ugro-finnic language, imported by the Magyars when they settled in 897 AD. Ugro-finnic languages, a major branch of the Uralic family, are spread on the northeastern part of the Baltic and the north of Scandinavia, where they probably arrived with reindeer shepherds. The other major anomaly in Europe is the already mentioned survival in the extreme west of a non Indo-European, probably very ancient language, Basque. It is stated to have similarities with other isolates of Asia (some Caucasian languages, an isolate in the Himalaya, Burushaski). Starostin has proposed that these languages are part of an old family called Dene-Caucasian that was spread very widely in Eurasia, including China (the Sino-Tibetan languages) and even North America (the Na-Dene family). At a time between 10,000 and 20,000 years ago this old family was replaced by a superfamily called Eurasiatic by Greenberg, Nostratic by Russian linguists. These two superfamilies include Indo-European, Altaic, Uralic and other east Asian languages. The major difference between the Eurasiatic and the Nostratic superfamily is that the latter includes also the Afroasiatic and the Dravidian families, which Greenberg believed separated earlier, while Eurasiatic may have split into its three major constituents in central Asia.

The very recent spread of some modern languages across wide regions, e.g. Indoeuropean languages in America, Oceania, South Africa was the result of transoceanic navigation and the use of military power. Other spreads were the consequence of colonization by relatively large groups. The switch to other languages was certainly favored by military conquest and the development of metals and, with them, of armies, but it did happen also spontaneously, mostly under economic consideration, in the absence of powerful armies. In the course of a survey of Pygmies in the African forest, I was using local dialects to carry out a simple demographic analysis and happened to discover, in a village near the boundary of the forest, between Ndele and Bambio in the south of the Central African Republic, that my questionnaire in the local dialect was useful only with the older half of the inhabitants of a camp. The younger half had made the transition to the dialect of the local Bantu farmers, which the older half also knew. African Pygmies, who were until a short while ago still living in a hunting-gathering economy, and still do where the forest is largely undisturbed, are well known for adopting the language of their farming neighbors, with whom they have economic exchanges (they barter the meat they hunt with other food, iron objects, etc., produced by the farmers, and often work for them in plantations in the dry season). The original Pygmy languages have completely disappeared, apart from words that only Pygmies know, like names of animals and plants of the forest, but the language spoken by a Pygmy group may be well that of the farmers' group near whom they lived before their last migration. Destruction or severe disturbance of the forest due to Bantu farmers, and more recently on a larger scale by white exploiters of the forest, has caused continuous displacement of Pygmy groups in the last centuries. Some former hunters of the Central African Republic (the Ngbaka) speak languages originally spoken in the south of Sudan (Thomas).

5 Agricultural expansions and the spread of language families in the last 10,000 years

The history of modern human expansions is based on archeological and genetic information, and will help to understand also the history of spread of languages. The spread of agriculture took place in many parts of the world: the Middle

East (wheat and barley, many domesticated animals), northern China (millet), S.E. Asia (rice), Mexico (maize and many other plants), Africa (probably in Mali and Burkina Faso, and also Ethiopia). The major ones originated around 10,000 years ago. The earliest was in the Middle East where the first known example of mixed economy (agriculture and animal breeding) is about 11,500 years ago in northern Syria. In Africa agriculture was early in the Sahara, then not a desert, probably with crops originated in the Middle East. Perhaps cattle had also an early, independent domestication in the Sahara, but the progressive drying made it necessary to abandon most of the area that had become a desert, 3,000–4,000 years ago.

The spread of agriculture from the centers of origin was mostly, but not exclusively, a spread of farmers, and therefore was rather slow, being caused by an increased birth rate made possible by the acquisition of more food, and by migration around in search of new fields. Being sustained by reproduction, it was of necessity slow, the speed of the spread being, in Europe, of the order of one km. per year (Ammerman and Cavalli-Sforza). We have called demic diffusion the spread of a culture by and with the people who practice a new technology, as contrasted with cultural diffusion, when the new technology is learnt by imitation or teaching. The spread was accompanied by genetic admixture with earlier local hunter gatherers, and presumably also cultural acquisition of the new culture by them. Admixture and/or partial cultural diffusion generated characteristic genetic gradients around the centers of origin of the expansions. The question of the participation of mid-eastern farmers to the population of Europe has raised much debate. Estimates have varied between 20% and 50–60% (Chickhi et al.). Naturally, in the most distant places from the center of origin, in England and Scandinavia the proportion of original farmers is minimal. Farmers took their languages along, as suggested by Renfrew for Europe, and this indicates the Middle East or Turkey as the place of origin of Indo-European languages (1987). Earlier, another archeologist, Gimbutas, had suggested that the center of origin of Indoeuropean languages was a region between the Volga and the Don. Gimbutas' hypothesis was well accepted by linguists (Mallory) and Renfrew's hypothesis raised much discussion, even though various linguists had independently suggested a Turkish origin. Renfrew, however, has criticized the hypothesis and especially the early dates proposed by Gimbutas on archeological grounds.

Naturally, in the absence of writing, which started much later (5000 years ago) archeology can give only indirect support to linguistic hypotheses, and the same is true of genetics. Genetics does, however, show five possible centers of demic expansion in Europe, suggested by an analysis of the European genetic map by principal components or PCs (Menozzi et al. 1978, Cavalli-Sforza et al. 1994). Statistically the most important one corresponds to the first PC, accounting for 26–28% of the genetic variation, and is located in the Middle East. It is thus close to Turkey and supports Renfrew's hypothesis. Two centers are suggested by the second PC, explaining 22% of the variation: one of them is in the Basque region and points to an expansion towards the North East, the other center is in North East and expands in the opposite direction, the South West. It is possible that the second PC does indicate two expansions in opposite directions, between Spain and Scandinavia, which cannot therefore be differentiated one from the other by PC analysis. An explanation for the direction from Spain to Scandinavia was suggested by Torroni: a postglacial expansion, which perhaps had no linguistic consequences observable today. The opposite one has some correlation with the expansion of Uralic languages, currently spoken in the area north and east of the Baltic, and also around the Urals. It pushed towards the south as far as Hungary. The third PC (11 % of the variation) corresponds very well with the hypothesis by Gimbutas on the center of origin of Indo-European languages. We have suggested (Cavalli-Sforza et al. 1994, Piazza et al.) that both hypotheses by Renfrew and Gimbutas are correct, one center, Turkey/the Middle East, being the primary one, and the other, the Volga/Don region, secondary to it, with perhaps a difference of 4,000–5000 years. An analysis of the tree of Indoeuropean languages suggests that this attempt at conciliating the two hypotheses is quite reasonable (Piazza et al.1995 and unpublished). A fifth center of expansion is shown by the fourth PC (7% of the variation in Europe) and corresponds to the Greek expansion to south Italy in the first millennium BC, which is well documented historically and archeologically. It was also clear linguistically until the late Middle Ages, when Greek was still spoken in the original Greek colonies of south Italy, and continued in the Eastern Roman Empire until the fall of Constantinople in 1453. In south Italy there is still a region where a Greek dialect is spoken in nine villages of the province of Lecce, centered around a village with the tale-telling name of Calimera, but the Greek language may have been re-imported there by a migration in byzantine times, in the 5th century AD.

Two other, more recent agricultural expansions have shown stronger correlation of archeological, genetic, and even more clearly linguistic histories. One is the Bantu expansion in Africa, beginning in the Nigeria/Cameroon border around 3,000 years ago that settled all central and southern Africa. The farmers did not quite reach the extreme south at the time Dutch farmers settled in Capetown, but were close to it. The other is the Austronesian expansion from Taiwan or the Philippines into northern Melanesia first, then Polynesia (and also into the Indian Ocean, reaching as far as Madagascar). It began 5,000–6,000 years ago.

6 Independent evolutionary histories confirming the standard model

The problem of reconstructing history is that it is impossible to reproduce historical events, which remain unique. The great strength of experimental science is that experiments can be repeated, and reproduction offers confirmation and the possibility of almost infinite extension of the analysis. But the examination of facts from very different sciences, like archeology, paleoanthropology, demography, genetics, linguistics, cultural anthropology gives a chance of reaching almost a 'reproduction' of historical phenomena even if in somewhat different form. It thus allows to look for a consensus among disciplines, which is a little similar to the confirmation of experiments by repetition, and change of experimental conditions in order to carry the analysis further. Thus multidisciplinary research can be of great help in providing clarification and support or rejection of historical hypotheses which are bound, otherwise, to remain a source of infinite debate without conclusion.

There are various independent sources of data that support the standard model of modern human evolution. The two most important ones are human parasites and commensals that have lived with humans since before the last expansion from Africa, and cultural evolution. Both allow to discover evidence derived from phenomena which are transmitted vertically, and therefore are expected, if they are sufficiently old in time, to show the same African initiated pattern of evolution, followed by spread to Asia and from there to the three other continents. Parasites and commensals that have lived a long time with humans, viruses like hepatitis B and polyoma, bacteria like Helicobacter pylori, and probably other ones show a pattern of geographic variation that is highly suggestive of the historical spread of modern humans. These parasites and commensals are in part transmitted vertically, and also horizontally, making them good candidates for study of their evolutionary pattern and its comparison with that of modern humans themselves. Naturally, if the horizontal component is too strong and cannot be dissected out from the vertical one the picture is blurred.

In cultural anthropology family and kinship characters, and some complex socioeconomic traits also give evidence of being mainly transmitted vertically, from studies so far limited to Africa (Guglielmino et al. 1995, 2002). They can be useful for identifying some areas of demic diffusion, in conjunction with languages.

References

Ammerman A. and L. L. Cavalli-Sforza, 1984. Neolithic Transition and the Genetics of Populations in Europe . Princeton Unversity Press, NJ.

Bateman R. J, I. Goddard, R. T. O'Grady, V. A Funk, R. Mooi, W. J. Kress and R. F. Cannell 1990. Speaking of forked tongues: the feasibility of reconciling human phylogeny and the history of language. Curr. Anthropol. 31:1-13

Cavalli-Sforza L. L, 1986. African Pygmies. Academic :Press, Orlando Fla.

Cavalli-Sforza L. L. 2001. Genes, Peoples and Languages . Penguin Press, London.

Cavalli-Sforza L. L. and M. W. Feldman 2003. The applicatioin of molecular genetic approaches to the study of human evolution. Nature Genetics Supplement 33: 266-275.

Cavalli-Sforza L. L., E. Minch, and J. Mountain 1992. Coevolution of genes and languages revisited. Proc.Nat.Acad.Sci.USA 89:5620-5624.

Cavalli-Sforza L. L., A. Piazza and P. Menozzi, 1994. History and Geography of Human Genes. Princeton University Press, Princeton NJ.

Cavalli-Sforza L. L., A. Piazza, P. Menozzi and J. Mountain, 1988. Reconstruction of human evolution; bringing together genetic, archeological and linguistic data. Proc Natl Acad..Sci.USA 85:6002-6006.

Cavalli-Sforza, L. L. and Wang, W. S-Y. 1986. Spatial distance and lexical replacement. Language 62 (1): 38-55.

Gimbutas M. in G. Cardona, H. M. Hoenigswald and A. Senn eds., pp 155-195, University of Pennsylvania Press, Philadelphia PA.

Guglielmino C. R., C. Viganotti, B. Hewlett and 1995. Cultural variation in Africa: Role of mechanisms of transmission and adaptation. Proceedings of the National Academy of Sciences U.S.A. 2 (16) : 7585-7589.

Hewlett B. S., De Silvestri A., Guglielmino C. R. 2002. Semes and Genes in Africa. Current Anthropology, 43: 313-321.

Mallory, J.P. 1989. In Search of the Indoeuropeans: Language,Archeology and Myth. Thomas and Hudson, London.

Menozzi P, A. Piazza and L. L. Cavalli Sforza 1978. Synthetic maps of human gene frequencies in Europe. Science 201: 786-792.

Renfrew C, 1987. Archaelogy and Language: the puzzle of European origins. Jonathan Cape, London.

Ruhlen M. 1997. L'Origine des Langues. Paris Gallimard.

Underhill, P. A., Shen, P., Lin, A. A., Jin, L., Passarino, G., Yang, W. H., Kauffman, E. Bonné-Tamir, B., Bertranpetit, J., Francalacci, P., Ibrahim, M., Jenkins, T., Kidd, J. R., Mehdi, S. Q., Seielstad, M. T., Wells, R. S., Piazza, A., Davis, R. W., Feldman, M. W., Cavalli-Sforza, L. L., Oefner, P. J. 2000. Y-Chromosome sequence variation and the history of human populations. Nat. Genet. (3) 26: 358-361.

Underhill, P. A., Passarino, G., Lin, A. A., Shen, P., Mirazon, L. M., Foley, R. A., Oefner, P. J., Cavalli-Sforza, L. L. 2001. The phylogeography of Y-Chromosome binary haplotypes and the origins of modern human populations. Ann. Hum. Genet. 65: 43-62.

3 Languages, genes, and prehistory, with special reference to Europe

Bernard Comrie
Max Planck Institute for Evolutionary Anthropology
and University of California Santa Barbara

1 Introduction

Linguists, in particular historical-comparative linguists, are accustomed to drawing conclusions regarding historical relations among languages from the comparison of those languages. For instance, by comparing the similarities among the attested Indo-European languages (English, German, French, Latin, Welsh, Greek, Russian, Persian, Sanskrit, etc.), they posit that all these languages must descend from a common ancestor, conventionally called Proto-Indo-European. By noting the greater similarities among some of these languages, such as English and German, the intermediate nodes of the Indo-European family can be established, in this case Proto-Germanic, a descendant of Proto-Indo-European and the common ancestor of English and German. In this way, a family tree can be constructed. The method is of course considerably more complex in practice, in that one has to exclude chance similarities, and also similarities that are due not to common inheritance but rather to language contact (as when German borrows the English word *cool*). But nonetheless the method provides a convenient way of representing certain aspects of the history of languages, with a single ancestor language changing — one is already tempted to say 'mutating' — in different ways to give rise to different descendants.

Population geneticists are accustomed to drawing similar trees in order to represent the relations among different human populations, especially when dealing with non-recombinant genetic material such as mitochondrial DNA or non-recombinant Y-chromosomal DNA, each of which is inherited from a single parent. One can thus reconstruct a mitochondrial Eve, the last common ancestor of all humans through the female line, and a corresponding Y-chromosomal Adam for the last common ancestor through the male line.

A crucial question that arises when one compares these two different approaches to different aspects of human prehistory is the following: Will the two trees, the one historical-comparative linguistic, the other population genetic, coincide in general, or will there be discrepancies between them? And further, How can such correspondences or discrepancies be explained?

Charles Darwin, writing in *The Origin of Species* (1859, Chapter 14) felt that there should in general be a correlation, an idea he expressed in the following quotation:

> If we possessed a perfect pedigree of mankind, a genealogical arrangement of the races of man would afford the best classification of the various languages now spoken throughout the world; and if all extinct languages, and all intermediate and slowly changing dialects had to be included, such an arrangement would be the only possible one … this would be strictly natural, as it would connect together all languages, extinct and recent, by the closest affinities, and would give the filiation and origin of each tongue.

By contrast, his close friend and colleague Thomas H. Huxley, in a piece entitled 'On the Methods and Results of Ethnology' that appeared in *The Fortnightly Review* 1 for 1865, expressed a very different view which, though couched in what strikes the modern reader as an archaic conceptual framework, allows ample room for populations to change their language but not, of course, their genes.

> It seems to me obvious that, though in the absence of any evidence to the contrary, unity of languages may afford a certain presumption in favour of the unity of stock of peoples speaking those languages, it cannot be held to prove that unity of stock, unless philologers are prepared to demonstrate that no nation can lose its language and acquire that of a distinct nation without a change of blood corresponding with the change of language.

One can readily recognize that there is no logical necessity for languages and genes to correlate. Genes are transmitted biologically from biological parent to biological offspring. Language (i.e. knowledge of a particular language) is transmitted culturally: a child will grow up speaking the language of the community in which it is brought up, irrespective of the language of its biological parents. It is also possible for an individual to change language in the course of a lifetime, acquiring one or more languages in addition to the native language, and perhaps even abandoning the original language (although the phenomenon of language shift, to which we return in the body of the article, is usually spread out across generations). Finally, a child's parents may speak different languages, with the child growing up speaking both languages, or just one of them (or indeed neither of them, if the child is adopted into a completely different speech community). It is an empirical question to what extent such social phenomena have disrupted the close correlation between language classification and population genetic classification in the history of humankind.

One of the aims of the present article is to revisit this controversy. The issue is important, because some of the early recent work investigating the relations between linguistic and genetic trees, such as Cavalli-Sforza et al. (1988), came to the conclusion that Darwin was basically right. In the present article, and in particular in Sections 2–4, I wish to investigate some instances that are more complex and suggest, with differing degrees of cogency, that populations may indeed have changed their language without changing their genes, thus leaving it as an empirical question for future investigation to what extent Darwin's scenario versus Huxley's scenario accounts for relevant aspects of human prehistory. In doing so, it will be necessary on occasion to bring in evidence from other disciplines, in particular archeology and ethnography, though also cognitive psychology, since it is only through the application of interdisciplinary research that questions like that posed in this introduction can be answered.

In the body of this article, I will concentrate on case studies from Europe, including peripheral areas of Europe such as the Caucasus. In the remainder of this introduction, I will examine briefly two rather straightforward cases, both involving overall correspondence between linguistic and genetic classifications, in order to illustrate some of the general questions involved.

1.1 Malagasy, the language of Madagascar

Somewhat surprisingly given the geographical location of the island of Madagascar off the east coast of Africa, its language, Malagasy, belongs to the Austronesian language family, whose other members stretch from Sumatra in the west to Easter Island in the east, from Hawaii in the north to New Zealand in the south, covering most of insular Southeast Asia (plus most of the Malay peninsula and a few other mainland Southeast Asian locations) and most of the Pacific with the exception of Australia and most of New Guinea. The fact that Malagasy is an Austronesian language is surprising given the great distance that separates Madagascar from any other Austronesian-speaking area, with the direct distance across the Indian Ocean being some 8000 kilometers, considerably longer if one makes intermediate landfalls on the Asian and African coasts.

The observation that Malagasy and Madagascar are related in this way to insular Southeast Asia was first made by linguists and represents a triumph of the application of comparative-historical linguistics that was only subsequently reconfirmed by the results of other disciplines. The early European sailors whose travels included both Madagascar and what is now Indonesia already remarked on the striking similarities between the languages of these lands so distant from one another geographically. But the detailed comparison that established the precise place of Malagasy within the Austronesian language family was worked out by the Norwegian linguist Otto Christian Dahl. Dahl (1951) showed that Malagasy is particularly closely related to the Barito languages, a group of Austronesian languages spoken in southeastern Borneo. In fact, it is not just that Malagasy is related to the Barito languages, rather, it is a Barito language.

Dahl based his conclusion on a comparison between Malagasy and one of the Barito languages spoken in Borneo, Ma'anyan. The examples in (1) show a small selection from Dahl's material, sufficient to show the striking similarities between the two languages.

(1)	Malagasy	Ma'anyan	English
	vava	wawa	mouth
	lela	lela	tongue
	taolana	taulang	bone
	volo	wulo	hair
	vato	watu	stone
	volana	wulan	moon
	aho	aku	I
	inona	inon	what
	tafa-	tapa-	accidentally

Some of the items are identical between the two languages, while others reflect minor but regular differences, such as the fact that Malagasy has *v* wherever Ma'anyan has *w*. Malagasy has lost the distinction preserved in Ma'anyan between *n* and *ng* (as in *sing*), and also that between *o* and *u* — Malagasy has the sound [u], written *o*, for both. In addition, Malagasy has added the vowel *a* to the end of words that would otherwise terminate in a consonant. Finally, there are a number of regular correspondences between consonants in the two languages: Malagasy *f* corresponds to Ma'anyan *p*, Malagasy *h* to Ma'anyan *k*.

It should be noted that the words cited in (1) belong to the most basic vocabulary, which is relatively unlikely to be borrowed (although such borrowings cannot be excluded a priori); in addition, it is of course difficult to imagine what contact there could have been between Malagasy and the languages of Borneo without positing a period of geographical proximity between them. The inclusion of the personal pronoun 'I' and of the interrogative pronoun 'what' is particularly striking. Moreover, the list includes not only free-standing words but also affixes, such as the prefix Malagasy *tafa-*, Ma'anyan *tapa-*, with affixes being even less likely to be borrowed than words. And finally, even the handful of words cited in (1) shows some surprising parallels between Malagasy and other Barito languages that contrast with other Austronesian languages and represent a common innovation within Barito. Thus, the word for 'tongue' would, by comparison with other Austronesian languages, have been expected to show up in Malagasy and Ma'anyan as *lila* (cp. Indonesian *lidah*) rather than the actual form *lela*, which represents an unexplained shift from *i* to *e*, but one that is shared by Malagasy and the other Barito languages. A common semantic shift concerns Malagasy *volo*, Ma'anyan *wulo*, whose cognate in other Austronesian languages (such as Indonesian *bulu*) refers exclusively to body hair, whereas in the Barito languages the word includes head hair.

The linguistic evidence is thus sufficient on its own to establish that Malagasy is a member of the Austronesian language family, more specifically of its Barito subgroup, suggesting that the Malagasy must have migrated from insular Southeast Asia to Madagascar. Dahl was able to add further detail to this in his estimation, on the basis of loan words shared versus those not shared by Malagasy and other Barito languages, that the Malagasy had probably arrived in Madagascar in the middle of the first millennium CE. Archeological investigations suggest that Madagascar was first occupied by humans around that time. While it may seem surprising that the island had not been colonized earlier from the African mainland, Madagascar is in fact invisible from the mainland, so that its very existence may not have been known to inhabitants of the African coast. Ethnographic research has also pointed to cultural similarities between the Malagasy and peoples of insular Southeast Asia, while most recently population genetic research has clearly identified genetic similarities between the Malagasy and other Austronesian speakers. (There is also a substantial African contribution to the Malagasy gene pool, not surprising given the continuous close contact between the island and the mainland since the settlement of Madagascar by the Malagasy; this contact also has its linguistic side, for instance in loan words from mainland Bantu languages into Malagasy, such as *kiso* 'knife', cf. Swahili *kisu*.) But it is important to bear in mind that in this case, linguistics on its own was able to establish the historical connection between the Malagasy and the rest of the Austronesian-speaking world.

1.2 The Haruai language of Papua New Guinea

However, it is not always the case that linguistics takes the leading role, as can be seen from the example of the Haruai language, spoken on the northern fringe of the Highlands of New Guinea, administratively in Madang province, Papua New Guinea. In the mid-1980s I had the opportunity to carry out a year's field work among the Haruai. While my main aim was to document the language, I was also interested in trying to work out its relations with neighboring languages, and in this I was able to establish a genealogical relationship with two neighboring languages in the small Piawi language family; more distant relationships, however, eluded me.

When my colleague William A. Foley (Sydney University) looked at some of my Haruai material, he suggested that there seemed to be striking similarities in the forms of the personal pronouns with those of a language he had been working on, Arafundi. Arafundi is separated from the Piawi languages by a sizable tract of uninhabited and, even by Highland New Guinea standards, difficult terrain, and the Haruai do not, to my knowledge, have any traditions of links with the Arafundi. Moreover, while the area where the Haruai live is unequivocally Highland, even if on the edge of the Highlands, the Arafundi live in a Lowland location. So an obvious question to ask is whether there is any evidence from other sources that might suggest a Lowland origin for the Haruai, thus reinforcing the possibility of a shared origin with the Arafundi.

There are some ethnographic respects in which the Haruai differ, or at least differed traditionally, from their Highland neighbors and are more similar to Lowland ethnic groups. Among Highlanders, for instance, the traditional marriage pattern is for marriages to be arranged, i.e. if a man wants to marry a woman he must seek the approval of the woman's family and, most importantly, pay a bride price, a considerable economic outlay that will only be possible with the cooperation of his own kin. By comparison, among Lowlanders, a common marriage pattern is by elopement, i.e. two people who want to get married run away together, their families are obliged to chase after them, and only subsequently will the bride price be negotiated. Elopement is, or at least was until recently, the Haruai pattern. While in practice the difference between the two patterns may be less than would seem to be the case at first sight — in New Guinea ethnic groups where marriages are arranged it is not customary for people to be married against their will, and in ethnic groups that practice elopement the fact that two people are likely to elope will often be a rather open secret — it is nonetheless considered an important cultural difference; some younger Haruai complained to me about the demise of the traditional pattern, under the influence of inter-marriage with Highland groups and of Christian missions.

Some traditional external physical measures would also suggest a Lowland origin for the Haruai. In New Guinea, in general body height correlates inversely with altitude, the tallest ethnic groups being found on the coasts and the shortest in the Highlands. The Haruai are on average noticeably taller than their Highland neighbors, although it should not be thought that they are giants: few adult Haruai males matched my 1.68 meters. Another physical anthropological parameter that correlates with altitude in New Guinea is skin pigmentation, with inhabitants of lower altitudes generally having darker skin pigmentation, and again the Haruai are on average noticeably darker than their Highland neigbors.

But clinching evidence has come from the work of a medical anthropological team that visited the Haruai soon after I left the area; the results of their work are published in Bhatia et al. (1989). In particular they found genetic material (alleles) among the Haruai that are otherwise only attested in Lowland populations, thus providing direct evidence in favor of the Lowland origin of the Haruai. The alleles in question involve alu-insertion, a mutation that is very unlikely to occur in the same form independently in two distinct populations. So here we have an example where the evidence from other disciplines was at best suggestive, but genetics has provided the decisive confirmation needed.

2 Languages of the Caucasus, with special reference to Azerbaijani

In the remainder of this article I will be looking at three test cases from Europe and the periphery of Europe, starting in the far southeast with the Caucasus, then moving to mainstream Europe by considering the Indo-European language family, and finally shifting to the northwestern periphery, more specifically England.

The Caucasus has long been noted for its linguistic diversity, contrasting with the broad sweeps of neighboring territories that are covered by large language families such as Indo-European, Semitic, or Turkic. Some of the languages of the Caucasus do indeed belong to these larger families, such as the Indo-European language Armenian or the Turkic language Azerbaijani, both in the South Caucasus. But the Caucasus also includes three language families that are not found outside the Caucasus, except as the result of sporadic recent emigration. These are the Kartvelian (formerly also called South Caucasian) languages, of which the best known member is Georgian, the dominant language of the Republic of Georgia; the West Caucasian (or Northwest Caucasian, or Abkhaz-Adyghe) languages, including Abkhaz and Circassian; and the East Caucasian (or Northeast Caucasian or Nakh-Daghestanian) languages, including Chechen and the languages of Daghestan, which include some languages spoken by just a few hundred people in a single village.

But our main concern here will be the Turkic language Azerbaijani, which is not only the dominant language of the Republic of Azerbaijan but is also spoken by a rather larger number of inhabitants of northwestern Iran. From the historical record, we know that Turkic languages first arrived in the territory of modern Azerbaijan about 1000 years ago, as part of the sudden expansion of Turkic languages that spread them from their original homeland in southern Siberia across Central Asia to the Caucasus and to present-day Turkey and parts of the Balkans. In other words, a thousand years ago Azerbaijan was not Turkic-speaking, whereas nowadays it is. How did this Turkic language come to establish itself in Azerbaijan? One could imagine two extreme possibilities. First, speakers of the Turkic language that was to become Azerbaijani could have arrived in this part of the Caucasus and have eliminated the previous population, killing them or driving them out. Second, the speakers of this Turkic language could have been a small group that established itself as an elite and gradually assimilated the existing population linguistically. This second possibility would illustrate the phenomenon of language shift, whereby an individual or a population abandons the original language in favor of another language. (In the linguistic literature the usual term is 'language shift', as used in the influential work of Thomason and Kaufman (1988). In the genetic literature the corresponding term is often 'language replacement'.) While linguists have traditionally often posed questions of this kind, it has usually been difficult or impossible to pin down cases of language shift that putatively took place more than a few hundreds of years ago. But recent developments in population genetics have enabled us to make more solid claims in this area, including the particular case of Azerbaijani.

Nasidze and Stoneking (2001) examine mitochondrial DNA (mt-DNA) from a number of populations in the Caucasus, in comparison with populations of Europe and the Middle East. Mt-DNA, though present in all humans, is inherited exclusively from the mother, so that it effectively traces the female line in the population, a point to which I return below. Their study shows that there is considerable variation in mt-DNA across different populations of the Caucasus, indeed the range of variation in such a small area and for such a relatively small population is surprising in comparison with larger neighboring areas such as Europe. However, despite the range of internal variation, mt-DNA of the Caucasus clearly forms a unified whole that contrasts both with mt-DNA from European populations and with that from populations of the Middle East. What is particularly striking is that the mt-DNA of Azerbaijani populations of the Caucasus is much closer to that of other populations of the Caucasus speaking non-Turkic languages, such as the Armenians, than it is to the mt-DNA of Turkic-speaking populations outside the Caucasus, including that of Turks from Turkey. In other words, while the language of the Azerbaijani population arrived in Azerbaijan within the last millennium, its genetic material is shared with other populations of the Caucasus and thus reflects genetic material that has been present in Caucasian populations for a much longer period.

(It should be noted that Nasidze and Stoneking's method operates by finding average values for each population studied. This does not exclude the possibility that there might be relatively small sub-groups within each population that are very distinct from this average.)

This feeds directly into the question of language shift. If Azerbaijani had been brought to the Caucasus by a new Turkic-speaking population which displaced the existing population, then we would expect this population to differ genetically from other populations of the Caucasus and be more similar to other Turkic-speaking populations (except to the extent that such other Turkic-speaking populations have resulted from language shift). But this is just the opposite of what we find, suggesting rather that we are dealing with a case of language shift: the population of Azerbaijan represents genetically a long-established population of the area, but one that has shifted its language to that of the Turkic-speaking newcomers. The precise details of the process of language shift are no longer recoverable, but presumably a small elite gradually assimilated larger and larger segments of the indigenous population. The last stages of this process are perhaps still to be seen in the small villages of northern Azerbaijan where East Caucasian languages are still spoken, but are under heavy pressure from Azerbaijani.

It was noted above that Nasidze and Stoneking (2001) refers exclusively to mt-DNA, i.e. that strictly speaking their conclusions concern only the female line of the Azerbaijani population. The mt-DNA material would still be consistent with a scenario whereby the female line of the Azerbaijani population was indigenous to the Caucasus, but the male line represented population replacement, i.e. Turkic-speaking men could have eliminated the original male population and mixed with the original female population to give rise to the present-day population. In order to test this hypothesis, it is necessary to examine Y-chromosomal DNA (more specifically: non-recombinant Y-chromosomal DNA), which is found exclusively in males and is passed exclusively down the male line of a population. Y-chromosomal DNA of populations of the Caucasus, including Azerbaijanis, is analyzed in Nasidze et al. (2003), with essentially the same result as was found for mt-DNA, namely that the genetic material patterns with that of other indigenous populations of the Caucasus. In other words, there was no substantial difference between male and female lines in the ethnogenesis of the Azerbaijanis, with an indigenous Caucasian population shifting to the language of a Turkic-speaking elite.

The combination of linguistic information (Azerbaijani is a Turkic language) and genetic information (this language is spoken by a population well within the range of variation found in populations of the Caucasus and distinct from Turkic-speaking populations outside the Caucasus) provides a clear resolution of the immediate population, namely that the 'Azerbaijanification' of Azerbaijan was an instance of language shift. But it still leaves open a number of other questions that only future research will (perhaps) be able to answer. In particular, it provides no evidence as to what language or languages was spoken by the population of Azerbaijan before this language shift. In some, especially northern parts of Azerbaijan, it might have been an East Caucasian language, and indeed we know from the historical record that some parts of northern Azerbaijan formed part of the Caucasian Albanian state — the similarity to the name *Albanian* in the Balkans is purely fortuitous — whose language, Caucasian Albanian, was perhaps an ancestor or near-ancestor of the present-day East Caucasian language Udi. In other parts of Azerbaijan the earlier language may well have been Iranian, and indeed it is Iranian influence that is most obvious in Azerbaijani as possible traces of the substrate, the language that was ultimately replaced by Azerbaijani but whose speakers carried over traces of their original language as part of the language shift process, a general phenomenon discussed in more detail in Section 4.

3 The Indo-Europeanization of Europe

If we look at the linguistic map of Europe today, then we find an area that is covered almost exclusively by Indo-European languages. In some peripheral parts of the continent we find other languages, in particular the Uralic languages in the northeast (such as Finnish and Estonian), though also Hungarian in the heart of Europe as the result of a unique migration pattern whose latest stages are part of recorded history, and of course the language isolate Basque in the Pyrenees. Now, it is generally acknowledged that Indo-European languages are not indigenous to Europe, so the question naturally arises where they came from and when. Most Indo-Europeanists would answer that Proto-Indo-European was spoken in the area to the north of the Black Sea around 6000 years ago, though Renfrew (1987), approaching the question from the perspective of an archeologist, has voiced a radically different view, locating Proto-Indo-European in Anatolia some 9000 years ago.

But the Indo-Europeanization of Europe, as a linguistic phenomenon, is only one of the major transformations undergone by Europe within the last 10,000 years. Early in this period Europe shifted its economic base, from being a continent primarily of hunter-gatherers to being a continent primarily of agriculturalists, the so-called Neolithic revolution, documented by archeology. Genetically, gene flow from the southeast seems to have substantially modified the genetic make-up of Europe's population. An obvious question to ask is whether these three major changes — linguistic, archeological, and genetic — can be correlated with each other. In this section I will try to answer this question from the perspective of a linguist, though drawing on results from the other disciplines. (For a more detailed discussion, see Comrie 2002.)

Of the three transformations, the introduction of agriculture is the easiest to document. The archeological record shows that agriculture entered Europe from the southeast about 9000 years ago and then gradually spread to the north and west, at an average rate of 1 kilometer per year. But this leaves open the question of exactly how agriculture spread in Europe. Was this a case of cultural diffusion, with each group taking up agriculture from its neighbors and little displacement of population? Or was it rather a case of population movement, with agriculturalists moving in from the southeast and displacing most of the original population, or at least reducing them to a minority? (Agricultural populations can under most circumstances support a much more rapid population growth than can hunter-gatherer populations, so that the meeting of the two kinds of societies almost invariably soon leads to a population advantage to the agriculturalists.)

(It should be noted that the model of demic diffusion espoused by Ammerman and Cavalli-Sforza (1984), though similar to population movement, is not quite the same. Under demic diffusion, it is the genes, rather than the individuals, that move. A simple illustration will clarify the difference. Imagine a chain of villages A–B–C–D–E–… in which a person is only allowed to marry someone from an immediately neighboring village. Given enough generations, the genetic material from someone born in village A may eventually diffuse to the far end of the chain, even though this individual may have traveled no further than village B. However, demic diffusion and population movement do have in common the feature that they represent biological spread, whereas cultural diffusion represents non-biological spread.)

Was the introduction of agriculture to Europe accompanied by a corresponding radical change in the genetic make-up of the population of Europe, such as would be consistent with widespread population movement or demic diffusion? Another way of asking the same question is: to what extent is the genetic make-up of the present-day European population of Paleolithic origin, reflecting population continuity from before the Neolithic, and to what extent is it of Neolithic origin, reflecting gene flow into Europe that accompanied the introduction of agriculture. Unfortunately, the answer provided by geneticists has been far from unanimous.

Two recent studies, Semino et al. (2000) and Chikhi et al. (2002), have examined this question, examining the same Y-chromosomal DNA data, and have come to radically different conclusions. Semino et al. conclude that the European genetic make-up is about 80% Paleolithic and about 20% Neolithic; Chikhi et al. conclude that it is about 30% Paleolithic and about 70% Neolithic. The one point on which both studies do agree is that the percentage of Neolithic decreases as one goes from southeast to northwest, so there is perhaps some evidence for gene flow accompanying the Neolithic revolution in Europe, although the very different percentages would point to quite different scenarios as regards the relative importance of cultural diffusion versus biological (population or gene) diffusion. One problem is that European populations are remarkably homogeneous with respect to their genetic make-up, indeed even more so with respect to mt-DNA than with respect to Y-chromosomal DNA, so that much can hinge on quite small differences, e.g. of chronology. Another is that some studies rely crucially on identifying particular present-day populations as direct descendants of pre-Neolithic European populations, with the Basques and Sardinians being the usual choices; unfortunately, this reliance is far from obviously justifiable, and without it one really has nothing by which to measure 'Paleolithicity' of genetic material. (Direct investigation of ancient DNA is problematic because of the danger of almost inevitable contamination from present-day genetic material.) About all that the outsider can do is to remain agnostically neutral between the competing claims (and perhaps others), at least until such time as geneticists reach consensus on the interpretation of data from this area.

So far we have seen that there may be a correlation between the Neolithic revolution in Europe starting 9000 years ago and at least some gene flow from the southeast, although the wide confidence intervals make it difficult to date the latter as accurately as the former. What does linguistics have to say?

Unfortunately, historical-comparative linguistics is notoriously bad at providing absolute chronologies. While linguists may be confident of many of their claims about what Proto-Indo-European was like, their assessments of when Proto-Indo-European was spoken are often based on subjective estimations of how much time would be required for languages to differentiate to a particular extent, although it is known that languages do not change overall at a constant rate — modern Lithuanian is much more archaic than modern Latvian, for instance, to take the two surviving members of the Baltic branch of the Indo-European language family. Moreover, methods that have tried to find fixed clocks for language change, such as glottochronology (with a fixed rate of replacement of basic vocabulary) have met with skepticism from most linguistics. (It should, however, be noted that chronologies placing Proto-Indo-European about 9000 years ago would require periods of development of early Indo-European considerably slower than that of the most archaic attested modern Indo-European language, Lithuanian (Mallory and Adams 1997: 585).)

However, it is possible to approach the problem from a somewhat less direct linguistic perspective. One of the techniques within the comparative-historical method, namely linguistic paleontology, enables us to reconstruct with reasonable certainty parts of the lexicon of the proto-language; the conclusion is then drawn that lexical items that can be reconstructed for the proto-language must represent concepts that were available to the speakers of the proto-language. Reconstruction involves careful control of the form and meaning of the items that are being compared in the individual languages — one would not, for instance, want to conclude that the Proto-Indo-Europeans were familiar with the telephone because a word something like *telephone* is widespread across Indo-European languages. Regular sound correspondences are one important tool in the linguist's tool box here: in English words that descend from Proto-Indo-European, word-initial *t* in English corresponds to word-initial *d* in non-Germanic languages, and to *ts* (written *z*) in German, e.g. English *ten*, Greek *deka*, German *zehn*; the fact that the word for 'telephone' begins with a *t* in all three languages suggests that it does not go back to Proto-Indo-European, but has been borrowed from one language into the others (in fact, it is composed of Greek elements).

To reconstruct a form back to Proto-Indo-European, reflexes must be attested in a sufficiently large number of branches of the family. Clearly, if an item is just attested in one branch (say, Germanic), then it may reflect an innovation of Germanic, rather than a feature of the proto-language. The attested branches of the Indo-European family are, going roughly from west to east, and with the abbreviations that will be used in examples below: Celtic (Celt), Italic (Ital), Germanic (Gmc), Balto-Slavic — with sub-branches Baltic (Balt) and Slavic (Slav) — Greek (Grk), Albanian (Alb), Armenian (Arm), Anatolian (Anat; extinct, including Hittite), Indo-Iranian — with sub-branches Indo-Aryan (IndA) and Iranian (Iran) — and Tocharian (Toch; extinct). How many branches should an item be attested in before we assign it to the proto-language? The great early twentieth-century Indo-Europeanist Antoine Meillet proposed a rule of thumb: three. However, in reconstructions it seems that not all branches are equal. In particular, some branches were in close contact for considerable periods and have shared innovations as a result of this; this applies in particular to the three western branches Celtic, Italic, and Germanic, so that something common to these three branches might well be an innovation later than Proto-Indo-European. On the other hand, some branches are generally considered to have split off from the rest very early, with Anatolian often considered the first, Tocharian the second. On this scenario, something attested in both Anatolian and Germanic stands a good chance of being Proto-Indo-European, even if not attested elsewhere in the family.

We can apply this terminology to agricultural terminology. Examples (2)–(5) show the application to words relating to animal husbandry. In each example, the form preceded by an asterisk is the reconstruction of the form of the word, the form in single quotes is its reconstructed meaning, while the list on the line below indicates the branches of the family in which reflexes are attested; a question mark indicates uncertainty. (The data are adapted from Mallory and Adams 1997.)

(2) *$h_1$ék´wos 'horse'
Anat, Toch, IndA, Iran, Arm, Grk, Balt, Gmc, Ital, Celt

(3) *pék´u 'cattle, domestic animal'
IndA, Iran, ?Balt, Gmc, Ital

(4) *g´hwer 'wild animal'
Toch, Grk, Slav, Balt, Ital

(5) *demh_x- 'to tame'
Anat ('push, press'), IndA, Iran, Grk, Gmc, Ital, Celt

The word for 'horse' is widely attested, so we can be reasonably certain that speakers of Proto-Indo-European were familiar with the horse, but it should be noted that it would be dangerous to go beyond this; for instance, this is not evidence that they were familiar with the domesticated horse, rather than just wild horses. However, the presence of reconstructable words differentiating 'cattle, domestic animal' from 'wild animal' is reasonable evidence that the speakers of Proto-Indo-European were familiar with domestication of animals. The possibility of reconstructing a verb meaning 'to tame' — the word is in fact the ancestor of English *tame* — points in the same direction, although the Anatolian cognate has a different meaning, which may represent the original meaning of the form, so that there may be somewhat more hesitation here.

Turning to cereal crops, we have the forms in (6)–(8).

(6) *yéwos/*yéwom 'grain, especially barley'
Anat, ?Toch, IndA, Iran, Grk, Slav, Balt

(7) *seh_1- 'to sow' (also 'to throw')
Anat, Slav, Balt, Gmc, Ital

(8) $*h_2\acute{e}rh_3ye$-/ $*h_2\acute{e}rh_3yo$- 'to plough'
?Anat, Toch, Arm, Grk, Slav, Balt, Gmc, Ital, Celt

The item in (6) represents a reconstructable grain type, but there are two problems: first, it is not entirely clear what grain is denoted, since the meaning is different in different languages, although the most likely is 'barley'. Second, as with 'horse' in (2), one cannot exclude the possibility that the word may originally have referred to a wild variety, and only subsequently been extended in meaning to include the domesticate, i.e. the word could be pre-agricultural. Something similar is true of 'sow' in (7), since this root also has the more general meaning 'throw', and sowing, especially early styles of sowing, would simply have involved throwing; on the other hand, the fact that this particular 'throw' root was selected in branches from Anatolian across to Germanic and Italic is indicative of a potentially significant shared innovation. But the last item is decisive: the only meaning is 'to plough', and the word is attested from Tocharian across to the western languages — the uncertainty surrounding the Anatolian term is unfortunate, but does not significantly affect the solidity of the reconstruction. In other words, the evidence seems good that speakers of Proto-Indo-European were familiar with agriculture, and are therefore available as candidates for having introduced agriculture into Europe.

But are they in fact the ones that did so? The reconstruction of a word for 'plough' is clear evidence that speakers of Proto-Indo-European were familiar with agriculture, but in fact it goes further: it is clear evidence that they were advanced agriculturalists, since the plough typically appears as an innovation around three millennia after the introduction of agriculture in the Middle East and Europe. (The earliest ploughs were wooden, and do not survive well in the archeological record, so the earliest evidence is often in the form of unmistakable plough marks, only occasionally actual plough remains where water has helped preserve the wood. See further Mallory and Adams (1997: 434–436), in particular for an argument that the Proto-Indo-European word did specifically denote a plough, and not some more primitive implement such as a digging stick, characteristic of the earliest agriculturalists.)

If the speakers of Proto-Indo-European were advanced agriculturalists, then they were not the people who initially introduced agriculture to Europe, some three millennia before the appearance of the plough. In other words, agriculture was introduced to Europe by some pre-Indo-European groups. The speakers of Indo-European languages who brought these languages to Europe were bearers of a more advanced form of agriculture, characterized inter alia by the plough, and indeed it may have been this more advanced agriculture that gave them the edge over the existing inhabitants, allowing their language to become the prestige language and eventually replace almost all its competition in Europe. This is not an unusual phenomenon in human history, whereby success in the long-term belongs not to those who first introduce an innovation (such as agriculture), but rather to those who improve upon it (as with the plough).

We can now try to draw together the various strands of the discussion in this section. The speakers of Proto-Indo-European were familiar with the plough, which would put them closer to the Indo-Europeanists' date of about 6000 years ago than to the introduction of agriculture around 9000 years ago. They entered a Europe that was already agricultural, although they almost certainly introduced improvements that led to their becoming the prestige group. If the geneticists are correct in claiming that there was a significant survival of Paleolithic genetic material into modern European populations, even if they disagree on the percentage — 30%, as concluded by Chikhi et al. (2002), is still high, and the percentage would have been higher in the north and west of the continent — then at least the bearers of this genetic material must have shifted language from whatever they spoke before to Indo-European. If there is no significant gene flow linked to the arrival of speakers of Indo-European, then there must have been even more widespread language shift, but this would require establishing reliably whether or not there was significant gene flow into Europe from the southeast around 6000 years ago. The information available at present does not quite allow us to tie all three strands — linguistic, genetic, and archeological — together. But it does point to what information we would need to complete the picture, and will hopefully also point specialists in the different disciplines to research that will fill in these gaps.

4 The anglicization of England

At the time of the Roman occupation of Britain (from the mid-first century CE to the beginning of the fifth century CE), the island that we now call Great Britain was almost exclusively, if not exclusively, Celtic-speaking, the one possible exception (apart, of course, from the Latin-speaking occupiers and the wide range of other languages likely to have been spoken by soldiers of the Roman army) being Pictish in the northeast of Scotland. Indeed, it was probable that the Celtic language of Roman Britain, usually called British, was relatively homogeneous: the poetry that is now considered the earliest Welsh poetry was composed in the kingdom of Strathclyde, around present-day Glasgow in Scotland, suggesting that the Celtic speech of one part of Britain would find ready acceptance elsewhere. Yet by only a few centuries after the collapse of Roman power in Britain, England (and parts of Scotland) were almost exclusively English-speaking, the result of the arrival of a Germanic language, the ancestor of present-day English and whose earliest stages in

England are referred to as Old English or Anglo-Saxon. The original Celtic language survives to the present day in Wales, as Welsh, and survived to around 1800 in Cornwall, as Cornish. (Scots Gaelic, the Celtic language that survives to the present in the Highlands of Scotland, was brought to Scotland from Ireland at about the same time as English was brought to England.) So it has been known for a long time that the Celtic language British was replaced by English in England.

But just as was done in Section 2 in the case of Azerbaijani, we can ask just what happened 'on the ground' when England became English-speaking. Did an incoming Germanic-speaking population eliminate the existing population, either killing them or driving them into peripheral areas like Wales and Cornwall? Or was it rather a smaller number of Germanic speakers who established themselves as an elite and gradually assimilated Celtic speakers linguistically? The issue has been much debated traditionally, but alas without any clear result. Indeed, I recall that as a student at the University of Cambridge I asked one of the lecturers in the history of the English language just this question, and got the answer that we don't know, and that we never will know. Perhaps it was dissatisfaction with this answer that set me to asking the kinds of questions that constitute the present article.

Unfortunately, in this case the evidence from disciplines outside linguistics is not particularly helpful. Archeology does provide some information, but the information is contradictory (see for instance Snyder 2003). The establishment of Anglo-Saxon England saw a massive abandonment of the towns in favor of rural dwelling, which might be taken as evidence of a change in population, with the new population having different residential preferences from its predecessor. On the other hand, use of cemeteries shows remarkable continuity, which would suggest a continuity of population. The evidence from genetic studies has been singularly inconclusive, with some suggesting that there is a significant genetic difference between populations located on the two sides of the Welsh–English border (e.g. Weale et al. 2002), others suggesting that any distinction is more gradual and that there is considerable retention of 'indigenous' genetic material in England (e.g. Capelli et al. 2003).

We may then ask whether linguistics is able to provide any further evidence. Some areas might seem promising. For instance, any dictionary of place names of England will show that a substantial number are of Celtic origin, but this is perhaps not in itself particularly telling, since it might just indicate that there was sufficient contact between Celtic and Anglo-Saxon populations for these place names to be transmitted, a phenomenon we know from many other parts of the world: in North America, many place names are of indigenous origin, but this is not indicative of substantial continuity of population from pre-Columbian times. A more striking piece of evidence does, however, come from place names, although this time from etymologically English place names that contain reflexes of Old English *Cumbre* or *Walh*, both terms used by the Germanic speakers to refer to the indigenous Celts — the latter is related to the word *Welsh* — and which therefore indicate settlements that were recognized by the Anglo-Saxons as being Celtic settlements. The map of the distribution of such place names given in Snyder (2003: 91) shows them across most of England with the exception of some eastern coastal areas, which one might well expect to have been more thoroughly settled by colonizers arriving from the Continent. So perhaps surprisingly, it is English place names that provide the more cogent evidence for late survival of Celtic settlements in England.

If the Anglicization of England did involve widespread language shift from British to English, then one might well expect that this would still be visible in the carry-over of features from British into English (but not into other Germanic languages whose history lacks such a shift). If we look at more recent instances of language shift, where the history is documented or at least more readily retrievable, then we do indeed find instances of just this type. In the course of the nineteenth century, Ireland shifted from being predominantly Irish-speaking to being predominantly English-speaking. But this shift led to considerable influence of Irish on the variety of English spoken in Ireland, Hiberno-English, as a result of individuals and groups undergoing language shift but carrying over features of their original language into the new language. The influence of Irish on the grammar of Hiberno-English is discussed in detail by Filppula (1999), and here only one example will be adduced to illustrate the phenomenon.

In Irish, it is possible to express an accompanying circumstance by means of the construction in (9), whereby a pronoun in the accusative is used together with a participle and no copular verb in order to express the attendant circumstance, the whole introduced by the coordinating conjunction *agus* 'and'; a literal translation into English would be something like 'John came and him drunk', a construction that is not possible in most varieties of English, but is found in Hiberno-English (and also, as one might expect, in some varieties of English spoken in Scotland where there has been language shift from Scots Gaelic, closely related to Irish).

(9) Tháinig Seán <u>agus é ólta</u>
came John and him drunk

'John arrived while (he was) drunk.'

Example (10) is from literary Hiberno-English, although examples from natural conversation are provided in Filppula (1999: 196–208) and references provided there. (Note that in Irish, the pronoun, as in (9), must be accusative, whereas in Hiberno-English it may be either nominative (as in (10)) or accusative; Filppula (1999: 200) discusses possible explanations for this slight difference.)

(10) ...you'd have as much chance o' movin' Fluther as a tune on a tinwhistle would move a deaf man an' he dead.
(Sean O'Casey, *The Plough and the Stars*, Act I, 148)

Do we find anything similar in English, or in varieties of English, that might be indicative of a similar shift from British to a Germanic language? Of course, since the attestation of British is minimal, we will need to find the next best evidence, namely that provided by Welsh. The search for evidence will also necessarily be more difficult, given the greater passage of time between the putative language shift from British to Old English in comparison with that from Irish to English. But one possible influence that has been suggested is the Northern Subject Rule (Klemola 2000), found in a number of dialects of English (but not the standard language), and otherwise quite isolated within the Germanic language family.

A number of regional dialects of English have the verb agreement pattern illustrated in (11). The pattern is basically the same as in the standard language, with one significant difference. When the subject is a non-pronominal noun phrase in the third person plural, the verb stands not in the expected third person plural form (which is found with third person pronouns), but rather in the third person singular, as in the bold-faced example in (11). (It is important to note the crucial difference between verb forms with a third person plural pronoun and with a third person non-pronominal noun phrase. Many other dialects of English have *the boys is*, but if they do not also have *they are*, but rather *they is*, then they do not exhibit the Northern Subject Rule.)

(11) S/he is.
The boy is.
They are.
The boys is.
I am. You are. We are.

At least in the kind of basic data shown in (11), the same pattern is found in Welsh, as illustrated in (12). Note that in the Welsh forms, the initial element is an affirmative particle, followed by the form of the verb 'to be', followed by the subject pronoun. The Welsh agreement system is richer than that of Modern English, but the crucial difference between the behavior of third person plural subject pronouns and non-pronominal noun phrases is clear. With a third person plural pronoun subject, the verb appears in the third person plural form, which is *maent* in the case of 'to be'. With a non-pronominal third person plural subject, however, the third person singular verb form is used, as in the bold-faced form in (12).

(12) Y mae ef/hi. 'He/She is.'
Y mae'r bachgen. 'The boy is.'
Y maent hwy. 'They are.'
Y mae'r bechgyn. 'The boys are.'
Yr wyf i. 'I am.' Yr wyt ti. 'You (SG) are.' Yr ydym ni. 'We are.' Yr ydych chwi. 'You (PL) are.'

The Northern Subject Rule thus provides suggestive evidence in favor of the transfer of one feature from British to some varieties of English. Of course, this is but a small beginning, and one would need far more evidence in order to build a convincing story of language shift from British to English. But this is research that should be done. Part of the problem is that surprisingly little is known about the syntax of English dialects, although a project currently underway at the University of Freiburg in Germany under the leadership of Bernd Kortmann should remedy this situation and provide the kind of information that we need in order to test further hypotheses of language shift in the formation of English; see http://www.anglistik.uni-freiburg.de/institut/lskortmann/index.htm.

It should be noted that in assessing the relevant contribution of population replacement versus language shift in the Anglicization of England (and likewise in other cases), it is not a simple choice between total population replacement or zero population replacement: at least some speakers of the Germanic ancestor of English must have entered Great Britain, otherwise there would have been no basis for language shift to have taken place. There must have been some contact between Celtic- and English-speaking populations, otherwise not even place names of Celtic origin would have made the transition. So the truth must lie somewhere in between these two extremes. What I have tried to suggest is that at least substantial language shift must have taken place. The same argument transfers, of course, to other instances of language shift, including the case of Azerbaijani discussed in Section 2.

In the course of this section, and more generally in the course of this article, frequent mention has been made of the phenomenon of language shift. Many non-linguists are often surprised at the frequency with which linguists (or at least some linguists) are prepared to consider the possibility of language shift, since many of those who have not studied the phenomenon believe that language shift should be a very rare phenomenon, at least other than under conditions of very strong social pressure of one language on another. This view is perhaps particularly strong among speakers of major world languages — and above all English — who find it hard to imagine a situation where they would abandon their language in favor of another. But this is viewing things from a perspective that is very much an aberration when viewed more broadly across the history of human language. Across most of human history bilingualism or multilingualism has probably been the natural state of humankind, as it is still is, for instance, among most indigenous communities of Australia, New Guinea, Amazonia, and many other parts of the world. And when one thinks about language shift, it is inappropriate to think of a monolingual speaker learning another language and then abandoning the first language. Rather, one needs to consider the shift of dominance from one language to another in the transmission of bilingual competence.

An interesting perspective on the notion of 'dominant language' in bilingual speakers is provided by Cutler et al. (1992). The subjects in this experiment were bilingual speakers who were judged to be native speakers by native speakers of each of the two languages involved. The subjects were asked to carry out speech perception tasks involving each of their two languages, and then involving nonsense sounds. They performed in each of their two languages like native speakers, but when faced with nonsense sounds each individual reverted consistently to one and only one of their two languages, thus providing clear evidence that this language was dominant. This suggests that the crucial change involved in language shift is not so much the replacement of one language by another, but rather the shift in the dominance relations between the two languages. In particular, parent and child may give the impression of both being equally bilingual, but the parent will be dominant in the traditional language, the child in the encroaching language. Paradoxically, the crucial step in language shift may be all but invisible to the observer. But once the dominance relation has shifted, the possibility is opened up for the recessive language to be lost in the process of transmission to future generations. Under this scenario, the first person or generation that acquires the second language may have no intention of having this language replace the original language; but they are setting into motion a process that may (but need not) have this end result, with a future generation becoming bilingual, and then a later generation switching the dominance values of the two languages.

5 Conclusions

While much can be learned about human prehistory by pursuing the implications of research within a single discipline, I have tried to show in this article that much requires the combination of results from different disciplines. In particular, I have tried to show how the combination of linguistic and genetic methods enables us to identify instances of language shift that occurred before or on the margins of recorded history. Wherever a particular language L1 is classified linguistically with language L2, but the speakers of L1 are classified genetically with speakers of L3, such that L2 is not classified linguistically with L3, then we have prima facie evidence for a case of language shift: the present-day speakers of L1 originally spoke a language related to L3, but shifted to their present language L1 (though of course more complicated scenarios, such as a sequence of language shifts, cannot be ruled out). Often, evidence from other disciplines, such as archeology and ethnography, will enrich the picture.

The discussion of the present article suggests a number of lines for future research. First, it is imperative to study a wide range of test cases to establish the extent to which genes and languages do correspond in historical classifications, but also to identify the circumstances — and here ethnography and archeology will play a particularly significant role — under which languages and genes do or do not correspond. Some obvious situations to examine would include linguistic exogamy (where one's marriage partner must be a speaker of a different language), attested in some Australian and Amazonian societies, or situations involving a breakdown in the regular transmission of language from parent to child, as in the formation of creole languages in plantation economies and elsewhere. At present we are barely on the threshold of the exciting developments that such interdisciplinary research promises in the investigation of human prehistory.

Acknowledgment

Versions of this article have been presented in numerous fora, including meetings of the Société Linguistique de Paris and of the Linguistic Society of America, invited lectures at La Trobe University, the University of California at Santa Barbara, and the University of Regensburg, and a meeting 'Humanities – Essential Research for Europe' organized by the Danish Research Council for the Humanities at the University of Southern Denmark. I am grateful to all those who have provided feedback.

References

Ammerman, A.J. and Cavalli-Sforza, L.L. (1984) *Neolithic Transition and the Genetics of Populations in Europe*. Princeton NJ: Princeton University Press.

Kuldeep, B., Jenkins, C., Prasad, M., Koki, G. and Lomange, J. (1989) Immunogentic studies of two recently contacted populations from Papua New Guinea. *Human Biology* 61: 45–64.

Capelli, C., Redhead, N., Abernethy, J.K., Gratrix, F., Wilson, J.F., Moen, T., Hervig, T., Richards, M., Stumpf, M.P.H., Underhill, P.A., Bradshaw, P., Shaha, A., Thomas, M.G., Bradman, N. and Goldstein, D.B. (2003) A Y chromosome census of the British Isles. *Current Biology* 13: 979–984.

Cavalli-Sforza, L.L., Piazza, A., Menozzi, P. and Mountain, J. (1988) Reconstruction of human evolution: bringing together genetic, archaeological, and linguistic data. *Proceedings of the National Academy of Sciences of the USA* 85: 6002–6006.

Chikhi, L., Nichols, R.A., Barbujani, G. and Beaumont, M.A. (2002) Y genetic data support the Neolithic demic diffusion model. *Proceedings of the National Academy of Sciences* 99: 11008–11013.

Comrie, B. (1988) Haruai verb structure and language classification in the Upper Yuat. *Language and Linguistics in Melanesia* 17: 140–160.

Comrie, B. (2002) Farming dispersal in Europe and the spread of the Indo-European language family. In P. Bellwood and C. Renfrew, eds, *Examining the Farming/Language Dispersal Hypothesis*, 409–419. Cambridge: McDonald Institute for Archaeological Research.

Cutler, A., Mehler, J., Norris, D. and Segui, J. (1992) The monolingual nature of speech segmentation by bilinguals. *Cognitive Psychology* 24: 381–410.

Dahl, O. C. (1951) *Malgache et Maanjan: une comparaison linguistique*. Oslo: Egede-Instituttet.

Filppula, M. (1999) *The Grammar of Irish English: language in Hibernian style*. London: Routledge.

Klemola, J. (2000) The origins of the Northern Subject Rule: a case of early contact? In Hildegard L.C. Tristram, ed., *Celtic Englishes II*, 329–346. Heidelberg: Universitätsverlag C. Winter.

Mallory, J.P. and Adams, D.Q. (1997) *Encyclopedia of Indo-European Culture*. London: Fitzroy Dearborn.

Nasidze, I. and Stoneking, M. (2001) Mitochondrial DNA variation and language replacements in the Caucasus. *Proceedings Royal Society London* B 268: 1197–1206.

Nasidze, I., Sarkisian, T., Kerimov, A. and Stoneking, M. (2003) Testing hypotheses of language replacement in the Caucasus: evidence from the Y-chromosome. *Human Genetics* 112: 255–261.

Renfrew, C. (1987) *Archaeology and Language: the puzzle of Indo-European origins*. London: Jonathan Cape.

Semino, O., Passarino, G., Oefner, P.J., Lin, A.A., Arbuzova, S., Beckman, L.E., De Benedictis, G., Francalacci, P., Kouvatsi, A., Limborska, S., Marcikic, M., Mika, A., Mika, B., Primorac, D., Santachiara-Benerecetti, A.S., Cavalli-Sforza, L.L. and Underhill, P.A. (2000) The genetic legacy of Paleolithic *Homo sapiens sapiens* in extant Europeans: a Y chromosome perspective. *Science* 290:1155–1159.

Snyder, C. A. (2003) *The Britons*. Oxford; Blackwell.

Thomason, S.G. and Kaufman, T. (1988) *Language Contact, Creolization, and Genetic Linguistics*. Berkeley: University of California Press.

Weale, M.E., Weiss, D.A., Jager, R.F., Bradman, N. and Thomas, M.G. (2002) Y chromosome evidence for Anglo-Saxon mass migration. *Molecular Biology and Evolution* 19: 1008–1021.

4 Poor design features in language as clues to its prehistory

Andrew Carstairs-McCarthy
University of Canterbury, NZ

1 Organisms as documents

Humans are peculiarly badly placed to understand why language is as it is. An ornithologist studying the nest-building habits of a particular bird species, for example, has ample evidence from other species to determine which habits of the bird in question are unique, which are unusual but shared with other species that may be closely related to it, and which are general, shared with many species. The unusual-but-shared habits will be particularly useful in establishing the species' prehistory and genetic relationships, especially if these habits serve no obvious contemporary function and are therefore unlikely to have been diffused independently through more than one bird population owing to similar selection pressures. But scientists studying the vocalisation and communication habits of humans have no such comparisons to assist them. No other species' communicative repertoire is anything like as elaborate as ours — or at least, any superficially comparable elaboration seems to serve much narrower ends, such as self-advertisement for mating purposes.

Noam Chomsky is fond of saying that an intelligent Martian, if it should come to earth, would regard all human languages as virtually identical, differing in only trivial details. Be that as it may, the intelligent Martian's form of language would at least provide something to compare our own with, analogous to the other bird species' nests with which the ornithologist can compare the nest of the bird that particularly interests her. For want of real-life Martians (or counterparts of the three intelligent Martian species that C.S. Lewis imagined in his novel *Out of the Silent Planet* (1943)), we have no direct evidence to distinguish those aspects of human language that are general, in the sense that we would expect to find them in any language-using species, and those that are peculiar, and hence clues to the historical accidents that shaped language evolution in humans but which would be unlikely to recur in the history of other hypothetical language-using species.

It is conceivable that nothing in the human capacity for language is the result of a historical accident in this sense. However, it is very unlikely. As the biologist George C. Williams puts it (1992:7):

> Many features of living organisms are functionally arbitrary or even maladaptive. ... All vertebrates are capable of choking on food, because digestive and respiratory systems cross in the throat. This ... is understandable as historical legacy, descent from an ancestor in which the anterior part of the alimentary tract was modified to form a previously unneeded respiratory system. This evolutionary short-sightedness has never been correctable. There has never been an initial step, towards uncrossing these systems, that could be favored by selection.

Similarly, bad design features in language may be clues to its history. This avenue of exploration has not been pursued enough, however, for the reason I suggested at the outset: humans, being the sole language-using species, are not well placed to identify which aspects of it are poorly designed.

Let me quote Williams again (1992:6):

> ... mechanistic biologists assume an *organism-as-crystal* and adaptationists an *organism-as-artifact* concept. An *organism-as-document* approach should also be recognized for biologists interested mainly in unique evolutionary histories.

The organism-as-crystal approach emphasizes characteristics such as the sturdiness of an elephant's legs, which is essential to support its massive weight. (A mouse the size of an elephant would collapse owing to gravity.) The organism-as-artifact approach emphasizes characteristics such as the streamlining of the body shape in seals and penguins, which has evolved independently in these two species in response to the same environmental pressures. Both these approaches are represented in recent comments on language evolution by linguists. A long-standing advocate of crystal-like (physical or mathematical) principles in language evolution is Chomsky, whose views are discussed critically by Newmeyer (1998) and favorably by Jenkins (2000). In a similar vein, Uriagereka (1998) has speculated that the Fibonacci series, implicated in the growth of sunflower heads and pine cones, plays a role in syntax too. By contrast, the adaptive characteristics of language are emphasized in a pioneering article by Steven Pinker and Paul Bloom (1990), and also by Newmeyer (1991) and by Derek Bickerton and William Calvin in various works (e.g. Calvin and Bickerton 2000). Both these approaches have attractions; but even when pursued in parallel, they are incomplete. Indeed, of the three approaches, it is the organism-as-document approach that will be most fruitful for the student of language evolution, because it is this approach that sheds most light on evolutionary prehistory.

The purpose of this article is to draw attention to three features of language that (I suggest) can be understood properly only by recourse to the organism-as-document approach. I hope thereby to stimulate more linguists who are interested in the history of language to look for other such features. Before embarking on the details, however, I will comment on what some may see as a fundamental difficulty. Given that we are speakers of some actual human language, will it be possible for us to recognize which aspects of language are designed well and which are designed badly? Will we not be fundamentally blinded by our own biological endowment, or by the absence of nonhuman languages for comparison?

This objection attributes to language a powerful stranglehold on our capacity to imagine alternatives to it. Benjamin Lee Whorf (Carroll 1956) suggested that individual languages could influence the thinking habits of their users in fundamental ways. This objection goes further, however: it is not individual languages but the language capacity itself that hampers us. In a similar vein, Ludwig Wittgenstein (1963a; 1963b) expressed radical skepticism about the possibility of ever getting outside language, so to speak, even while emphasizing the need to avoid 'bewitchment' by it — an insoluble dilemma. But this view is over-pessimistic, and deserves brisk rejection. Humans have successfully, for a variety of reasons, devised and investigated grammatical and semantic frameworks that are language-like but do not follow the pattern of any actual human language. For example, the so-called 'Polish notation' for propositional calculus (Prior 1962), in which the logical operators consistently precede all their arguments, permits complex expressions that are built up in a fashion alien to the syntax of any actual language, but nevertheless not difficult for students of logic to grasp. Predicate calculus, too, combines predicates and arguments in a readily graspable fashion, even though it incorporates no counterpart for grammatical functions such as subject and object (discussed in Section 3).

Even if we are prepared to recognize poor design in language as a possibility, a criterion for determining prima facie instances of it is needed. I suggest the following format for appropriate thought experiments. Assume some alternative world in which (a) a certain feature is absent from all human languages, and (b) linguists are invited by a colleague to contemplate the possibility that all or some languages possess this feature. Within the range of possible reactions, one extreme would be: 'Yes, that would be an improvement. I can see at once what selective advantage this feature might confer, from the point of view of either communication or the mental representation of experience.' The other extreme would be: 'No, I can see no advantage in this feature. If it were possible for languages to possess it, that could only be because it is a residue of a historical situation that natural selection has not been able to alter, much like the cross-over of the alimentary and respiratory channels in vertebrates.' Intermediate reactions would include variations on the following: 'Well, it's hardly surprising that languages lack this feature, but if some or all of them possessed it, one can envisage ways in which it might be exploited advantageously.'

2 A poor design feature: tolerance of allomorphy

Let us consider some characteristics of the artificial international language Esperanto. Nearly all the grammatical characteristics of Esperanto (e.g. basic subject-verb-object order, tense distinctions in verbs, singular and plural number and nominative and accusative case in nouns, case-number agreement in adjectives) are found among western European languages, and its vocabulary is overwhelmingly European-sourced too. But one characteristic it lacks: allomorphy. There is no counterpart in Esperanto to the morphological alternations exhibited in *wife~wives*, or *foot~feet*, or *leave~left* (by contrast with *fife~fifes*, *boot~boots*, and *heave~heaved*). Why not? The answer that Ludwig Zamenhof, the inventor of Esperanto, would surely have given is: 'Those variations in shape are a pointless complication. Natural languages acquire them as a residue of phonological change, mainly, but there is no reason why an artificial language should be burdened with complications that merely make the learner's task harder.' And Zamenhof would surely be right. There is an obvious sense in which allomorphy constitutes poor design. Reflecting this, there is an established research programme in morphological theory of seeking to reconcile the existence of allomorphy with the view that the most 'natural' kind of morphological expression obeys the principle 'one form, one meaning' (Dressler 1985; Dressler et al. 1987).

At one level, the explanation for allomorphy that I have put in Zamenhof's mouth is correct: it typically comes about through phonological change. Yet there are circumstances in which allomorphy is drastically and suddenly reduced: in creole formation, for instance. So let us imagine an alternative world in which the biological capacity for language is such that allomorphy is not tolerated. In practice, this would mean that, whenever some alternation risks arising through phonological change, it will be immediately eliminated through one of the processes that in historical linguistics have traditionally been lumped together as 'analogy'. In this world, the plurals of *wife* and *foot* would be *wifes* and *foots*, and the past tense of *leave* would be *leaved*, just as in the 'Newspeak' of George Orwell's *Nineteen Eighty-Four* (1949). Let us imagine also that some linguist in this world invited his colleagues to contemplate the possibility that allomorphic alternations of the *leave~left* kind could remain in existence and be perpetuated from one generation of speakers to another. What would be the reaction? 'That could never happen!', they would say. 'The linguistic sign, whether lexical or grammatical, is at the heart of how language operates, and it is scarcely conceivable that the relationship between the signifiant and the signifié should be complicated so as to allow one signifiant to have more than one signifié! There would be no cognitive or communicative advantage in that — certainly no advantage sufficient to outweigh the disadvantage for the learner of having to master all the irregularities that would arise. It is hardly surprising that our biological endowment for language enforces the immediate abolition through analogical regularization of any potential variations in shape that sound change may engender. As it is, language-learning is a massive task for the brain to complete in a remarkably short period of years, and the 'allomorphy' that you envisage would make the task even more massive!'

By the criterion proposed in the previous section, tolerance of allomorphy is thus a remarkably poor design feature of grammar. By what historical route, then, have humans evolved so as to possess a capacity for language that tolerates it? This is an 'organism-as-document' question that has scarcely been raised, let alone answered. It is linked to the question why language has not one but two kinds of grammatical organization: syntax and morphology. The seemingly unnecessary complexity of morphological alternation and of morphology in general has led Comrie (1992) to suggest that they appeared relatively late in linguistic evolution. My own view contrasts with this. The answer, I suggest, lies in the human brain's powerful capacity to categorize, that is, to recognize distinct items as related (Carstairs-McCarthy 2005b). To illustrate what I mean by 'distinct but related' I will use a historical example; but I ask readers to bear in mind that what is at issue is the language-evolutionary reason why allomorphy is tolerated, not how it has arisen in individual historical instances.

The English pair of allomorphs *foot* (singular) versus *feet* (plural) arose through a process in which a corresponding Proto-Germanic pair with a uniform stem and a plural suffix *-i* (*[fo:t] versus *[fo:t-i]) acquired two stems, a singular and a plural one, through the kind of phonological assimilation known as umlaut (*[fo:t]~*[fø:t-i]). This assimilation reflects the fact that the vocal apparatus does not operate in such a way as to yield clearcut boundaries between successive sounds, either in articulation or in the acoustics of the speech signal, even though at some level of representation the brain may impose such boundaries. At some point in the prehistory of English, the vowel difference between [fo:t] and [fø:t-] became sufficiently salient so that the brain recognized the two forms as distinct, though still clearly related in their lexical meaning and hence assigned to the same category, in some sense. This relationship was established sufficiently firmly so that [fo:t] and [fø:t], or their modern English counterparts *foot* and *feet*, could carry on as expressions of 'foot, singular' and 'foot, plural', even though the plural suffix has now disappeared entirely. The child's capacity for language learning operates in such a way that a pressure to 'repair' such allomorphy, and to create a Newspeak-style regular plural form *foots*, is not sufficient to overwhelm the readiness to preserve *foot* and *feet* as distinct but related linguistic items, belonging to the same category. (In more technical terms of morphological theory, the relevant categories are lexemes: both *foot* and *feet* are forms of the lexeme FOOT.) However, if the medium of linguistic expression had a digital rather than an analogue character, then there would be no reason for words or morphemes to affect the pronunciation of their neighbors in the speech chain. In that case, even given the brain's readiness to categorize, an essential factor in the origin of allomorphy (and hence the origin of morphology, as distinct from syntax) would have been missing. According to this scenario, tolerance for allomorphy is a byproduct of the way in which successive individual linguistic items (words or morphemes) can influence each other phonologically, combined with the brain's readiness to categorize distinct forms as related.

Even if this story is on the right lines, there is vastly more to be said about how morphology works and how it may have originated. The alternation between *foot* and *feet* coincides exactly with a grammatical distinction, between singular and plural. Such neat correlations are not always found, however. For example, the Italian verb *fuggire* 'to flee' has two allomorphs [fugg] and [fuddʒ], the first of which is used just in the 1st singular and 3rd plural of the present indicative, and the singular and 3rd plural of the present subjunctive. But, even if the brain is willing to categorize these as different forms of the item FUGG-, why does it tolerate such a messy distribution? The crucial point seems to be that the messiness of FUGG- is not unique: several other Italian verbs show the same pattern of distribution of alternants (Maiden 1992). Useless though it may be for cognitive and communicative purposes, this pattern of distribution is itself what the [fugg]~[fuddʒ] alternation signals, it seems; and the pattern is sufficiently widespread and consistent to make the alternation learnable.

No sane person designing a language system from scratch would incorporate as a characteristic of it allomorphy of the kind just described. It is a remarkable example of unintelligent design. But just for that reason it sheds light on how two factors interacted in the prehistory of language so as to produce it: the brain's readiness to categorize, and the analogue character of the speech signal.

(Alternatively, if one believes that the origins of language are gestural, the same point can be made, relying on the analogue character of gesture. What I have said about how allomorphy may have become entrenched does not discriminate between gestural-origin and vocal-origin theories of language evolution.) So allomorphy, although widely regarded in recent decades as one of the messy peripheral aspects of language that are irrelevant to its essential nature, turns out to provide striking evidence of the brain's readiness to luxuriate in categorization, even at the cost of devising communicatively and cognitively pointless rationales for the choice between distinct forms categorized as belonging to the same word. Tolerance for allomorphy also shows that, even if many of the central features of grammar derive from the status of language as a mental phenomenon, there are nevertheless some central features that are tightly bound up with how it is externalized, in speech or gesture.

3 A poor design feature: grammatical functions

Let us assume, at least for the moment, that any sort of syntax must distinguish between arguments and argument-takers. (I use the term 'argument-taker' rather than 'predicate' because the latter is ambiguous, depending on whether it contrasts with 'argument' or with 'subject', and because it has associations with notions such as 'sentence' and 'proposition' that I would like to avoid.) That is, there must be some distinction between one the one hand 'nouns' and on the other hand 'verbs' or 'adjectives'. (The scare quotes are a warning to treat these terms with caution, given that I am using them outside the framework of the syntax of any actual modern language.) Let us assume also an alternative world in which syntax provides no more than this; that is, that the distinction between arguments and argument-takers is signaled, but the semantic roles of the arguments (as agent, patient, instrument, etc.) are not, and nor are their information-structural roles (as shared versus new information, or as topic verus comment). For example, in this alternative world there exist complex expressions such as *kick girl horse*, in which the role of *kick* as an argument-taker is signaled by its initial position (let's assume), but which are equally applicable to any kicking event with a girl and a horse as participants, and in which there is no convention to distinguish new from old information.

Imagine now that in this alternative world a linguist invites fellow-linguists to contemplate a kind of language in which the role of the horse and the girl in the event would be consistently and reliably signaled, so there would never be any doubt about who is kicking whom. Would that innovation be seen as functional? The answer is, surely, yes. A kind of syntax with no differentiation of semantic roles is better than no syntax at all (just as an eye sensitive to just light and dark is better than no eye at all), but a syntax that encodes semantic roles reliably is clearly better.

Now, by contrast, imagine that in this same world, what fellow-linguists are invited to contemplate is the possibility of encoding not semantic roles but information structure. Old and new information would be clearly signaled in the syntax, whether by word order or by particles. That would open the way for (for example) the omission of arguments that are part of the information shared by speaker and hearer. Again, the consensus would surely be that this would be an advantageous innovation.

At first sight, it may seem that both these 'innovations' are features of syntax in our actual world. It is true that both semantic roles and information structure are signaled more or less efficiently in many languages. But the emphasis should be on 'more or less'. Typically, the mechanism through which both of these kinds of encoding is achieved is that of the so-called 'grammatical functions', such as 'subject', 'direct object' and 'indirect object'. Thus, in English, it is usual for grammatical subject status to signal an argument as both an agent and part of the shared information in a discourse. Here is an illustration. Consider the relative likelihood of sentences (1) and (2) occurring in a description by me of what I was doing yesterday afternoon:

(1) Between three and four o'clock I wrote a letter.

(2) Between three and four o'clock a letter was written.

Example (1) seems more plausible than (2), because in (1) the grammatical subject *I* represents not only the agent but also shared information (since it is my activities that my discourse is describing). Yet the very fact that this information is shared would seem to render it a prime candidate for omission. So why does (2) not sound more acceptable than it does? And (3), where the topic is likewise omitted, is even less acceptable because it is ungrammatical (an overt grammatical subject being compulsory in English):

(3) *Between three and four o'clock wrote a letter.

Suppose, then, that in the same alternative world we proffer for consideration neither a direct mechanism for encoding semantic roles nor a direct mechanism for encoding information structure, but rather the sort of grammatical-function mechanism just exhibited in English (and in all languages, one way or another, according to some linguists). What would be the reaction of our alternative-world linguist colleagues? It seems likely that they would say: 'Well, that's not so good! These things you call 'grammatical functions' seem to be a sort of mish-mash, trying to fulfill two purposes simultaneously. It would be much better to encode information structure and semantic roles separately, since, even if there is a statistical tendency for (for example) agents to be topics, clearly the two parameters can vary independently.'

This negative reaction is sensible, in the light of linguists' difficulty in arriving at stable and workable criteria for identifying grammatical functions in language-as-it-is (Davies and Dubinsky 2001). This applies particularly to the notion 'subject' (Keenan 1976). So, despite the pervasiveness of the notions 'subject' and 'object' in linguistic description within almost every theoretical framework, we should take seriously the possibility that grammatical functions are a relatively poor design feature. We fail to recognize them as such only because (as I suggested at the start) we as humans are so badly placed to study human language. There are indeed uses to which grammatical functions are regularly put, and a rationale can be found for why certain uses seem to be preferred over others. For example, if topics and agents coincide more often than topics and patients do, it is not surprising that the combination of semantic and information-structural values that the grammatical subject typically expresses should be 'topic-agent' rather than 'topic-patient'. But this does no more than demonstrate that sensible use can be made of less-than-ideal raw materials, in language as elsewhere. It does not tell us where the raw materials came from in the first place. That is the question that interests the student of language evolution. In respect of grammatical subjects, I have suggested an answer to the question elsewhere (Carstairs-McCarthy 1999). My present aim, however, is not to propose an answer but to persuade readers that the question is genuine and important.

4 A poor design feature: the distinction between sentences and nominal expressions

It may seem that there is a straightforward answer to the question just posed, on the following lines: the notion 'grammatical subject' is indispensable in any sort of syntax, because any sort of structured assertion, in our actual world or an alternative world, must distinguish between what is mentioned (the 'subject') and what is said about what is mentioned (the 'predicate'). Thus, Bowers defines 'predication' as follows (2001:299):

> I will take for granted the traditional view that a proposition in a natural language consists minimally of a distinguished nominal expression referred to as the 'subject' and another expression referred to as the 'predicate'. Predication is the relation between these two constituents.

He goes on to say later (2001:328):

> There could hardly be a relation more fundamental to grammar than predication. Indeed, it could be argued that predication is, in a certain sense, *the* most fundamental relation in both syntax and semantics. Though there are many features of natural language systems that one could imagine eliminating without seriously impairing communication, predication is surely not one of them.

In contrast to Bowers, I will argue that it is possible to imagine an alternative world in which successful linguistic communication is achieved without predication, at least in its most conventional syntactic sense. I will also argue that linguists in this alternative world, when invited to contemplate incorporating a syntactic subject-predicate distinction into the kind of syntax that they are familiar with, would by no means be inclined to greet it as an improvement.

My argument starts with an observation about the relationship between sentences and some nominal expressions. In many if not all languages in our actual world, it is possible to identify, for any sentence, one or more nominal expressions with just the same semantic content, including (at least according to some analyses) the same argument structure. Thus, corresponding to the sentences at (4) are the nominal expressions at (5):

(4) a. Columbus discovered America.
  b. It is raining.
  c. The dog is dying.

(5) a. Columbus's discovery of America
  b. rain
  c. i. the dying dog
   ii. the death of the dog

In some instances it seems most natural to think of the nominal expression as being derived from the corresponding sentence, as in (5a), but this is not essential, as (5b) shows. In some instances also there appears to be just one obvious corresponding nominal expression, but this is not essential either, as (5c) shows. The essential point is that nominal counterparts to sentences are easy to find.

Consider now an alternative world in which only the nominal counterparts of sentences exist. In this alternative world, English would not be a possible language, but a language that we may call Nominalized English would be. In circumstances where a speaker of English would utter (4a), a speaker of Nominalized English could utter (5a), and so on. In this alternative world, would communication be seriously impaired, by comparison with the communication we can achieve in this world? I can see no reason why it should be. Even for complex English sentences such as in (6), a Nominalized English counterpart can be imagined, as in (7):

(6) a. If it rains tomorrow, we won't want to go to the beach.
b. Why do you think Sally refused to marry Bruce?
c. Give that to me!

(7) a. an entailment by eventual rain tomorrow of absence of a desire for a beach trip on our part
b. my curiosity about your opinion on Sally's refusal of a marriage with Bruce
c. my insistence on your handover of that

This sounds quaint and cumbersome. But Nominalized English is of course a makeshift, contrived simply to give some feel for what syntax would be like in a world without any distinction between sentences and nominal expressions. The important question is: would communication be seriously impaired in such a world?

Our first reaction may be that merely to mention an event or a situation is not to connect with the world in the way we do when we make an assertion, or ask a question, or issue a command, as in (6). But that reaction is born out of nothing more fundamental than unfamiliarity. If we assume that an expression such as (7a) is used in the alternative world with the intention of communicating, the most natural expectation about what an appropriate rendering would be in actual English for the content communicated is as in (6a).

Another reaction may be that the distinction between nominal expressions and sentences must reflect a fundamental cognitive distinction between things (physical objects) on the one hand and events or situations on the other. But, even supposing such a cognitive distinction exists independently of the linguistic devices that supposedly encode it, it is a distinction that is equally expressible in Nominalized English, through a distinction between argument-takers (e.g. *discovery* and *dying/death* at (5)) and arguments (e.g. *Columbus*, *America*, and *dog*). (Semantically, *rain* is perhaps best seen as an 'argument-taker' with zero arguments.) So, if satisfactory communication is possible with English in the actual world, it is equally possible with something resembling Nominalized English in the alternative world.

A counter to this, in defense of Bowers's position, might run as follows: 'That may be so, but even in the alternative world a subject-predicate distinction exists. For example, in the nominal expression *Columbus's discovery of America* at (5a), *Columbus* is semantically the subject, and *discovery of America* (or rather the semantic content of these words) is the predicate. The subject-predicate distinction does not depend crucially on a syntactic distinction between sentences and nominal expressions.' My response is: 'That may be so. If you tell me that in the alternative world it will be possible to identify unambiguously in linguistic expressions a counterpart to what Bowers calls the 'distinguished nominal expression', I will not disagree with you, though I will raise my eyebrows skeptically. But that does not affect my point. People in the alternative world seem to be able to communicate quite effectively without any counterpart to the distinction between nominal expressions and sentences.'

It is now time to conduct our regular thought-experiment. Let us suppose that, in the alternative world, a linguist invites his colleagues to contemplate the importation into their languages of the distinction between sentences and nominal expressions. 'What sort of advantage would that bring?', they ask. 'Well', says the imaginative linguist, 'these items that I will call 'sentences' will be used when an expression is intended to connect with the world seriously, conveying or requesting information about it, while 'nominal expressions' will be used when their content is merely being mentioned or contemplated or mused over, without that intention. That would certainly be an advantage.'

We in the actual world may be inclined to agree with the imaginative alternative-world linguist. With the contemplated innovation (we may think), people in the alternative world would now for the first time be able to distinguish between asserting and merely mentioning. Before we agree too hastily, however, we should examine how close the correlation is in our own world between sentencehood and assertion, and between nounhood and mere mentioning. Our terminology for labeling speech acts risks making this correlation seem more exact than it is. The term 'assert' expects a clause or a proposition as its complement, rather than a nominal expression. We can assert that it is raining or that Archduke Ferdinand was assassinated, but we cannot assert rain, nor the Archduke's assassination. That makes it seem as if a serious intention to convey information must inevitably require the use of a sentence. In reality, however, it reflects only something more modest and parochial: certain grammatical restrictions on the English verb 'assert'. So, in order to avoid any covert biases in terminology, I propose to use the terms 'announcement' and 'envisagement' in a new technical fashion. A linguistic expression is used to announce (let us say) if it is used with the intention that its contents should convey or request information. A linguistic expression that is used without that intention is being used only to envisage.

We are now in a position to ask: in our actual world, are announcements always expressed sententially, and are envisagements always expressed non-sententially (in particular, through a nominal expression)? The answer is no. Announcements are routinely expressed nominally in certain conventional contexts: for example, newspaper hoardings (e.g. 'Brazil victory in World

Cup'), book titles (e.g. *The Decline and Fall of the Roman Empire*), and when guests arrive at certain formal gatherings ('The Prime Minister and Mrs. Blair!'). Conversely, envisagements are routinely expressed in sentences, sometimes but not always accompanied by a warning label such as 'Suppose...' or 'perhaps'. What's more, there are many embedded contexts in English and in other languages where syntax permits or requires the use of a sentence to express what is clearly only an envisagement. This applies to the bracketed sentences in the following examples:

(8) The people in that village believe that [the world is flat].

(9) If [I were you], I wouldn't do that.

(10) We still hope that [war will be avoided], but it seems increasingly unlikely.

Let us now grant to the assembled linguists of the alternative world a glimpse of how sentences and nominal expressions are distributed in the linguistic usage of our own world. They may decide that the innovation that their imaginative colleague has invited them to contemplate would not be so advantageous after all. At the very least, they would conclude that in our world, having been given the opportunity (so to speak) to exploit the distinction between sentences and nominal expressions to fulfill a clearcut function, we have wasted that opportunity. So the distinction between sentences and nominal expressions, despite what Bowers says about propositions and predication, is not so obviously a good design feature of language after all.

I am conscious that what I have said raises issues in the philosophy of language, logic and semantics that have been discussed ever since the days of Plato and Aristotle. I have not begun to do justice to those issues here, though I treat them more fully elsewhere (Carstairs-McCarthy 1999; 2005a). What matters for present purposes is that readers should think seriously about the possibility that even something so apparently central to language as the distinction between sentences and nominal expressions may be dispensable. If so, then its origin is a real puzzle whose solution (if it can be achieved) will be historically enlightening.

5 Conclusion

In section 1 I introduced George Williams's distinction between the organism-as-crystal, the organism-as-artifact and the organism-as-document. Language is not an organism, but a salient characteristic of a particular species of organism. It is legitimate therefore to think in evolutionary terms of language-as-crystal, language-as-artifact, and language-as-document. This three-way distinction corresponds exactly to a distinction drawn recently by Chomsky (2001:3) with regard to 'the initial conditions on language acquisition'. He uses the symbol S_0 to stand for the genetically determined initial state of the faculty of language and the abbreviation IC to stand for the 'interface conditions' that ensure that the expressions generated by a language are accessible to 'the sensorimotor and conceptual-intentional systems that enter into thought and action'. The initial conditions are divided among three classes:

(i) unexplained elements of S_0

(ii) IC (the principled, or well designed, part of S_0)

(iii) general properties, i.e. 'general principles (physical, chemical, mathematical)'

Initial conditions of class (iii) belong to language-as-crystal. Conditions of class (ii) belong to language-as-artifact; they are the conditions emphasized by Pinker and Bloom (1990). Our concern in this chapter, however, has been with conditions of class (i). Concerning these, Chomsky is pessimistic. He says: 'Principled explanation, going beyond explanatory adequacy, keeps to (ii) and (iii). An extremely strong minimalist thesis ... — too much to expect — would be [that class (i)] is empty.'

I call this view pessimistic because it assumes that nothing interesting can be said about those aspects of language that belong to language-as-document. On the contrary: it is precisely language-as-document, rather than language-as-crystal or language-as-artifact, that will be most revealing about how language originated. Similarly, it is precisely because the QWERTY keyboard layout is unprincipled, or seemingly arbitrary, that a correct explanation for it is historically revealing — hence Dennett's (1995) use of the term 'QWERTY phenomenon' for the kind of historically revealing biological trait whose counterpart in language I have been discussing. So the first step in a linguistic contribution to understanding how language originated (to set alongside contributions from archaeology, anthropology, neurology and primatology) is to identify characteristics of language that are 'unprincipled' in Chomsky's sense. There are more of them than one at first suspects; but finding them may require us to cast off our human-language blinkers.

Acknowledgment

I am grateful to Fritz Newmeyer for comments on an earlier draft. He is not to be assumed to agree with what I say.

References

Bowers, J. (2001) Predication, in Baltin, M. and Collins, C. (eds), *Contemporary Syntactic Theory.* Oxford: Blackwell, 299–333.

Calvin, W. and Bickerton, D. (2000) *Lingua ex Machina: Reconciling Darwin and Chomsky with the Human Brain.* Cambridge, MA: MIT Press.

Carroll, J. (ed.) (1956) *Language, Thought and Reality: Selected Writings of Benjamin Lee Whorf.* Cambridge, MA: MIT Press.

Carstairs-McCarthy, A. (1999) *The Origins of Complex Language: An Inquiry into the Evolutionary Beginnings of Sentences, Syllables and Truth.* Oxford: Oxford University Press.

Carstairs-McCarthy, A. (2005)a The link between sentences and 'assertion': an evolutionary accident?, in Elugardo, R. and Stainton, R. (eds), *Ellipsis and Non-Sentential Speech.* Dordrecht: Kluwer, 149–162.

Carstairs-McCarthy, A. (2005)b The evolutionary origin of morphology, in Tallerman, M. (ed.), *Language Origins: Perspectives on Evolution.* Oxford: Oxford University Press, 166–184.

Chomsky, N. (2001) Beyond explanatory adequacy, *MIT Occasional Papers in Linguistics* 20: 1–28.

Comrie, B. (1992) Before complexity, in Hawkins, J. and Gell-Mann, M. (eds), *The Evolution of Human Languages.* Redwood City: Addison-Wesley, 193–211.

Davies, W. and Dubinsky, S. (2001) Remarks on grammatical functions in transformational syntax, in Davies, W. and Dubinsky, S. (eds), *Objects and Other Subjects: Grammatical Funcions, Functional Categories and Configurationality.* Dordrecht: Kluwer, 1–19.

Dennett, D. (1995) *Darwin's Dangerous Idea: Evolution and the Meanings of Life.* New York: Simon and Schuster.

Dressler, W. (1985) *Morphonology: The Dynamics of Derivation.* Ann Arbor: Karoma.

Dressler, W., Mayerhaler, W., Panagl, O. and Wurzel, W. (eds) (1987) *Leitmotifs in Natural Morphology.* Amsterdam: Benjamins.

Jenkins, L. (2000) *Biolinguistics: Exploring the Biology of Language.* Cambridge: Cambridge University Press.

Keenan, E. (1976) Towards a universal definition of 'subject', in Li, C. (ed.), *Subject and Topic.* New York: Academic Press, 303–333.

Lewis, C. S. (1943) *Out of the Silent Planet.* London: J. Lane.

Maiden, M. (1992) Irregularity as a determinant of morphological change, *Journal of Linguistics* 28: 285–312.

Newmeyer, F. J. (1991) Functional explanation in linguistics and the origins of language, *Language and Communication* 11: 3–28.

Newmeyer, F. J. (1998) On the supposed 'counterfunctionality' of universal grammar, in Hurford, J., Studdert-Kennedy, M. and Knight, C. (eds), *Approaches to the Evolution of Language: Social and Cognitive Bases.* Cambridge: Cambridge University Press, 305–319.

Orwell, G. (1949) *Nineteen Eighty-Four*. London: Secker & Warburg.
Pinker, S. and Bloom, P. (1990) Natural language and natural selection [with peer commentary], *Behavioral and Brain Sciences* 13: 707–784.
Prior, A. (1962) *Formal Logic* (2nd ed.). Oxford: Oxford University Press.
Uriagereka, J. (1998) *Rhyme and Reason: An Introduction to Minimalist Syntax*. Cambridge, MA: MIT Press.
Williams, G. C. (1992) *Natural Selection: Domains, Levels and Challenges*. New York: Oxford University Press.
Wittgenstein, L. (1963a) *Tractatus Logico-Philosophicus* (with translation by D. F. Pears and B. F. McGuinness) (2nd corrected impression). London: Routledge & Kegan Paul.
Wittgenstein, L. (1963b) *Philosophical Investigations* (with translation by G. E. M. Anscombe) Oxford: Blackwell.

5 What can we learn about the earliest human language by comparing languages known today?

Lyle Campbell
University of Utah

1 Introduction

Looking back from modern languages, what can we find out about the earliest human language? The goal of this paper is to determine what, if anything, can be learned about the earliest human language(s) from evidence extant in modern and older attested languages. It evaluates attempts to arrive at the origins of language through such comparisons. The main finding is negative: because of so much change over such a long time, nothing of the original language(s) survives in modern languages in any form that could be usefully compared across-linguistically to give any indication of the lexical or structural content of the original language(s).

2 Methodological issues

A number of linguists have attempted to find deep genetic relationships, so-called 'macrofamilies', and some go even further, attempting to trace all human languages back to a single origin. 'Global etymologies' have been presented as evidence for 'Proto-World' (see Bengtson and Ruhlen 1994a, 1994b, Ruhlen 1987, 1994a, 1994b, Ruhlen's homepage [1]). 'Proto-World' is receiving considerable attention, and therefore it is important to scrutinize it carefully. I argue (see also Bender 1993, Hock 1993, Picard 1998, Rosenfelder 1999, Salmons 1992a, 1992b, Trask 1996:391–6, McWhorter 2001:287–303) that such a scrutiny reveals that claims about global etymologies are mistaken and cannot teach us anything about the origins of human language.

Both friends and foes acknowledge that the principal method employed in global etymologies is 'mass [or multilateral] comparison' (cf. Ruhlen 1987:258). Ruhlen (1992:178) says, 'John Bengtson and I, operating in a Greenbergian tradition of multilateral comparison, have proposed some thirty etymologies connecting all the world's language families' (see Bengtson and Ruhlen 1994a, Ruhlen 1987:261, 1994a, 1994b). Aitchison (1996:172) calls this the "lucky dip' approach: trawling through dictionaries, and coming across superficial resemblances between words in far-flung languages'. The criticisms of mass (multilateral) comparison are well-known and need not be repeated here (see Aitchison 1996:172–3, Campbell 1988, 1998a, 1998b, 1999, Campbell and Poser forthcoming, Matisoff 1990, McMahon and McMahon 1995, Rankin 1992, Ringe 1992, 1995, 1996, 1998, 1999, Trask 1996:376–403, etc.). Most linguists reject the global etymologies because they do not find the method used reliable (cf. McWhorter 2001:288). Aitchison (1996:173) summarizes the problems:

> Chance resemblances are easy to find among different languages if only vague likenesses among shortish words are selected ... sounds change radically over the centuries. Words which existed so long ago are unlikely to have survived in anything like their original state ... the 'lucky dip' approach does not make any attempt to eliminate accidental correspondences, nor does it control for phonetic probability or taboo ... meanings tend to be reduced to fairly simple, straightforward items, with a limited number of phonetic shapes. In these circumstances, chance similarities are likely to play a worryingly high role, and this 'mass comparison' method is unlikely to stand the test of time.

2.1 Global etymologies: the 'strong' cases

There is not space to evaluate each proposed global etymology; however, a few examples are sufficient to reveal the problems. The two strongest (most cited) have already been evaluated rigorously, **tik* 'finger' (Bender 1993, Salmons 1992a, 1992b) and **maliq'a* 'to suck(le), nurse, breast' (Hock 1993, Hock and Joseph 1996:498–502). As critics show, the data (Bengtson and Ruhlen 1994a:322–3) are much weaker than they at first appear, and the methods employed are unable to show that chance is not a more plausible explanation than genetic relationship.

In standard etymological criteria used among languages known to be related, purely accidental lexical matchings are constrained by the demands of sound correspondences and semantic equivalence (see Goddard 1975:254–5, Salmons 1992a). The numerous non-cognate lexical similarities in closely related languages show why such criteria are necessary, e.g.: English *day*: Spanish *día* 'day' (these do not obey Grimm's law as true cognates do, English < Old English *dæg* < Germanic **dagaz* 'day' < Proto-Indo-European (PIE) **agh* 'day'; Spanish < Latin *dies* 'day' < PIE **dyē-*, **deiw-* 'to shine'); Spanish *mucho* 'much': English *much* (Spanish < Latin *multus* 'much, many' < PIE **ml̥-to-* 'great, strong', English < Old English *micel*, *mycel* 'great', 'much' < Gemanic **mik-ila* < PIE **meg-* 'great'); Hungarian *fiú* 'boy': Romanian *fiu* 'boy, son' (Hungarian < Proto-Finno-Ugric **poyi* 'boy, son'; Romanian < Latin *filius* 'son' < PIE **dhi:-lyo-* < **dhe(i)-* 'to suck, suckle').

Global etymology does not heed these constraints known to be necessary even in closely related languages, as seen from the example **kuna* 'woman'. This is one of the strongest cases (cf. Allman 1990, Bengtson 1991). Bengtson and Ruhlen (1994a:306) list for this words of the following shapes from various languages: *knw*, *eq*^{w}*en*, *xuonā*, *teknē*, *wanā*, *gerim*, *grua*, *ben*, *kin*, *žena*, *günü*, *arnaq*, *chana-da*, *k'uwi*, *hun*, *ʔunu*, *huini*, *kuyã*, *ekwaʔa*, *hanökö*, etc. While global etymologists do not spell out what criteria they follow to determine whether something fits, the target is CVC(V), where differences in the vowels are ignored. For **kuna* 'woman', the target is approximately *KVN(V)*, where '*K*' is any velar-like sound, '*N*' some *n*-like sound. However, matches are not tight, since for the '*K*', any of the following fits: *k, k', g, q, x, h, w, b, ž, ʔ, č*. For the final '*N*', any of the following count: *n, r, m, ã, w, ʔ*, and Ø. Even '*KV*' seems to be accepted. As for the glosses accepted which allow a form of this vague phonological shape to be selected as a match, all of the following are encountered among the forms for the 'woman' global etymology: 'wife', 'woman', 'lady', 'mother', 'female' (any species), 'spirit of dead woman', 'girl', 'daughter', 'maiden', 'daughter-in-law', 'small girl', 'young woman', 'old woman'.

Salmons' (1997:5) understanding of global etymologists' principles for whether something is a 'cognate' agree with mine:

> A. Ignore vowels entirely: Any vowel matches any other vowel …
>
> B. For consonants, roughly similar place of articulation suffices to establish cognates [though non-initial consonants are sometimes allowed drastic differences]. Minor place changes are acceptable: Velars match uvulars, palatals, etc. Other features play no role whatsoever, so that oral stops correspond to nasals, etc.

> C. Any differences in place which parallel widely attested sound changes such as lenition are acceptable, so that any consonant can be reflected by [h] …
>
> D. In semantics, any narrowing or any metaphorical extension is acceptable without further justification (such as cultural or historical arguments), so that 'dog' corresponds to 'fox, lynx, deer', etc. and 'arm' to 'elbow/hand, fingernail, foot, armpit, shoulder/arm' and so forth.[2]

So, how difficult can it be to find forms that fit the range of permitted sounds and meanings by accident for **kuna* 'woman'? Answer, easy. The following from Spanish illustrates how easy it is:

> *cónyuge* 'wife'
> *cuñada* 'sister-in-law'
> *china* 'girl, young woman' (and *chinita* 'Indian girl')
> *cana* 'old woman' (adjective)
> *canuda* 'old woman'

These are just accidentally similar to the forms in the **kuna* 'woman' global etymology, since we know their history and it shows the forms have etymologies where the sounds and meanings in question do not originally match the target of the global etymology. *Cónyuge* is from Latin *con-* 'with' + *jugum* 'yoke', where these pieces have nothing to do with 'woman'. Similarly, *cuñada* is from Latin *cognātus/cognāta* 'consanguineal relative' (*con-* 'with' + *nātus* 'born'), and so in origin has nothing to do with the sound-meaning equation of the global etymology for 'woman'. *China* is a loanword from Quechua *čina* 'female of animals', and thus cannot be a direct inheritance in Spanish from Proto-World. *Cana* is from Latin *canus/cana* 'white' (with the sense 'old' through 'grey hair'), with no connection originally with 'woman'.

2.2 Criticisms

Hock (1993) demonstrated the point that seeming fits are easy to find by accident for the various proposed global etymologies using such procedures; he showed in a comparison of Hindi and English (IE languages) that 65% of the items that would be identified as 'cognates' by the methods of global etymology are 'false friends,' i.e. non-genetic similarities. The excessive generosity in deciding what fits phonologically and semantically has frequently been criticized (cf. Aitchison 1996:173, Bender 1993, Trask 1996:395).

The exercise – as in the Spanish examples above – of finding various words with disparate known histories which nevertheless fit proposed global etymologies reveals the severest criticism, namely that global etymologies cannot be tested. 'The methods of 'global etymology' remove all controls on accidental similarity' (Salmons 1992b:1). Without the constraints of standard methods, claims that something fits a putative global etymology are not falsifiable, since their fit cannot be checked against proposed sound correspondences or constraints on semantic shift (Salmons 1992a). Moreover, even if we eliminate all the forms whose history does not fit, using the same techniques, it is always possible to generate new examples to replace them. For example, even if we demonstrate that because of their history forms cannot be connected, as with the Spanish forms that fit **kuna* 'woman', this method can nevertheless just produce more examples of the same sort, whose histories may not be so well known (Spanish *cañenga* 'old woman', *changa* 'girl', unclear etymologies; see Salmons 1992a for many in the **tik* 'finger' set; Hock's 1993 criticism of the **maliq'a* 'suck(le), nurse, breast' set). Thus the supporters' allegation that 'you have to take our claims seriously, we have so many examples' (Bender 1993:192) is hardly compelling, given the nearly inexhaustible source of new examples which are accidentally similar but where there are no constraints on how to restrict such accidents.

In spite of the evidence to the contrary, Bengtson and Ruhlen (1994a:281) believe that 'the failure of our critics to appreciate the truly minuscule probability of accidental similarities is the chief impediment to their understanding why all the world's languages must derive from a common origin'. The longish lists of 'so many examples' at first strike the uninitiated as impressive. However, the fact is, given the looseness of the semantics and phonetics permitted for matches, large numbers of forms accidentally similar can easily be found. Thus, falsifiability is not possible (cf. Salmons 1992a:217). 'It is impossible to distinguish between significant and chance resemblances' (McWhorter 2001:297). 'How do we constrain our imagination and ingenuity if we lack explicit controls?' (Bender 1993:195).[3]

2.2.1 A test

Bengtson and Ruhlen (1994a:290) suggest tests which could falsify their claims, but which they believe will bear out their belief that their findings cannot be due to a mere assembly of accidentally similar forms. For the first test, in response to those who say 'one can find anything in linguistic data if one looks for it hard enough,' they say:

> 'Wanting' to find something is of very little help if it is not there ... that the Amerind family has two general words for females, TUNA 'girl' and KUNA 'woman' ... whereas KUNA is widely attested in the Old World ... we have found no trace of TUNA in the Old World. If it is so

> easy to find anything one looks for, why did we fail to find TUNA in roughly 4,500 Old World languages ... That there is no trace of TUNA 'girl' in the Old World is because it never existed there. (Bengtson and Ruhlen 1994a:290)

So, if we do find words from Old World languages which fit the range of glosses and phonetic forms of the TUNA material presented for Amerind, Bengtson and Ruhlen would concede that it is possible to find accidentally similar forms. It is not difficult to meet this challenge. This set is one of the weakest in Greenberg (1987), with examples presented from only four of Greenberg's eleven branches (Greenberg 1987:225, #125). The forms presented for the assumed Amerind etymology includes: *tun*, *tana*, *-tsan*, *šan*, *tsini*, *tu:ne*, *tele*, *suri-s*, *teŋ*, *tunna*, *t'an'a*, etc. The glosses covers: 'son, daughter, diminutive, small, child, be small, mother, daughter'. It is not difficult to find similar words in non-Amerind languages. A quick look at a few dictionaries in my office turns up: Finnish *tenava* 'kid, child', German *Tante* 'aunt'; Japanese *tyoonan* 'eldest son'; Malay *dayang* 'damsel'; Maori *teina* 'younger sister', 'younger brother', Somali *dállàan* 'child'; even English *son* fits.[4]

2.2.2 Another test

Bengtson and Ruhlen claim in several works that it would be impossible to take their list of proposed global etymologies and produce equally impressive lists of words if the meaning is shifted one number in each case, that is, where instead of their (1) AJA 'mother, older female relative', (2) BU(N)KA 'knee, to bend', etc., rather we should assemble sets similar to theirs but with (1) AJA 'knee', (2) BU(N)KA 'ashes, etc. In fact, Bender (1993) took up this challenge and demonstrated that such sets of similarities can be assembled easily, showing that accidental similarity is at stake in much of what they present.

2.2.3 'Reaching down'

Another criticism is 'reaching down' (Trask 1999), accepting forms as evidence of Proto-World which are found only in a single language or in a single branch of a family. This violates Meillet's (1925:38) heuristic that evidence is needed from more than one branch, and the more languages and branches represented, the better as evidence of cognacy (Salmons 1992a, Trask 1996:394).

2.2.4 Unlikely semantics

Another criticism is that the semantics in well-studied families often reveal problems with forms selected as support for global etymologies (Salmons 1992a). For example, PIE **deik-* is listed as evidence of the **tik* 'finger, one' global etymology; however within IE languages, the meanings 'finger' and 'point' upon which Bengtson and Ruhlen focus are secondary, attested only in Latin and Sanskrit. The meaning supported by the other branches is 'to pronounce solemnly, to show', with 'derivatives referring to the directing of words and objects' (Watkins 1985:10; cf. Trask 1996:394). Lack of constraints on accident and semantic latitude 'leads to such absurdities such as accepting that Amerind Tikuna 'elbow' is genetically related to Latin 'to say'' (Bender 1993:196).

2.2.5 Errors in data

Bengtson and Ruhlen's (1994a) global etymologies have been criticized for the many errors in the data. For example, Picard (1998:146) found in the 9 Algonquian forms listed in their 27 global etymologies, 3 were attributed to the wrong language, 4 were given with the wrong gloss, 4 had errors of morphological segmentation, 3 were transcribed wrongly, and all 9 have serious problems of this sort. In general, mistakes of these sorts are found throughout the words presented for the 27 proposed global etymologies.

2.2.6 Short forms

Another criticism is that short forms are not sufficiently long to eliminate chance as a possible explanation for similarities perceived. The length of proposed cognates and the number of matched segments within them are important, since the greater the number of matched segments in a proposed cognate set, the less likely it is that accident may account for the similarity (cf. Meillet 1958:89–90); as Greenberg (1996:134) put it, 'the longer an item, the greater its weight' (cf. Ringe 1992, 1995, 1996, 1999, Nichols 1996). Unfortunately short form examples are common in proposed global etymologies. Ryan's (2001) 90 monosyllabic words of 'Proto-language' are all CV or similar. Several of Bengtson and Ruhlen's (1994a) 27 proposed global etymologies are short. Only one is longer than two syllables, **maliq'a* 'suck(le), nurse, breast', which has been thoroughly discredited (Hock 1993, Hock and Joseph 1996:498–502). Most are intended to be bisyllabic (19), though occasional CV words are cited (e.g. Korean *ka* 'dog' for global **kuan* 'dog'); 4 are monosyllabic CVC shape (with occasional CV examples, e.g. Proto-Yao **(w)i* 'two' and Mak *wa* 'twin' in support of global **pal* 'two'); and 2 are CV(C).

For **ku(n)* 'who?' (Bengtson and Ruhlen 1994a:303–5) we find: *xa, ka, kí/ká, k(w)/q(w), gin, ka:na,* k^{w}*o/*k^{w}*i, ke/ki, ku/ko, hu, kua, kutte, kun, quɳ, kon, ken, gi, gæ, xaj, aj, udu, i:, adi, ono, o:n(i), k'e, mik/mek, ajkia, qa-, kjei, gyis-oto, gùsú, gigi, gunuga, kamu, o-ko-e, ku'a('), gu-, jus, ke*k^{w}*, ka-n, a:č'is, kwanu, go:š, xaŋ, key, ki:, kia, k'owa, kin, kai, karea, karo, kejaito, go:si, kate, kia, koide, katsik, kona, gaga, kepia*, etc. Clearly it is possible by chance to find similar forms in many languages; the *-n* is not necessary for a match, and any vowel counts; for initial **k*, it appears a wide range of consonants qualifies. As for the meanings, anything vaguely interrogative seems accepted – '*who, what, when, which, where, why, how, how much, how many, interrogative particles, whither, whence, someone, either or, anything*', etc. In short, if anything from *i:*, *udu*, and *aj* to *qanangun*, *kiš-to*, and *ekkwarijawa* meaning anything from 'who' to 'anything' can be seen as evidence in favor of this set, then it is indeed difficult to imagine how chance as a possible explanation for forms such as these could be denied.

The treatment of **mi(n)* 'what?' (Bengtson and Ruhlen 1994a:313–5) is similar. Among the forms presented are: *kama, ma, m(j), mann, mi, mah-ma:, mi:t, miya, mena, -ma, maj, mo-, ma/mo, -u:, mida:, wi-/we-, amin, minh/minya, amae, mu, a:mai, m'as, matswɛ, mi:š, maua, manti, mato, may, mano, muski, makaya, maap, mukat, muda, manpat, miki, muru, mba'e, mukoka, mi, muena, ampô-ny, matuni, mašika*. The glosses include: '*if, when, where, who, which, what, how much, when, what kind of, sentence interrogative, thing, this, something*', etc. To find a match by accident, one need only find some form in any language which means something interrogative or 'if, something, thing, whether', with *m*, although the *m* is not strictly required, since some forms listed lack it. Again, chance is surely a major factor behind the grouping of many of these examples.

In the often-cited **tik* 'finger, one' case, the forms demonstrate that a match need have little in common with the final *-k*: *tsiho, ɗẽ́, ɗèʔ, ti, tu, (s-)*t^{l}*a, tay, (tu-)diŋ, (pɨ-)*t^{s}*i*, etc. The assumption that sound changes produced these forms gives the investigator excessive power to imagine matches where chance is probable.

The failure of the methods to distinguish chance from real history as the explanations of the sets of compared words offered as global etymologies is a devastating criticism. Much work has shown such methods incapable, even remotely, of exceeding chance as the probable explanation for the forms cited: Nichols 1996, Ringe 1992, 1999, Salmons 1992a (cf. McWhorter 2001:292–303).

3 Some things that are not reliable evidence

3.1 Nursery words

It has been recognized for centuries that nursery formations (the *mama-nana-papa-dada-caca* sort) should be avoided as evidence of genetic relationship, since they typically share a high degree of cross-linguistic similarity which is not due to common ancestry (cf. Greenberg 1957:36). Nevertheless, such words are frequent in the evidence put forward for hypotheses of distant genetic relationship, including Proto-World (cf. Bengtson and Ruhlen 1994a:292–3, Ruhlen 1994b:122–4, 2000).

Murdock (1959) investigated 531 terms for 'mother' and 541 for 'father' in different languages and concluded that the data 'confirm the hypothesis [of] a striking convergence in the structure of these parental kin terms throughout historically unrelated languages' (Jakobson 1962[1960]:538). Jakobson explained the non-genetic similarity cross-linguistically among such terms as nursery forms which enter common adult vocabulary:

> Often the sucking activities of a child are accompanied by a slight nasal murmur, the only phonation which can be produced when the lips are pressed to mother's breast or to feeding bottle and the mouth is full. Later, this phonatory reaction to nursing is reproduced as an anticipatory signal at the mere sight of food and finally as a manifestation of a desire to eat, or more generally, as an expression of discontent and impatient longing for missing food or absent nurser, and any ungranted wish ... Since the mother is ... *la grande dispensatrice*, most of the infant's longings are addressed to her, and children ... gradually turn the nasal interjection into a parental term, and adapt its expressive make-up to their regular phonemic pattern. (Jakobson 1962[1960]:542–3.)

The forms with nasals are found more frequently in terms for females, stops for males, but not exclusively so. Because these kinship terms are often found to be phonetically similar across genetically unrelated languages, and because this non-genetic similarity has plausible explanations, such nursery words are not considered viable evidence in proposals of distant genetic relationship (see Campbell 1997:227–9). The cases put forward as evidence of Proto-World are not reliable evidence; the following from Bengtson and Ruhlen's (1994a, Ruhlen 1994b, 2000) global etymologies are challenged: **aya* 'mother', older female relative', **mama* 'mother', **papa* 'father', and **kaka* 'older brother', 4 of 27 sets.

3.2 Onomatopoeia

Onomatopoetic forms may be similar because the words in different languages have independently approximated sounds of nature; such cases must be eliminated from proposals of genetic relationship. As Swadesh (1954:313) advised, 'a simple way to reduce the sound-imitative factor to a negligible minimum is to omit from consideration all such words as 'blow, breathe, suck, laugh' and the like, that is all words which are known to lean toward sound imitation'. Judgements of what is onomatopoetic may be subjective; however, forms whose meaning plausibly lends itself to mimicking the sounds of nature are often found in proposals of distant genetic relationship, e.g. comparisons among languages of words meaning 'blow/wind' which approximate *p(h)u(h/x/w/f)* phonetically, and of 'breast/suckle, nurse/suck' *(V)m/nVm/n, s/ʃ/ts/č/Vp/b/k*, or *s/ʃ/ts/č/Vs/ʃ/ts/č*, as seen in numerous forms presented as putative cognate sets in proposed but controversial 'macrofamily' hypotheses (cf. Rosenfelder 1999). Some words which frequently are similar across languages due to onomatopoeia are: 'break/cut/chop/split', 'baby', 'breathe', 'choke', 'cough', 'cry', 'cricket', 'crow' (and many bird names in general), 'frog/toad', 'lungs', 'beat/hit/pound', 'call/shout', 'drip', 'hiccough', 'kiss', 'nose/smell', 'shoot', 'sneeze', 'snore', 'spit', 'whistle'.

Proposed global etymologies must contend with the question of possible onomatopoeia (and of affective, expressive, or sound symbolic forms) among the words from various languages listed. Here, I list some of examples from the proposed global etymologies together with a brief indication of why some scholars see onomatopoeia or affective forms in these cases. Some of these will be more persuasive than others, though all warrant serious consideration. To the extent that onomatopoeia and affective formation are involved, the similarities seen in cross-linguistic comparisons owe their origin to later developments, not to inheritance from 'Proto-World'. These include the following (from Bengtson and Ruhlen 1994a:277–336, Ruhlen 1994b:101–24).

'Breast/suck(le)/nurse' **maliq'a* (see Hock 1993), illustrated by: *maal-, melu-t, mellu, mekku, umlix, mik'-is, murgi, mallaqa*, etc. Similarities among these words across various languages are generally thought to be due to imitation of the noises children make when nursing, sucking. In this case it is complicated by the fact that many of the words given (see Bengtson and Ruhlen 1994a:308–9) mean 'swallow', 'food', 'chew', 'eat', 'throat', 'neck', and 'chest', and thus have no particular motivation to mimic sucking/nursing noises, but, then, this only means that onomatopoeia and accidental similarities both are involved.

'Dog' **kuan*, with forms: *!gwaĩ, gwí, kwon, ka, x^woʔi, kawun, kwi*, etc. Some linguists believe similarities such as these are imitative of dogs 'hauling' and 'barking' and 'growling', perhaps with a nursery component, since children have affective associations with household pets. As Hock and Joseph (1996:498) point out, 'in a number of Indo-European languages, the original word for 'dog' was replaced by words with initial *ku-* such as Sanskrit *kurkura-* 'the one that snarls, growls, or barks, i.e. makes a sound [kurkur]"; they cite as further examples English *cur*, German *Köter*, Modern Hindi *kutta:*, Tamil *kurai* 'to bark' / *ku:r̥an* 'dog'; many other 'dog' examples could be added, e.g. Finnish *koira*, Māori *kuri:*, etc.

'Fly' (verb) **par*, illustrated with: *pil, far, ferfir, par, -biri, phur, aphir, bin, ʔbil, pen, pau, pal, parpal, purupuru, piropir*, etc. Many see in such words (which include in Bengtson and Ruhlen's lists also 'wing', 'butterfly', 'flee', 'moth', 'bird') both onomatopoetic and affective, sound symbolic aspects. Such words for 'fly' and 'wing' suggest the imitation of the sounds of 'flapping', 'fluttering', 'flying' made by birds' wings, thus explaining (1) the similarity found among unrelated languages, and (2) why the same language can have multiple non-inherited words of this sort (compare for example English's: *fly, flap, flutter, flit, flicker, whoosh*, etc.).

That affective sound play is involved in some cases cited as evidence is especially evident cross-linguistically in words for 'butterfly' (cf. folk-etymological *flutterby*) (some examples are in Bengtson and Ruhlen's 1994a:317–8 global etymology for 'to fly'):

> 'butterfly': Albanian *flutur*, Arabic (Moroccan) *fertattu*, Bunabun *piropir*, Dravidian (Kolami *gu:ge*, Gondi *gu:ge*, Parji *gogava:la*; Tamil *pa:ppa:tti*, Malayalam *pa:ppa:tti*, Kodagu *pa:pïli*, Gonid *pa:pe:*, *pipri:*, Kurux *papla:*), Estionian *liblikas*, Finnish *perhonen*, French *papillon* (< Latin *pāpillō*), Guarao *guaroguaro*, Hindi *tiitri/titli*, Indonesian *kupu-kupu*, *rama-rama*, Italian *farfalla*, Māori *pu:rerehua*, *pe:pe*, Mískito *pulpul, dildil*, Nahuatl *papalo:-tl*, Paya *waruwaru*, Portuguese *borboleta*, Proto-Austronesian **qaLi-baŋbaŋ*, Proto-Lezghian **pa(r)pul-*, Proto-Mayan **pehpen*, Proto-Zoquean **me:meʔ*, Quechua *pilʸpintu*, Sumu *saisai*, Swedish *fjäril*, Tequistlatec *-bobolóh*, Totonac *špiʔpiʔle:ʔqa*, Ulwa (Sumu) *kublamhlamh*, Welsh *pilipala*.

'Smell/nose' **čuna/*čunga,* with: *sun, sina, snā, čona, sányuu, sinqa, tsinyu*, etc. These comparisons suggest imitation of the sounds of 'sniffing', 'snuffling', and 'smelling', which in many languages have affective and nursery-word connections from the runny noses associated with children and their numerous childhood illnesses. (cf. English phonaesthetic forms with no regular etymologies: *sneer, sneeze, sniff, sniffle, snivel, snot, snotty, snort, snuff, snuffle*).

'Water' **aq'wa* (with forms such as *akwa, okho, gugu, k'a*, etc.). The similarity of sound suggests to many the imitation of the sound of swallowing water, a nursery form, or of gurgling running water.

4 The futility of modern lexical comparisons as evidence of Proto-World

Can lexical comparisons across known languages offer any insight into Proto-World or the origin of human language(s)? Lexical comparisons have seldom been considered convincing proof of genetic relationship without additional support, e.g. from sound correspondences and shared irregularities in morphological elements. It is easy to see why this should be even more the case with global etymologies. By glottochronology, after about 14,000 years, nearly all of a language's basic vocabulary will be replaced, so in related languages which split up before 15,000 years ago, we will not find recognizable cognates.[5] Glottochronology may not be supported, but this illustrates the point that over vocabulary is replaced and the lexical comparisons of global etymologies must expect cognate vocabulary to survive in modern languages for tens of thousands of years unreplaced and in recognizable form – extremely unlikely given the amount of normal lexical replacement and phonological change that take place in far shorter lengths of time (see below).[6]

Given the extremely long time since the origin of human language, absolutely all lexical items from that period will have been replaced or changed beyond recognition in all languages. Others make the same point about so much change over such a long time leaving no residue in modern languages or leaving whatever survivals could be imagined too garbled through the regular workings of linguistic changes to be recognizable (cf. Trask 1996:392, McWhorter 2001:292, Hock 1993:218).

The extent of this problem can be appreciated from Hindi and English, languages known to be related.[7] I mark the forms compared in the Swadesh 100-word list with the following codes before the numbers:[8]

+: true cognate which would be recognized by the methods utilized by global etymologists

+?: true cognate which might be accepted by global etymologists, though are by no means obvious

-: non-cognate form which would nevertheless be accepted by the methods

-?: non-cognate form which perhaps would be accepted by the methods, though it should not be

#: true cognates which would be missed by the methods of global etymology

#?: true cognates which very likely would be missed by the methods, though perhaps not.

Equivalents from Māori (an Austronesian language) are also compared. I code English-Māori similarities with <-> for cases which would be accepted by the method, though they are not cognates, and <-?> for weaker cases that perhaps would be accepted. For Hindi-Māori similarities, in order to distinguish them form those with English, the symbol <%> is used for those the method would accept, and <%?> for those it might accept.[9]

	English	Hindi	Māori
1	I	maĩ (but see *me*)	ahau
2	you	a:p (polite), tum, tu: (informal)	koe (singular)
#3	we	ham (cf. Sanskrit *vayam* 'we')	ma:tou (exclusive several), ta:tou (inclusive several)
4	this	yah	-? te:nei
5	that	vah, voh	i?te:ra: (that away), te:na: (that near)
+? 6	what	kya:	%? he aha?
+? 7	who	kaun	- wai
+8	not	nahĩ	ka:hore, ka:o
9	all	sab	katoa
10	many	bahut	- maha
#11	one	e:k	tahi
+12	two	do:	-? rua
-? 13	big	baṛa:	- pi:ki, nui
-? 14	long	lamba:	-? roa
15	small	choṭa:	iti
16	woman	stri:, aurat	- wa:hine
17	man	a:dmi:, puruṣ	ta:ne
18	person	vyakti:, log, insan	tangata
19	fish	machli:	ika
20	bird	pakśi:	manu
21	dog	kutta:	% kuri: (cf. English *cur*)
22	louse	jũ:	%? kutu
23	tree	pe:ṛ	ra:kau (cf. to:tara 'tree' (podocarpus)

	English	Hindi	Māori
24	seed	bi:j	%? pua
25	leaf	patta:	wha:rangi
26	root	mu:l	pakiaka (cf. rauruhe 'fern root')
27	bark	chha:l(f.)/kha:l	-? pa:pa:kiri, kiripaka, kiri, hiako
29	flesh *	mã:s	- mi:ti (English loan)
30	blood	xu:n, lahu, rekt	toto
31	bone	haḍḍi:	-? poroiwi, wheua, iwi
#32	egg	aṇḍa:10	– he:ki, hua manu
33	grease	charbi/chikna:'i	hinu
#34	horn	sĩ:g	- haona, maire, pi:hi
35	tail	dum/pũ:chh	- te:ra (English loan), waero, whiore
+?36	feather	par	piki
37	hair	ba:l	- huruhuru
38	head	sir	ma:tenga
39	ear	kan	taringa
#?40	eye	ã:kh	%? kanohi
+?41	nose	na:k	ihu
-42	mouth	mũh	-? ma:ngai
+?43	tooth	dã:t	niho
#44	tongue	ji:bh, zaba:n[11]	arero
45	claw	chã:gul/na:xun/pã:jah	maikuku
#?46	foot	pã:v, pair	-?/% pu:, waewae, take
-?47	knee	ghuṭna	turi, pona
-48	hand	ha:th	ringa
-?49	belly	pe:ṭ	-? puku, %? ho:para
50	neck	gardan	kaki:
51	breast	chha:ti:	uma,poho
52	heart	dil[12]	nga:kau
53	liver	jigar/kaleyja	ate
54	drink	pi:-	inu, unu
55	eat	kha:-	% kai
56	bite	ka:ṭ-	% kakati, ngau
57	see	de:kh-	kite
58	hear	sun-	rongo
#59	know	ja:n-	mo:hio
60	sleep	so:-	moe
61	die	mar-	% mate
62	kill	ma:r-/ma:r ḍa:l-na:	% whakamate, -mate
63	swim	tair-	kaukau
64	fly	uṛ-	rere, tere

	English	Hindi	Māori
65	walk	chal- 'walk', ja:- 'walk, go'	- wa:ke (English loan), %? haere
66	come	a:-	heke, kuhu
-67	lie	leṭ-	takoto
68	sit	baiṭh-	noho
69	stand	khaṛa + ho- 'standing'	tu:, tu:tu:
70	give	de:-	%? tapae
71	say	kah-	%? ko:rero
+72	sun	su:raj, su:rya	%? ra:
73	moon	chã:d	- marama
+/-74	star	ta:r, sita:ra:[13]	whetu:
75	water	pa:ni:	- wai
76	rain	ba:riś	ua
77	stone	patthar	% po:hatu, ko:hatu
78	sand	ba:lu	onepu:
79	earth	zami:n, prithvi:, mitti	oneone, paru
80	cloud	ba:dal	kapua, ao
81	smoke	dhuã:[14]	paoa
82	fire	a:g	% ahi, -? ka:pura
83	ash	ra:kh	%? pungarehu
84	burn	jal-	%? ka:, ngiha, tahu, wera
-85	path	pagḍaṇḍi:, pa:th	huanui
86	mountain	paha:ṛ	- maunga
87	red	la:l	%? whero
-?88	green	hara:	- kiri:ni (English loan), % karera, ka:riki
89	yellow	pi:la:	%? Punga, ko:whai
90	white	safe:d	ma:, tea
91	black	ka:la:	pango, mangu
92	night	ra:t	po:
93	hot	garm (gerem)	%? wera (cf. *warm*)
94	cold	ṭhaṇḍa:	makariri
+?95	full	pu:ra:	-/% puhapuha
96	good	accha:	pai, tika
+?97	new	naya:	ho:u
98	round	go:l	porotaka
99	dry	su:kha:	maroke
+100	name	na:m	ingoa

* Note: if 'meat' could be substituted, one gets a <-> for the English-Hindi comparison)

The ancestor of English and Hindi did not begin to diversify into separate languages until some 5,000 or 6,000 years ago, but we find only some five clear cognates on the Swadesh list (those marked <+>), only some 13 by generous criteria (marked <+?>), several of which would only be chosen by someone utilizing liberal notions of phonetic similarity. If the impact on the vocabulary of clearly related languages is so great after only a few millennia, surely there is no hope for comparisons at the level of Proto-World, comparisons in which the languages involved are assumed to have separated from one another some 100,000 years ago or more (see below). It is clear that the English-Hindi comparison – with only 9 cases clearly selected by the method (those marked <+> or <->) – fares worse than the English-Māori comparisons (15 cases accepted, marked <->; not counting the 'maybes', marked <-?>) and than the Hindi-Māori comparisons (10 cases, marked <%>). The differences between English-Hindi and Māori with the other two languages are so striking that a shift in coding for a few items would not greatly alter the outcome that looks as similar to English and Hindi, to which it is not related, as related English and Hindi do to one another. Clearly if unrelated Māori exhibits more matchings with both English and Hindi of the sort the method accepts than these two IE languages do with each other, then there is something alarmingly wrong with this method. This comparison demonstrates that it cannot perform better on related languages than on unrelated ones and therefore sheer accident must be the explanation for many of the matchings accepted as global etymologies.

Taking into account what is known of IE would reveal more English-Hindi cognates, but also would expose additional similarities known not to be cognates. As Hock (1993) pointed out, often the cognates are changed so much by sound changes that they would not be recognized by search for superficial similarity followed by global etymologists. For example, the following English-Hindi cognates are not phonetically similar enough to be selected by such methods (from Hock 1993:218): horn : *sĩ:g* (< Sanskrit *śṛṅga* - 'horn'), *sister : bahan* (< Sanskrit *svasar*, cf. Old English *sweostor*), *be* : *ho*:- (< Sanskrit *bhavati* < PIE **bhu*:), *we* : *ham* (< Sanskrit *vayam*), etc. Hock (1993) and Hock and Joseph (1996:469, 491–3) list several others.[15] Hock and Joseph (1996:492–3) report that in an open-ended search, some 55 genuine cognates turn up which are still similar enough phonetically and semantically to appear related, plus some 30 other cognates so altered by linguistic change that they would probably not be recognized without historical knowledge. However, this is complicated by:

1 more than 45 loanwords in Hindi from Sanskrit which have English cognates, but are not direct inheritances in Hindi;

2 5 loans from Persian into Hindi;

3 10 or more loans from other sources;

4 60 cases of phonetically and semantically similar forms known from their history to be purely accidentally similar.

As Hock and Joseph (1996:493) show, no matter how the genuine cognates are balanced against accidental similarities and loans, there is less than a 50:50 chance that similarities that would be selected by the method used to identify global etymologies would select genuine cognates.

The argument of too much garbling having taken place since Proto-World for anything to survive or be recognizable depends in part on the date assigned to Proto-World. Clearly if human language is 100,000 (coeval with anatomically modern humans) or older, as some claim, then the amount of garbling and replacement are surely far too much to imagine the survival of anything like a recognizable cognate. There is, however, an interesting twist on views of the date. Researchers of the Santa Fe Institute reason in reverse. Since they believe that real evidence of Proto-World survives in today's languages, they argue that the date of human language must be much later than commonly thought in order to accommodate these assumed linguistic survivals:

> here are serious indications that all existing human languages are descended from a single ancestor, 'Proto-World', which would have been spoken some tens of thousands of years ago. (It seems that an age of one or two hundred thousand years can be ruled out: there would not be any significant amount of evidence remaining.)
>
> http://www.santafe.edu/sfi/organization/annualReport/00/activities/evolution.html.

Bengtson and Ruhlen (1997:4, 57) also suggest that the date involved is not so early, that 'the origin of modern linguistic diversity is to be traced only to the advent of *behaviorally*-modern humans, who appear in the archaeological record between 50,000 and 40,000 years ago.' They ask, might not linguists 'be able to perceive similarities going back 40,000 years?'

The answer is almost certainly 'no' (seen in the Hindi-English-Māori comparisons). However, this dating is also too recent. Australian aboriginal peoples reached Australia by 50,000 years ago. This means that human language must be at least as old as their arrival, since no one imagines they arrived and then developed language subsequently. This probably took place considerably before the rock painting, venus and animal figurines, and burial rites of the European Upper Paleolithic, from ca. 35,000 years ago (mentioned in the Santa Fe Institute's report) sometimes associated with early human language. Even if human language were as young as 40,000 years, this length of time would be more than sufficient to produce the same result, so much lexical replacement and change that nothing reliable could be inferred for Proto-World from lexical comparisons. The extent of the English-Hindi differences after only a fraction of that time, some 5,000 years, should be sobering for anyone who expects recognizable lexical survivals some 35,000 years or more further into the past.

5 Structural speculations

What would the structure of 'Proto-World' ('proto-language') look like? Can we get an idea looking back from structural traits of modern languages? Would 'Proto-World' be simple or complex? Both views have been favored, though the simple-to-complex view has dominated. A third view imagines that whatever in today's language has functional or typologically motivation would also have characterized early human language. I consider each, beginning with the last.

5.1 Functional-typological accounts

To illustrate this sort of argument, consider the claim that Proto-World had SOV word order (cf. Newmeyer 2000). One reason for suspecting this has to do with the claim that changes from OV > VO are more common and natural than VO > OV. A more extreme form of the claim is that languages can only acquire SOV order through language contact, that SOV does not arise through internal developments (cf. Faarlund 1990:84, Tai 1976). However, this claim is incorrect (Campbell, Bubenik, and Saxon 1988, Harris and Campbell 1995:405). While borrowing is a prominent path for the development of new SOV languages, there are other pathways. Another reason is that 'SOV order predominates among the world's languages today' (Newmeyer 2000:372; see Song 2001:49–137). Nevertheless, the following are relevant: (1) some languages have shifted their word order thoroughly even more than once, meaning it is difficult to project their histories from their current state of affairs. (2) There are strong functional typological motivations for why some languages will prefer SOV over the other logically possible word orders (see Song 2001), meaning that regardless of the word order it starts out with, a language may have changed to SOV for good reasons. (3) The number of logically possible orders available is small (only two, OV or VO, in some interpretations), constrained further by the typological tendencies mentioned. Taken together, these considerations make it clear that word order in Proto-World need not have been SOV. That is, from what we know of possible word-order changes and typological motivation, and given the time depth, human language could have started with any word order and we could easily get to today's distribution of word orders in the world's languages.

Another example involves Nichols' 'stable features'. Nichols (1992, 1995, 1998) argues that certain typological traits are 'relatively persistent in language families, of relatively low frequency worldwide, not readily diffused, and not likely to arise spontaneously' (Nichols 1998:143–4). These include: head/dependent marking, typological alignment (nominative-accusative, ergative, active), morphological complexity, inclusive/exclusive, alienable/inalienable, noun classes, numeral classifiers, etc. Some have speculated that Proto-World would have been characterized by these 'stable' traits, either because these traits represent retentions in modern languages, or because, given their stability and utility, languages of the remote past as now would tend to have such traits, even if those in today's languages do not reflect direct survivals. This does not represent Nichols' own view; she rather concludes that 'nongenealogical comparison [among these 'stable' traits] can tell us a good deal about when and where modern language arose and about the proximate and ultimate major geographical contributors to large populations of languages' (Nichols 1998:165). Nevertheless, there is an implication in her 'nongenealogical comparison' that many of these will be traits of early human language, in Africa, which after initial spread tended to persist with subsequent change delivering the geographical distributions of the traits; she focuses on this distribution, though the origin is implied.

A serious problem for relating the 'stable traits' to Proto-World is that there is nothing particularly stable about most of them. For example, the inclusive/exclusive first person pronoun contrast is not stable, but can develop or be lost easily. The same language can differ in that some dialects have the contrast and others lack it, where the change is very recent. For example, some Mam (Mayan) dialects have the contrast, 'exclusive' clitic *-a*/*-ya*, 'inclusive' Ø; other Mam dialects lack it. The inclusive/exclusive contrast is typically superficial, not deeply integrated in the fabric of the grammar; there is nothing about it which would lead us to expect long-term 'stability' (see Jacobsen 1980:204, Foley 2000:392 for other examples).

Notwithstanding, Nichols 'turns this one example [inclusive/exclusive opposition as a global cline] into a more general model of the history of diversity' (Nichols 1992:215). However, given the apparent general instability of this feature, the conclusion is not warranted.

The claim of stability for a number of other traits is also unsupported (see Campbell and Poser 2008).

If these traits turn out not to be stable, then the speculation that they provide some insight into the structural contents of early human language is without foundation.[16]

5.2 Simple-to-complex

Views common in the 19th century and resurrected in grammaticalization see language as formerly simple, made more complex through time as morpho-syntactic elements were created through grammaticalization (see Heine and Kuteva 2002; Comrie 1992). Heine and Kuteva (2002:394) do not insist overtly on the simple-to-complex trajectory in language evolution, but do argue on the basis of 'grammaticalization theory' for a concrete-to-abstract direction in language evolution and believe that 'at the earliest conceivable stage human language(s) might have lacked grammatical forms such as case inflections, agreement, voice markers, etc., so that there may have existed only two types of linguistic entities: one denoting thing-like, time-stable entities (i.e. nouns), and another one for non-time-stable concepts such as events (i.e. verbs)' – that is, simple-to-complex via grammaticalization.

While it is reasonable to suspect that human language may have began as something more simple that evolved to something more elaborate, it is by no means a necessary assumption, as observed in the complex-to-simple views held by some (below). Speculation along this line sometimes reasons that anything not common in today's languages, or not needed for effective communication, would not yet have emerged in early human language. Thus, for example, it has been supposed that Proto-World would have lacked morphophonemic alternations, tones, vowel nasalization, clicks and various other complex sounds, and affixes (see Comrie 1992); it would have had no tense markers, no aspect markers, definitely no evidential markers, no future markers; it would probably have had only main clauses, or conjunction/subordination only by juxtaposition; no overt copula; etc. While this is not an unreasonable possibility, there is no compelling reason why it had to be the case. For example, for those who believe human emotion played a role in the emergence of language, perhaps early tonal contrasts would not seem unlikely, if they evolved from emotion-laden intonational differences. Evidential markers, for example visible vs. non-visible, could be extremely useful to a hunting society.

Simplicity for ease of production makes a good story, but more complexity for ease of understanding is also reasonable. In the end we shall never know! Would a very simple Proto-World have been mangled beyond recognition by massive later accretions and changes, or would structurally more elaborate language in its early stages have been distorted far beyond recognition because of loss, replacement, and normal analogical and phonological change? Either way, too much change has taken place since the origins of human language ever to know where the truth may lie.

6 Society and language complexity

That early stages of human language(s) may have been complex in structure has also been alleged by some. This view takes encouragement from the often repeated opinion that language becomes more complex in isolated communities or in small-scale societies where most members interact with one another face to face (see Andersen 1988, Hymes 1974, Nettle 1999, Nettle and Romaine 2000, Ross 1996, 1997, Trudgill 1989). Hymes (1974:50) asserted 'the surface structures of languages spoken in small, cheek-by-jowl communities so often are markedly complex, and the surface structures of languages spoken over wide ranges less so.' The earliest speakers of human language(s) probably were members of such small-scale isolated communities, and consequently, according to this claim, may have had complex language(s). But does this view have merit?

The view is often attributed to Jakobson (1929[1962]:82): 'dialects which serve as vehicles of communication in large areas and gravitate towards the role of koiné tend to develop simpler systems than dialects that serve purely local purposes' (Andersen 1988:37), to which Andersen (1988:60) adds, 'dialects that serve predominantly local functions are more prone to elaborate phonetic detail rules.' Later versions of the claim lean not to the tendency towards conservativism but to develop complexity. Andersen speaks of 'relatively open' and 'relatively closed communities,' arguing that 'the greater potential for variablility of usage in open communities favors a more active leveling of irregularities in these, and the lesser variablility a more faithful transmission of morphological irregularity in closed communities' (Andersen 1988:61). He asserts that 'the conservativism of relatively closed dialects is common knowledge' but argues that 'phonetic norm elaboration' is also common in closed dialects (Andersen 1988:62), including "exorbitant' phonetic changes' (Andersen 1988:73–4). Trudgill (1989:227), speaking of 'high- and low-contact varieties,' extends Andersen's dichotomy to include different languages. For Trudgill, high contact leads to simpler systems: 'dialects which serve a relatively wide socio-spatial function tend to have simpler systems than dialects with a more restricted function' (p.228), that 'in low-contact situations we know that the speed of linguistic change will typically be slow' (p.229), and that 'many of the changes that take place in this sort of situation [low-contact] are of the type that move in the opposite direction complication as opposed to simplification' (p.229). In this way Trudgill sees how the relative greater isolation of Faroese over Danish could perhaps explain the seeming less conservativeness of Danish (p.231), but, how, then, are we to understand the fact that higher-contact Danish is linguistically more conservative in some regards than some of its lower-contact Scandinavian sisters, e.g. in Danish

/k/ is preserved before front vowels, where Swedish and Norwegian have changed it to a fricative.

This notion of isolated, low-contact varieties being conservative is just to opposite of Nettle and Romaine's view (below). Nevertheless, Trudgill (1989:234) does suggest some kinds of 'changes typical of low-contact social contexts.' One is the development of grammatical agreement; however, for example, case and number agreement on adjectives in Finnic languages is generally understood to be due to contact with IE languages. That is, due not a low-contact, but a high-contact phenomenon. Another is the 'proliferation of clicks in the Khoisan languages,' but, then, the many clicks in southern Bantu languages are due to language contact, with Koisan languages. The Northwest Coast Linguistic Area of North America is characterized by extensive language contact and extremely elaborates phonemic inventories. Clearly there is no easy correlation of the sort envisaged by Trudgill between relative contact or isolation and structural complexity.

Nettle (1999:138) also argues for 'community size' as a cultural or social variable which may correlate with language structure:

> If a group consists of just a few hundred people, the idiosyncracies of one very influential individual can spread through it very easily. This is not the case if the group consists of thousands or tens of thousands of people. In general, the smaller the community, the greater the probability that a given variant that has no functional advantage at all, but is neutral or slightly disadvantageous, can replace the existing item and become the norm. (Nettle 1999:139)

Nettle and Romaine (2000:12) add 'languages which are used only for in-group communication in small groups can afford complexity.' 'In small language groups innovations and new usages can quickly spread throughout a whole village.' The basic idea in this literature is that such communities, isolated or characterized by face-to-face communication, tolerate eccentricities, and so complexity can grow and highly unusual linguistic traits can become part of the structure of the language.

A problem is that there are many counterexamples, many simple but relatively isolated small languages and many large and non-isolated but complex languages. For example, looking at phonological complexity (from which some of the proponents take their inspiration), we see counterexamples in numerous small and isolated languages such as Rotokas, Pirahã, Hawai'ian, Māori, etc. which have extremely limited phonemic inventories. Rotokas (a 'Papuan' language of Bougainville, 4,000 speakers), has only 7 segments, only 6 consonants; Pirahã (of the small Muran family in Brazil, spoken by only about 150 speakers) has only 8 consonants and 3 vowels (cf. Maddieson

1984). Hawai'ian has only 8 consonants. Isolated South Island Māori, instead of becoming more complex, reduced its 10 consonants, merging /ŋ/ with /k/, leaving 9: /p, t, k, ɸ, h, m, n, r, w/. On the other hand, there are plenty of large non-isolated languages which are complex or exhibit unusual traits, some having become more complex over time. For example, of the Quechua languages, the one spread by the Inca Empire, spoken by several millions, is phonologically very complex, 3 series of obstruents, plain, glottalized and aspirated, at 5 points of articulation (6 in some varieties). Zulu, not small (6,000,000 speakers) nor isolated, with 35 consonants, acquired an extremely elaborate system of click consonants. Eastern Armenian added glottalized stops (under influence from Caucasian languages), now with 29 consonants, which include the 3 series, plain, aspirated, and glottalized stops and affricates, both dental and palato-alveolar affricates and fricatives, etc. Georgian (4,000,000 speakers) is complex (29 consonants), with 3 series of stops and affricates, plain, voiced, and glottalized; uvular stops, etc., and, in morphosyntax, a rich case system, exceptionally complex verb morphology, etc. Even English, probably one of the least isolated languages, has unusual phonological traits, e.g. interdentals, /θ/, /ð/, and 'r' rare in other languages. Arabic, with many millions of speakers, a language of civilization and empire for centuries, not only has interdentals, /θ/, /ð/, it has them and the other coronal fricatives and stops in plain and 'emphatic' (pharyngealized) versison, plus it has pharyngeal fricatives (/ʕ/ and /ħ/). There is far from an easy correlation between size/isolation and complexity. Nothing follows for the structure of Proto-World.

7 What of the structure of the earliest human language(s)?

As just seen, there is good reason to be skeptical about many claims about structural properties of the earliest human language. So, is there anything we can know or reasonably infer about the structure of the earliest human language(s), looking back from modern and attested older languages? The answer is a qualified 'yes,' limited by both logic and content in ways language evolution enthusiasts may not find exciting. This has to do with the design features of human languages. It is argued that the earliest human language will have had the design features of human language and this gives us some clues to its nature.

The logical limitation has to do with definitions and the problem of 'emergence.' Uniformitarianism holds that things about language that are possible today were not impossible in the past and that things impossible today were not possible in the past. This means that whatever is diagnostic of human language today would also have been among the properties of the earliest human language(s) and that the earliest language(s) would not be characterized by either the presence of things not known in modern languages nor by the absence of things present in all modern languages. So, logically, the earliest language(s) must have exhibited the design features characteristic of human languages today. However, abiding by uniformitarianism means we cannot address 'emergence.' That is, it is generally assumed that there was some earlier non-language communication system (perhaps like other primates' call and display systems) which did not have all the design features of human language but which evolved so that it emerged, as new biological species emerge, crossing the line from non-language to language. However likely it is that such emergence took place, by the uniformitarian principle the point of inquiry is cut off as we go back in time at the point where any form of communication ceases to have the requisite design features that qualify it as language as known today. Thus, while we can speculate about the nature of the earliest human language, looking back from what is known from known languages, we cannot go beyond the logical boundary defined by uniformitarianism without losing empirical constraints and being left in the realm of speculation. We can assume that the earliest language(s) did meet the design feature requirements of human language, but this is in a sense a definitional demarcation which says anything else is not human language, which cuts off access before emergence, leaving unaddressed the question most fascinating to many, of how human language originated and evolved from something that was not (yet) human language.

Accepting the uniformitarian constraint, that anything lacking the design features of human language is not human language, imposes the limitation that the earliest human language that qualifies as such will not have been different in design from languages known in modern times, and that therefore we can assume, though only by default, that the earliest human language which qualifies as language was characterized by these same design features. Let us look at some of the design features that have been proposed and consider what they might mean for the structure of the earliest language(s) (cf. Hockett 1960):

Duality of patterning (double articulation) (recombination of sounds in association with meaning to allow an open-ended number of linguistic signs)

Grammar (fixed or preferred sequences of linguistic elements)

Open-ended word classes (probably at least noun or noun-like and verb or verb-like categories)

Verbal channel (with consonant or consonant-like and vowel or vowel-like segments)

Discourse function of categories (e.g. subject vs. object, agent vs. patient, predicate, etc.)

Multimodality (statements, questions, commands, negation; narrative, conversation)

Synonymy (rephrasability)

Recursion (clauses embedded in other clauses)

Productivity (ability to produce utterly new utterances)

Pantopicality (unlimited by context or topic)

Displacement (reference to the imperceptible things, not in the here and now)

Metalanguage (ability to talk about talking)

Prevarication (verbal deception)

This constitutes my guess as to what 'Proto-World' must have been like: it must have had design features such as these. However, since these features are broad, they do not constrain the form of the earliest human language(s) very much with respect to specific structural traits. They do not help us select the most likely earliest structures from among the variants/parameters known in human languages today. For example, from the design feature of a verbal channel with consonants and vowels, we may infer that probably the earliest human language had consonants and vowels, but whether it had a simple or complex phonemic inventory cannot to be known from this. In the design trait of multimodality, we can infer that the earliest language presumably had means for forming questions, but whether this was with intonation, question particles, inversion of elements, or something else, we cannot know. In the discourse function of categories, presumably the earliest language had means for hearers to distinguish agents from patients, but from this we cannot know whether this may have involved ergative-absolutive, nominative-accusative, or active-stative alignment, whether it involved word order, case marking, cross-referencing, or context and semantic clues. In short, the design features give us some ideas of the nature of the first language(s), but nothing specific, and even relying on them for our guesses about the nature of early language is strained, since by definition, anything not (yet) fitting these conditions is eliminated from consideration. Surely for language evolution, it is precisely those pre-language developments which led to language(s) with all these design features which are most interesting, but about which we can know next to nothing.

8 Conclusion

So, what can we find out or reasonably hypothesize about the earliest human language(s) from looking back from evidence in modern and attested older languages? We can speculate, perhaps even reasonably in some cases, but we can 'know' extremely little. What can we find out from lexical comparisons? Answer: essentially nothing, though we can learn object lessons from the many problems found in the methods which have been utilized to attempt to get at 'global etymologies.' Perhaps because of the assumption that all the world's languages are genetically related, descendants of 'Proto-World,' global etymologists are disposed to believe in etymological connections among words in contemporary languages, and this will to believe permits them to accept as related forms which do not exceed sheer accidental similarity as a more plausible explanation. I conclude with Bender (1993:203), "global etymologies' are an illusion. They are an artifact of too much freedom of choice and the loss of control.' The global etymologists have not met their burden of proof. In the long time since the origin of human language(s), so much vocabulary replacement has taken place that in effect no forms once found in 'Proto-World' could have survived. Moreover, if some form had survived (and I assert it did not), after so much change it could not be recognized, and, if it should preserve a recognizable shape (and again I assert it could not), there would be so few such surviving forms that it would be impossible to distinguish successful survivors from forms similar by sheer accident. In short, the search for global etymologies is at best a waste of time, at worst an embarrassment to linguistics as a discipline, confusing and misleading those who might look to linguistics for understanding in this area.

What can we find out Proto-World from structural comparisons? Answer: nothing especially useful, though functional typological and structural considerations may provide broad guidelines to what even the earliest human language would have to have in order to qualify as a human language. Again, though, we learn object lessons from the problems encountered in such structural comparisons. In particular, we learn that there is no correlation to be found between size of speech community or social organization and structural aspects of languages. We can speculate that the design features of human language give us a small handle on the necessary nature of the earliest human language(s), but these are so broad that essentially any linguistic structure known in any language today would qualify as possible.

Notes

1 http://members.aol.com/_ht_a/yahyam/page24/protoworld.htm

2 Similar points are made by Rosenfelder 1999. As he explains, based on the **maliq'a* 'suck(le), nurse, breast' example:

> Take a closer look at the list; the rules for this game are evidently quite lax. The vowels are completely ignored. The middle consonant varies from l to ly to lh to n to r to zero. The end consonant ranges from g to j to d to k to q to q' to kh to k' to X to zero. Switching around medial consonants seems to be allowed; extra consonants and syllables can appear where needed. Observe the semantic variation as well: body parts ranging from neck to nape to throat to breast to cheek; actions including swallowing, milking, drinking, chewing, and sucking. Some defenders of Ruhlen and Greenberg make much of the probability of finding such lists among given numbers of families; but notice that one can pretty much pick and choose what languages from a family to include. If Greek doesn't do it for you, try Latin; if Hebrew doesn't work, use Arabic. (Rosenfelder 1999)

3 It might be asked, does not the case become stronger when so many words from so many languages are piled onto a particular putative global etymology? The answer is no: an error does not become a truth through the addition of many more errors of the same sort. 'A bad methodology doesn't become more respectable just by repeating it' (Rosenfelder 1999a). This has been demonstrated often in critiques of mass or multilateral comparison (see Ringe 1992, 1999, for example).

4 Even English *daughter* (Old English *dohtor*, PIE **dhughə̑ter*) fits in view of such forms as *tsuh-ki* and *u-tse-kwa* in the list. Note, incidentally, the considerable overlap between this and Ruhlan's (1994a:192–206) proposed Amerind **t'aʔna* 'child, sibling'. Note also, incidentally, that it does not mean 'girl' in any of the languages Greenberg cited, though 'girl' is the gloss assigned to the overall set.

5 Nichols (1998:128) points out that, according to the method, 'after 6,000 years of separation, two languages are expected to exhibit only 7% shared cognates; and 7% represents the lowest number of resemblant items that can safely be considered distinct from chance.'

6 Moreover, given that languages have some vocabulary similarities due to chance, any word that did manage to persist unreplaced since the dawn of human language so many long millennia ago could not be reliably distinguished from sheer accidental similarities. That is, given the extremely small number of such putative survivals, it would be impossible to determine whether they are due to accidental similarity or to inheritance from the very distant past.

7 Baxter and Manaster-Ramer (2000) also compare English and Hindi vocabulary, but their purpose is different from mine. They argue that it is possible to detect the genetic relationship between English and Hindi based on modern data; they compare Hindi and English in a list of 33 'especially basic word-meanings' (p.174) utilizing probabilistic techniques. My point is rather, how little recognizable cognate material remains in these two languages known to be related and how it fares on the methods of global etymology when compared with unrelated languages.

8 I do not have access to Hindi etymological materials, and therefore make judgements about cognacy based on limited knowledge of Indo-European and Sanskrit; I may have missed some true cognates or perhaps misassigned a form as a cognate which is only accidentally similar; I believe, however, not many such errors occur.

9 I thank Miriam Butt, Stephen Fennell, Mate Kapovic, David Nash, Roger Lass, Robert Rankin, and Larry Trask for helpful comments and information with the Hindi forms and their history. Errors are mine.

10 Baxter and Manaster-Ramer (2000:177) identify this set as true cognates, though it is by no means obvious. The PIE form from which English egg comes is **əyo-*, from **ō̆wyo-*, not an obvious source for the Hindi form, but possible.

11 Hindi *ji:bh* comes from Sanskrit *jihva:*, from pie **dn̥ghū̆*, from whence English *tongue*.

12 Hindi has *her̥day* 'heart', which is cognate, but *dil* is the common form in use.

13 Hindi *ta:r* may be cognate with *star*, though it is not certain; but *sita:ra:* is a persian loanword, not a direct cognate.

14 The Hindi form is cognate with English *fume*, but this is a loanword in English.

15 For example, if we do not rely strictly on the forms that appear on the Swadesh list, but on what we know from other facts about the history of English and of Hindi, we could extend the list of cognates somewhat, for example:

1	I / maĩ (cf. *me*)
61	die / mar- (cf. *murder*)
69	stand / khaṛa 'standing' (cf. Hindi *tha:* 'was', the true cognate of English *stand*)
93	hot / garm (cf. *warm*)

However, historical facts such as these are not known in the vast majority of comparisons undertaken in attempts to establish global etymologies, and so these forms could not legitimately be used to increase the apparent similarity between English and Hindi for this test. Also, when known historical facts are taken into account, some cases that might have seemed likely drop out, for example, Hindi *hath*: English *hand*, when we see that Hindi comes from Sanskrit *hásta*, cf. Hittite *kkessar* < PIE **ghesor*.

16 Moreover, even if any did prove stable in Nichols' sense (though the evidence is against this), it could still well be the case that the modern distribution of these traits reflects changes much later in time, recent acquisitions or losses of the traits, much after the advent of Proto-World. Indeed there is historical linguistic documentation to this end for many of these traits in numerous languages (e.g changes to ergativity, development of inclusive/exclusive contrasts, of numeral classifiers, etc.; see Campbell and Poser 2008 for details).

References

Aitchison, J. (1996) *The Seeds of Speech: Language Origin and Evolution.* Cambridge: Cambridge University Press.

Allman, W. F. (1990) *The Mother Tongue.* U.S. News and World Report, Nov. 5, 1990. 109.18:60–70.

Andersen, H. (1988) Center and periphery: adoption, diffusion and spread. *Historical Dialectology,* ed. by Fisiak, J. 39–83. Berlin: Mouton de Gruyter.

Baxter, W. H. and Ramer, A. M. (2000) Beyond lumping and splitting: probabilistic issues in historical linguistics. *Time Depth in Historical Linguistics*, ed. by Renfrew, C., McMahon, A. and Trask, L., 167–88. Cambridge: The McDonald Institute for Archaeological Research.

Bender, M. L. (1993) Are global etymologies valid? *General Linguistics* 33.191–219.

Bengtson, J. D. (1991) Paleolexicology: a tool towards language origins. *Studies in Language Origins*, vol. 2, ed. by von Raffler-Engel, W., Wind, J. and Jonker, A., 175–86. Amsterdam: Benjamin, J.

Bengtson, J. D. and Ruhlen, M. (1994a) Global etymologies. *On the Origin of Languages: Studies in Linguistic Taxonomy*, ed. by Ruhlen, M., 277–336. Stanford: Stanford University Press.

Bengtson, J. D. and Ruhlen, M (1994b) Another look at *TIK 'Finger, One'. *California Linguistics Newsletter* 24.2:9–11.

Bengtson, J. D. and Ruhlen, M (1997) In defense of multilateral comparison. *California Linguistics Newsletter* 25.1:3–4, 57

Campbell, L. (1988) Review of Language in the Americas, by Joseph Greenberg. *Language* 64, 591–615.

Campbell, L. (1997) *American Indian Languages: The Historical Linguistics of Native America.* Oxford: Oxford University Press.

Campbell, L. (1998) Nostratic: a personal assessment. *Nostratic: Sifting the Evidence*, ed. by Joseph B. and Salmons J., 107–152. Amsterdam: John Benjamins.

Campbell, L. (1999) Nostratic and linguistic palaeontology in methodological perspective. *Nostratic: Evaluating a Linguistic Macrofamily*, ed. by Renfrew, C. and Nettle, D.179–230. Cambridge: The McDonald Institute for Archaeological Research.

Campbell, L. (2004) *Historical Linguistics*. (2nd edn) Edinburgh: Edinburgh University Press and Cambridge, MA: MIT Press.

Campbell, L. (2005) How to show languages are related: methods for distant genetic relationship. *Handbook of Historical Linguistics*, ed. by B. D. Joseph and Janda, R. D. 262–82. Oxford: Blackwell.

Campbell, L. and Poser, W. (2008) *Language Classification: Method and History*. Cambridge: Cambridge University Press.

Campbell, L, Bubenik, V. and Saxon L. (1988) Word order universals: refinements and clarifications. *Canadian Journal of Linguistics* 33:209–230.

Comrie, B. (1992) Before complexity. *The Evolution of Human Languages*, ed. by Hawkins, J. A. and Murray Gell-Mann, 193–210. Redwood City, CA: Addison-Wesley Publishing Co.

Faarlund, J. T. (1990) Syntactic and pragmatic principles as arguments in the interpretation of runic inscriptions. *Historical Linguistics and Philology*, ed. by Fisiak, J. 165–86. Berlin: Mouton de Gruyter.

Foley, W. A. (2000) The languages of New Guinea. *Annual Review of Anthropology* 29.357–404.

Goddard, I. (1975) Algonquian, Wiyot, and Yurok: proving a distant genetic relationship. *Linguistics and Anthropology in Honor of C. F. Voegelin*, ed. by Kinkade, M. D., Hale, K. L. and Werner, O. 249–62. Lisse: de Ridder, P., Press.

Greenberg, J. H. (1957) Genetic relationship among languages. *Essays in Linguistics*, Chapter 3, 35–45. Chicago: University of Chicago Press.

Greenberg, J. H. (1987) *Language in the Americas*. Stanford: Stanford University Press.

Greenberg, J. H. (1996) In defense of Amerind. *International Journal of American Linguistics* 62.131–64.

Harris, A. C. and Campbell, L. (1995) *Historical Syntax in Cross-Linguistic Perspective.* Cambridge: Cambridge University Press.

Heine, B. and Kuteva, T. (2002) On the evolution of grammatical forms. *The Transition to Language*, ed. by Wray, A., 376–97. Oxford: Oxford University Press.

Hock, H. H. (1993) Swallow tales: chance and the 'World Etymology' MALIQ'A 'swallow, throat'. *Chicago Linguistic Society* 29.215–9.

Hock, H. H. and Joseph, B. (1996) *Language History, Language Change, and Language Relationship: An Introduction to Historical and Comparative Linguistics*. Berlin: Mouton de Gruyter.

Hockett, C. F. (1960) The origin of speech. *Scientific American* 203.88–96.

Hymes, D. (1974) Speech and language: on the origins and foundations of inequality among speakers. *Language as a Human Problem*, ed. by Morton Bloomfield and Einar Haugen, 45–71. New York: W. W. Norton & Co.

Jacobsen, W. R., Jr. (1980) Inclusive/exclusive: a diffused pronominal category in native Western North America. *Papers from the Parasession on Pronouns and Anaphora,* ed. by Kreiman, J. and. Ojeda, A. E., 204–27. Chicago: Chicago Linguistic Society.

Jakobson, R. (1929) Remarques sur l'évolution phonologique du russe comparée à celle des autres langues slaves. (*Travaux du Cercle Linguistique de Prague,* 2) [Reprinted 1962 *Selected writings of Roman Jakobson*, I: Phonological studies. The Hague: Mouton.]

Jakobson, R. (1960) Why 'mama' and 'papa'? *Perspectives in Psychological Theory*, ed. by Kaplan, B. and Wapner, S., 21–9. New York: International Universities Press. [Reprinted 1962 *Selected writings of Roman Jakobson,* I: Phonological studies, 538–45. The Hague: Mouton.]

Maddieson, I. (1984) *Patterns of Sounds*. Cambridge: Cambridge University Press.

Matisoff, J. A. (1990) On megalo-comparison: a discussion note. *Language* 66.106–20.

McMahon, A. and McMahon S. (1995) Linguistics, genetics and archaeology: internal and external evidence in the Amerind controversy. *Transactions of the Philological Society* 93.125–225.

McWhorter, J. (2001) *The Power of Babel: A Natural History of Language.* New York: Time Books.

Meillet, A. (1925) *La Méthode Comparative en Linguistique Historique*. Paris: Champion. (Translation 1967: *The Comparative Method in Historical Linguistics*. Paris: Champion.)

Meillet, A. (1958) *Linguistique historique et linguistique générale.* (Société Linguistique de Paris, Collection Linguistique, 8.) Paris: Champion.

Murdock, G. P. (1959) Cross-language parallels in parental kin terms. *Anthropological Linguistics* 1.9:1–5.

Nettle, D. (1999)a. *Linguistic Diversity*. Oxford: Oxford University Press.

Nettle, D. and Romaine S. (2000) *Vanishing Voices: the Extinction of the World's Languages*. Oxford: Oxford University Press.

Newmeyer, F. J. (2000) On the reconstruction of 'Proto-World' word order. *The Evolutionary Emergence of Language: Social Function and the Origins of Linguistic Form*, ed. by Knight, C., Studdert-Kennedy, M., and Hurford, J. R. 372–90. Cambridge: Cambridge University Press.

Nichols, J. (1992) *Linguistic Diversity in Time and Space*. Chicago: University of Chicago Press.

Nichols, J. (1995) Diachronically stable structural features. *Historical Linguistics 1993: Selected Papers from the 11th International Conference on Historical Linguistics*, ed. by Andersen H., 337–56. Amsterdam: John Benjamins.

Nichols, J. (1996) The comparative method as heuristic. *The Comparative Method Revised*, ed. by Durie, M. and Ross, M., 39–71. Oxford: Oxford University Press.

Nichols, J. (1998) The origins and dispersal of languages: linguistic evidence. *The Origin and Diversification of Language*, ed. by Jablonski, N. and Aiello, L., 127–70. San Francisco, CA: California Academy of Sciences.

Picard, M. (1998) The case against global etymologies: evidence from Algonquian. *International Journal of American Linguistics* 64:141–7. [Published also 1995, On the nature of the Algonquian evidence for global etymologies. *Mother Tongue* 24:50–4.]

Rankin, R. L. (1992) Review of language in the Americas, ed. by Greenberg, J. H. *International Journal of American Linguistics* 58:324–51.

Ringe, D.A., Jr. (1992) On calculating the factor of chance in language comparison. *Transactions of the American Philosophical Society* 82.1:1–110.

Ringe, D.A., Jr. (1995) 'Nostratic' and the factor of change. *Diachronica* 12.55–74.

Ringe, D.A., Jr. (1996) The mathematics of 'Amerind'. *Diachronica* 13.135–54.

Ringe, D.A., Jr. (1998) Probabilistic evidence for Indo-Uralic. *Nostratic: Sifting the Evidence*, ed. by Joseph, B. and Salmons, J., 153–97. Amsterdam: John Benjamins.

Ringe, D.A., Jr. (1999) How hard is it to match CVC-roots? *Transactions of the Philological Society* 97.213–44.

Rosenfelder, M. (1999) Deriving Proto-World with tools you probably have at home *http://www.zompist.com/proto.html*

Ross, M. (1996) Contact-induced change and the comparative method: cases from Papua New Guinea. *The Comparative Method Reviewed: Regularity and Irregularity in Language Change*, ed. by Mark Durie and Malcolm Ross, 180–217. Oxford: Oxford University Press.

Ross, M. (1997) Social networks and kinds of speech community events. *Archaeology and Language I: Theoretical and Methodological Orientations*, ed. by Blench, R. and Spriggs, M., 209–61. London: Routledge.

Ruhlen, M. (1987a) *A Guide to the World's Languages, volume 1: Classification.* Stanford: Stanford University Press.

Ruhlen, M. (1987b) Voices from the past. *Natural History* 96(3):6–10.

Ruhlen, M. (1992) An overview of genetic classification. *The Evolution of Human Languages*, ed. by Hawkins, J. A. and Gell-Mann, M., 159–89. Redwood City, CA: Addison-Wesley Publishing Co.

Ruhlen, M. (1994b) On the Origin of Languages: Studies in Linguistic Taxonomy. Stanford: Stanford University Press.

Ruhlen, M. (1994b) *The Origin of Language: Tracing the Evolution of the Mother Tongue*. New York: John Wiley & Sons.

Ruhlen, M. (2000) Why kaka and aya? Functional Approaches to Language, *Culture and Cognition: Papers in Honor of Sydney B. Lamb*, ed. by Lockwood, D. G., Fries, P. H., and Copeland, J. E., 521–5. Amsterdam: John Benjamins.

Ryan, P. (2001) Proto-language monosyllables: with their principal meanings. http://www.geocities.com/Athens/Forum/2803/ProtoLanguage-Monosyllables.htm

Salmons, J. (1992a) A look at the data for a global etymology: *tik 'finger'. *Explanation in Historical Linguistics*, ed. by Davis, G. W and Iverson, G. K., 208–28. Amesterdam: John Benjamins.

Salmons, J. (1992b) Theory and practice of global etymology. *Proceedings of the 15th International Congress of Linguists* 1.153–5.

Salmons, J. (1997) Global etymology as pre-Copernican linguistics. *California Linguistic Notes* 25.1, 5–7.

Santa Fe Institute (2000) *Annual Research Report*. http://www.santafe.edu/sfi/organization/annualReport/00/activities/evolution.html.

Song, J. J. (2001) *Linguistic Typology: Morphology and Syntax*. Harlow, England: Longman.

Swadesh, M. (1954) Perspectives and problems of Amerindian comparative linguistics. *Word* 10.306–32.

Tai, J. H.-Y. (1976) On the change from SVO to SOV in Chinese. *Papers from the Parasession on Diachronic Syntax*, ed. by Steever, S. B. Walker, C. A. and Mufwene, S. S. 291–304. Chicago: Chicago Linguistic Society.

Trask, L. (1996) *Historical Linguistics*. London: Arnold.

Trask, L. (1999) *Nostratic: Examining a Linguistic Macrofamily*, ed. by Renfrew, C. and Nettle, D., 157–76. Cambridge: The McDonald Institute for Achaeological Research.

Trudgill, P. (1989) Contact and isolation in linguistic change. *Language Change: Contributions to the Study of its Causes*, ed. by Breivik, L. E. and Jahr, E. H., 227–38. Berlin: Mouton de Gruyter.

Watkins, C. (1985) *The American Heritage Dictionary of Indo-European Roots*. Boston: Houghton Mifflin.

6 Conceptualization, communication, and the origins of grammar

Frederick J. Newmeyer
University of Washington, University of British Columbia, Simon Fraser University

1 The evolutionary grounding of grammar in conceptual structure

When linguists started turning to questions of language origins and evolution in early 1990s, a near consensus began to develop on a central issue.[1] In a nutshell, the idea was the roots of grammar lay in hominid conceptual representations and that the shaping of grammar for communicative purposes was a later development. For the most part that was taken to mean that syntax is grounded in predicate-argument structure, that is, representations embodying actors, actions, and entities acted upon, though other aspects of conceptualization were sometimes pointed to as possible antecedents of grammar.

The idea that grammar is grounded in conceptual structure is sometimes referred to as the position that the origins of language are in thought, but one needs to be careful here. Surely conceptual representations are an ingredient of thought, but thought itself is a poorly understood process, which should not be equated with those representations. However, for this short paper we can gloss over the differences between the claim that grammar derives from conceptual structure and the claim that grammar derives from thought.

Here are some quotes from representative work from that period, with key passages italicized:

> We should search for the ancestry of language not in prior systems of animal communication but *in prior representational systems* (Bickerton 1990: 23)

> A far better case could be made that grammar exploited mechanisms *originally used* for the conceptualization of topology and antagonistic forces [than for motor control] (Jackendoff 1983; Pinker 1989; Talmy 1983; 1988), but that is another story. (Pinker and Bloom 1990: 726)

> The conditions for the *subsequent development* of language as a medium of communication were set by the evolution of ... the level of conceptual structure ...*A first step* toward the evolution of this system for communication was undoubtedly the linking up of individual bits of conceptual structure to individual vocalizations ... (Newmeyer 1991: 10)

> [T]he emergent ability, driven by the evolutionary appearance of C[onceptual] S[tructure], was the capacity to acquire meaningful, symbolic, abstract units ... *it would be appropriate to expect adaptation-based explanations to come into play at a later stage, once language came to be used preferentially as the human communication system.* (Wilkins and Wakefield 1995: 179)

Let me summarize the reasons for the belief that the roots of grammar lie in pre-human conceptual structure rather than in pre-human communication. First, we have learned that the conceptual abilities of the higher apes are surprisingly sophisticated (Cheney and Seyfarth 1990; Tomasello 2000; Waal 1996). Each passing year leads to new discoveries about their capacity for problem solving, social interaction, and so on. Not human-level, but sophisticated nevertheless. In other words, as Jackendoff 2002: 238 has stressed, human evolution — in particular human *language* evolution — begins with our ancestors possessing a complex combinatorial conceptual structure. As he points out, a precondition for language is that 'there must be a community of individuals who have thoughts worth communicating to each other' (238).

Chimpanzees meet that precondition — and so, presumably, our immediate anccstors did as well.

Second, the *communicative* abilities of the higher apes are remarkably primitive (Hauser 1996). There is very little calling on their conceptual structures in communicative settings.

Now let us look ahead to human language. What almost all theories of grammar have in common is a tight linkage between syntactic structure and certain aspects of conceptual structure. Of course Pinker and Bloom (1990: 714) and Hurford 2002 are absolutely right when they point out that grammars are cluttered with devices that are irrelevant to the reasoning process or even impede it — phonology and irregular morphology, to state the obvious. But at a gross level, the basic categories of reasoning — agents, entities, patients, actions, modalities, and so on — tend to be encoded as elements of grammar.

This encoding is directly built in into theories like cognitive grammar and construction grammar, which do not even allow for an independent level of morphosyntactic patterning. But it is true of standard generative models too. No one denies that the links between syntactic structure and whatever one might want to call it — conceptual structure / logical structure / semantic representation — are very direct. Ray Jackendoff's principle of Argument Fusion is typical in this respect:

(1) Argument Fusion. To form the conceptual structure of a syntactic phrase that has been linked with LCS (Lexical Conceptual Structure), fuse the conceptual structure of each indexed syntactic position into the coindexed conceptual constituent in the LCS. (Jackendoff 1990: 264)

The degree of match up between syntactic and conceptual structure points to the origins of the former in the latter. Jackendoff, in fact, was explicit about the evolutionary implications of this match up:

> The syntactic category system and the conceptual category system match up fairly well. In a way, the relation between the two systems serves as a partial explication of the categorial and functional properties of syntax: syntax presumably evolved as a means to express conceptual structure, so it is natural to expect that some of the structural properties of concepts would be mirrored in the organization of syntax. (Jackendoff 1990: 27)

The purpose of this paper is to defend the position that the evolutionary roots of grammar lie in conceptual structure.

2 The role of communication in language origins

Few linguists would deny that over time (possibly evolutionary time, but surely historical time) the needs of communication *have* shaped the properties of grammars. This shaping is manifested by the fact that grammars allow the more rapid expression of frequently-used meaningful elements than of those less frequently used ones. Thus it is auxiliaries and negative elements that tend to contract in English, not full lexical nouns and verbs. Many languages have affixes for the most commonly-used concepts: negation, causation, comparison, and so on, but rarely for more complex infrequent concepts (Bybee 1985: 202). Pressure for the rapid processing of spoken language has also helped to shape grammars profoundly. For example, universal or near-universal constraints seem designed — intuitively speaking — to 'help' the hearer recover pairings of fillers and gaps. Many languages allow structures like (2a), fewer like (2b), and fewer still like (2c):

(2) a. What$_i$ did you eat ___$_i$?
b. What$_i$ did you ask John to eat ___$_i$?
c. What$_i$ did you wonder whether John ate ___$_i$?

The constraint known as 'Subjacency' developed, presumably, to eliminate from grammars the possibility of sentences like (2c), which pose a serious processing strain on language users. There are also good parsing explanations for some of the most uncontroversial typological generalizations in syntax. For example VO languages tend to have prepositions and OV languages tend to have postpositions. Let us assume with Hawkins 1994 that it is in the language user's interest to recognize the major constituents of the sentence as rapidly as possible. There are four logical possibilities, illustrated in (3a-d): VO and prepositional (3a); OV and postpositional (3b); VO and postpositional (3c); and OV and prepositional (3d):

(3) a. b.

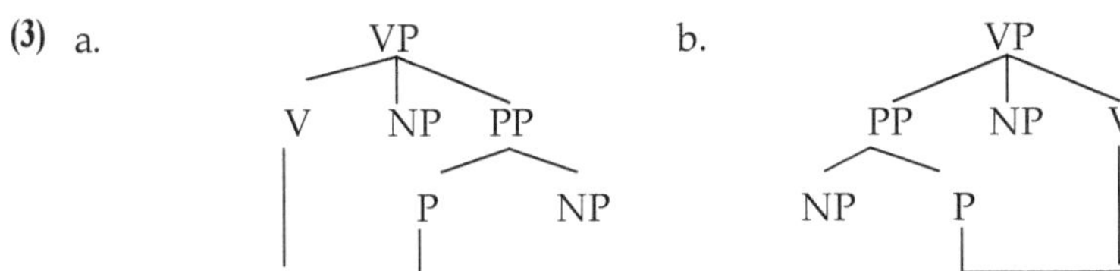

VO and prepositional (common) OV and postpositional (common)

c. d.

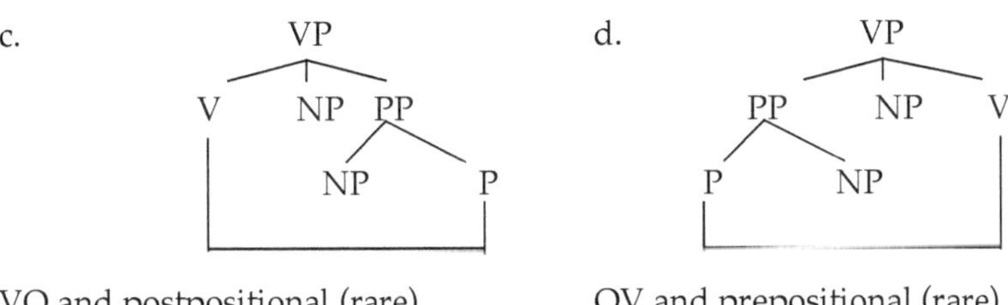

VO and postpositional (rare) OV and prepositional (rare)

In (3a) and (3b), the two common structures, the recognition domain for the VP is just the distance between V and P, crossing over the object NP. But in (3c) and (3d), the uncommon structures, the recognition domain is longer — it involves the object of the preposition as well. So we see grammars adapting themselves to efficient communication.

The view that grammars have been shaped by communicative needs is, of course, the hallmark of the functionalist school. But few formalists would question that communicative pressure has shaped language. One of the first functional explanations for Subjacency was put forward by two 'orthodox'

MIT linguists, Bob Berwick and Amy Weinberg (Berwick and Weinberg 1984). And Chomsky has never questioned the idea that language structure has been influenced by the functions that it needs to serve. As long ago as 1975 he wrote:

> Surely there are significant connections between structure and function; this is not and has never been in doubt. … Searle argues that 'it is reasonable to suppose that the needs of communication influenced [language] structure'. I agree. (Chomsky 1975: 56–58).

More recently (Chomsky 1995) and in subsequent work, he suggests that displacement phenomena — that is movement rules — probably exist to facilitate language use, both in terms of parsing needs and the demands of information structure.

So, we have what I will call the 'Classical Position' on the origins of grammar — the position that the remainder of this paper will be devoted to defending:

(4) The 'Classical Position' on the origins of grammar:
 a. The roots of grammar lie in conceptual structure.
 b. Grammar was subsequently shaped by the demands of efficient communication.

3 The rejection of the classical position on the origins of grammar

Clause (4a) of the classical position is under attack. Functional linguists seem to reject it outright. Charles Li, for example, could not be any more explicit (see also Li and Hombert 2002):

> Scholars who recognize the merit of functional linguistics agree that language emerged evolutionarily first and foremost as a vehicle of human communication, *not* as an instrument of thought. The claim of language as an instrument of thought is an intuitive and a priori claim that defies scientific verification. (Li 2002: ms., p. 5)

It is not at all clear to me why the claim that language emerged from thought is any more 'intuitive and a priori' than the claim that it emerged from communication. But Li's views dovetail perfectly with the view expressed by many functionalists that *grammar itself* bears no relation to the propositional structures posited by formal linguists, that is, structures embodied by formal rules that consider the sentence to be the basic unit of grammar and subjects, verbs, and objects to be its basic division (structures in which sentences are in a rough mapping with propositions, verbs with predicates, and noun phrases with logical arguments). The priority of the sentence is dismissed by some critics of the generative program as a carryover from the Western logical tradition, reinforced by the conventions of written language (see especially Harris 1980; 1981 and Hopper 1988: 131–132).

Why would anyone draw that conclusion? It is apparently the case that in *actual speech* speakers rarely utter sentences with a subject, a verb, and an object, where the two arguments are full lexical items, even though that is what grammars generate. Rather, what one finds the most is what Du Bois 1987 calls 'Preferred Argument Structure'. Most utterances consist of a verb with one full argument, which is either the subject of an intransitive verb or the object of a transitive verb. Other arguments are either reduced to clitic or affix status or omitted entirely. Examples are provided in (5):

(5) Examples of 'Preferred Argument Structure'

Cayuga (Iroquoian)	1–2% of clauses contain 3 major constituents (Mithun 1987)
Chamorro (Austronesian)	10% of transitives have 2 lexical arguments (Scancarelli 1985)
Hebrew (Semitic)	93% of transitive clauses lack a subject NP (Smith 1996)
French (Romance)	French preferred clause structure is [(COMP) clitic+Verb (X)]. Only 3% of clauses contain lexical subjects (Lambrecht 1987)
German (Germanic)	even ditransitive verbs in spoken discourse tend to follow Preferred Argument Structure (Schuetze-Coburn 1987)
Huallaga Quechua (Andean)	in one corpus, only 8% of sentences contained both a noun subject and a noun object (Weber 1989)
Coos (Penutian)	2–3% of clauses contain 3 major constituents (Mithun 1987)
Mam (Mayan)	1% of clauses have 2 lexical arguments (England 1988)

Malay (Austronesian)	'Malay is thus similar to what Du Bois (1985) has described for Sacapultec Maya: it has a 'Preferred Argument Structure'' (Hopper 1988: 126)
Ngandi (Australian)	2% of clauses contain 3 major constituents (Mithun 1987)
'O'odham = Papago (Uto-Aztecan)	only 9% of transitives have 2 overt arguments (Payne 1992)
Rama (Chibchan)	transitive clauses with 2 NPs are rare (Craig 1987)
Sacapultec (Mayan)	in connected discourse, only 1.1% of clauses have 2 lexical arguments (Du Bois 1985; 1987)
Yagua (Peba-Yaguan)	in a corpus of 1516 clauses, only 3% contained both a noun subject and a noun object (Payne 1990)

Even English, which is non-null-subject and considered rigidly SVO, manifests preferred argument structure. A corpus of 20,794 sentences (from telephone conversations) included only 5,975 (29%) that were SVO (Dick and Elman 2001; see also Thompson and Hopper 2001 for similar figures). So if real speech, the argument goes, is not propositional, then grammars should not be either. And if grammars are not propositional, then it is safe to conclude that they could not have their roots in conceptual structures representing full scenes embodying actors, actions, and entities acted upon. Many more studies of language in use (e.g. Fox 1994; Thompson and Hopper 2001) lead to similar conclusions.

Interestingly, recent work by formal linguists on language evolution implicitly rejects the first clause of the classical position. For Berwick 1998 all that is needed to get syntax is a pre-existing lexicon and a single combinatorial operation of concatenation called 'Merge'. The meanings of the elements involved play no role at all in shaping properties of syntax. Berwick's position is developed further in a paper co-authored by Chomsky (Hauser, Chomsky and Fitch 2002), which is Chomsky's first full-length paper on language evolution. For Hauser, Chomsky, and Fitch the only uniquely human component of the language faculty is recursion. While they make no concrete proposal on how this component may have arisen evolutionarily, it clearly bears no mark of an origin in propositional structure.

The remainder of this paper will argue for idea that roots of grammar do indeed lie in conceptual structure. The first part of my strategy will be to argue that language users represent the full propositional structure of sentences, even though doing so serves no apparent communicative use. Likewise, they are capable of making reliable judgments about communicatively useless sentences. I will suggest that these facts might reflect the existence of conceptual structure from before the time of vocal communication and will point to two facts about language that seem to bear out this hypothesis. The first is the fact that language change is largely syntagmatic, rather than paradigmatic, and the second is the fact that when grammatical structure does depart from conceptual structure, it is almost always in the interest of serving communication. My conclusion will be that the independent level of conceptual structure both antedates grammar and is responsible for some of its most distinguishing properties. It was only later that the needs of communication shaped language.

4 Language users represent full grammatical structure, however pared down their actual utterances are

My first argument is based on typology. Since Greenberg 1963, it has been customary to divide languages into their basic ordering of subject, verb, and object. From this ordering, certain predictions tend to follow: SOV languages are more likely to have postpositions than prepositions, SVO languages are more likely to have *Wh*-Movement than SOV languages and VSO languages more likely to have it than SVO languages, and so on. But as we have seen, very few utterances in natural language actually have the full subject, verb, and object. If speakers do not mentally represent the full propositional structure, then a prediction follows. The prediction is that the ordering of full subject, verb, and object should be irrelevant to typology. But that prediction is false, as a look at French indicates. French is SVO when the object is lexical, but SOV when the object is prepositional:

(6) a. Marie voit Jean.
b. Marie le voit.

Text counts show that sentences like (6b) are vastly more likely to be uttered than those like (6a). But French is archetypically an VO language in its typological behavior. In other words, in this case actual language use is irrelevant. What is important is the ordering of elements in sentences with full propositional and lexical structure, rare as they are in actual discourse. The reason is that it is this full structure that is called upon in speech production. According to Levelt 1989, a central part of planning a speech act involves retrieving lexical information, what he calls 'lemmas', essentially predicates and their argument structure. In other words, for transitive verbs like *hit*, *know*, *eat*, and so on the speaker has a mental representation of the full argument structure of the sentence:

> Lemma structure plays a central role in the generation of surface structure. In particular, the main verb dictates what arguments have to be checked in the message, and which grammatical functions will be assigned to them. (Levelt 1989: 244)

The 'formulator', the formulating component of speech production, takes this information as input. Because of that, sentences with full argument structure are psychologically more basic than others, even though efficient discourse packaging keeps them from being used very often. But for typological purposes, it does not matter that fully elaborated sentences are rarely actually used. It is the most frequently used canonical ordering of subject, verb, and object that drives typology, not the most frequently used utterance type in general. The speaker of French might rarely utter sentences like (6a), but he or she does so more far more often than those like:

(7) *Marie Jean voit.

And because of that, French behaves typologically like a VO language, not like an OV language.

The way that sentence fragments are processed also points to the centrality of fully specified grammatical representations, as work such as Pope 1971 and Morgan 1973 reveals. Consider some possible answers to the question in (8):

(8) Who does John$_i$ want to shave?

Those in (9a-c) are possible, but not those in (9d-e):

(9) a. Himself$_i$
b. Him$_j$
c. Me
d. *Myself
e. *Him$_i$

How can one explain that? The generalization, of course, is that the possible pronoun corresponds to the one usable in full sentences, with all arguments expressed:

(10) a. John$_i$ wants to shave himself$_i$.
b. John$_i$ wants to shave him$_j$.
c. John$_i$ wants to shave me.
d. *John$_i$ wants to shave myself.
e. *John$_i$ wants to shave him$_i$.

In other words, whatever one might do in actual speech, one's cognitive representation embodies all the arguments and the principles for assigning the proper pronominal form to the direct object. Clearly, we mentally represent the full grammatical structure, even if we utter only fragments.

Let's look at another piece of evidence that language users have representations that are not predictable from usage-based facts about language. Generative grammarians have long been castigated by other linguists for working with sentences that we make up out of our heads, rather than those taken from actual texts. Now, there are lots of pros and lots of cons to the use of introspective data and is not my intention to review them here (for a good discussion, see Schütze 1996). I just want to point out a remarkable fact about the human language faculty, and one that would never have been unearthed if we just confined our attention to usage. Speakers have the remarkable ability to make reliable judgments about sentence types that they only rarely hear or utter. Take sentences with parasitic gaps, as in (11):

(11) This is the paper$_i$ that I filed ___$_i$ before reading ___$_i$.

I believe that these are rare in actual speech, though I do not know of any statistical studies to confirm that claim. But I doubt that there exists an adult speaker of English who does not know that (11) is a better sentence than (12a-b), despite their superficial similarities:

(12) a. *I filed the paper$_i$ before reading ___$_i$
b. *This is the paper$_i$ that I filed the notes before reading ___$_i$

'Useless' as it is to know the facts surrounding (11) and (12), we know them anyway. Recent experimental work has confirmed that speakers can make reliable introspective judgments, even about rarely occurring sentence types. Cowart 1997 took some sentence types that have loomed large in theoretical discussions (the examples of 13 to 15) and showed that there was a stable pattern of response to them among his subjects:

Subjacency:

(13) a. Why did the Duchess sell a portrait of Max?
b. Who did the Duchess sell a portrait of?
c. Who did the Duchess sell the portrait of?
d. Who did the Duchess sell Max's portrait of?

That-trace phenomena:

(14) a. I wonder who you think likes John.
b. I wonder who you think John likes.
c. I wonder who you think that likes John.
d. I wonder who you think that John likes.

Coordination and binding theory:

(15) a. Cathy's parents require that Paul support himself.
b. Paul requires that Cathy's parents support himself.
c. Cathy's parents require that Paul support himself and the child.
d. Paul requires that Cathy's parents support himself and the child.

These are not particularly common sentence types in use, and yet experimental subjects are quite consistent as to how they judge them. By the way, these results do not always support intuitions reported in generative literature, but that is another story.

Along the same lines, McDaniel and Cowart 1999 found that subjects can reliably rate sentences like (16) and (17) in terms of degree of acceptability:

Resumptive pronouns:

(16) a. That is the girl that I wonder when met you.
b. That is the girl that I wonder when she met you.

(17) a. That is the girl that I wonder when you met.
b. That is the girl that I wonder when you met her.

What this shows is that there is a lot more to grammar than can be predicted from use in naturally occurring discourse. More importantly, what it shows is that the human language faculty is designed — at least in part — for something other than communication.

Do reliable judgments about little-used sentences also point to the evolutionary roots of grammar in conceptual structure? That is a little more tricky. To the extent that our grammars let us say and understand utterances that we would have little reason to need to say and understand, the tentative answer has to be 'yes'. It shows that we have a built-in meaning-generator independent of communication. The links between this meaning-generator and our grammars are extremely direct. Indeed, they would have to be, given the speed with which we can understand sentences with parasitic gaps. It is highly plausible, then, that this meaning-generator and its linkage to grammar arose in evolutionary time, before, or at least independently, of the use of grammars for communicative purposes.

5 A three-stage model for the evolution of grammar

Let us look a little more carefully at our working hypothesis that grammar originated as a representation of conceptual structure and became shaped to facilitate communication. I propose a three-stage process in language evolution. First, there existed a level of conceptual structure:

(18)

CONCEPTUAL STRUCTURE

Secondly came the principal evolutionary event. Conceptual structure was linked to the vocal output channel, creating for the first time a grammar that was independent of the combinatorial possibilities of conceptual structure per se, and making possible the *conveying* of thought. That is, it made vocal communication possible. Diagram (19) illustrates:

(19)

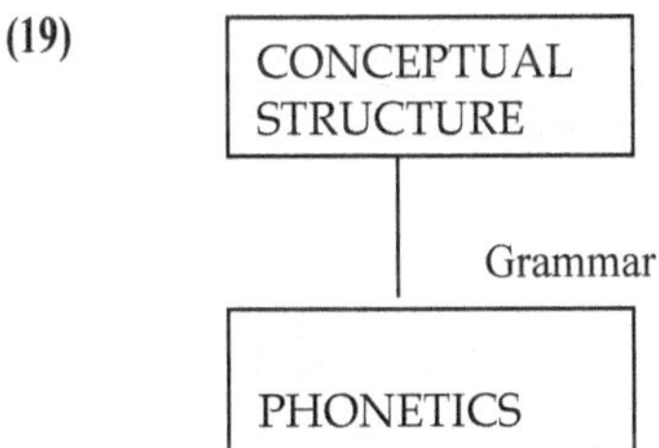

But once grammars started to be drawn upon for real-time purposes, the constraints of real-time use began to affect their properties. In particular, grammars began to be shaped to facilitate processing, frequently used elements become shorter, and so on (20):

(20)

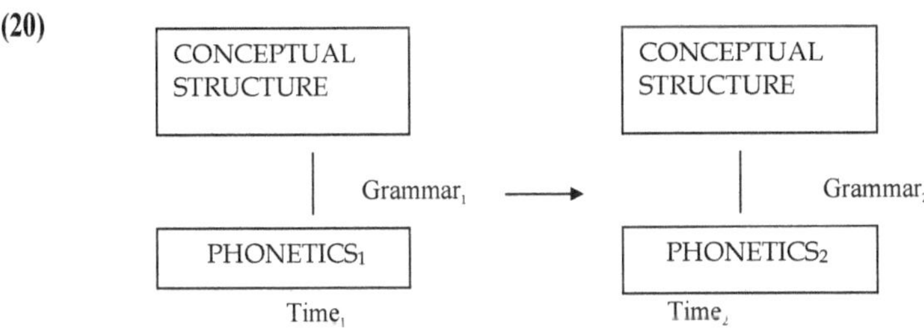

The importance of conceptual structures: their antedating language per se and their forming the basis on which syntax developed, combined with the derivative appearance of language for communicative purposes, provides the evolutionary-historical basis for the disparity between grammar and usage that I have been stressing.

6 Grammatical change is syntagmatic, not paradigmatic

Implicit in this model is the idea that grammatical change is a *syntagmatic* process, not a *paradigmatic* one. By that I mean that grammars change to 'improve', so to speak, the speed or effectiveness of the sequence of grammatical elements in real-time communication, but not to 'improve' (again, so to speak) the directness of the link between sound and meaning. This link will change, of course, as a *result* of a syntagmatically-induced change, at times giving the appearance of paradigmatically-induced change, but we are talking about results, not causes.

One prediction of such a model is that the desire to reduce ambiguity will not drive language change. And that seems quite right, given the extreme amount of ambiguity that language is willing to tolerate. This approach to language change is broadly compatible with that outlined in Croft 2000, which also stresses syntagmatic over paradigmatic change:

> Form-function reanalysis [one of Croft's principal mechanisms of change — FJN] is syntagmatic: it arises from the (re)mapping of form-function relations of combinations of syntactic units and semantic components. The *process may nevertheless have an apparently paradigmatic result*, for example, a change of meaning of a syntactic unit … (Croft 2000: 120; emphasis added)

Or again, commenting on an experiment reported on in Bybee and Slobin 1982, in which subjects were asked to produce past tense forms as quickly as possible, Croft wrote:

> Thus, speakers produced innovations. But the innovations were a result of speakers attempting to produce 'correct' forms — conforming to linguistic norms — in (accelerated) real time. *They were not the result of speakers trying — intending — to make past tense forms more similar to base forms, although that was in fact the result in many instances*. (Croft 2000: 119; emphasis added)

In support of Croft, let me present what looks like a compelling example of paradigmatic pressure on morphosyntax and show how the facts can be reanalyzed in syntagmatic terms. Faltz 1977/1985 and Comrie 1998 point out that if a language has 1st and 2nd person reflexives, it will also have 3rd person reflexives, as (21) illustrates:

(21) Occurrence of distinctive reflexives

	Third person	First/Second Person
English	yes	yes
Old English	no	no
French	yes	no
*	no	yes

Faltz's and Comrie's explanation for (21) is based on the idea that 1st and 2nd person referents are unique. But 3rd person referents are open-ended. In principle, a 3rd person referent could be any entity other than the speaker or the hearer. So it would seem to be more 'useful' to have 3rd person reflexives, since they narrow down the class of possible referents. Hence it appears that grammars are serving our needs by reducing potential ambiguity.

I can offer a syntagmatic explanation of these facts, that is, an explanation that does not involve problematic appeals to ambiguity-reduction. In languages that have reflexive pronouns in all three persons, 3rd person reflexives are used more frequently than 1st and 2nd. Consider English. In a million-word collection of British English texts, 3rd person singular reflexives were 5.8 times more likely to occur than 1st person and 10.5 times more likely to occur than 2nd person (22 gives the facts).

(22) Reflexive Pronoun Occurrence in English (Johansson and Hofland 1989)

Reflexive pronoun	**Number of occurrences in corpus**
myself	169
yourself	94
himself	511
herself	203
itself	272
TOTAL 3RD PERS. SG.	986

Language users (for whatever reason) more frequently use identical subjects and objects in the 3rd person than in the 1st or 2nd. Given that more frequently appealed to concepts are more likely to be lexicalized than those that are less frequently appealed to, the implicational relationship among reflexive pronouns follows automatically. There is no need to appeal to ambiguity-reducing 'usefulness'. Also, it is worth asking how much ambiguity is reduced by a 3rd person reflexive anyway. It eliminates one possible referent for the object, leaving an indefinite number of possibilities remaining.

7 Grammars do not necessarily do what is useful for the language user

Notice that Faltz and Comrie's argument depends crucially on paradigmatic ambiguity-reduction as a motivating force. But it is well known that language tolerates a tremendous amount of (formal) ambiguity, particularly in the reference system. Consider the inclusive/exclusive pronoun distinction:

(23) The inclusive-exclusive pronoun distinction in Washo (Jacobsen 1980)

	Sg.	Dual	Pl.
1st exclusive	lé'	léši (= I and one other)	léw (= I and others)
1st inclusive		léšiši (= I and you [sg.])	léwhu (= I and you [pl.])

According to Nichols 1992, only a minority of languages (about 42%) make this distinction. And it is heavily areal — only in Australia, Oceania, and South America do more than 60% of languages manifest it. Yet the distinction is quite 'useful' from an ambiguity-reduction perspective. We all have been in situations where we or someone else has said 'We are going to do X, Y, and Z' and it has not been clear whether the person addressed was included in the 'we' or not. So a distinction that we 'need' is not generally lexicalized.

One could make the same point about the falling together of 2nd person singular and plural pronouns in English (where it is total) and in other European languages (where it affects the polite form). How useful is that? Consider also the fact that a majority of the world's languages are null subject (Gilligan 1987). That might make language faster to use, even though it creates more potential ambiguity in doing so.

Notice that in their argument based on reflexives, Faltz and Comrie make the implicit assumption that grammars will do what is 'useful' to language users.

That is, they assume that within a given domain if a language makes a less-than-useful distinction, it will also make a useful one. So — their argument goes — grammars accommodate themselves to what speakers need to do — what they find most useful in communicative settings. Such is a standard assumption in functionalist writing and is enshrined in a famous dictum from Jack Du Bois:

> Grammars provide the most economical coding mechanism … for those speech functions which speakers most often need to perform. More succinctly: Grammars code best what speakers do most. (Du Bois 1985: 362–363)

But how generally true is that dictum? To begin with, unlike appeals to parsing-efficiency as a functional explanation, say, which are predictive, general appeals to 'usefulness' and 'need' have a post-facto feel to them. One observes a generalization and comes up with a plausible story to account for it. But there is nothing predictive about accounts like Comrie's. One can come up with any number of things that it would be useful for a language to do (or for language in general to do), but which never occur. One needs a theory — which is now lacking — of why some useful features result in grammatical coding, and some do not.

Take deictic systems. They do not seem particularly designed to meet language users' needs either. They are typically organized in terms of distance from speaker or hearer. The height of an object in relation to the speech participants seems like a useful distinction for grammars to make. But according to Anderson and Keenan 1985, only a small handful of languages encode this distinction grammatically. Speakers could also avoid potential ambiguity by means of a grammatical marker specifying whether an object is on their left side or their right side. But according to Hawkins 1988, no language grammaticalizes this distinction.

Another striking fact, reported in Talmy 1985/2000, is that no language has markers or incorporations that are not related either to the referent event or to the speech event itself. In other words, no matter how useful it would be to provide grammars with the possibility of sentences like (24) with meanings like (25) and (26), no language allows that possibility:

(24) The chair broke-ka

(25) The chair broke and I'm currently bored.

(26) The chair broke and it was raining yesterday.

It would be interesting to speculate if the impossibility of such sentences hearkens back to constraints on the conceptual structure – phonetic structure mapping that were forged in evolutionary time.

8 Departures from strict conceptual structure – grammatical structure match ups

There is an interesting prediction that follows from the claim that departures from a strict conceptual structure – grammatical structure match up were made primarily in the interest of allowing rapid communication. The prediction is that most such departures should be in the interest of language processing. I think that such is correct. Displacements provide the best examples. So take displacements to the right — extrapositions of constituents like those in (27a-b) are the best examples:

(27) a. [It] seems to me [that we are in for a lot of trouble]
b. [The computer] crashed [that you left in the student lounge]

In (27a) the phrase *that we are in for a lot of trouble* is displaced from logical subject position. In (27b) the relative clause *that you left in the student lounge* occurs separated from its head noun *the computer*. The parsing theory of Hawkins 1994 provides a straightforward explanation for these displacements. In both cases the postpositions of the heavy elements allow for the rapid recognition of the major constituents of the sentence. Now consider preposings of topicalized and focused elements as in (28a-b):

(28) a. That mistake$_i$, I'll never make ___$_i$ again.
b. Who$_i$ did you give the book to ___$_i$?

Here theories differ as to the relative role of parsing and discourse-oriented explanations. But all agree that the preposing facilitates the communicative process.

Before concluding, it would be worthwhile writing a few words of comparison between the position that I have been arguing for and the position that Ray Jackendoff takes in a recent book (Jackendoff 2002). Jackendoff, like me (and like Bickerton 1990 and Wray 2000; 2002 before him), is searching for 'fossils' in modern-day language that point back to its earlier stages. Jackendoff points to principles arguably governing proto-language such as 'Agent First', 'Focus Last', 'Grouping', the use of compound nouns, and so on. These are still found in modern human languages and are especially evident in what Klein and Perdue 1997 call 'The Basic Variety' — the stage arrived at (and often never left) by second-language learners. There is no incompatibility between Jackendoff's proposals and mine. He is looking back to the earliest stages of the use of language for communication. I am looking back to an even earlier stage, one where our ancestors had a recursive conceptual structure which had not yet been called into play for communicative purposes.

9 Conclusion

So let us recapitulate and conclude. Pre-humans possessed a rich conceptual structure representing predicates and their accompanying arguments.

I postulate that the evolutionary 'event' that underlies human language was the forging of a link between conceptual structures and the vocal output channel — in other words, the beginnings of grammar per se. But early grammar was extremely unstable. Once it was put to use for communicative purposes, which presumably this happened very early on, it began to be shaped by those purposes. In particular, it was shaped by the need to allow language to be produced and comprehended as rapidly as possible. But conceptual structures did not 'go away'; they continued to exert a stabilizing effect on language. That effect is seen in the importance to the nature of grammar of full argument structure, even if that full argument structure is rarely expressed. It is seen in the fact that speakers can make reliable judgments about sentences they would never use. And it is seen in the limited place for the drive to reduce ambiguity as a functional force affecting language.

In other words, we have good reason to believe that the Classical Position is right. The roots of grammar lie in hominid conceptual representations and its adaptation for communication took place as a subsequent development.

Notes

1 Some of the material in this essay has appeared in Newmeyer 2003 and is reprinted with permission.

References

Anderson, S. R. and Keenan, E. L. (1985) 'Deixis', Shopen, T. (ed.), *Language, Typology and Syntactic Description. Volume 3: Grammatical Categories and the Lexicon.* Cambridge: Cambridge University Press, 259–308.

Berwick, R. C. (1998) Language evolution and the minimalist program: the origins of syntax, Hurford, J. R., Studdert-Kennedy, M. and Knight, C. (eds), *Approaches to the Evolution of Language: Social and Cognitive Bases*. Cambridge: Cambridge University Press, 320–340.

Berwick, R. C. and Weinberg, A. (1984) *The Grammatical Basis of Linguistic Performance*. Cambridge, MA: MIT Press.

Bickerton, D. (1990) *Language and Species*. Chicago: University of Chicago Press.

Bybee, J. L. (1985) Morphology: a study of the relation between meaning and form, typological studies, *Language*, Vol. 9. Amsterdam: John Benjamins.

Bybee, J. L. and Slobin, D. I. (1982) Rules and schemas in the development and use of the English past tense, *Language*, 58: 265–289.

Cheney, D. and Seyfarth, R. (1990) *How Monkeys See the World.* Chicago: University of Chicago Press.

Chomsky, N. (1975) *Reflections on Language*. New York: Pantheon.

Chomsky, N. (1995) *The Minimalist Program*. Cambridge, MA: MIT Press.

Comrie, B. (1998) Reference-tracking: description and explanation, *Sprachtypologie und Universalienforschung*, 51: 335–346.

Cowart, W. (1997) *Experimental Syntax: Applying Objective Methods to Sentence Judgments*. Newbury Park, CA: SAGE Publications.

Craig, C. G. (1987) The Rama language: a text with grammatical notes, *Journal of Chibchan Studies,* 5.

Croft, W. (2000) *Explaining Language Change: An Evolutionary Approach.* London: Longman.

Dick, F. and Elman, J. L. (2001) The frequency of major sentence types over discourse levels: a corpus analysis. *Newsletter of the Center for Research Language*, University of California, San Diego, 13: 3–19.

Du Bois, J. (1985) Competing motivations, Haiman, J. (ed.), *Iconicity in Syntax.* Amsterdam: John Benjamins. 343–365.

Du Bois, J. (1987) The discourse basis of ergativity, *Language*, 63: 805–855.
England, N. C. (1988) Mam Voice, Shibatani, M. (ed.), *Passive and Voice*. Amsterdam: John Benjamins. 525–545.
Faltz, L. M. (1977/1985) *Reflexivization: A Study in Universal Syntax, Outstanding Dissertations in Linguistics*. New York: Garland.
Fox, B. A. (1994) Contextualization, indexicality, and the distributed nature of grammar, *Language Sciences*, 16: 1–38.
Gilligan, G. M. (1987) A cross-linguistic approach to the pro-drop parameter, *Ph. D. dissertation*, University of Southern California.
Greenberg, J. H. (1963) Some universals of language with special reference to the order of meaningful elements, Greenberg, J. (ed.), *Universals of Language*. Cambridge, MA: MIT Press, 73–113.
Harris, R. (1980) *The Language–Makers*. Ithaca: Cornell University Press.
Harris, R.(1981) *The Language Myth*. London: Duckworth.
Hauser, M. D. (1996) *The Evolution of Communication*. Cambridge, MA: MIT Press.
Hauser, M. D., Chomsky, N. and Fitch, W. T. (2002) The faculty of language: what is it, who has it, and how did it evolve?, *Science*, 1569–1579.
Hawkins, J. A. (1988) Explaining language universals, J. A. Hawkins (ed.), *Explaining Language Universals*. Oxford: Blackwell, B. 3–28.
Hawkins, J. A. (1994) A performance theory of order and constituency, *Cambridge Studies in Linguistics*, Vol. 73. Cambridge: Cambridge University Press.
Hopper, P. J. (1988) Emergent grammar and the apriori grammar postulate, Tannen, D. (ed.), *Linguistics in Context: Connecting Observation and Understanding*. Norwood, NJ: Ablex, 117–134.
Hurford, J. R. (2002) The roles of expression and representation in language evolution, Wray, A. (ed.*), The Transition to Language*. Oxford: Oxford University Press, 311–334.
Jackendoff, R. (1983) *Semantics and Cognition*. Cambridge, MA: MIT Press.
Jackendoff, R.(1990) *Semantic Structures*. Cambridge, MA: MIT Press.
Jackendoff, R. (2002) *Foundations of Language: Brain, Meaning, Grammar, Evolution*. Oxford: Oxford University Press.
Jacobsen Jr., W. H. (1980) Inclusive/exclusive: a diffused pronominal category in native western North America, Ojeda, A. E. (ed.), *Papers from the Parasession on Pronouns and Anaphora*. Chicago: Chicago Linguistic Society, 204–227.
Johansson, S. and Hofland, K. (1989) *Frequency Analysis of English Vocabulary and Grammar Based on the Lob Corpus. Volume 1: Tag Frequencies and Word Frequencies*. Oxford: Clarendon Press.
Klein, W. and Perdue, C. (1997) The basic variety, or: couldn't language be much simpler?, *Second Language Research*, 13: 301–347.

Lambrecht, K. (1987) On the status of SVO sentences in French discourse, R. Tomlin (ed.), *Coherence and Grounding in Discourse*. Amsterdam: John Benjamins. 217–262.

Levelt, W. J. M. (1989) *Speaking: From Intention to Articulation*. Cambridge, MA: MIT Press.

Li, C. N. (2002) Missing links, issues, and hypotheses in the evolutionary origin of language, *Symposium on the Evolution of Language*, Düsseldorf.

Li, C. N. and Hombert, J-M. (2002) On the evolutionary origin of language, Stamenov, M. and Gallese, V. (eds), *Mirror Neurons and the Evolution of Brain and Language*. Amsterdam: John Benjamins.

McDaniel, D. and Cowart, W. (1999) Experimental evidence for a minimalist account of English resumptive pronouns, *Cognition*, 70: B15–B24.

Mithun, M. (1987) Is basic word order universal? Tomlin, R. (ed.), *Coherence and Grounding in Discourse*. Amsterdam: John Benjamins. 281–328.

Morgan, J. L. (1973) Sentence fragments and the notion sentence, Kachru, B. B. Lees, R. B. Malkiel, Y. Pietrangeli, A. and Saporta, S. (eds), *Issues in Linguistics: Papers in Honor of Henry and Renée Kahane*. Urbana: University of Illinois Press, 719–751.

Newmeyer, F. J. (1991) Functional explanation in linguistics and the origins of language, *Language and Communication*, 11: 3–28.

Newmeyer, F. J. (2003) Grammar is grammar and usage is usage, *Language*, 79: 682–707

Nichols, J. (1992) *Linguistic Diversity in Space and Time*. Chicago: University of Chicago Press.

Payne, D. L. (1990) *The Pragmatics of Word Order: Typological Dimensions of Verb-Initial Languages*. Berlin: de Gruyter, M.

Payne, D. L. (1992) Nonidentifiable information and pragmatic order rules in O'odham, Payne, D. L. (ed.), *Pragmatics of Word Order Flexibility*. Amsterdam: John Benjamins. 137–166.

Pinker, S. (1989) *Learnability and Cognition: The Acquisition of Argument Structure*. Cambridge, MA: MIT Press.

Pinker, S. and Bloom, P. (1990) Natural language and natural selection, *Behavioral and Brain Sciences*, 13: 707–784.

Pope, E. (1971) Answers to yes-no questions, *Linguistic Inquiry*, 2: 69–82.

Scancarelli, S. (1985) Referential strategies in chamorro narratives: preferred clause structure and ergativity, *Studies in Language*, 9: 335–362.

Schuetze-Coburn, S. (1987) Topic management and the lexicon: a discourse profile of three-argument verbs in German, *Ph. D. dissertation*, UCLA.

Schütze, C. (1996) *The Empirical Basis of Linguistics: Grammaticality Judgments and Linguistic Methodology*. Chicago: University of Chicago Press.

Smith, W. (1996) Spoken narrative and preferred clause structure: evidence from Modern Hebrew discourse, *Studies in Language*, 20: 163–189.

Talmy, L. (1983) How language structures space, Pick, H. L. and Acredolo, L. P. (eds), *Spatial Orientation: Theory, Research, and Application*. New York: Plenum Press, 225–282.

Talmy, L.(1985/2000) Lexicalization patterns: semantic structure in lexical forms, Talmy, L. (ed.), *Toward a Cognitive Semantics*. Cambridge, MA: MIT Press, 21–212.

Talmy, L. (1988) Force dynamics in language and cognition, *Cognitive Science*, 12: 49–100.

Thompson, S. A. and Hopper, P. J. (2001) Transitivity, clause structure, and argument structure: evidence from conversation, Bybee, J. L. and Hopper, P. (eds), *Frequency and the Emergence of Linguistic Structure*. Amsterdam: John Benjamins. 27–60.

Tomasello, M. (2000) Primate cognition (special issue), *Cognitive Science*, 24: (3).

Waal, F. B. M. de (1996) *Good Natured: The Origins of Right and Wrong in Humans and Other Animals*. Cambridge, MA: Harvard University Press.

Weber, D. J. (1989) *A Grammar of Huallaga (Huánaco) Quechua*. Berkeley: University of California Press.

Wilkins, W. K. and Wakefield, J. (1995) Brain evolution and neurolinguistic preconditions, *Behavioral and Brain Sciences*, 18: 161–226.

Wray, A. (2000) *Holistic Utterances in Proto-language: The Link from Primates to Humans*, Knight, C. Studdert-Kennedy, M. and Hurford, J. R. (eds). Cambridge: Cambridge University Press, 285–302.

Wray, A. (2002) Dual processing in Proto-Language: performance without competence, Wray, A. (ed.), *The Transition to Language*. Oxford: Oxford University Press, 113–137.

7 The origin of language as a product of the evolution of modern cognition

Gilles Fauconnier
University of California San Diego

Mark Turner
Case Western Reserve University

To ask where language comes from is to raise the question of the origin of the cognitively modern human mind. Recent work in conceptual integration theory (CIT) shows that cognitively modern human beings are equipped with an advanced form of a basic mental operation that makes it possible for them to develop a number of human singularities: art, music, science, fashions of dress, dance, mathematics. This basic mental operation is *conceptual integration*, and the advanced form is *Double-Scope* integration. Human singularities are not independent. They precipitate as products of Double-Scope conceptual integration.

Here, we will explore the implications of these findings for the origin of language. There are many problems besetting theories of the origin of language. These problems include the absence of intermediate stages in the appearance of language, the absence of existing languages more rudimentary than others, the appeal to some extraordinary genetic event unlike any other we know of, and the difficulty of finding a defensible story of adaptation. CIT opens up a different way of looking at the origin of language that is free of such problems.

Conceptual integration[1] is an operation with principles and constraints. It creates dynamic networks. The mechanics of such networks and the emergent structure they produce are a complex branch of cognitive science that we cannot study here in any detail. The gist of the operation is that two or more mental spaces can be partially matched and their structure can be partially projected to a new, blended space that develops emergent structure. These mental spaces and their relations constitute a conceptual integration network. Human beings are especially adept at creating and using such networks routinely in thought and action.

Here is a simple example: in *Aesop's Fables,* animals preach, complain, beseech, cajole, implore, and argue. When the shaman talks to animal spirits, or when the serpent whispers in Eve's ear, a similar integration is taking place. One input mental space has ordinary human beings, who eat, compete, talk, listen, preach, cajole. Another has animals, who eat, compete, vocalize, and interact. Partial matching connects humans with animals, talking with making noise, and so on. In the blended mental space ('blend' for short), we have talking animals! Such networks are found throughout all cultures. Whether it be the talking fox or the animal spirit, the emergent structure is both easily achieved and extremely complex if you begin to analyze it. Researchers have shown, as we survey in *The Way We Think* (2002), that exactly the same type of networks arise in the evolution of mathematics, scientific discovery, visual representation, and, as we will see, grammar. In the case of mathematics, which is so thoroughly admired, we have no difficulty imagining that there is creativity, discovery, and emergent structure. For example, complex numbers and non-Euclidean geometry, which are products of Double-Scope integration, were clearly great conceptual achievements. The talking fox is in every way as complex and creative — only our species can do it — but this complexity goes unnoticed precisely because everyone can do it.

1 Central discoveries of CIT

Here are some of the findings from CIT that we will need in order to demonstrate how language originated as a product of the capacity for Double-Scope integration.

> **Finding 1:** Thinkers have been fascinated and puzzled since even before the time of *Aesop's Fables* by mental patterns that are commonly classified under labels such as analogy, category extension, metaphor, framing, counterfactuals, and grammatical constructions. It has been assumed that these names refer to separate kinds of things. Typically, these things are considered part of distinct disciplines: counterfactuals in philosophy and logic, metaphor in literature, analogy in psychology, framing in sociology and artificial intelligence, grammatical constructions in linguistics. A remarkable result of CIT is that, at a deeper level, all of these patterns are products of conceptual integration networks. The mental principles of their origin are uniform.

Finding 2: A central feature of integration networks is their ability to compress diffuse conceptual structure into intelligible and manipulable human-scale situations in the blended space. These compressed blends are memorable and can be expanded flexibly to manage their integration networks. Compressions have been studied in great detail. They operate on a set of twenty or so vital conceptual relations, such as Cause-Effect, Analogy and Disanalogy, Time, Space, Change, Identity, Part-Whole, and Representation. Relations can be compressed into a human-scale version of themselves, or into different vital relations. As an example of compression, consider a statement like 'Dinosaurs changed into birds,' used to suggest the new theory according to which birds are descendants of dinosaurs. At one level, this evolutionary story spans millions of years, in which many organisms lived and died, none of them actually 'changing' into anything. These organisms are connected by Cause-Effect (progeneration), Analogy and Disanalogy (offspring are analogous and disanalogous to their ancestors), and Time. In the blend, the Analogy is compressed into Identity (a single dinosaur becomes a single bird) and the Disanalogy is compressed into Change. Time is compressed into the lifetime of an animal, which at the beginning is a dinosaur and at the end is a bird. There are many standard patterns of compression, and this is one of the most common. In ordinary language, we say 'My tax return gets longer every year'. A number of analogous tax returns at the end of every year, no one of which gets longer, but each of which is longer than the previous one, are compressed in the blend into a single tax return that changes. Conceptual integration networks with useful compressions are the rule in human thought and action, as has been shown for domains as different as material anchors (edwin Hutchins), sign language (Scott Liddell), and magic and religious practices (Jesper Sørensen).

Finding 3: Conceptual integration networks fall on a complexity gradient. There are some focal positions on this continuum: Simplex networks, Mirror networks, Single-Scope networks, and Double-Scope networks. The blended spaces of simplex networks provide framings, as in 'Paul is the father of Sally'. Mirror networks have inputs that have the same frame, and their blended spaces also have that frame, often with a slight extension. So, for example, the familiar behavior of talking to oneself is made possible by mirror networks. Single-scope and Double-Scope networks can work on inputs that have very different frames or even frames with clashes in their central structures. Double-scope networks, as we will see, are the most important for explaining the origin of language. Human beings became cognitively modern when they acquired the capacity to do Double-Scope integration. Human language, spoken or signed, is a product of that ability.

2 The mystery of language

Language is a mystery because it is a singularity: only human beings have grammar of the sort we find in natural languages. But language is not the only singularity: the considerable efforts of animal psychologists have uncovered no evidence that other species can reach very far in conceiving of counterfactual scenarios (like those underlying pretense), metaphors, analogies, or category extensions. Even the most impressive nonhuman species have very limited abilities to use tools, let alone design and make them. Human beings have elaborate rituals that constitute cultural meaning without being tied to immediate circumstances of feeding, fighting, or mating, but the nearest that other species can come to 'rituals' are instinctive displays that are directly tied to such immediate circumstances. As Merlin Donald puts it, 'Our genes may be largely identical to those of a chimp or gorilla, but our cognitive architecture is not. And having reached a critical point in our cognitive evolution, we are symbol-using, networked creatures, unlike any that went before us'.[2]

It is hard to get an explanation of language that sees it as the product of gradual steps, each producing a grammar by making the previous grammar a little more complicated. Such an explanation would ask us to imagine that a group of human beings began with a very simple grammar that gradually, generation after generation, grew ever more complex, until it reached the level we see in the languages in the world today. Such an explanation runs up against the fact that we can point to no simple languages, or even ones that are simpler than others. There are many evolutionary developments for which it is relatively easy to see a gradual path: we can see gradual steps by which early mammals plausibly evolved into primates or cetaceans. But we do not see any gradual path in mammalian history for the development over many generations of ever more complex grammars.

3 Existing theories

The hunt is on for the origin of language. What could have caused this singularity to come into existence? One line of thinking looks at language as a very specific human production and asks how it could have arisen. The language faculty is viewed as distinct from other human capacities, and so the correlation with the other human singularities has no theoretical place: those other abilities are distinct from language and call for other explanations. This line of exploration has room for many different kinds of theories.

Nativist theories — Chomksy is the preeminent name here — place the distinctiveness of language in specific genetic endowment for a specifically genetically instructed language module. Under that view, there is minimal learning involved in acquiring a language. Most of the language module is already in place. Which language actually gets spoken — Chinese, Bantu, English — is relatively superficial: very thin exposure to a given language sets parameters that control the output of the language module, that is, gives us one language instead of an alternative language. But it is not clear what, in the evolution of the human brain, could have been the precursor of the language module. Nor is it clear what pressures from natural selection would have produced such a module, given that we find no intermediate stages. This is why many nativists have embraced the view that a sudden, dramatic, perhaps unique event in human evolutionary history produced in one leap a language module resembling nothing like the brain's previous resources.

Other nativist views of language see it as having arisen by gradual natural selection. Stephen Pinker and Paul Bloom argue that 'there must have been a series of steps leading from no language at all to language as we now find it, each step small enough to have been produced by a random mutation or recombination'.[3]

Although viewing language as a specific production distinct from other human capacities is associated with nativist theories of language as modular, neither nativism nor modularity is crucial for the view of language as a distinct capacity. A radical associative theorist who sees cognition as developing during childhood through the forming, strengthening, and weakening of connections between neurons might easily view language as a very special set of operations that arise in a network. On this view, language would be essentially distinct from other capacities of the network, even though all of them would share a common denominator in the basic associative operations. While the language faculty would not be localized in any area of the network, it would still be distinct operationally.

Some associative theories emphasize the role of evolution in developing powerful learning mechanisms that perform statistical inferences on experiences. In these views, the brain has evolved rich, specific architectures for statistical extraction, and language is one of the things that can be learned through those domain-general processes of statistical inferencing. Language is intricate and depends upon the evolution of those learning abilities, but the way we learn it is not specific to language. The language the child hears — far from impoverished — is adequate for the purpose of converging on grammatical patterns by doing statistical inferencing.[4] The evolutionary story here is that the brain evolved learning abilities with some bias for learning things like language, but did not evolve 'language' or a neural 'language module'. As Terrence Deacon writes, 'The relevant biases must be unlike those of any other species, and exaggerated in peculiar ways, given the unusual nature of symbolic learning'.[5] It remains a challenge, of course, to explain how those particular learning abilities and biases for language could have evolved, and it is still not clear under this explanation why we have no evidence of intermediate, simpler forms of language.

One line of thinking, associated with theorists like William Calvin and Derek Bickerton[6] in *Lingua ex Machina* and Frank R. Wilson[7] in *The Hand*, tries to find preadaptations for language — such as the development of the hand, of reciprocal altruism — that could have put in place some of the computational ability that language needs. In this way of thinking, there were gradual steps to language, but the early steps did not look like language because they weren't. They had some powers that later on made sophisticated language possible.

There are also coevolutionary proposals, including an influential recent proposal by Terrence Deacon.[8] Language, he argues, is not an instinct and there is no genetically installed linguistic black box in our brains. Language arose slowly through cognitive and cultural inventiveness. Two million years ago, australopithecines, equipped with nonlinguistic ape-like mental abilities, struggled to assemble, by fits and starts, an extremely crude symbolic system — fragile, difficult to learn, inefficient, slow, inflexible, and tied to ritual representation of social contracts like marriage. We would not have recognized it as language. Language then improved by two means. First, invented linguistic forms were subjected to a long process of selection. Generation after generation, the newborn brain deflected linguistic inventions it found uncongenial. The guessing abilities and intricate nonlinguistic biases of the newborn brain acted as filters on the products of linguistic invention. Today's languages are systems of linguistic forms that have survived. The child's mind does not embody innate language structures. Rather, language has come to embody the predispositions of the child's mind.

The second, subordinate means, by which language improved, in Deacon's view, had to do with changes in the brain. Crude and difficult language imposed the persistent cognitive burden of erecting and maintaining a relational network of symbols. That demanding environment favored genetic variations that rendered brains more adept at language. Language began as a cognitive adaptation and genetic assimilation then eased some of the burden. Cognitive effort and genetic assimilation interacted as language and brain co-evolved. In Deacon's view, language was 'acquired with the aid of flexible ape-learning abilities'. It was grafted onto an ape-like brain. It is not walled off from other cognitive functions such as interpreting and reasoning. Grammatical form is not independent of conceptual meaning. There is no linguistic black box and there was no insertion.

4 A range of arresting human singularities

Three of the biggest singularities that seem to enter explosively on the human stage around the same time in human prehistory are art, religion, and science. As Stephen Mithen writes in 'A Creative Explosion?',

Art makes a dramatic appearance in the archaeological record. For over 2.5 million years after the first stone tools appear, the closest we get to art are a few scratches on unshaped pieces of bone and stone. It is possible that these scratches have symbolic significance — but this is highly unlikely. They may not even be intentionally made. And then, a mere 30,000 years ago, at least 70,000 years after the appearance of anatomically modern humans, we find cave paintings in southwest France — paintings that are technically masterful and full of emotive power.[9]

Mithen makes the same claim for religion and science, and naturally asks what could have led to these singularities. His answer is that human beings suddenly developed a totally new capacity for 'cognitive fluidity,' that is, a capacity for the 'flow of knowledge and ideas between behavioral domains,' such as 'social intelligence' and 'natural history intelligence'. Although Mithen offers no theory about the principles or operation of 'cognitive fluidity,' and views it as a higher-order operation used for the special purpose of putting different domains together, there are interesting parallels between the general notion of cognitive fluidity and the idea of conceptual integration. What caused cognitive fluidity? In Mithen's view, there must have been some singular, explosive evolutionary event that produced a quite different sort of brain.

Mithen observes that time and again, theorists have confidently if vaguely located the exceptional cognitive abilities of human beings in their ability to put two things together. Aristotle wrote that metaphor is the hallmark of genius. Koestler proposed that the act of creation is the result of bisociating different matrices.

The prehistoric picture we are left with is one of mysterious singularities: explosions, some perhaps simultaneous, in new human performances. We also have, for all these singularities, the problem that there is essentially no record of intermediate stages between the absence of the ability and its full flowering. And this prehistoric story has, at least for language, its contemporary parallel: we find no human groups, however isolated, that have only rudimentary language. We find no primates with rudimentary language. At first glance, this is a completely abnormal situation. We find no parallels in evolution of species, for example — no complex organisms that leap without precursors out of the slime. What kind of theory do we need in order to account for such a strange and unprecedented picture?

5 What should a proper theory of language look like?

As Darwin noted, evolution's main trick seems to be gradual change, so that an adaptationist account is obliged to show that each step would have been adaptive. Evolution is never allowed to think, 'Well, if I could get to stage ten, it would be good, so give me a break while I go through the first nine'. Other things being equal, we prefer an evolutionary account that shows continuity of change rather than a spectacular singularity. Even 'punctuated equilibrium' theories propose only relatively minor jumps — not jumps that produce an eye or language out of nothing.

But we face a problem: how do we explain the arresting human singularities as arising out of relatively continuous changes in brain and cognition?

To think about this question, we must put aside two major fallacies. The first is the fallacy of Cause-Effect Isomorphism. Compressing cause and effect is indispensable to cognition, but it often has the bad consequence for scientific thinking that, recognizing an effect, we conceive of the cause as having much of the same status as the effect. So if the effect is dramatic, we expect a dramatic causal event. If the effect is unusual, we expect an unusual causal event. This way of thinking is so common that popular science accounts routinely offer entertaining demonstrations of the way in which unusual cases come from boring, routine causes. This is always the story for popular accounts of evolution or chaos theory — the beetle whose abdomen has grown into a covering costume that makes it look like a termite so it can live in termite nests arose through the most routine operations of gradual natural selection.

The Cause-Effect Isomorphism fallacy leads us to think that a discontinuity in effects must come from a discontinuity in causes, and therefore that the sudden appearance of language must be linked to a catastrophic neural event. The only evidence we need against this fallacy is the straw that broke the camel's back, but we see such evidence everywhere in science. Under heat, there is a smooth continuity of causation as ice goes abruptly from solid to liquid. The change from solid to liquid is a singularity, but there is no underlying singularity in the causes or in the causal process. One more drop of water in a full cup causes a lot of water to flow suddenly out onto the table, not just the one drop that was added. One more gram of body fat can make it possible for you to float on your back without effort in the middle of the South Pacific; a gram fewer and you sink down. In this case, a life-and-death singularity arises from smooth continuity in causes and causal operations. Nothing has changed about the principles of hydrodynamics or buoyancy when you drown.

So, in principle, the sudden appearance of language is not evidence against evolutionary continuity. Singularity from continuity is a normal occurrence. The only remaining question is, can biological evolution also work this way?

Are there specific evolutionary processes that give us remarkable singularities out of causal continuities? Here, we encounter a second major fallacy, the Function-Organ Isomorphism Fallacy. This is the well-known idea that the onset of a new organismic function requires the evolution of a new organ. Under this fallacy, because opossums hang from trees by their tails, tails are organs for performing the function of hanging from trees; because people speak with their tongues, tongues are organs for talking. As biologists routinely point out, as an organ evolves it may acquire new functions or lose old functions or both. There were intricate mammalian tongues before there was language; the tongue did not need to be invented afresh. The ancestors of opossums had tails before opossums hung from trees. The continuous evolution of an organ does not necessarily correlate with a continuous evolution of a function. Functions can be singularities while the evolution of an organ is continuous. Like the body in the water, an organ may need only the tiniest increment of change to subserve a striking new function, like floating.

We see this in the case of the proposed theory of how dinosaurs evolved into birds. Nobody proposes a theory of discontinuity for the organ (wings) but nobody proposes a theory of continuity for the function (flight). According to all these theories, wings came gradually — scales seem to have developed slowly into feathers, feathers provided warmth, the existence of longer arms and feathers made it possible to flap for a little extra ground speed and so the arms got longer and more feathery. Flight in all these theories came at one swoop — at a critical point, the organism could become truly airborne, and so now it could fly after the dragonfly and gobble it up. It occurs to no one to propose that flight — a spectacular singularity of function — came about because an organ for flight suddenly evolved from scratch. It also occurs to no one to propose that since modern birds fly higher than one hundred feet, there must have been intermediate stages in which birds could attain heights of first of one foot, then many generations later two feet, and so on up to one hundred feet. Being truly airborne is all-or-nothing, and so the behavior of flying is also basically all-or-nothing. An organism either flies or does not.

In thinking about the origin of language, we must put aside the fallacies of Cause-Effect Isomorphism and Function-Organ Isomorphism. Language is not an organ. The brain is the organ, and language is a function subserved by it, with the help of various other organs. Language is the surface manifestation of a capacity. It is a singularity of function, and so nothing prevents it from having arisen from a basically continuous and adaptive process of evolution. The function can have arisen recently in human evolution even though the continuous changes that brought it about can have been working for many millions of years. The causes are very old but one particular effect showed up just yesterday. This is what we propose.

The best theory of the origin of language would have the following features:

- A recognition of the singularity of language. There is no evidence of sustained intermediate stages phylogenetically, and no evidence of present human languages that are rudimentary.
- Rejection of an extraordinary event as responsible for the extraordinary capacity. In other words, no Cause-Effect Isomorphism.
- A continuous path of evolutionary change over a very long period as the cause of language, since that is how evolution almost always works.
- A path that is a plausible adaptive story: each change along the path must have been adaptive in itself, regardless of where the path ultimately led.
- Hence a continuous evolutionary path that produces singularities.
- A model of what mental operations developed along that path, and in what order.
- An explicit account of what continuous changes produced what singularities, and how they did it.
- Robust evidence from many quarters that human beings actually perform the mental operations on that hypothetical path.
- Intermediate steps not for the function of language itself but for the cognitive abilities that finally led to the precipitation of language as a product.
- Evidence in the anatomy or behavior of today's human beings pointing to the history of these steps, just as anatomical evidence in today's human beings points to our once having had tails.
- Other things being equal, a parsimonious way of explaining the emergence of many related human singularities as products that arise along the same continuous evolutionary path.

6 The central problem of language

The world of human meaning is incomparably richer than language forms. Although it is sometimes said that language makes an infinite number of forms available, it is a lesser infinity than the infinity of situations offered by the very rich physical mental world that we live in. To see that, take any form, like 'My cow is brown' and try to imagine all the possible people, cows, shades of brown to which it might apply, as well as the different uses of the phrase as ironic or categorical or metaphoric, including its use as an example in this paragraph.

A word like 'food' or 'there' must apply very widely if it is to do its job. The same is true of grammatical patterns independent of the words we put in them. Take the Resultative construction in English, which has the form A-Verb-B-Adjective, where the Adjective denotes a property C.[10] It means *A do something to B with the result that B have property C*, as in 'Kathy painted the wall white'. We want it to prompt for conceptions of actions and results over vast ranges of human life: 'She kissed him unconscious', 'Last night's meal made me sick', 'He hammered it flat', 'I boiled the pan dry', 'The earthquake shook the building apart', 'Roman imperialism made Latin universal'. We find it obvious that the meaning of the resultative construction could apply to all these different domains, but applying it thus requires complex cognitive operations. The events described here are in completely different domains (Roman politics versus blacksmithing) and have strikingly different time spans (the era in which a language rises versus a few seconds of earthquake), different spatial environments (most of Europe versus the stovetop), different degrees of intentionality (Roman imperialism versus a forgetful cook versus an earthquake), and very different kinds of connection between cause and effect (the hammer blow causes the immediate flatness of the object, but eating the meal one day causes sickness later through a long chain of biological events).

This very simple grammatical construction allows us to perform a complex conceptual integration which in effect compresses over Identity (e.g. Roman imperialism), Time, Space, Change, Cause-Effect, and Intentionality. The grammatical construction provides a compressed input space with a corresponding language form. It is then blended in a network with another input that typically contains an unintegrated and relatively diffuse chain of events. So, if it is our job to turn off the burner under the pan that has zucchini in boiling water, and we forget about it and all the water evaporates, we can say, confessionally, 'No zucchini tonight. I boiled the pan dry. Sorry'. In the diffuse input, the causal chain runs from forgetting to the invariant position of the burner knob, to the flow of gas, to the flame, to the temperature of the pan, to the temperature of the water, to the level of the water, to the dryness of the pan. The agent performs no direct or indirect action on the pan at all. But in the blend, the compressed structure associated with the grammatical construction is projected together with some selected participants from the diffuse chain of events in the diffuse input. In the blend, the agent acts directly on the pan. Moreover, although the boiling of the water is an event and its cause was something the agent did or did not do, there is cause-effect compression in the blend so that in the blend, although not in the input spaces, *boiling* is an action the agent performed on the pan. As this example shows, the simplest grammatical constructions require high abstraction over domains and complex Double-Scope integration.

Paradoxically, language is possible only if it allows a limited number of combinable language forms to cover a very large number of meaningful situations.

There is every reason to think that some species are able to operate efficiently in separate domains of, say, tool use, mating, and eating without being able to perform these abstractions and integrations. If that is so, then grammar would be of no use to them, because they cannot perform the conceptual integrations that grammar serves to prompt. But couldn't they just have a simpler grammar? The only way they could have a simpler grammar and yet have descriptions in language for what happens would be by having separate forms and words for everything that happens in all the different domains. But the world is infinitely too rich for that to be of any use. Trying to carry around 'language' of that size would be crippling. The evidence does not suggest that primates have compensated for lack of language by developing, for example, one million special-purpose words, each conveying a special scenario. On the contrary, while primate species have some specific 'vocalizations' (e.g., in response to a potential predator), the best efforts to teach words to chimpanzees cannot get them past a vocabulary of about two hundred items. Having a handful of vocalizations is clearly a help, but evolution has found no use in trying to extend that strategy very far. The extraordinary evolutionary advantage of language lies in its amazing ability to be put to use in *any* situation. We will call this crucial property of language 'equipotentiality'. For any situation, real or imaginary, there is always a way to use language to express thoughts about that situation. Double-Scope conceptual integration is the key to the amazing power of the equipotentiality of language, which we take for granted and use effortlessly in all circumstances.

7 Gradients of conceptual integration and the emergence of language

On independent grounds, we must grant that human beings today have powerful and general abilities of conceptual integration. In particular, Double-Scope networks are the kind of mental feat that human beings perform with the greatest of ease but that other species are unable to achieve. Blending research has shown how Double Scope networks play a role in grammatical constructions, the invention of scientific and mathematical concepts, religious rituals, counterfactual scenarios, persuasive representations, and vital relation compressions.

It has also shown that networks of conceptual integration fall along gradients of complexity. At the top end are networks whose inputs have clashing organizing frames and blends that draw on both of those frames, the Double Scopes. At the bottom end are Simplex networks with conventional frames and ordinary values for their roles.

Our hypothesis for the origin of language is as follows:

- Double-Scope conceptual integration is characteristic of human beings as compared with other species and is indispensable across art, religion, reasoning, science, and the other singular mental feats that are characteristic of human beings.
- The hallmark virtue of advanced blending capacity is its provision of efficient, intelligible, strong compressions across ranges of meaning that are otherwise diffuse and unmanageable. There are many scenes that are immediately apprehensible to human beings: throwing a stone in a direction, breaking open a nut to get the meat, grabbing an object, walking to a visible location, killing an animal, recognizing a mate, distinguishing friend from foe. Double-Scope blending gives us the supremely valuable, perhaps species-defining cognitive instrument of anchoring other meanings in a highly compressed blend that is like the immediately apprehensible basic human scenes, often because those scenes are used to help frame the blend.
- The development of blending capacity was gradual and required a long expanse of evolutionary time: basic blending is evident as far back as the evolution of mammals.
- Each step in the development of blending capacity was adaptive. From very simple Simplex blends to very creative Double-Scopes, each step of the capacity would have been adaptive because each step gives increasing cognitive ability to compress, remember, reason, categorize, and analogize.
- There is ample evidence of intermediate stages in the development of blending capacity. Some species, for example, seem able to do only simple Simplex networks. Others seem able to do slightly more unusual Simplex networks.
- There is also ample evidence of intermediate stages in human beings, in the sense that although we can do Double-Scope blending, we can of course still do Simplex blending.

- A special level of capacity for conceptual integration must be achieved before a system of expression with a limited number of combinable forms can cover an open-ended number of situations and framings.
- The indispensable capacity needed for language is the capacity to do Double-Scope blending.
- The development of Double-Scope blending is not a cataclysmic event but rather an achievement along a continuous scale of blending capacity, and so there is no Cause-Effect Isomorphism in the origin of language: the cause was continuous but the effect was a singularity.
- Language arose as a singularity. It was a new behavior that emerged naturally once the capacity of blending had developed to the critical level of Double-Scope blending.
- Language is like flight: an all-or-nothing behavior. If the species has not reached the stage of Double-Scope blending, it will not develop language at all, since the least aspects of grammar require it. But if it has reached the stage of Double-Scope blending, it can very rapidly develop a full language in cultural time because it has *all* the necessary prerequisites for a full set of grammatical integrations. The culture cannot stop at a 'simpler' language, for example one that has only the Subject-Verb clausal construction. A grammatical system, to meet the crucial condition of equipotentiality, must be a full set of possible integrations and corresponding forms that can combine to give expressions suitable for any situation. Therefore, language will automatically be multiply Double-Scope and complex. And there will be no stopping the development of language from achieving that level, since the engine of Double-Scope blending that produces equipotentiality will be fully in place.
- The story of the origin of language does have room for intermediate stages, in the capacity: human beings still have the capacity to do simple forms of blending. But no intermediate stages will be found in the languages because full grammar precipitates quickly as a singular product of the blending capacity once it reaches the critical stage. 'Quickly' here does not mean instantaneously, but within cultural rather than evolutionary time.
- The hallmark virtue of language is its ability to use grammatical patterns suitable for basic human scenes, to capture and convey much less tidy meanings. This is done through the massive compression offered by Double-Scope blending, which can achieve blends that fit

the grammatical patterns associated with those basic human scenes. Language, in the strong sense, must be equipotential. It must be serviceable for the new situations we encounter. The only way for it to be equipotential is for the human mind to be able to blend those new situations with what we already know to give us intelligible blends with attached grammatical patterns so those existing grammatical patterns can express the new situations. To say something new, we do not need to invent new grammar — and a good thing, too! Rather, we need to conceive of a blend that lets existing grammar come into play. Only in this way can an individual with a small, relatively fixed vocabulary of words and basic grammatical patterns cope with an extremely rich and open-ended world.

- If we follow the view of Stephen Mithen, according to which other singular explosions in human capacity and society, such as tool design, art, religion, and scientific knowledge, were the result of 'cognitive fluidity', then it is plausible that all these spectacular changes in human performance came about once the continuous improvement of blending capacity reached the critical level of Double-Scope blending. Mithen explicitly places the origin of language far before the development of 'cognitive fluidity'. For him, it is an input to 'cognitive fluidity'. For us, by contrast, it is the most impressive behavioral product of Double-Scope blending.

In summary, continuous improvement of blending capacity reached the critical level of Double-Scope blending, and language precipitated as a singularity. Why should Double-Scope blending have been the critical level of blending that made language possible? The central problem of expression is that we and perhaps other mammals have a vast, open-ended number of frames and provisional conceptual assemblies that we manipulate. Even if we had only one word per frame, the result would be too many words to manage. Double-Scope integration permits us to use vocabulary and grammar for one frame or domain or conceptual assembly to say things about others. It brings a level of efficiency and generality that suddenly makes the challenging mental logistics of expression tractable. The forms of language work not because we have managed to encode in them these vast and open-ended ranges of meaning, but because they make it possible to prompt for high-level integrations over conceptual arrays we already command. Neither the conceptual operations nor the conceptual arrays are encoded, carried, contained, or otherwise captured by the forms of language. The forms need not and cannot carry the full construal of the specific situation, but instead consist of prompts for thinking about situations in the appropriate way to arrive at a construal.

Our proposal would explain the apparent discontinuity of the appearance of language: no 'fossils' of early simple language have been found because there were none. The appearance of language is a singularity like rapid crystallization in a super-saturated solution when a dust speck is dropped into it. When a community graduates to Double-Scope integration at the conceptual level, any local problem of expression that is solved by a specific Double-Scope integration gives the pattern for solving the general problem of expression, making that general problem tractable, and resulting in the complex singularity of the appearance of a system that uses a limited number of combinable forms to cover an open-ended number of situations. It 'covers' these situations not by encoding construals of them (through, for example, truth-conditional compositionality) but rather by using a limited number of forms to prompt for on-line inventive integrations that are full construals.

8 The origin of cognitively modern humans

Here are some fascinating individual truths about evolution and the origin of modern human beings that have been widely, if disparately, recognized but that have never been combined into a single coherent story:

- Biological evolution happens gradually.
- Human language appears, in evolutionary terms, very suddenly in recent prehistory.
- Art, science, religion, and tool use also appear very suddenly in recent prehistory.
- Human beings differ strikingly from all other species in having these behavioral singularities, and their performances in these areas are extraordinarily advanced.
- Anatomically modern human beings arose 150,000 years ago.
- But behaviorally modern human beings date from around 50,000 years ago. That is, evidence of advanced modern behavior in tool use, art, and religious practices appears in the archaeological record around 50,000 years ago.
- There is no evidence of 'simple' languages in other species.
- There is no evidence of 'simpler' languages in other human groups.
- Children learn complex languages remarkably easily. But they go through what look like intermediate stages.

None of the previous theories puts all these truths together, and the theories that do exist conflict with each other, sometimes in extreme ways.

Some theorists propose that a dramatic biological event produced dramatically different human beings who had language. Chomsky is one of them. Mithen, by contrast, proposes a neurological 'big bang' for cognitive fluidity but *not* for language. According to Mithen, the earliest anatomically modern human beings already have language, but it takes them another hundred thousand years to get art, religion, science, and elaborate tool use, and when they do get those performances, it happens overnight. That change in behavior is triggered by an exceptional, singular change in the human brain that was highly adaptive. For Mithen, that dramatic biological change is unrelated to the origin of language but instead produces remarkable and noticeable human creative abilities. Language, already available, latches on to these new abilities. It is a beneficiary of 'cognitive fluidity' but is not in itself creative under this account. For Chomsky, by contrast, the dramatic biological event has only syntax as its direct product. He is also skeptical of accounts that adaptation played any role in the appearance of language. Both Chomsky and Mithen look at a singular result or results and explain them by postulating a singular biological cause. In this way, they deal efficiently with the absence of intermediate stages — the full results followed quickly from the causes. For Chomsky, the singular result of the dramatic biological change is language, which appears explosively on the human stage. For Mithen, art, science, and religion appear explosively on the human stage, but not language. But these theories do not come without cost. They go against the principle of gradualism in evolution. Chomsky even seems to go against natural selection. Both pull a speculative, catastrophic, indeterminate, but all-powerful biological event out of a hat. The explanations have built-in limits and cannot be pushed beyond them. Chomsky would need an extra theory for all the other human singularities, and Mithen would need an extra theory for language. These theories are driven by Cause-Effect Isomorphism. Chomsky additionally adds Function-Organ Isomorphism of the strongest possible sort. Since these isomorphisms give us compressions and hence global insights, they are seductive.

Some theories, like those of Terrence Deacon on one hand and Steven Pinker and Paul Bloom on the other, propose gradual evolutionary or co-evolutionary development of language ability. These theories avoid the trap of proposing dramatic biological causes, but they do face the problem of explaining why there are no surviving intermediate stages. Both theories propose that there were intermediate stages, but that the people who had them are gone and left no trace of those stages. Pinker and Bloom additionally face the difficulty of explaining the other human singularities — their theory, like Chomsky's, is directed exclusively at the origin of language and not at the development of certain forms of conceptual thought. Deacon is the one theorist in our list who leaves ample room for relating the origin of language to the origin of other cultural behaviors. He proposes the gradual, adaptive evolution of a relational ability that underlies a range of human performances. Those performances then co-evolved with that mental and biological capacity. From our point of view, Deacon has the right overall frame for the origin of language, but his theory is missing an explanation of the mental operations underlying this relational ability. The findings we present in this book were not available when Deacon was developing his views. More generally, the notion that human mental feats as disparate as simple framing, counterfactual thinking, and event integration could fall out of the same cognitive ability and lie on a common continuum was unavailable in the cognitive neuroscience community. We have seen that conceptual blending is a good candidate for a continually evolving mental ability that could produce the singularity of language. This opens up possibilities that Deacon could not have considered. Another consequence of our findings is that language would have precipitated much more quickly than Deacon proposes, over a span of thousands of years rather than millions. But on the other hand, the evolution of the cognitive capacity that yields language as a singularity could have begun long before there were human beings, hominids, or even primates.

Some other theories, like the *Lingua ex Machina* proposal of William Calvin and Derek Bickerton, offer a preadaptation story. In these theories, evolution labored long to produce abilities that ended up subserving syntax. These theories thereby avoid postulating a singular cataclysmic cause. On the contrary, they are gradualist stories. Calvin and Bickerton also go into the details of what those evolved capacities were — e.g., the ability to throw a projectile, the ability for reciprocal altruism — and what computational abilities they could provide to syntax. There is certainly nothing wrong with thinking that preadaptations played an important role in making the origin of language possible. In fact, the capacity we invoke, conceptual blending, far from being limited to language, extends to action, reasoning, social interaction, and so on. The emergence of conceptual blending would have been favored by preadaptations. Where we differ with Calvin and Bickerton is that they propose that evolution delivered an ability for grammar, while we propose that evolution delivered an ability for conceptual blending which, once it reached the stage of Double-Scope integrations, had grammar as a product.

None of the proposals we have seen explicitly links all the singularities — language, science, religion, the arts — as deriving from a common cause. But there are other accounts that do see that linking as a priority. For example,

Richard Klein, in *The Human Career*, offers the hypothesis that there was a dramatic mutation that produced neurological change about 50,000 years ago, and that this neurological change gave human beings some signal capacity such as language. Once that particular capacity was in place, it led to the development of advanced tool use and the invention of art and perhaps other abilities, and these neurologically advanced human beings spread throughout the world.[11]

Our proposal for the origin of language has ample room for full linkage across the singularities in human performance that arose around 50,000 years ago, but does not require any one of them to have been the cause of the others. On the contrary, there is a deeper, underlying cause, namely the continuous development of blending capacity until it arrived at the critical point of Double-Scope blending, and all these staggering new performances of human beings fall out of that capacity as products developed in parallel. On our view, these new performances reinforced each other in cultural time. The evolutionary achievement of Double-Scope blending still needs cultural time in which to bear all its fruit. The visible products of the new cognitive capacity are all social and external — art, religion, language, tool use. There is every reason to think that once the capacity was achieved and the cultural products started to emerge, they reinforced each other. Language assisted social interaction, social interaction assisted the cultural development of language and language assisted the elaboration of tool use, as the tree of culture put forward these exceptional new products. Language and art became part of religion, religion part of art, language part of the technology of tools, all intertwined. Certainly this is the picture we see when we look at human beings today.

We agree with Klein that the singularities are linked, but this does not imply that one of them caused the others. They are all products of the underlying evolution of the capacity for Double-Scope blending. There is another aspect of Klein's work, however, that is crucial to our account. He places the origin of language near in date to the origin of the other singularities. Why would a theorist like Mithen, who saw cognitive fluidity as the 'big bang of human evolution,' not have considered language as part of the constellation of singularities like art, science, and religion that resulted from that big bang? The answer is simple: he assumes that language falls out of a combination of big brains and modern vocal apparatus. Mithen writes, 'During the last few years the argument that both archaic *H. sapiens* and Neanderthals had the brain capacity, neural structure and vocal apparatus for an advanced form of vocalization, that should be called language, is compelling'.[12] This would place the origin of language in the range of 100,000 to 400,000 years ago, and perhaps even as much as 780,000 years ago. Therefore, language must have arisen, on his view, at least 50,000 years before the explosion of art, science, and religion in the human record.

Yet Mithen himself takes the view that human beings about 50,000 years ago developed striking new mental abilities that did not require a change in brain size or in anatomy. We think that is exactly right, but that language was part of the suite of products that flowed from that evolution. This unifying hypothesis receives strong support from recent archaeological and genetic studies that were not available to Mithen.

Klein provides archaeological evidence that there are two distinct types of modern human beings — anatomically modern and behaviorally modern. Anatomically modern humans have our anatomy, but not our characteristic behaviors. Behaviorally modern humans have both. The anatomically modern human beings, dating from about 200,000 years ago, at some point cohabited with more archaic human beings, like Neanderthals. The behaviorally modern human beings originated much more recently, say about 50,000 years ago, and dispersed eastward from Africa, ultimately supplanting all other human beings.

Klein's view receives even stronger support from two genetics studies, one by Silvana Santachiara-Benerecetti, the other by Russell Thomson, Jonathan Pritchard, Peidong Shen, Peter Oefner, and Marcus Feldman. Santachiara-Benerecetti's work on mitochondrial DNA leads her to the conclusion that behaviorally modern human beings arose about 50,000 years ago out of Africa and migrated eastward into Asia, not northward into Europe as had been previously found for the more ancient anatomically modern human beings.[13] The study by Russell Thomson and his colleagues looked at Y chromosomes in people around the world today and computed an expected time on the order of 50,000 years to our most recent common ancestor.[14] That dating falls within a large range of uncertainty, but in any event moves the origin of behaviorally modern human beings closer to us by many tens of thousands of years. Luigi Luca Cavalli-Sforza takes the final step and locates language as an invention of behaviorally modern human beings.[15] He places it alongside the invention of boats and rafts and Aurignacian technology, which is to say, beads and pendants and other items of personal decoration used for social and ritual purposes. While Cavalli-Sforza brings the origin of language forward to about 50,000 years ago, other researchers would push the date of the invention of craft technologies like making string and weaving back by several tens of thousand years. James M. Adavaso, an anthropologist specializing in textiles, estimates that weaving and cord-making probably date from 40,000 BC, 'at a minimum', and possibly much further. [16]

These new findings converge to suggest the rapid cultural invention of a coordinated suite of modern human performances, dating from the same epoch, perhaps about 50,000 years ago. We have argued that all of these modern human performances, which appear as singularities in human evolution, are the common consequence of the human mind's reaching a critical level of blending capacity, Double-Scope conceptual integration.

Acknowledgement

The present chapter is adapted from Chapter 9 of *The Way We Think* (Fauconnier and Turner 2002).

Notes

1 See Fauconnier & Turner 2002 and http://blending.stanford.edu for an extensive bibliography.

2 Donald 1991, p. 382.

3 Pinker & Bloom 1990.

4 Elman et al. 1996.

5 Deacon 1997, p. 142.

6 Calvin & Bickerton 2000.

7 Wilson 1999.

8 Deacon 1997.

9 Mithen 1998, p. 165.

10 See Goldberg 1994.

11 'Thus,' says Klein, 'the text argues that after an initial human dispersal from Africa by 1 million years ago, at least three geographically distinct human lineages emerged. These culminated in three separate species: *Homo sapiens* in Africa, *Homo neanderthalensis* in Europe, and *Homo erectus* in eastern Asia. *Homo sapiens* then spread from Africa, beginning perhaps 50,000 years ago to extinguish or swamp its archaic Eurasian contemporaries. The spread was prompted by the development of the uniquely modern ability to innovate and to manipulate culture in adaptation. This ability may have followed on a neural transformation or on social and technological changes among Africans who already had modern brains. Whichever alternative is favored, the fossil, archeological, and genetic data now show that African *H. sapiens* largely or wholly replaced European *H. neanderthalensis*.' (Richard Klein 1999, p. xxiv.) Klein further argues that 'only fully modern humans after 50 ky ago possessed fully modern language ability, and that the development of this ability may underlie their modernity' (p. 348). He also writes: 'But even if important

details remain to be fixed, the significance of modern human origins cannot be overstated. Before the emergence of modern people, the human form and human behavior evolved together slowly, hand in hand. Afterward, fundamental evolutionary change in body form ceased, while behavioral (cultural) evolution accelerated dramatically. The most likely explanation is that the modern human form — or more precisely the modern human brain — permitted the full development of culture in the modern sense and that culture then became the primary means by which people responded to natural selective pressures. As an adaptive mechanism, not only is culture far more malleable than the body, but cultural innovations can accumulate far more rapidly than genetic ones, and this explains how, in a remarkably short time, the human species has transformed itself from a relatively rare, even insignificant large mammal to the dominant life form on the planet' (1999, p. 494). In an earlier work, Klein similarly notes that '[t]he archeological record is geographically uneven, but where it is most complete and best-dated, it implies that a radical transformation in human behavior occurred 50,000 to 40,000 years ago, the exact time perhaps depending on the place. Arguably, barring the development of those typically human traits that produced the oldest known archeological sites between 2.5 and 2 million years ago, this transformation represents the most dramatic behavioral shift that archaeologists will ever detect' (1992, p. 5). 'Thus, while both Mousterians and Upper Paleolithic people buried their dead, Upper Paleolithic graves tend to be significantly more elaborate. These graves are the first to suggest a burial ritual or ceremony, with its obvious implications of religion or ideology in the ethnographic sense of the term' (1992, 7). 'The list of contrasts can be extended, and in each case the conclusion is not just that Upper Paleolithic people were qualitatively different, but also that they were behaviorally more advanced than Mousterians and earlier people in the same way that living people are. The evidence does not demonstrate that every known Upper Paleolithic trait was present from the very beginning. It is, in fact, only logical that many features, particularly those involving advances in technology, took time to accumulate. What the evidence does show is that, compared to their antecedents, Upper Paleolithic people were remarkably innovative and inventive; this characteristic, more than any other, is their hallmark. In the broad sweep of European prehistory, they were the first people for whom archeology clearly implies the presence of both 'Culture' and 'cultures' (or ethnicity) in the classic anthropological sense.' (1992, p. 7).

12 Mithen 1996, p. 142.

13 We quote from 'Out of Africa: Part 2', a website press release from *Nature Genetics* dated November 29, 1999: 'Fossil evidence indicates that modern humans originated in Africa and then expanded from North Africa into the Middle East about 100,000 years ago. Silvana Santachiara-Benerecetti (of the University of Pavia) and colleagues now provide evidence that supports

a second route of exit from Africa, whereby ancient peoples dispersed from eastern Africa and migrated along the coast to South Asia.

'Mitochondria are tiny intracellular bodies that generate the energy needed to drive the activities of a cell. They have their own DNA, distinct and independent from nuclear DNA. Mitochondrial DNA can be 'fingerprinted' according to small variations in sequence and, because mitochondria are only inherited from the mother, used to trace maternal ancestry. Closely related mitochondrial DNA sequences fall within the same 'haplogroup', and insinuate – but do not prove – a close genetic relationship between the people who carry them. People in Asia and Ethiopia carry the 'M' mitochondrial haplogroup, which raises the question: how has this come about? Have their mitochondrial DNAs evolved independently, but, through coincidence, converged onto the same haplotype? Or does the similarity reflect a genetic relationship?

'On scrutinizing the region of mitochondrial sequence in Africans and Indians, Santachiara-Benerecetti and coworkers ruled out the possibility that the M haplogroups in eastern-African and Asian populations arose independently — rather, they have a common African origin. These findings, together with the observation that the M haplogroup is virtually absent in Middle-Eastern populations, support the idea that there was a second route of migration out of Africa, approximately 60,000 years ago, exiting from eastern Africa along the coast towards Southeast Asia, Australia and the Pacific Islands. 'Out of Africa: Part 2.' Press release from *Nature Genetics* (web site), November 29, 1999, p. 437.

14 'We focused on estimating the expected time to the most recent common ancestor and the expected ages of certain mutations with interesting geographic distributions. Although the geographic structure of the inferred haplotype tree is reminiscent of that obtained for other loci (the root is in Africa, and most of the oldest non-African lineages are Asian), the expected time to the most recent common ancestor is remarkably short, on the order of 50,000 years. Thus, although previous studies have noted that Y chromosome variation shows extreme geographic structure, we estimate that the spread of Y chromosomes out of Africa is much more recent than previously was thought.' (Thomson et al. 2000 p. 736).

15 Cavalli-Sforza 2000.

16 As reported in Angier, 1999.

References

Angier, N. (1999) Furs for evening, but cloth was the Stone Age standby. *The New York Times on the Web*, December 14.

Calvin, W. and Bickerton, D. (2000) Lingua ex Machina: reconciling Darwin and Chomsky with the human brain. Cambridge: MIT Press.

Cavalli-Sforza, L. L. (2000) *Genes, Peoples, and Languages*. NY: Farrar, Straus, and Giroux.
Deacon, T. (1997) *The Symbolic Species: The Co-Evolution of Language and the Brain*. NY: W. W. Norton.
Donald, M. (1991) Origins of the modern mind: three stages in the evolution of culture and cognition. Cambridge: Harvard University Press.
Elman, J. L., Bates, E. A., Johnson, M. H., Karmiloff-Smith, A., Parisi, D. and Plunkett, K. (1996) *Rethinking Innateness: A Connectionist Perspective on Development*. Cambridge: MIT Press.
Fauconnier, G. and Turner, M., (2002) *The Way We Think*. New York: Basic Books.
Goldberg, A. (1994) *Constructions: A Construction Grammar Approach to Argument Structure*. Chicago: University of Chicago Press.
Klein, R. G. (1999) *The Human Career: Human Biological and Cultural Origins*. Second Edition. Chicago: The University of Chicago Press.
Klein, R. G. (1992) The archeology of modern human origins. *Evolutionary Anthropology*, 1(1): 5–14.
Mithen, S. (1998) A creative explosion? Theory of mind, language, and the disembodied mind of the Upper Paleolithic. In Mithen, S. (ed.) *Creativity in Human Evolution and Prehistory*. London and New York: Routledge, 165–191.
Pinker, S. and Bloom, P. (1990) Natural language and natural selection. *Behavioral & Brain Sciences* 13, 707–784.
Wilson, F. R. (1999) *The Hand*. New York: Vintage.

8 Comparativism: from genealogy to genetics

Bernard Laks
University of Paris X, and CNRS MODYCO[1]

'The Sanskrit language, whatever be its antiquity, is of a wonderful structure; more perfect than the Greek, more copious than the Latin, and more exquisitely refined than either, yet bearing to both of them a stronger affinity, both in the roots of verbs and in the forms of grammar, than could possibly have been produced by accident; so strong indeed, that no philologer could examine them all three, without believing them to have sprung from some common source, which, perhaps, no longer exists: there is a similar reason, though not quite so forcible, for supposing that both the Gothic and the Celtic, though blended with a very different idiom, had the same origin with the Sanskrit; and the old Persian might be added to the same family.'

William Jones, 1786, the 3rd anniversary discourse, *Royal Asiatic Society* of Calcutta[2]

1 The genealogical model

Nowadays it is difficult to imagine the revolutionary effect that Jones' proposal had in the academic world. Beyond circles of philologists and grammarians, it inaugurated a new way of thinking, both deductive and inferential, of which it could be said that it constituted the precursor of scientific thought[3] throughout the 19th and 20th centuries. In effect, it had a profound influence across all academic circles, and one can find a definite echo of it in the work of Darwin, for example. Such spontaneous genealogical thinking must have been expressed particularly forcefully in the work of Schleicher and Müller, even before having been revitalized and motivated anew in contact with the scientific theory of evolution[4]. Understood as the comparative description and analysis of languages that existed or had died out, analyzed in terms of their dynamic evolutions and family resemblances, linguistic comparativism, irrespective of the form it took, was from then on at the very heart of linguistic thinking for over a century; and the metaphor of the genealogical tree of languages (*Stammbaum*) became to be seen as so obviously correct, even well beyond linguistic circles, that none of the internal objections to it, however conclusive they may have been, were able to cast doubt upon it. The triumph of post-Saussurian linguistics (in the widest sense of the term, i.e. structural then generativist), despite its relative recency, nevertheless marks a profound rupture with comparativist modes of reasoning. Even when such linguistic research aims to compare languages in terms of modern linguistic classificatory systems, the search for universals and comparative grammatical analysis have little in common with the theoretical background of classical comparativism. Despite this fact, the genealogical model, together with the tree metaphor as its founding principle, seems to persist in linguistics as elsewhere, and to be only asking to reappear[5]. In a sense that goes beyond the status of hypotheses linked to a specific theoretical framework, the model and its attendant metaphor comprise a *doxastic* construction that seems to be ready to rise to the surface once the question of origins is reactivated.

A case in point is the work of Ruhlen[6]. Whilst being couched in the dynamic approach initiated by Greenberg[7], Ruhlen nevertheless emphasizes — often in a particularly strong manner — his theoretical and methodological rupture with what he terms specifically European 'classical comparativism'. At the same time, he nevertheless bases his work on the genealogical model and the tree metaphor in their more recent and supposedly significantly more convincing forms, when hybridized with population genetics[8].

Throughout the previous ten years a particularly prolific field of research has been explored concerning the question of the origins of languages and their diverse classifications. Linguistic genetics has been confronted with neo-comparativism and linguistic reconstruction; and archaeology has encountered the dynamics of human habitation of geographical space and population genetics. The evolutionist — and henceforth genetic — *Stammbaum* metaphor, whether vigorously defended or criticized using new arguments derived from such cross-disciplinary links, has thus found itself at the centre of numerous reflections. Such recent work is unfortunately associated with significant historical and epistemological deficiencies that greatly handicap it. Counter-arguments and alternatives that had been put forward since the end of the 19th century have unfortunately been completely ignored. More contemporary divergences and counter-proposals are neither taken into account nor debated. This article has therefore the modest aim of contributing to a more informed critical discussion in the light of the principal arguments at stake here, by bringing out some of the issues that can be discerned across previous or present day themes.

2 Classical comparativism and its critics

2.1 Comparing and reconstructing

Comparativism attained its apotheosis[9] with the historical and comparative grammar of Indo-European languages, and it is also in such a terrain that its evolutionist vulgate took root. In order to clarify the debate, it is possible to summarize this approach in the form of a few key themes and forceful ideas. Languages are thus organisms that *live*, *develop* and *die*[10]. Carried by *migrations* of peoples, they *move* and *spread out* in space. In the manner of living species, they allow themselves to be *grouped together* into branches, families and sub-families[11]. As is the case for natural species, linguistic evolution manifests an increasing degree of *complexity*[12]. The comparison of sibling languages demonstrates common *lineage* and allows the mother tongue to be reconstructed, even when the latter is no longer claimed to exist[13]. Against this common evolutionist background, it is important to be particularly attentive to the methodology employed. In effect, once the genealogical model is unraveled with the inexorable logic of common sense given that the organic metaphor on which it is based is accepted as a starting point, the comparativist method appears, on the other hand, to be more rigorous and constrained. Recall some of the criteria the most cruelly ignored by contemporary neo-comparativism. The 'healthy comparativist method' (Vendryes 1921, 329–37) necessarily bases its work on Indo-European reconstruction on more local comparative grammars (for example on Slavic, Romance or Germanic languages) that themselves depend on one-to-one comparison between each of the languages and dialects of which the family is composed. In other words, comparativism does not involve vast multilateral comparisons between a large number of languages whose degree of resemblance is presupposed *a priori*. Quite to the contrary: the comparativist method making successive *bilateral comparisons* between two grammars with respect to which there are solid *external reasons* for thinking that they are related, and proceeds step by step. At each stage, grammatical foundations and the relatedness hypothesis are thus put to the test on the basis of two grammars. Comparativist analysis implies two grammatical systems understood in their multiple dimensions (phonological, morphological, syntactical and semantic). This was what was intended to give certain credibility to the reconstruction of common Germanic or Slavic, to the Proto-Languages from which they were derived and, in the final analysis, to the Indo-European language thus reconstructed. It was therefore never etymology in itself that could alone demonstrate common ancestry[14].

The initial hypothesis of common ancestors, on the other hand, is neither fortuitous nor *purely internal*. For Indo-Europeanists, it is motivated by historical or prehistoric data, as well as by all kinds of evidence from archaeology, literature and inscriptions, that play the roles of indispensable external proofs[15]. In effect, grammatical proximity between two languages does not alone permit the conclusion of common ancestry with certainty[16]. Finally, the richness of dialectological documentation with respect to Indo-European languages is such that it is never in fact the case that two languages are compared, considered in isolation, but rather linguistic groups that display a high degree of internal differentiation across a continuum. The variants internal to each linguistic domain often appear as a series of intermediary stages that reinforce the hypothesis of common family membership.

Such hypotheses nevertheless will remain only hypotheses so long as the linguist is not able to state scientific laws — essentially phonetic ones — that, in *explaining* linguistic change, prove that the variants are derived from the same source, and that the languages in question are effectively genetically related[17]. In the final analysis, for comparativists it is the phonetic law that provides internal *proof* of the validity of the reconstruction. In this case, precise classifications exist that, whilst being perhaps mechanical, blind and unpredictable from the point of view of neogrammarians, are nonetheless coherent, and provide the central *explanatory* principle of this approach. Above and beyond the reconstruction of a common etymological source, fundamentally, the goal of the comparativist is to establish such linguistic laws[18].

The absolute necessity of disposing of external evidence and proof, and the role of dialectological knowledge, limit the comparativist's horizon to approximately five thousand years, and to the only linguistic family for which such historical, cultural and geographical data is available and abundant. The limitation of application of the comparativist model to the Indo-European family is thus not the outcome of an ideological choice. Rather, it is a consequence of the strict application of its own criteria[19].

The comparativist methodology thus appears as particularly precise, constrained and demanding from a linguistic point of view. Being relatively independent from the *Stammbaum* genealogical model, it exerts a strong influence on the development of the field of linguistics and on the construction of modern linguistics as a science[20]. Quite to the contrary, however, the genealogical model was criticized from the time that it was formulated. It was destined to be pushed completely to the fringes of research, if not quite simply abandoned, under the conjunction of attacks from the synchronic reorientation of linguistic research, the development of structuralism then generativism, and the emergence of new classificatory and comparativist work that was allowed by these modern theoretical frameworks.

2.2 Criticisms of the naturalist metaphor

The genealogical model of comparativism is thus organized in terms of the following organicist and naturalist thesis: languages are living organisms[21] that are subjected to the natural laws of evolution. What the often radical critic of genealogical comparativism contests is primarily the conception of the object of study, 'language', that is implied by these metaphors[22].

Following Whitney[23], Saussure defends forcefully the idea that language is a social institution. From this follows a set of distinctive traits whose expression establishes a rupture and a polemical debate with comparativism[24]. The first of these traits is usage: language has a function, that function is communication between the members of a given community. However, the very notions of communicative function and usage are deeply foreign to naturalism, and can not be assimilated into organicist comparativism[25]. Nevertheless, it is usage, that is to say the real life of language in a community, and not the chronological time of physics, that explains and motivates linguistic change. Given that it has not grasped this fact, comparativism works on uncovering *causalities without real causes*. In effect, for naturalists, once conceived outside usages and real communities that speak them, the evolution of languages takes place over perfectly abstract genealogical time that has nothing to do with historical time, understood in its full depth and its cultural and social complexity (Vendryes 1921, 334; Sériot 1999, 114).

However, as Saussure (2001, 122) insists, there is no other time in languages than that of history, and the history of languages is nothing other than that of their *continuous transformation*. From usage results the character of absolute *continuity* of languages, in *time*[26] as in *space*[27]. This is such that strictly speaking, there is no meaning in constructing genealogies[28], however banal they may be, such as, that which links French to Latin[29]. Contemporary French is not the daughter of Latin, it *is* contemporary Latin, as it has evolved continuously in and with that historical, cultural and geopolitical space. The naïve genealogical conception of the *Stammbaum* is thus opposed to a phylogenetic conception of continuous evolving lineages, the evolution of family trees accounting for the cladogenesis and the multiple branching out of the contemporary linguistic field[30].

Because nowhere, nor never, have languages been born or died, but have always changed[31], taxonomies and linguistic genealogies only classify *illusions*, which are misguided sub-products of a discontinuist, anhistorical and linguistically absurd conception of time. In effect, from a linguistic point of view, the most fundamental character of historical time[32] is the absence of rupture, that allows different linguistic objects to be distinguished amongst the continuity of usages. In manipulating nevertheless arbitrarily delimited objects, taxonomy and genealogy posit artificial discontinuities, homogeneities and heterogeneities (i.e. 15th and 20th century French are the same language, but 11th century French and Late Latin are two different languages). They presuppose immobility followed by discontinuity, together with sudden leaps that never exist[33]: *natura non facit saltus*. Thus succession of languages does not exist, but rather *divergent continuity* over time, such that all the languages that are concurrently spoken have the same age, that of the origin of language and of languages themselves (Saussure 2001; 121).

This is also true with respect to space. The usage and the permanency of communication ensure mutual understanding point by point over very large areas: this is the principle of spatial continuity. *A contrario*, no linguistic domain is homogeneous and between two points, however close they are, grammatical differences of all kinds indefinitely divided up linguistic space[34]. The two forces that thus act in space, local characteristics, being the sources of differences (the parochial mind of Saussure) and diffusion, being the source of similarity (the force of intercourse)[35] feed and constrain geographical variation by their dynamic opposition. Likewise with respect to social space (Labov 1994; 2001). In the most delimited and isolated linguistic community, in the most circumscribed geographical space — nevertheless, synchronic unity of speaking does not exist (Gauchat 1905)[36] ; and as Saussure (Ibid., 122) points out, nothing allows us to believe that things have ever or anywhere been otherwise, throughout all the life of human languages.

One of the most well established results of descriptive linguistics of the 19th century, geographical dialectology, offers new and overwhelming number of proofs (Gilliéron and Edmond 1902–1912). Isoglosses *do not coincide,* and each word, each linguistic mechanism patiently built on field studies, possesses its own spatial extension. It follows that the notions of limits of dialects and linguistic frontiers lose all coherence[37]. Even the concept of groups of isoglosses, which was subsequently proposed by Italian neolinguists, did not manage to preserve the solidity of spatial delineation of languages and to restore some degree of credibility to the geolinguistic *doxa* (Sériot 1999, 127–32).

The lack of absence of concurrence of isoglosses and the correlative impossibility of marking out linguistic frontiers found itself at the heart of the polemic between on the one hand Gaston Paris and Paul Meyer, and on the other hand, Graziadio Ascoli, concerning the existence of franco-provençal (Bergounioux 1994). The French, together with Saussure and the majority of young linguists of the period, contested jointly the existence of languages and dialects that were clearly separated in time and in space, together with the existence of distinct linguistic families, and thus refused to even comment on the most widely accepted filiations of genealogical linguistics[38].

This historical and geographical refusal to comment is also demographical, so much is it true that the genealogical conception of the *Stammbaum* is profoundly linked to a vulgate concerning movements of populations (invasions and migrations). Physical time of the succession of generations does not take usage into account. It is situated, as we have already mentioned, outside history, outside geographical, social or cultural space. It constitutes a somewhat paltry driving force of change and creation of linguistic 'species', that are nevertheless patently obvious. It is thus necessary to substitute for it a different explanatory principle: historical demography. In the static conception of genealogical linguistics, where languages, linguistic areas and peoples are perfectly co-defined and co-delineated, change and divergence can only come from major displacements of populations. In the continuity without history of genealogy, migrations, invasions and conquests introduce the only catastrophic principle that is available: invaders impose their language that in the end is bastardized by the invaded[39]. The criticisms of genealogical linguistics that we have recalled here extend logically to calling into question the prevalent conception of the history of languages, that is linked only to demography. Saussure thus derides a theory that he qualifies as 'infantile, from the simple fact that it is useless'. Indeed, it does not have the explanatory power that one might confer on it in as much as one recuses all the other mechanisms that generate linguistic change, heterogeneity and variation. In a continuist theory, based on usage, where historical, social and cultural dimensions interact with each other, dialectisation constitutes a central phenomenon, as an inevitable consequence of diffusion throughout space. Thus, if there had been neither migrations nor invasions, the Indo-European arena would have remained identical; the wave theory (*Wellentheorie*[40]) alone sufficed in order to account for its diversity and organization (Saussure Ibid., 240).

2.3 Alternatives

The various arguments that we have just mentioned all bring us back to the polemic between genealogical comparativism and general linguistics in gestation. This polemic was all the more virulent given that for young linguists of that period, it was clear that the *Stammbaum* theory bore within itself a conception that, although it went in the same direction as, nevertheless was an obstacle to the development of a veritable science of language. As is well known, for those young linguists, the explicit construction and the precise definition of the object of study that is known as 'language', constituted a crucial point in time for any genuinely scientific linguistic thought. In that respect, they were opposed to comparativism that contented itself with giving substance to the genealogical *doxa*. From a doxastic point of view, there is no need to inquire as to the status of the object 'language', to define it or to construct its contours. From a common sense point of view, there would be no question of doubting for a single instant that *languages exist*, that they are definable and circumscribable objects, just as much in time as in geographical and social space. A certain Darwinian vulgate came to reinforce such a non-linguistic way of thinking.

It is well known that Darwin devoted very few pages to the subject of language (cf. Bergounioux 2001). Besides what Cavalli-Sforza (1993, 276) calls the 'prophesy of Darwin'[41], they are principally devoted to establishing fifteen criteria whose aim is to justify a close parallel between languages and species (Darwin 1871, 176). This parallel, that has been unceasingly resumed and quoted ever since, confers scientific legitimacy, in the minds of those who adhere to it, on genealogical comparativism (Cavalli-Sforza 1996, 1993; Ruhlen 1997). However, nothing undoubtedly expresses better its purely metaphorical content than its total absence of re-evaluation over more than 130 years. Now, as (Labov 2001, 10–14) has insisted, even if one agrees with Darwin on the 15 criteria that he proposes[42], it is the cornerstone itself of Darwinian thinking — natural selection and adaptation as the unique driving forces of evolution — that is definitively ruined by this simplistic parallel[43]. As Labov shows additionally, the Darwinian paradox can be effectively understood such that linguistic change, seen as the driving force of the evolution of languages, possesses *none* of the characteristics of functionality and adaptation that are required by natural selection, but reveal themselves to be, to the contrary, absolutely dysfunctional, anomalous, destructive and fundamentally ill-adapted.[44] However, without the principle of natural selection and without the criterion of the best ecological adaptation, Darwinism is no more! Thus, genealogical comparativism finds itself contested by the very theoretical paradigm on which it claims to depend. All that thus remains is a set of common sense claims supported by uncontrolled metaphors. As we have seen, it was just such a critique of metaphors that led newly emerging linguistics to question itself with respect to its object of study and to propose other approaches to the interactions between languages than that of simple filiation.

We have already pointed out that the wave theory constituted a credible alternative to the *Stammbaum* model. This alternative took continuist dimensions into account, linked to usage, heterogeneity and variation over temporal, spatial and social dimensions, as well as modalities of diffusion and of standardization relating to idioms. Such a model leads to totally rethinking the concept of language, since it denies that one could ever define its perimeters. Indeed, as soon as the qualities of homogeneity, temporal and spatial stability and normative circumscription are called into question, the notion of language loses all coherence. It is then replaced at the centre of the theoretical machinery by the notions of diffusion (across all dimensions), of force of intercourse and force of homogenization. Different idioms, the synchronic characteristics and their diachronic evolutions are henceforth nothing but sub-products of these forces, only particular and ephemeral crystallizations of the equilibrium between variation and homogeneity, of heterogeneity and mutual understanding. Diffusion and intercourse, as well as their dynamic correlates in terms of power relationships, also account for the interaction and the competition between idioms, in other words, for the phenomena of borrowing, superimposition, mixture, and more generally intersection, between languages. Indeed, whilst the genealogical model only recognizes filiation and degree of kinship as relations between languages, these being necessarily static and fixed, a diffusionist model, integrating socio-historical and cultural dimensions of communicative usage, allows a large range of more or less conflictual dynamic relations to be taken into account. As Whitney had already insisted, in the matter of language, everything can be exchanged and mixed together, this being inherent in the social and cultural nature of these institutions.

Examples of massive lexical borrowings between related languages, with or without re-phonologisation, are legendary, and do not need to be evoked here (cf. for example, Vendryes 1921). It must be emphasized, however, that the situation is not different when it is a question of languages that belong to clearly differentiated phyla[45]. If mixtures between languages were limited to lexical borrowings, then the genealogical model would be already in difficulty. Now phenomena of mixing are much more common than is ordinarily supposed, and can attain every level of grammatical organization, when understood as a coherent whole. Tesnière (1939) has thus analyzed numerous examples involving mixture of phonetic, phonological, morphological, syntactic and semantic mixtures from very different origins[46]. Far from being peripheral or secondary phenomena, linguistic mixtures of all kinds and at all levels appear to be central, just as much for analysis of linguistic evolution as for the construction of an adequate typology. It is within this line of reasoning that Baudouin de Courtenay (1901) defended forcefully the ' mixed character of all languages', thus taking on board the argumentation of Schuchardt, whose work, unanimously famous in its time, yet most unfortunately ignored since, has made a remarkable reappearance at the heart of the debate on creolization.

Schuchardt (1922) generalized and conceptualized the notion of mixture. He was radically opposed to genealogical comparativism. On the basis of very impressive empirical studies in Slavic, Germanic and Roman domains, he elaborated a model of generalized hybridization. To the genealogical metaphor of *Stammbaum* and the Darwinian parallel with species that was supposed to reinforce it, he opposed the *total absence of barriers between species* in matter of languages: all mixtures are possible and many are attested. If hybridization reigns everywhere in the order of languages, this is precisely because languages are not living organisms that can be typologically classified into family trees. They are social, cultural and historical systems that, whatever their degree of proximity, can interpenetrate each other and mix together[47]. Their basic kinship being that of each belonging to humankind, allows all types of crossings and all kinds of re-combinations[48]. It is thus the force of intercourse — the ambiguity and the sexual connotations of the term are in this case most appropriate — that constitutes the driving force of such re-combinations, where communication and exchange thereby play the roles of sexual reproduction (Croft 2000).

Given that it establishes a fundamental rupture with any organic and genealogical conception, the hybridization model can also just as much give rise to (neo-)Darwinian linguistics (cf. *infra*) as to some other anti-Darwinian linguistics. As Sériot, (1999, 186 et seq.) has emphasized, it was on an anti-Darwinian basis that what Jakobson called 'the Russian science' comprehended the relationships between languages. Without taking up here the critical analysis of the ideological foundations and the geopolitical objectives of the Eurasian movement (cf. Sériot, Ibid.), it is nevertheless evident that the diachronic and geolinguistic work of Jakobson, Troubetzkoy and Savickij depends on phonological and morphological analyses that are quite solid from an empirical point of view: in the Eurasian spatial domain, languages belong to very different genealogical families. Nevertheless, all the languages situated in the centre are all characterized by strong systematic convergences, amongst the most important of which should be cited is the phenomenon of the correlation of soft consonants (*palatalisation*), whereas the peripheral languages, being in contact with Germanic domains to the west and Asiatic ones to the east, are all denuded of these characteristics and are by contrast marked by a type of polytonality that is unknown in the centre. One could certainly evoke here the notion of convergence between languages belonging to clearly distinct genetic lineages, and this would be already sufficient to shake to its foundations the family tree proposed by genealogical comparativism. But let us emphasize yet again that the Darwinian notion of convergence presupposes the existence of external pressure of natural selection whose counterpart on the linguistic terrain is difficult to imagine and has never been brought to light. In addition, the phenomena analyzed by Jakobson are too important and too general to enable an explanation in terms of marginal convergence to be satisfactory.

In the line of research opened up by Schuchardt, with his hybridization model, Jakobson, Troubetzkoy and Savickij were to elaborate a theory of linguistic affinities that also separated radically from genealogical comparativism, contested fundamentally its typology and challenged the Darwinian metaphor upon which it was based. The fundamental phenomenon to be taken into account is the *coexistence* of different dialects belonging to distinct evolutionary lineages, in the *same ecological niche*. Since there is no barrier between species, such dialects will converge, mix together, import and export abstract structures, etc.; the cultural, political or religious prestige of these dialects, as well as 'community spirit' (Jakobson 1938, 354) are explanatory factors for these relations of affinity[49]. In this framework, the evolution of languages is thus not brought about and conditioned by kinship origins. Further, it is defined in abstraction from them[50]. The theory of affinities has thus radically destructive typological consequences for comparativism. In bringing together languages according to relations of affinity between systems, whatever their genetic parenthood may be, one constructs alliances between languages (*Sprachbünde*) that are much more coherent than linguistic families (*Sprachfamilien*) that often share only a few common lexical elements[51]. A given language could thus belong to totally distinct classificatory groups[52]. This superior coherence of *Sprachbünde*, including from a diachronic point of view, results from the fact that structural affinities do nothing more than retranscribe, in the very interior of linguistic systems, the existence of real and partly shared linguistic histories. Thus, taxonomical principles can be brought forth that are freed from any specific genealogical references, and that pave the way towards another form of comparativism, i.e. a form of structuralist comparativism, with respect to which current research on linguistic universals and typologies of languages appear as its heirs.

2.4 Comparativism and nominalism

If it were necessary to summarize the principal arguments that have been leveled against genealogical comparativism from the outset, one could say that in the final analysis, it is a question of a simple verbal quarrel. ' One day there will be a very unusual and very interesting book to be written on the role of the word as a perturbatory principle of the science of words' wrote Saussure (2000, 127), who deplored in a famous letter to Meillet 'the immensity of the work that would be required to show linguists what they themselves do [...] the ineptitude of current terminology, the necessity of reforming it and of showing what kind of object is language in general' (Ibid., 14). From this point of view, the preliminary error of genealogical comparativism consists in believing that languages *exist* in themselves, that they are natural and concrete objects, and that as soon as one has named them, one has circumscribed and defined them. The definition of language thus corresponds to a *definitio rei*, and one can manipulate it without further ado. From this initial typically nominalist error[53] result all the others, by uncontrolled metaphorical filtering: languages are living entities that are perfectly defined and delimited in time and space. Homogeneous and invariant, they are transported unchanged by peoples. They end up by dying but allow themselves to be seen in their descendents. One can thus classify them and account for their interrelationships by genealogical taxonomies.

Now this is a quite commonsense idea; and yet modern linguistics was constructed from the end of the 19th century onwards precisely within a properly scientific effort to detach itself from this *doxa*. Languages are not defined and clearly delimited objects. Dialects are heterogeneous and variable, change and evolution are continuous. In the linguistic continuum of communication, no caesura allows stable entities to be extracted to which one could assign the names of languages. Borrowings, convergences, mixtures, hybridization, affinities, and so on, enter into play to befuddle the map of linguistic phenomena and relations between dialects, to such an extent that it is not false to say that the notion of language does not appear as a linguistic concept, but rather as a *fictio nominis*[54].

Thus, it is not the case that the most radical criticism of genealogical comparativism results directly from the criticism of the concept of language: if languages are not defined, circumscribed and stable objects, it is illusory to aim to classify them, and family trees only link quixotic constructions together. In addition, whilst one might all the same still attempt to save such a classification by attributing a weak or approximate meaning to it, it would be then genealogical criteria of classification that would be lacking. Indeed, once one has recognized this, mixtures and hybridizations between unrelated languages no longer allow any similarity at all to be assigned with certainty to such kinship. Genealogical comparativism thus loses its method of investigation together with its unique proof criterion.

But as is well known, it is the defining characteristic of the *doxa* to be inaccessible to scientific argumentation and to resist any form of critical analysis. One can thus understand the resignation of Saussure when he exclaimed (Ibid., 127) 'The denominations '*French*' and '*Latin*' are infinitely stronger, will always or for a long time remain a thousand times more powerful in your mind than all the examples to which I could have recourse as a linguist, in order to make such cardboard dualism crumble into ruins, that obsesses us under the names of *French* and *Latin*.'

3 Genealogical comparativism: the comeback

3.1 Explaining its marginalization

However, Saussurian pessimism had been caught out, and during half a century, the critical deconstruction of genealogical comparativism by general linguistics had come to confine it to a more than peripheral position. It was only during the 1960s, with the work of Greenberg, that the situation began to evolve ; and it was during the 1980s that genealogical comparativism — with the halo given to it once it was taken up by population genetics — came back to the centre stage with, notably, the work of Ruhlen and Cavalli-Sforza. For the initiators of this comeback, and for all the current defenders of this paradigm, it is obviously crucial to be able to explain such marginalization and such a longstanding neglect.

The argument put forward here, and above all the constancy with which it is taken up, will not leave the attentive reader astonished. There is no book or article, however restricted, that does not take up the same old tune: whilst flourishing during the 19th century, genealogical comparativism was ostracized by the *Société Linguistique de Paris* (SLP) in 1866. Thenceforth, it could only survive at the periphery of academia, and it took the return of 'hard' science on the terrain of linguistics for this unavoidable political taboo to be broken[55]. In the final analysis, it matters little that the prohibition only lasted five years, and above all that historians of linguistics had patiently shown that it was a quite different matter from that of prohibition[56]. It matters little that the argument put forward explains nothing, since in reality it would be to confer an outrageous universal power to this small Parisian academic society to think that it could have imposed anything at all over more than a century on the entire planet. The argument allows genealogical comparativism to be seen to have been in opposition to the linguistic establishment in a way that goes against any historical evidence, and situates the debate against the backdrop of the fight for the freedom of scientific thinking against the sclerosis of politically correctness institutionalized by the University. Ruhlen (1997, 75) thus exploits particularly excessively a political argument that would no longer retain our attention had it not been for the precise function that it fulfilled in the scientific debate that concerns us here. Indeed, for all zealots of neo-comparativism, denouncing the political ostracism that it has suffered obviates the necessity for inquiry as to the precise epistemological and theoretical reasons for the marginalization of this paradigm. Such amnesia with respect to the genesis of intellectual history thus has a deeply ideological function, and as is often the case also a healthily cathartic function. Calling into question the real effectiveness of the decision of the SLP thus leads, in order to explain the marginalization of comparativism, to reviving the debate that opposed it to *la linguistique générale*, but on a new basis, to replying to fundamental arguments that were leveled against it, whose logic we have attempted to recall above. Now, this is precisely what is never done by those who defend the new genealogical paradigm[57], which is no doubt why it suffers from the same drawbacks as its predecessor. Our previously mentioned criticisms thus apply in the same manner to neo-comparativism, a point upon which it is not necessary to dwell here. Yet it is still necessary to linger on what constituted its proper methodological innovation.

3.2 Neo-comparativism and its method

Besides being anchored in the field of descriptive, contrastive and typological studies bearing on the languages of the five continents, the work of Greenberg finds its origins partly in lexico-statistical methods and also in glottochronological studies to which they are linked. On the basis of the hypothesis that the basic deictic lexicon (parts of nature, parts of the body, food, everyday bestiary, etc.) comprise the most diachronically stable part of the vocabulary, (Swadesh 1952; Swadesh and Sherzer 1972) has compiled a list of 200 items and proposes on this basis to apply methods of statistical comparison to two kindred languages in order to determine their relative degree of relatedness[58]. These methods have then allowed the coherence of family groupings to be tested in the Indo-European domain, and elsewhere[59]. They have been generalized and developed by (Lees 1953) under the name of glottochronology, in order to evaluate what one might term in modern vocabulary *linguistic drift* (i.e. the time that has elapsed since separation into two languages). Indeed, by applying lexico-statistical methods to pairs of languages (in the case in point, Romance languages) whose external history is well known and whose lexica are relatively well dated, one can define a temporal value for such 'drift'. In claiming that the velocity of divergence is just about the same for all pairs of languages, one defines this temporal value as a *constant*. By inferential reasoning, one could thus estimate the time of separation for all pairs of kindred languages. lexico-statistical methods and glottochronology raise acute mathematical, semantic and lexical problems[60]. Purely for purposes of the present debate let us restrict ourselves to the fact that for numerous researchers working in these frameworks, the validity of these methods is strictly bilateral, *i.e.* limited to *pairs* of languages where we have external proof that they effectively have a *family relationship*, and to items with respect to which it can be etymologically proven that they are cognates[61], a generalized and multilateral evaluation of linguistic drift being by definition not meaningful.

It is precisely the extension of these methods to languages whose kinship is not ensured, and by consequence their application to lexical items when it is not known whether or not they are cognates, that comprise, together with generalized multilateralism, the bases for the very virulent criticisms that have been leveled against the work of Greenberg[62]. Accused of violating the very method that it stakes a claim on, indeed, it presupposes implicitly as a primitive what it claims to demonstrate explicitly. The point is not innocuous since, as Vendryes[63] had already underlined, no hypothesis concerning relatedness, including the most preposterous, is formally *refutable*. Supposing a case of relatedness with no external proof can not therefore lead to validating it. In addition, the exaggerated importance given to the lexicon, to the detriment of other linguistic levels, renders almost any demonstration possible and leads to seriously underestimating systemic and typological arguments[64]. Finally, the extension to multilateral analyses leads to singularly weakening criteria of semantic correspondence that are already difficult to deal with when cognates are at issue for which a common etymology is indubitable.

Such critiques did not lead Ruhlen (1991; 1994) to modify the 'impressionist' and 'unorthodox' (Pinker 1999, 243–44) lexico-statistical and glottochronological method of Greenberg[65]. Quite to the contrary, in his recent work, he radicalizes this method, simplifying and reducing it up to the point of a simple multilateral comparison between a few tens of lexical entries[66]. The comparison also involves an extremely fragile and fuzzy notion of phonic resemblance, for which no fixed metric of comparison, leading to the acceptance of one correspondence and the *refusal* of another has ever been proposed. The overabundance in the list of compared mono and disyllable items also raises a serious problem. Given the limits of the universal phonetic inventory, the magnitude of the combinations for items of one or two syllables is necessarily limited, and leads to calling into question the probabilistic relevance of the claimed resemblances[67].

But Ruhlen's most problematic innovation of all undoubtedly consists in having rendered the comparative and the reconstructive phases autonomous, as well as the strongly claimed[68] inversion of their respective priorities. Let us recall that in classical comparativist approaches, the strictly bilateral comparison of languages is totally linked to the reconstruction of the common source language. Since we know, by external proof, that the two languages are related, one compares their lexicons and their grammatical systems with the sole aim of hypothetically reconstructing their common ancestor. These two aspects of the analysis are linked and logically constrain each other, reconstruction acting as a verification of relatedness and inversely. Finally, the reconstruction is entirely wagered on the formulation of rules that motivate the attested changes. As we have already mentioned, this method can not, in principle, go beyond the barrier of around 5000 years.

In claiming the comparison phase to be primary and completely autonomous, and in freeing it from the necessity of postulating the forms reconstructed by plausible diachronic rules, Ruhlen removes all the constraints and barriers that weighed upon the classical method. Thenceforth, the multilateral comparison of languages is no longer, as he himself asserts (cf. Note 58) only a simple matter of common sense: recognizing the existence of a small number of words whose forms and meanings are more or less alike[69]. No metric is used to organize and to constrain such a comparison, and since one has no external hypothesis of a priori relatedness available, one treats etymological attested cognates and purely hazardous similarities in the same way[70]. In postulating a case of relatedness on the basis of a simple multilateral comparison of a few dozen items, one would thus be led to reconstruct source languages without being limited by the historical horizon of 5000 years. The reconstruction of the original language, this being a recurrent fantasy of 19th century linguistics, thenceforth finds itself reactivated.

The weakening of the comparative method is such that for Ruhlen himself it is no longer a question of comparison but rather of simple classification. The first stage of his method is thus constituted by an entirely autonomous classification of languages on the basis of similitude. This first order typology then forms the basis for the work of reconstruction. The recourse to typological vocabulary never fails to astonish. Indeed, the recent evolution of typological work seems to distance it even further from neo-comparativism: such typologies precisely depend on strictly bilateral comparisons, and far from limiting themselves to a few lexical elements, they insist on the comparison of different *linguistic sub-systems*. Moreover, contrary to what Ruhlen might imply, all typologies and all taxonomies are not necessarily genealogical. Quite to the contrary, numerous modern typological approaches aim to uncover universal patterns that allow the classification of languages in a universalist framework freed from any genealogical commitment.

In rendering the comparative stage autonomous and in reducing it to a simple family classification, one also modifies the status of reconstructions. For classical comparativism, establishing commonalities and reconstruction were, as we have already mentioned, strongly intertwined and completely dependent on a proof system constituted by rules of phonetic change. The set of source/form relations thus derived was thus *calculable* and *refutable*. In such an approach, comparativists were less concerned with reconstructing languages than with calculating, by a doubly oriented derivational system, abstract explicative hypotheses for claimed states of affairs. Generative and transformational grammars have besides drawn from such work part of their formal inspiration[71]. It remains to be said therefore that it is only by an abusive nominalist interpretation that one could term such a body of formal hypotheses and abstract correspondences a 'reconstructed language'[72]. In the positivist logic of neo-comparativism, quite the other way around. The classification in a given group of languages by simple lexical comparison justifies relatedness, which in turn justifies the reconstruction of what are then presented as veritable languages, or fragments of archaic languages, that can in turn be compared with each other. It is no longer necessary to construct a proof system[73] and, once the constraints imposed on the comparativist method are removed, neo-comparativism can reactivate with incomparable power the metaphor of the genealogical tree. Paradoxically, such methodological weakening has negative consequences for neo-comparativism itself, which, lacking an apparatus for proof or an internal metric, can no longer decide between mutually contradictory classificatory hypotheses, such as those that oppose the hypothesis of a Eurasian family (Greenberg 2002) to that of a Nostratic family (Kaiser & Chevrochkine 1988)[74].

3.3 Languages and peoples: the genetic argument

It is to Theodosius Dobzhansky that has been attributed the elaboration of the Synthetic Theory of Evolution (STE) that combines Darwinian evolutionism and natural selection with Mendelian biology and genetics[75]. In this systematic taxonomy, population genetics takes the place of an essentialist conception of species and types. The notion of genetic fluctuation, with its implied exchange, recombination, ecological pressure and modification, gives rise to the construction of complex genetic trees. Different molecular clocks (biological and genetic) allow the dynamics of evolution to be modeled within such taxonomies, to date bifurcations and to calculate the emergence of new species. In sum, such a population genetics puts the notion of *genetic drift* at the heart of its theoretical and methodological approach, which can thus be calculated and modeled[76]. It is then extremely tempting to establish a parallel between such genetic drift and the linguistic drift that we mentioned previously.

This is what has been done over the last twenty years by numerous researchers in population genetics, who have thus provided new arguments for linguistic comparativism, notably in giving the latter a genetic coloring. The combination of techniques for analyzing genetic drift of populations with those for the classification of families of languages and the reconstruction of archaic languages, taken up in and archaeological framework, has given rise to a new field of scientific investigation that (Renfrew 2001) has termed 'archeogenetics'. It is in this methodological and theoretical framework that he has, for example, formulated a new thesis of the joint origin of agriculture and Indo-European in Anatolia, and of their rapid diffusion from this initial common home, in the European space[77].

Contrary to what Ruhlen's (1994) presentation might lead one to believe, such a 'New Synthesis' does not demonstrate the validity of neo-comparativism. It concerns purely external arguments, which are most often compatible with several linguistic genealogies and classifications, and that do not lead to refutation of the internal methodological criticisms that we have expressed throughout this chapter. By way of conclusion, we shall only mention a few examples of them. The correspondence between the classificatory units 'species' and 'language' (Cavalli-Sforza 1993; 1994), which is the principle upon which the comparison of genetic and linguistic drift depends, needs to be treated with caution, for reasons relating to internal heterogeneity, variation and mixing throughout time and space, as we have mentioned previously. More specifically, whilst the driving force of genetic dynamics is that of sexual reproduction, presupposing the co-presence of individuals, there is an additional force of intercourse in the case of linguistic evolution, this being a principle of diffusion across distance, that demands reflection within quite different historical, cultural and social frameworks. In addition, biological and molecular clocks, on one hand, and glottochronological clocks, on the other, have quite different granularities and degrees of systematicity: the nucleotides of DNA are primary and strongly systemic units with respect to their possibilities of combining with each other, whereas words are not. Even if one maintains such a parallel, with Cavalli-Sforza, one is obliged to recognize, as he does himself (Cavalli-Sforza et al. 1992, 5623), that the correlation between genetic distance and linguistic distance is 'extremely weak if not null'. These distances measure the degree of similarity between units belonging to the same families or sub-families. In other words, whilst recognizing that genetic trees and linguistic trees allow one to perceive some classificatory similarities, that are besides difficult to measure statistically (Cavalli-Sforza ibid., 5620)[78], parallelism between their *internal structures* can not be achieved because their branching out principles do not correspond.

The correspondences between genetic trees and linguistic trees are therefore rather crude, notwithstanding several methodological biases. It was because population genetics was searching for principles of tree-like classification in order to account for numerous genetic data that had been collected that it seized upon existing linguistic family trees, whilst at the same time recognizing their fragility and controversial nature[79]. Given that linguistic trees have thus, to some extent, served as the bases for formatting genetic trees, the risk of a circular argument based on their convergences is thus not null[80]. One should also add that for population geneticists themselves, the reconstruction of genetic trees does not represent a unique and universally accepted solution. From a point of view that is strictly internal to this discipline, debate and alternative solutions exist, which renders correspondence with linguistic trees even more problematic[81]. Finally, it should be noted that models of genetic drift, implying sexual reproduction, depend on strictly demographic expansion of the populations concerned[82]. Now, we have pointed out above, following notably in the footsteps of Saussure, that linguistic evolution and change do not necessarily rely on invasions and transfers of populations. Since the impetus of intercourse reproduces the same results, when considered in isolation it can neither invalidate nor confirm this hypothesis.

4 Opening

At the end of this chapter, it remains to be underlined that the relationship between human inhabitation and languages, however complex and problematic it may be, must be studied with precision. It is also the case that the Darwinian paradigm, notably in its so-called neo-Darwinian version, constitutes one of the major explanatory paradigms of our times. We shall reserve a detailed presentation of these approaches for another occasion. But for the present, we simply highlight the fact that some recent research attempts precisely to take up anew the questions that we have raised here, but in a new light, freed notably from the *Stammbaum* metaphor, with the numerous pitfalls with which it is associated.

We have already mentioned the work of Croft (2000) which elaborates a new analytical framework for the analysis of linguistic change, beginning from Dobzhansky's STE. The social, cultural, variationist and dynamic nature of linguistic phenomena play central roles in such an approach, where hybridisation and mixture are the main driving forces. Thus, the work of Croft proposes a neo-darwinian synthesis of the evolution of languages, which integrates many of the topical critiques mentioned above.

In a more directly comparativist perspective, one could also cite the work of (Nakleh et al. 2005; Ringe and Warnow 2002; Warnow 1997), that whilst integrating the original constraints of the comparativist method (bilateralism, external proof, etc.), proposes extremely sophisticated formal multivariate algorithms for formal comparativist analysis, which allow a large number of factors and different linguistic levels (phonological, morphological, syntactic, lexical) to be taken into account. The outcome of such an approach is an extremely precise and detailed comparison, calling into question one of the most widely accepted typological hypotheses[83]. In particular, Warnow builds on the work of (Nichols 1992), who applies a very detailed comparativist methodology.

In distinguishing several types of linguistic expansion and contact, with very different rhythms and dynamics, such an approach leads to profound rethinking of the internal relationships between languages belonging to a given family. In particular, his methodology enables languages to be taken into account with respect to which it is not known whether they are related or not, and to take decisions concerning their relatedness.

As has been seen from this too brief mention of recent research, the *Stammbaum* metaphor, together with the crude Darwinian vulgate on which it is based, are far from forming required frameworks for all reflection on the history and the evolution of languages. Quite to the contrary, it is via the deconstruction of tools that have for too long cluttered up the historical or typological terrain that the present renewal of such research has found its way forward. The current development of research on the origin and the evolution of languages bears witness to this fact.

Notes

1 I would like to thank the following colleagues with whom I have been able to discuss preliminary versions of this article, especially: Christian Abry, Gabriel Bergounioux, Annie Delaveau, Jean-Paul Demoule, Pierre Encrevé, John Goldsmith, Françoise Kerleroux, Christiane Marchello-Nizia, François Muller, Jean-Emmanuel Tyvaert and Bernard Victorri. Translated from French by Michael Baker.

2 Quoted from Lehmann (1967).

3 As Sériot points out, relevantly, all things taken into consideration, Jones in fact has discovered nothing: he only takes fragmentary, disparate and more or less well known data into account, yet in a radically new way.

4 Cf. Bergounioux (2001).

5 'Même chez ceux qui ne prennent plus au sérieux la généalogie simpliste des langues, l'image du S*tammbaum*, de l'arbre généalogique, selon la juste remarque de Schuchardt, reste malgré tout en vigueur; le problème du patrimoine commun dû à une souche unique persiste à être la préoccupation essentielle de l'étude comparative des langues.' Jakobson (1938, 351).

6 Ruhlen (1991; 1994; 1997).

7 Greenberg (1966; 1971; 1987); Greenberg and Ruhlen (1992).

8 Cavalli-Sforza (1996; 1997); Cavalli-Sforza and Cavalli-Sforza (1993); Cavalli-Sforza et al. (1992); Cavalli-Sforza et al. (1994) and Dupanloup et al. (2001).

9 Brugmann and Delbrück (1896), Schleicher (1861), Meillet (1903).

10 For example Hovelacque, quoted by Saussure (2001, 120). cf. *infra* note 22.

11 'Nous en inférons donc que tous les dialectes en question sont les représentants multipliés d'une même langue appartenant, à une certaine époque et dans un certain pays, à une certaine société, dont la dispersion a produit avec le temps, toutes ces discordances; et à cette grande collection de dialectes qui se ressemblent plus ou moins, nous donnons, par figure permise, le nom de famille, terme emprunté au vocabulaire de la généalogie' Whitney (1875, 143).

12 As Sériot (1999, 200) points out, in the work of Schleicher the succession of isolated stages, agglutinants, flexionnels marks an evolution in the complexity of languages that parallels the transition from the mineral to the plant and then the animal kingdoms.

13 'la présence de mots véritablement correspondants, si éloignés que puissent être leurs rapports, dans différentes langues, prouve que ces mots ont une racine commune, puisque la parenté des mots comme chez les hommes indique qu'ils ont eu un ancêtre commun. Et ce qui est vrai des mots d'une langue est vrai des langues elles-mêmes: les langues dans lesquelles il se trouve en majorité des mots de même origine sont filles d'une même mère.' Whitney (1875, 130).

14 'L'étymologie des mots isolés n'a pas d'intérêt en elle-même: un fait particulier, même s'il est scientifiquement établi, n'est qu'une amusette si l'on ne dégage pas un principe général qui puisse s'appliquer à d'autres faits.' Vendryes (1921, 218).

15 'Il y a peut-être sur la surface du globe des langues indo-européennes insoupçonnées, lesquelles, dépourvues d'histoire et réduites à des populations illettrées, auraient perdu tout caractère capable de dénoncer leur origine. En appliquant la saine méthode, *nous n'aurions aucun moyen* de prouver qu'elles sont parentes du grec, du latin ou du sanskrit.' Vendryes (Ibid., 337, our italics).

16 'En l'absence de toute donnée précise sur les conditions du développement historique, les conclusions qu'on peut tirer de la méthode comparative en ce qui concerne la détermination de la parenté linguistique se trouvent beaucoup atténuées. On en est réduit alors à déterminer la parenté par les ressemblances que les langues présentent entre elles. C'est une méthode dangereuse. Il y a parfois dans la nature des parents qui se ressemblent au point d'être pris l'un pour l'autre. Mais tous les sosies ne sont pas des parents. En linguistique aussi les ressemblances sont souvent trompeuses.' Vendryes (Ibid., 334).

17 'La philologie pourrait ainsi s'efforcer de restituer la préhistoire oubliée des langues. Elle tire cette confiance en ses possibilités de la découverte de la régularité des altérations sonores et des lois phonétiques qui sont à l'œuvre dans le cours de l'histoire des langues, lois dans lesquelles les néogrammairiens ont vu un équivalent de celle de la nature.' Pande (1965, 199).

18 'Le linguiste ne fait de l'étymologie que pour réunir le grand nombre possible de procès sémantiques semblables et pour dégager de cette étude les lois générales suivant lesquelles le sens des mots évolue.' Vendryes (1921, 218).

19 'Dans l'état actuel de la science linguistique, la comparaison des éléments radicaux entre diverses langues est entourée de trop d'incertitude et de dangers pour avoir la moindre valeur. Tout ce qui a été fait en ce sens jusqu'à ce jour est non avenu [...]qu'on ne prenne pas des inventions plausibles pour des faits établis. Celui qui sait combien est immense la difficulté d'arriver aux racines, même dans des langues aussi connues que celles de la famille indo-européenne, et cela malgré la conservation exceptionnelle de ses plus anciens dialectes, celui-là n'est point exposé à fonder son espoir sur la comparaison des racines.' Whitney (1885, 221).

20 Concerning phonology (cf. Laks 2001).

21 As Victorri points out (personal communication), the uncontrolled use of organicist metaphors confutes the debate to an even greater extent given that it maintains a systematic confusion between ' species' and ' organism'. Darwinism and the theory of evolution do not deal with (concrete) organisms but rather with abstract constructed classes that are termed species. This confusion has multiple consequences that we shall analyse elsewhere.

22 'On ne saurait considérer un mot comme un être vivant. L'analogie entre les deux n'est qu'apparente. Les mots ne naissent ni ne meurent à la façon des hommes.' Vendryes (1921, 216).

23 'Nous considérons donc chaque langue comme une institution, et une de celles qui, dans chaque société, constituent la civilisation. '[...] Les caractères physiques de la race ne peuvent se transmettre qu'avec le sang; mais les acquisitions de la race – langue, religion, science – peuvent être empruntés et prêtées.' Whitney (1875, 231).

24 'Non, la langue n'est pas un organisme, elle n'est pas une végétation qui existe indépendamment de l'homme, elle n'a pas une vie à elle entraînant une naissance et une mort. Tout est faux dans la phrase [de Hovelacque] que j'ai lue: la langue n'est pas un être organisé, elle ne meurt pas d'elle même, elle ne dépérit pas d'elle même, elle ne croît pas, en ce sens qu'elle n'a pas plus une enfance qu'un âge mûr ou une vieillesse et enfin elle ne naît pas. [...] Jamais on a signalé sur le globe la naissance d'une langue nouvelle. Saussure (2001, 120).

25 'Quand on lit Bopp et son école, on en arriverait à croire que les Grecs avaient apporté avec eux, depuis un temps infini, un bagage de racines, thèmes et suffixes, et *qu'au lieu de se servir des mots pour parler, ils s'occupaient de les confectionner.*' Saussure in Godel (1969, 29, our italics).

26 [A propos du français et du latin] 'Nous nous figurons alors assez volontiers qu'il y a deux choses, dont l'une a pris la succession de l'autre. Or qu'il y

ait *succession*, c'est là ce qui est indubitable et évident, mais qu'il y ait *deux choses dans cette succession, c'est ce qui est faux*, radicalement faux, et dangereusement faux, du point de vue de toutes les conceptions qui s'ensuivent. Il suffit d'y réfléchir un instant, puisque tout est contenu dans cette simple observation: chaque individu emploie le lendemain le même idiome que la veille et cela s'est toujours vu. Il n'y a donc aucun jour où on ait pu dresser l'acte de décès de la langue latine et il n'y a eu également aucun jour où on ait pu enregistrer la naissance de la langue française. Il n'est jamais arrivé que les gens de France se soient réveillé, en se disant *bonjour* en français, après s'être endormis la veille en se disant *bonne nuit* en latin.' Saussure (2001, 119, our italics).

27 'La conséquence de cette observation c'est qu'il n'existe pas; régulièrement, de frontière entre ce qu'on appelle deux langues par opposition à deux dialectes, quand ces langues sont de même origine et parlées par des populations sédentaires. Par exemple il n'existe pas de frontière entre l'italien et le français [...] De même qu'il n'y a pas de dialectes délimités, *il n'y a pas de langue délimitées dans les conditions normales.*' Saussure (Ibid., 131, our italics).

28 'Il n'y a pas de langue filles ni de langues mères, il n'y en a nulle part, il n'y en a jamais eu. Il y a dans chaque région du globe un état de langue qui se transforme lentement, de semaine en semaine, de mois en mois, d'année en année et de siècle en siècle [...] mais il n'y a jamais eu nulle part parturition ou procréation d'un idiome nouveau par un idiome antérieur.' Saussure (Ibid., 119).

29 'Gaston Paris a déclaré une guerre impitoyable à 'le français vient du latin' ou 'chanter vient du latin *cantare*' 'Le français ne *vient* pas du latin, mais il *est* le latin, le latin qui se trouve être parlé à telle date déterminée et dans telles et telles limites géographiques déterminées. *Chanter* ne vient pas du latin *cantare* mais il *est* le latin *cantare.*' Saussure (Ibid., 119).

30 The intuition of the criticisms of genealogical comparativism thus encounters some of the most modern conclusions of paleontology and neodarwinism. Cf. for example Thaler (1985, 604): 'We now know of numerous examples of such continuous evolutions that allow links to be established, via successive populations, between a very different ancestor species and a descendent species. This means of expression is besides not entirely satisfactory: from an ancestor to its descendent, however different they may be, is it not in a certain sense the same species that one is following? It should thus be quite clear that the natural object that is being considered here is the specific lineage. *It is only for linguistic convenience that one arbitrarily gives a specific name to different successive segments of such a lineage*' (our italics).

31 'Il y a *transformation*, et toujours et encore transformation, mais il n'y a nulle part reproduction ou production d'un être linguistique nouveau, ayant une existence distincte de ce qui l'a précédé et de ce qui suivra. Pas de langues

mères, pas de langues filles, mais une langue une fois donnée qui roulera et se déroulera indéfiniment dans le temps, sans aucun terme préfixé à son existence, sans qu'il y ait même de possibilité intérieure pour qu'elle finisse, s'il n'y a pas accident, et violence, s'il n'y a pas force majeure, supérieure et extérieure qui vienne l'abolir.' Saussure (Ibid., 122).

32 'Le *premier aspect* en effet sous lequel doit être envisagée l'idée *d'Histoire* quand il s'agit de la langue ou la première chose qui fait que la langue a une histoire, c'est le fait fondamental de sa *continuité dans le temps* [...] Il vaut la peine de nous arrêter un instant devant ce principe élémentaire et essentiel de la continuité ou de *l'ininterruption* forcée qui est le premier caractère ou la première loi de transmission du parler humain et cela quelles que soient autour de la langue, les révolutions et les secousses de tout genre qui peuvent changer toutes les conditions. Qu'un peuple vive paisible au fond d'une vallée retirée, qu'il soit un peuple agriculteur, guerrier, nomade, qu'il change subitement de civilisation, qu'il change de patrie et de climat, qu'il change même de *langue*, – car alors il ne fera que continuer en l'adoptant celle d'un autre peuple – jamais et nulle part on ne connaît historiquement de rupture dans la trame continue du langage, et on ne peut logiquement et a priori concevoir qu'il puisse jamais et nulle part s'en produire.' Saussure (Ibid., 118).

33 De même [le linguiste] s'il commence par supprimer l'idée de *continuité*, en imaginant qu'un jour le français sortit comme Minerve du cerveau de Jupiter armé de toutes pièces des flancs de la langue latine, il tombe régulièrement dans le sophisme de *l'immobilité*; il suppose naturellement qu'entre deux de ces sauts imaginaires, la langue est dans un état *d'équilibre* et de repos, ou au moins d'équilibre opposable à ces sauts, tandis qu'il n'y a jamais en réalité un équilibre, un point permanent, stable dans aucun langage. Nous posons donc le principe de la transformation incessante des langues comme absolu.' Saussure (Ibid., 122).

34 Gaston Paris has defended this idea very forcefully. Cf. for example Paris (1888, 13) and *infra*.

35 'Il est connu que le langage n'est pas le même chez deux sujets parlants entre eux la même langue [...] deux forces agissent sans cesse simultanément, et en sens contraire: c'est d'une part l'esprit particulariste ou en d'autres termes, 'l'esprit de clocher' – et de l'autre l'esprit de communauté ou la force unifiante dont l'intercourse [...] n'est qu'une manifestation typique.' Jakobson (1938, 355).

36 For a more recent analysis of the heterogeneity that is intrinsic to a group of speakers cf. Laks (1983).

37 'Une des conquêtes les plus appréciables, et les plus récentes de la linguistique, due principalement à M. Paul Meyer de l'Ecole des Chartes, c'est que les dialectes ne sont pas en réalité des unités définies, qu'il *n'existe pas*

géographiquement de dialectes; mais qu'il existe en revanche géographiquement des *caractères* dialectaux. [...] On arrivera donc enfin à comprendre que l'aire géographique des *phénomènes* peut parfaitement elle, être tracée sur la carte, mais qu'entreprendre de distinguer des unités dialectales est absolument chimérique et vain.' Saussure (2001, 130).

38 'Il n'y a que des traits linguistiques qui entrent respectivement dans des combinaison diverses, de telle sorte que le parler d'un endroit contiendra un certain nombre de traits qui lui seront communs, par exemple avec le parler de chacun des quatre endroits les plus voisins, et un certain nombre de traits qui différeront du parler de chacun d'eux. Chaque trait linguistique occupe d'ailleurs une certaine étendue de terrain dont on peut reconnaître les limites, mais ces limites ne coïncident que très rarement avec celles d'un autre trait ou de plusieurs autres traits; elle ne coïncident pas surtout, comme on se l'imagine souvent encore, avec les limites politiques anciennes ou modernes (il en est parfois autrement, au moins dans une certaine mesure, pour les limites naturelles, telles que montagnes, grands fleuves, espaces inhabités).[...] Cette observation bien simple, que chacun peut vérifier est d'une importance capitale; elle a permis à mon savant confrère et ami, M. Paul Meyer, de formuler une loi qui toute négative qu'elle soit en apparence, est singulièrement féconde et doit renouveler toutes les méthodes dialectologiques: cette loi, c'est que, dans une masse linguistique de même origine que la notre, il n'y a réellement pas de dialectes; il n'y a que des traits linguistiques qui entrent respectivement dans des combinaisons diverses.' Paris (130).

39 'L'histoire de la linguistique indo-européenne montre que les linguistes eux-mêmes n'ont cessé, chose curieuse, de vouloir qu'une différence de langue correspondît à une séparation géographique matérielle. Pendant toute la première période où exista une sciences des langues indo-européennes il était entendu que chaque peuple, Celtes, Germains, Grecs, etc. avec sa langue représentait une *migration*, comme qui dirait un essaim d'abeilles, ayant transporté au loin la langue reçue partant des plateaux du Pamir. Un beau jour, les *Celtes*, un autre jour les *Slaves* etc. étaient partis du pied gauche de ces hauteurs asiatiques complètement indépendamment les uns des autres et comme si c'était chose essentielle qu'ils fussent détachés géographiquement de la masse. Cet exemple prouve une seule chose, c'est que notre esprit aime les représentations qui peuvent se traduire visuellement: voici deux langues différentes d'une précédente, eh bien nous allons colloquer la première ici, puis faire partir des ballons qui transportent l'indo-européen ailleurs, et expliquent soi-disant qu'il ne soit plus identique à lui même, par le fait de la séparation géographique.' Saussure (Ibid., 240).

40 'Pour [Schmidt], les langues indo-européennes ne doivent pas être représentées comme des branches qui se séparent d'un tronc, mais comme une chaîne faite d'anneaux et n'ayant ni début ni fin, ni centre ni périphérie. Contrairement à ce que la théorie de l'arbre généalogique permettait de prévoir, des innovations

apparues dans une langue séparée, distincte peuvent s'étendre, *se diffuser* à d'autres langues voisines spatialement, comme des ondes qui se propagent à la surface de l'eau. Chaque onde en gagnant de proche en proche par un mouvement insensible, ne comporte *aucune limite.*' Sériot (Ibid, 126).

41 Curiously, this prophesy, often cited in support of linguistic comparativism, in fact works in the opposite direction since for Darwin (1859, 480), only the complete knowledge of the genealogy of humanity could make a rigorous and complete classification of languages possible.

42 Each criterion would merit deeper critical examination. The 10th, for example, that stipulates that once extinct, languages like species are not challenged, seems to strike a note of commonsense. But once one remembers that languages are social and cultural objects, one understands that everything is a matter of social and political investment. The example of Modern Hebrew, a dead language fifty years ago, provides striking proof of this.

43 The arguments invoked by Darwin in support of his parallel often leave more than one linguist in a state of perplexity: 'The survival or the preservation of certain words, favoured in the struggle for existence, is a fact of natural selection'. Darwin (1871, 173).

44 'The general consensus of 20th Century linguists gives no support to this contention, and finds no evidence for natural selection or progress in linguistic evolution. [...] Thus we cannot support Darwin's hope to complete the fifteen parallels between biological and linguistic evolution by including a sixteenth parallel: natural selection. We might sum up the situation as Darwin's paradox: [...] The evolution of species and the evolution of language are identical in form, although their fundamental causes are completely different' Labov (2001, 14).

45 'On sait que le vocabulaire arabe de l'Islam s'est allié à une grammaire indo-européenne dans le persan et à une grammaire turco-tatare dans le turc [...] Hugo Schuchardt donne d'innombrables faits de ce type.' Tesnière (1939, 207).

46 L'arménien présente un système morphologique dont l'indo-européanisme est indéniable. Mais il a une phonétique qui ressemble étrangement à celle des langues caucasiennes voisines [...] Le germanique allie à une morphologie nettement indo-européenne un système phonétique d'origine différente, et qu'il est logique d'attribuer au type articulatoire d'une population dont la langue n'était pas l'indo-européen.' Tesnière (Ibid., 207).

47 'Hugo Schuchardt [...] est porté à nier, non seulement un rapport de causalité nécessaire entre les hybridations linguistiques et biologiques, mais même la possibilité d'un tel rapport: 'Wo Blutmischung im Verein mit Sprachmischung auftritt, beruht diese nicht auf jener, sondern beide auf einem dritten. Die Ursache der Sprachmischung ist immer sozialer, nicht physiologischer Art.' Jakobson 1938, 361).

48 'Mischung durchsetzt überhaupt alle Sprachentwickelung, sie tritt ein zwischen Einzelsprachen, zwischen nahen Mundarten, zwischen verwandten und selbst zwischen unverwandten Sprachen.' Schuchardt (1922, 171).

49 'Ainsi l'étude de la répartition géographique des faits phonologiques fait ressortir que plusieurs de ces faits dépassent d'ordinaire les limites d'une langue et tendent à réunir plusieurs langues contiguës, indépendamment de leurs rapports génétiques ou de l'absence de ces rapports.' Jakobson (1938, 363).

50 ' Cela revient à dire que la similitude de structure est indépendante du rapport génétique des langues en question et peut indifféremment relier des langues de même origine ou d'ascendance différente. La similitude de structure ne s'oppose donc pas mais se superpose à la 'parenté originaire' des langues. Cela rend nécessaire la notion *d'affinité linguistique* (Ayala and Fitch) l'affinité n'exclut pas la parenté d'origine, mais en fait seulement abstraction.' Jakobson (1938, 353).

51 'Nous appelons *groupe langues* tout ensemble (*Gesamheit)* de langues qui sont liées par un nombre important de correspondances systématiques. Parmi les groupes de langues, deux types sont à distinguer: Nous appelons *union de langues (Sprachbund)* les groupes de langues qui manifestent une grande similitude dans les relations syntaxiques, une ressemblance dans les principes de construction morphologique et qui possèdent une grande quantité de termes de culture communs, parfois aussi une ressemblance apparente dans le système phonique, tout en ne manifestant pas de correspondances phoniques systématiques, aucune correspondance dans l'enveloppe phonologique de leurs éléments morphologiques et qui ne possèdent pas de mots élémentaires communs. Nous appelons *familles de langues* des groupes de langues qui possèdent un nombre considérable de mots élémentaires communs, qui présentent des concordances (*Übereinstimmungen*) dans l'expression phonique des catégories morphologiques et, surtout des correspondances phoniques *(Lautentsprechungen)* constantes. [...] Ces dénominations, ou ces concepts, sont à distinguer soigneusement. Lorsqu'il établit l'appartenance d'une langue à un certain groupe de langues, le linguiste doit scrupuleusement indiquer s'il considère ce groupe de langues comme une famille ou une union. C'est ainsi qu'on évitera bien des déclarations hâtives et inconsidérées' (Troubezkoy 1928), 18) cité par Sériot (1999).

52 Thus, for example, Bulgarian belongs on one hand to the Slavic family of languages (with Serbo-Croatian, Polish, Russian, etc.) and on the other hand, to the union of Balkanic languages (with modern Greek, Albanian and Rumanian).Troubezkoy (Ibid., 18).

53 'On dira que nier dans ce sens qu'aucune langue soit née c'est jouer sur les mots, et qu'il suffit de définir ce qu'on entend par naissance pour ne pouvoir nier la naissance ou le développement progressif d'une langue comme l'allemand, le français. Je réponds que dans ce cas on joue sur un autre mot qui

est le mot *langue*; en réalité la langue n'est pas un être défini et délimité dans le temps; on distingue la langue française et la langue latine, l'allemand moderne et le germain d'Arminius [...] et alors on admet que l'un commence et que l'autre finit quelque part, ce qui est arbitraire. [...]Je rappellerais surtout, [...] qu'il n'arrive jamais qu'une *langue succède à une autre*; par exemple que le *français* succède au *latin*; mais que cette succession imaginaire de deux choses vient uniquement de ce qu'il nous plait de donner deux noms successifs au même idiome, et par conséquent d'en faire arbitrairement deux choses séparées dans le temps.' Saussure (2000, 120–126).

54 More recently, this position has often been defended very vigorously by Chomsky (cf. for example Chomsky 1995).

55 The list of authors that take up this argument is so long that it is out of the question, due to restrictions of space, to repeat it here. By way of example, one could consult Pande (1965), Cavalli-Sforza (1996; 1997); Cavalli-Sforza and Cavalli-Sforza (1993, 251); Cavalli-Sforza et al. (1992, 5620); Cavalli-Sforza et al. (1994); Ruhlen (1997); Aitchison (1998); Pinker (1999); Dessalles (2000); Kaplan (2001). One can also find more than 700 websites that take up the argument, and one can even find the '*banishment article*' there: ftp://www.cogsci.soton.ac.uk/pub/psycoloquy/1999.volume.10/Pictures

56 Cf. Bergounioux (1996). Opposing genealogical comparativism to the 19th century university establishment could only at best raise a smile from an historian of linguistics.

57 The criticism of 'politically correctness' thus takes the place of an epistemological debate. Beyond the stylistic effects specific to the author, it is within such a 'logic of circumvention' that the populist excesses of Ruhlen (1997) can best be understood. In the name of a fight against the linguistic establishment, one thus learns that no comparativist PhD thesis in linguistics would be accepted today by a jury (p. 10, 27, 75), that the recognition of relatedness is simply a matter of commonsense, that the reader knows more than any 'small-minded academic' (p. 10, 27, 54, 82, 87, 110), that Meillet was ignorant with respect to taxonomy (p. 91) even if one concedes to him some ancillary knowledge (p. 278), that the arguments against comparativism are 'double-talk', 'hoaxes' or 'far-fetched requirements' (p. 75, 151), and finally, that classical comparativists limited their method to the Indo-European family for defeatist, ideological or even racist reasons (p. 26, 82, 141). (References and pages from the French translation.)

58 Cf. also Gudschinsky (1956).

59 For example Dyen (1975; 1976); Dyen et al. (1992).

60 Chretien (1962); Dobson et al. (1972).

61 One of the thorniest questions concerns the possible polysemantism of cognates: do the different meanings of an item have the same drift, and in the two languages being considered. Cf. Sankoff (1970; 1973).

62 Cf. Campbell (1988; 1997); Campbell and Mithum (1979). Poser (LINGUIST List 3.327, 1992) writes for example that: 'Studies of the sorts that Alexis Manaster-Ramer mentions are to be welcomed, and add to similar studies that have previously been made. An early one is Callaghan & Miller (1962), which argues that by Swadesh's criteria English is Macro-Mixtecan. Campbell (1973) argues that using criteria proposed by Bender, Finnish, Cakchiquel (a Mayan language), and Quechua are related. Campbell (1988) argues that by Greenberg's criteria Finnish is Amerind. Campbell (1988) has also argued, as Alexis does, that Greenberg did not really follow his own method. However, I am reluctant to accept Alexis' tentative conclusion that it is only Greenberg's application of the method rather than the method itself that is at fault.'

63 'Mais la méthode nous impose en revanche cette conclusion, qu'il est également impossible de prouver jamais que deux langues ne sont pas parentes.' Vendryes (1921, 337).

64 The relatedness of lexica is in fact based on the quantitative analysis of the small number of correspondances sufficient for establishing it, whereas in the case of syntax, morphology and phonology across languages, relatedness is established on the basis of qualitative analysis of structures and systems. Besides the lexical point of view, one is always lead to discuss a ratio of related vs. non-related forms. Convergences, borrowings, remotivations, re-lexicalisations, mixtures and simple chance lead to weakening the argumentative force of the comparison of lexica.

65 Justice must no doubt be rendered to the recurrent argument according to which the family groupings proposed by Greenberg would be accepted today, even by its detractors. If it is true that his analysis with respect to Africa is generally accepted, in fact it only takes up again and develops hypotheses that have already been strongly argued by africanists, for example Westermann. In the Amerindian domain, the grouping that he proposes should be treated with caution, whereas in the Indo-Pacific domain it appears to have been universally rejected (cf. Poser Ibid.).

66 'Cette exigence de produire, pour établir des relations génétiques, des reconstructions accompagnées de correspondances phonétiques régulières a encore une autre conséquence désastreuse. Pour reconstruire une protolangue avec des correspondances phonétiques régulières, il faut disposer d'un corps de données assez étendues[...] selon Kaufman [...] au moins cinq cents mots de vocabulaire et cent points de grammaire sont nécessaires avant de pouvoir commencer 'un travail comparatif sérieux'. [...] il est impossible de prendre au sérieux de telles exigences *a priori*. [...] Qu'on puisse classer correctement les langues sur

la base d'une douzaine de mots ne devrait pas vous surprendre.' Ruhlen (1994, 146).

67 Cf. Victorri (2000) and references cited *supra* notes 61, 62.

68 'D'une façon ou d'une autre on a confondu la reconstruction, qui est en réalité la deuxième étape de la linguistique historique, avec la première étape, c'est à dire la classification.' Ruhlen (1994, 144).

69 'La véritable base de l'affinité génétique entre langues n'a rien à voir avec les exigences loufoques posées par les indo-européanistes et leurs partisans. C'est bien plutôt la présence, dans le vocabulaire de base de différentes langues ou familles de langues, de nombreuses ressemblances qui détermine leur classification, et partant leur parenté. Darwin avait reconnu cette base simple de la taxinomie biologique dès 1871.' Ruhlen (Ibid., 151).

70 'A l'exemple souvent cité du mot *bad* qui en anglais et en persan signifie également 'mauvais' sans aucun rapport étymologique, on peut joindre celui du mot allemand *Feuer*, qui n'a originellement rien de commun avec le mot français de même sens, feu. De même il n'y a qu'une ressemblance extérieure fortuite entre l'anglais *whole* et le grec '*ὅλος*' 'tout entier', entre le latin *femina* et le vieux-saxon *fêmea fêmia*, même sens, entre le latin *locus* et le sanskrit *lokas* 'monde', entre le grec moderne μάτι 'œil' et le polynésien *mata* 'voir', etc.' Vendryes (1921, 334).

Il en est de même entre la racine grecque *πνευ* et le klamath *pniw,* entre l'anglais *dog* et le mbabaram *dog.* Pinker (1999, 254).

71 Cf. Halle (1962); Laks (1996) and also Bloomfield (1939).

72 'Comme ils n'opèrent aussi en général que sur les langues communes reconstituées par hypothèse, les linguistes qui reconstituent l'indo-européen se trouvent à un degré supérieur condamnés à un travail purement schématique. L'indo-européen des linguistes n'a aucune réalité concrète: ce n'est comme on l'a dit qu'un 'système de correspondances'. Il suit de là que le plus savant connaisseur de l'indo-européen serait incapable d'exprimer dans cette langue une phrase aussi simple que le 'cheval court' ou 'la maison est grande.' (Vendryes 1921, 330).

73 'Cette exigence d'une 'preuve' est complètement à côté de la plaque: la notion de 'preuve' est un concept mathématique qui n'a pas d'application dans les sciences empiriques telles que la linguistique, la biologie ou même la physique. Dans ces domaines du savoir, on ne cherche pas tant à prouver quelque chose qu'à fournir l'explication la plus vraisemblable à une série non aléatoire de données.' Ruhlen (Ibid., 151).

74 'La famille eurasiatique de Greenberg représente *sa vision personnelle* des parents les plus proches de l'indo-européen.' Ruhlen (Ibid., 82, our italics).

75 Cf. Ayala and Fitch (1997) for a presentation. Cf. also Mayr (1982) and Croft (2000) for a critical discussion.

76 Cf. for example Cavalli-Sforza (1996; 1993).

77 The Anatolian thesis (Renfrew 1987) is opposed to the more classical thesis of Gimbutas (1991), who defends a Kourganian origin for the language of the Indo-European civilisation.

78 Cf. also Barbujani and Sokal (1990).

79 'Ce qui manque encore cependant, c'est un arbre de classification de toutes les langues auxquelles on peut reconnaître de façon certaine une signification évolutive – c'est à dire une classification qui rende compte de leur origine et de leur histoire – [...] Les méthodes [de la linguistique] auraient tout à gagner en devenant plus quantitatives qu'elles ne le sont à l'heure actuelle; elles y gagneraient peut-être aussi en objectivité.' Cavalli-Sforza (1994, 239, 251).

80 'Nous nous sommes servis [de Ruhlen] pour organiser en une hiérarchie simple les données biologiques recueillies sur les populations du monde en ne lui attribuant cependant qu'une valeur formelle. [...] Grâce à notre classement linguistique initial, il nous a été facile de vérifier si notre arbre génétique avait un rapport avec l'arbre linguistique. Et la réponse a été positive.' Cavalli-Sforza (1994, 239, 270).

81 Cf. for example Cavalli-Sforza (1994, 97); Barbujani and Sokal (1990, 1816); Harpending et al. (1998, 5–6). For a genetic evaluation of opposed hypotheses concerning nostratic and euroasiatic cf. also Barbujani and Pilastro (1993).

82 The demic hypothesis seems to be nevertheless less strongly involved in the work of Renfrew than in that of Cavalli-Sforza. The importance granted to the demic thesis sometimes produces hazardous results, such as the case where Ruhlen (1994, 24) treats simultaneously as demic the diffusion of Indo-European and that of Latin. The invasion of the roman space by populations of latium can only raise a smile. As for the linguistic homogeneity of roman armies, it would suffice to open Flaubert's *Salambô* in order to have a literary idea of the linguistic and cultural melting pot of which they consisted.

83 In Warnow's model, the place of germanic is extremely problematic. Although the model pleads in favour of close relationships with the Italo-Celtic group, the best analysis seems to be the one that positions it as a sister branch from the Balto-Slavic node.

References

Aitchison, J., Hurford, J. R., Studdert-Kennedy, M. and Knight, C. (1998) *On Discontinuing the Continuity-Discontinuity Debate.* Approaches to the evolution of languages, Cambridge, Cambridge University Press. 17–30.

Ayala, F., Fitch, J. and Walter, M. (1997) Genetics and the origin of species: an introduction, *Proceedings of the National Academy of Science* 94/15, 7691–97.

Barbujani, G. and Pilastro, A. (1993) Genetic evidence on origin and dispersal of human populations speaking languages of the Nostratic macrofamily, *Proceedings of the National Academy of Science* 90, 4670–73.

Barbujani, G. and Sokal, R. (1990) Zones of sharp genetic change in Europe are also linguistic boundaries, *Proceedings of the National Academy of Science* 87, 1816–19.

Bergounioux, G. (1994) *Aux origines de la linguistique française.* Paris, Pocket.

Bergounioux, G. (1996) Aux origines de la Société de Lingüistique de Paris (1864–1876), *Bulletin de la Société de Linguistique de Paris* XCI, 1 1–36.

Bergounioux, G. (2001) La sélection des langues: darwinisme et linguistique, *Langages* 125.

Bloomfield, L. (1939) Menomini morphophomemics, *Travaux du cercle linguistique de Prague* 8 105–15.

Brugmann, K. and Delbrück, B. (1896) *Grundriss der vergleichenden Grammatik der indogermanischen Sprachen.* Strasbourg.

Campbell, L. (1988) Review of Greenberg J. H. Language in the Americas, *Language* 64 591–615.

Campbell, L. (1997) *American Indian Languages: The Historical Linguistics of Native America.* Oxford, Oxford University Press.

Campbell, L. and Mithum, M. (1979) *The Languages of Native Americas.* University of Texas.

Cannon, G. (1990) *The Life and Mind of Oriental Jones.* Cambridge, Cambridge University Press.

Cavalli-Sforza, L. L. (1996) *Gènes et peuples.* Paris, Odile Jacob.

Cavalli-Sforza, L. L. (1997) Genes, peoples and languages, *Proceedings of the National Academy of Science* 94, 7719–24.

Cavalli-Sforza, L. L. and Cavalli-Sforza, F. (1993) *Qui sommes nous? Une histoire de la diversité humaine.* Traduction française 1994 Albin Michel, Edition 1997. Paris, Flammarion.

Cavalli-Sforza, L. L., Menozzi, P. and Piazza, A. (1994) *The History and Geography of Human Genes.* Princeton, Princeton University Press.

Cavalli-Sforza, L. L., Minch, E. and Moutain, J. (1992) Coevolution of genes and languages revisited, *Proceedings of the National Academy of Science* 89, 5620–24.

Chomsky, N. (1995) *The Minimalist Program.* Cambridge, Mass., MIT Press.

Chretien, C. D. (1962) The mathematical models of glottochronology, *Language* 38, 11–37.

Courtenay, B. de (1901) O messannom charaktere vsech jazyko (Sur le caractère mixte de toutes les langues), *Zurnal Ministerstva Narodnago Prosvescenija.*
Croft, W. (2000) *Explaining Language Change: An Evolutionary Approach.* Londres, Longman.
Darwin, C. (1859) *L'origine des espèces au moyen de la sélection naturelle ou la préservation des races favorisées dans la lutte pour la vie.* Traduction Barbier, E., Nouvelle édition Becquemont, D., 1992. Paris, Flammarion.
Darwin, C. (1871) *La filiation de l'homme et la sélection liée au sexe.* Nouvelle traduction Prum M., 1999. Paris, Institut Charles Darwin International / Syllepse.
Dessalles, J. L. (2000) *Aux origines du langage: une histoire naturelle de la parole.* Paris, Hermès.
Dobson, A., Kruskal, J. B., Sankoff, D. and J. Savage, L. (1972) The mathematics of glottochronology revisited, *Anthropological Linguistics* 14 6, 205–12.
Dupanloup, I., Poloni, E. S., Schneider, S., Excoffier, L. and Langaney, A. (2001) Génétique, linguistique et histoire des peuplements humains, *Langages* 125.
Dyen, I. (1975) *Linguistics Subgrouping and Lexicostatistics.* La Haye, Mouton.
Dyen, I. and Jucquois, G. (1976) *Lexicostatistics: Present and Prospects.* Lexicostatistics in genetic linguistics, Centre de Recherches Mathématiques, Université de Montréal.
Dyen, I., Kruskal, J. B. and Black, P. (1992) An indoeuropean classification: a lexicostastical experiment, *Transactions of the American Philosophical Society* 82 5.
Gauchat, L. (1905) L'unité phonétique dans le patois d'une commune. *Aus Romanischen Sprachen und Literaturen.* Festschrift H. Mort.
Gilliéron, J. and Edmont, E. (1902–1912) *Atlas Linguistique de la France.* Paris, Champion. 12 Vol.
Gimbutas, M. (1991) *The Civilization of the Goddess: The World of Old Europe.* San Francisco, Harper.
Godel, R. (1969) *A Geneva School Reader in Linguistics.* Bloomington, Indiana University Press.
Greenberg, J. H. (1966) *Language Universals, with Special References to Feature Hierarchies.* Janua Linguarum Series Minor n°59 La Haye, Mouton.
Greenberg, J. H. and Sebeok, T. F. (1971) *The Indo-Pacific Hypothesis.* Current Trends in Linguistics 8 La Haye, Mouton.
Greenberg, J. H. (1987) *Language in the Americas.* Stanford, Stanford University Press.
Greenberg, J. H. (2000) *Indo-European and Its Closest Relatives: The Eurasiatic Language Family.* Stanford, Stanford University Press.
Greenberg, J. H. and Ruhlen, M. (1992) Linguistic origins of native Americans, *Scientific American* 94–99. 1993 L'origine linguististique des Amérindiens, Pour la science 183, 48–55.

Gudschinsky, S. (1956) The ABC's of lexicostatistics (glottochronology), *Word* 12, 175–210.
Halle, M. (1962) Phonology in generative grammar, *Word* 18 1/2, 54–72.
Harpending, H. C., Batzer, M. A., Gurven, M., Jorde, L. B., Rogers, A. R. and Sherry, S. T. (1998) Genetic traces of ancient demography, *Proceedings of the National Academy of Science* 95 4, 1961–67.
Jakobson, R. (1938) Sur la théorie des affinités phonologiques entre les langues, *Actes du 4ème congrès international des linguistes* 48–58, Copenhague, Repris dans Troubetzkoy Nicolaï Sergeivicth, Principes de Phonologie, Paris, Klincksieck 1947, 351–65.
Kaiser, M. and Chevorochkine, V. (1988) Nostratic, *Annual Review of Anthropology* 17, 309–29.
Kaplan, F. (2001) *La naissance d'une langue chez les robots*. Paris, Hermès.
Labov, W. (1994) *Principles of Linguistic Change: Internal Factors*. Oxford, Blackwell.
Labov, W. (2001) *Principle of Linguistic Change: Social Factors*. Oxford, Blackwell.
Laks, B. (1983) Langage et pratiques sociales: étude sociolinguistique d'un groupe d'adolescents, *Actes de la Recherche en Sciences Sociales* 46, 73–97.
Laks, B. (1996) *Langage et cognition: l'approche connexionniste*. Paris, Hermès.
Laks, B. (2001) Un siècle de phonologie, *Modèles Linguistiques*.
Lees, R. (1953) On the basis of glottochronology, *Language* 29, 113–27.
Lehmann, W. P. (ed.) (1967) *A Reader in Nineteenth Century Historical Indo-European Linguistics.* Bloomington, Indiana University Press.
Mayr, E. (1982) *The Growth of Biological Thought: Diversity Evolution, Inheritance*. Cambridge MA, Belknap Press.
Meillet, A. (1903) *Introduction à l'étude comparative des langues indo-européennes*. Paris, Hachette. 8ème édition 1953.
Nakleh, L., Ringe, D. and Warnow, T. (2005) Perfect phylogenetic network: a new methodology for reconstructing the evolutionary history of languages. *Language* 81, 382–420.
Nichols, J. (1992) *Linguistic Diversity in Space and Time*. Chicago, University of Chicago Press.
Ostoff, H. and Brugmann, K. (1898) *Morphologische Untersuchungen auf den Gebiete des Indogermanischen Sprachen. I.* Leipzig.
Pande, G. C. (1965) Vie et mort des langues, *Diogène* 51, 197–214.
Paris, G. (1888) Les parlers de France, *Revue des Patois Gallo-romans* 2, 161–75.
Pinker, S. (1999) *L'instinct du langage*. Paris, Editions Odile Jacob.
Pinker, S. (1994) The language instinct. New York, William Morrow and Company.

Renfrew, C. (2001) From molecular genetics to archeogenetics, *Proceedings of the National Academy of Science* 98 9, 4830–32.
Ringe, D. and Warnow, T. (2002) Indo-European and computational cladistics. Transactions of the Philological Society.
Ruhlen, M. (1991) *A Guide to the World's Languages: Classification.* Stanford, Stanford University Press.
Ruhlen, M. (1994) *On the Origin of Languages: Studies in Linguistic Taxonomy.* Stanford, Stanford University Press.
Ruhlen, M. (1997) *L'origine des langues.* Paris, Belin.
Sankoff, D. (1970) *Historical Linguistics as a Stochastic Process.* Phd McGill.
Sankoff, D. (1973) On the rate of replacement in word-meaning relationship, *Language* 46, 564–69.
Saussure, F. de (2001) *Ecrits de linguistique générale.* Bouquet, S. and Engler, R. (eds) Paris, Gallimard.
Schleicher, A. (1861/1862) *Compendium der vergleichenden Grammatik der indogermanischen Sprachen.* Weimar, Böhlau.
Schuchardt, H. (1922) *Hugo Schuchardt-Brevier. Ein vademekum der allgemeinen Sprachwissenschaft.* Spitzer L. (ed.) Halle, M., Niemeyer, F., J.
Sériot, P. (1999) *Structure et totalité.* Paris, PUF.
Swadesh, M. (1952) Lexico-statistical dating of prehistoric ethnic contacts: With special reference to North American Indians and Eskimos dialects, *Proceedings of the American Philosophical Society* 96, 452–63.
Swadesh, M. and Sherzer, J. (1972) *The Origin and Diversification of Language.* London, Routledge and Paul.
Tesnière, L. (1939) Phonologie et mélange de langues, *Travaux du Cercle Linguistique de Prague* 8, 83–93.
Thaler, L. (1985) *Phylogénèse.* Encyclopaedia Universalis, 14 603–7.
Troubezkoy, N. S. (1928) Proposition 16, *Actes du Premier Congrès International des Linguistes, La Haye du 10 au 15 avril 1928* Leiden, Sijthoff.
Vendryes, J. (1921) *Le Langage: Introduction linguistique à l'histoire.* Paris, La renaissance du livre.
Victorri, B. (2000) La langue originelle, *Sciences et Avenir* numéro spécial 37–41.
Warnow, T. (1997) Mathematical approaches to comparative linguistics, *Proceedings of the National Academy of Science* 95, 6585–90.
Whitney, W. D. (1875) *La vie du langage.* Paris, Librairie Germer Baillière et compagnie. Facsimile Didier Erudition.

9 Simulating the expansion of farming and the differentiation of European languages

Domenico Parisi, Francesco Antinucci, Francesco Natale, Federico Cecconi
Institute of Cognitive Sciences and Technologies, National Research Council

1 Simulations as theories

Theories in science are traditionally expressed using either everyday language or mathematical equations, with sometimes the help of visual tools such as pictures and flow charts. Many phenomena of human behavior and human societies are too complicated to be captured by mathematical equations while verbally formulated theories tend to be vague and with little empirical content and pictures and flow charts only capture static properties but not the dynamics of mechanisms and processes. Computer simulations are a new way of expressing scientific theories that may help solve the problem of how to formulate theories in the social sciences. Simulations are theories expressed as computer programs. When the program runs in the computer, the results of the simulation are the empirical predictions derived from the theory incorporated in the simulation. For those who are interested in the phenomena of human behavior and societies, simulations offer three important advantages. First, simulations force the researcher to make his or her theory explicit, consistent, precise, and complete, because otherwise the theory/simulation will not run in the computer or will not generate the expected results. Secondly, theories expressed as simulations are necessarily rich in empirical content in that, by manipulating the conditions and variables of the simulation and the value of the parameters, much as one does in a laboratory experiment, the researcher can generate a rich and detailed set of simulation results which, as already noted, are the empirical predictions of the theory incorporated in the simulation. Of course, the final test of a simulation is the demonstrated correspondence between the simulation results and the actual empirical or historical facts. But computer simulations can amplify and strengthen the dialogue between theory and empirical facts which is critical for scientific progress. A third advantage of simulations for the study of human behavior and societies is that simulations can reproduce the manner in which phenomena develop, their dynamics in space and time, which is a critical requirement given the historical character of many human phenomena.

Cellular automata[1,2] are a useful tool for doing simulations of processes of geographical expansion and of cultural/linguistic change. A grid of cells is superimposed on a specific geographical region, with each cell covering an area comprising a given number of square kilometers. Each cell is assigned the same set of properties with a specific value for each property which can vary from cell to cell. These properties may represent the geographical characteristics or the resources present in the area covered by the cell, the number of people living in the cell, their culture or language, their political or technological expansion potential, and so on. Furthermore, the model includes a set of rules for modifying, in a succession of update cycles, some or all of the properties of each cell as a function of the properties of the neighboring cells – for example, the eight cells surrounding a square cell. This produces change in space and time in the region covered by the cellular automaton that may help us understand actual historical changes.

In this chapter we will first briefly present a simulation based on a cellular automaton that tries to reproduce (explain) the expansion of the Neo-Assyrian empire in the Ancient Near East but we will dedicate most of the chapter to describing a simulation model of the expansion of farming in Ancient Europe with possible links to the origin and differentiation of European languages. In both cases our main goal is methodological, i.e., to illustrate the potential of simulations as a research tool in the social and historical sciences, not to claim the validity of any particular model which may seem to be supported by the simulations.

2 The expansion of the Assyrian empire

Consider the geographical region of the ancient Near East and the phenomenon of the expansion of the Assyrian empire which took place in that region from the XIV to the VII century before Christ. The entire region is divided up into hexagonal cells of 50 sq. km.[3] At the beginning of the simulation only a single cell in the Upper Tigris is occupied (controlled) by the Assyrians. All the cells occupied by the Assyrians have a property called 'expansion potential' with a value that, locally, can go from 1 (maximum expansion potential) to 0 (no expansion potential). The value of the expansion potential for the initial cell is 1. This means that in the next cycle the Assyrians will expand to the 6 neighboring cells with probability of 100%. However, the expansion potential of the 6 newly occupied cells will not be 1 but it will only be 0.98. The rule is that the expansion potential of a newly occupied cell is the same as that of the occupying cell with a decrement of 0.02. This decrement captures the logistic costs of maintaining transportation and communication links between subsequently occupied cells and the point of origin of the Assyrian expansion, i.e., the initial Assyrian cell. These costs increase with the distance of each Assyrian cell from the center of the empire on the Upper Tigris. The expansion potential of a cell determines the probability that the cell will occupy a new, previously unoccupied, cell. As we have said, an expansion potential of 1 signifies a probability of expansion of 100%. A value of 0.98 a 98% probability, a value of 0.10 a 10% probability, etc. The progressive decrement in the expansion potential of progressively more distant cells signifies that the expansion process will spontaneously arrive to an end when the logistic costs of maintaining a large empire become too large.

But the model includes other factors. Each cell has two additional properties, each with its own local value: the geographical penetrability of the cell and its political penetrability. Geographical penetrability means that the nature of the terrain (mountains, plains, rivers, desert, etc.) makes the expansion to a particular unoccupied cell more or less probable. Cells with mountains, desert areas, large rivers, have a low geographical penetrability index. Cells covering easily accessible terrain have a higher index. Political penetrability refers to the presence of other peoples already occupying a given cell, and the value of this property reflects the demographic density and the level of political and military organization of these peoples. Numerous and well organized people already living in a given cell reduce the political penetrability of the cell. Hence, the probability that a given Assyrian cell will expand to a new, previously unoccupied, cell is a function not only of the expansion potential of the Assyrian cell but also of the two indices of geographical and political penetrability of the cell to be occupied.

Another aspect of the model is that the expansion potential of an Assyrian cell is not only a function of the distance of the cell from the center of the Assyrian empire, reflecting increasing logistic costs, but it also depends on natural and, possibly, other types of resources (e.g., artifacts and other resources constituting the 'wealth' of the people originally occupying the cell) which are present in the territory covered by the cell. The expansion potential of an

Assyrian cell does not only decrease with the distance from the center of the empire but it can also increase because the Assyrians acquire these resources. Hence, every cell is assigned a further quantitative index which reflects the quantity of resources present in the cell and this index influences the expansion potential of the Assyrians when they happen to occupy the cell.

There are two versions of the model: monocentric and polycentric. In the monocentric model only the Assyrians expand. The presence of other peoples in the region (Babylonians, Egyptians, Hittites, Aramaic, etc.) is only passive and is reflected in the political penetrability index and, in some cases, in the resource index of the cells to be occupied by the Assyrians. In the polycentric model all the peoples of the ancient Near East may expand like the Assyrians – or fail to expand. Each people is represented by an initial cell in a specific geographical region and the cell is assigned a certain expansion potential, which may vary from 1 to 0 depending on the people. All the cells still have a political penetrability index but this index is not assigned once and for all at the beginning of the simulation, as in the monocentric model, but it changes dynamically during the historical process the simulation is trying to reproduce. If a cell is 'empty', i.e., it is not occupied by anyone, the index has its maximum value: 1. If the cell happens to be occupied by some people, its current political penetrability index reflects the local expansion potential of the people occupying the cell. When two peoples occupy neighboring cells and therefore each people tries to expand to the cell occupied by the other people, the people that 'wins' is the one with a greater local expansion potential.

To run a simulation using the monocentric model the researcher initially defines three maps: the map of the geographical penetrability of the cells, the map of their political penetrability, the map of the resources present in each cell. To run the polycentric model, the map of political penetrability is omitted but one has to assign to each people of the region an expansion potential index for their initial cell. Furthermore, the cellular automata model has to be temporally calibrated. The simulation runs in cycles. In each cycle all the cells are updated, i.e., their properties that need to be modified are modified. The temporal calibration of the model means that one has to decide how many years are covered by each update cycle. Then the simulation begins. The initial year for the expansion of the Assyrian empire is 1350 B.C. Its end is the end of the VII century.

A basic result of the simulation is how the size and shape of the Assyrian empire changes at various successive dates during the period considered. The simulation generates a succession of maps of the (simulated) Assyrian empire at various dates which can be compared with the succession of historical maps. A more global but quantitative result is how the total size of the empire changes in each of the successive dates. The resulting curve can be compared with the corresponding historical curve. In fact, using the monocentric model the simulation generates a curve of historical changes in the size of the Assyrian empire which closely matches the actual historical data.

Two aspects of the actual historical phenomena are not captured by the simulation. First, it is known that, while the total size of the Assyrian empire tends generally to increase in the period considered, a couple of times during the period there is contraction rather than expansion of the territory controlled by the Assyrians. And, second, at the end of the period considered there is a rather sudden collapse of the entire empire which disappears as a unified political entity in only a few years towards the end of the VII century. Both phenomena are not, and could not, be replicated in the simulation we have described. The first phenomenon is likely to be due to contingent factors such as succession crises or ascent to power of inadequate emperors. The terminal collapse tends to be interpreted as either due to external factors such as the emergence of new powerful neighbors or to internal reasons such as an excessive growth of logistic and administrative costs for maintaining such a large empire. Contingent factors that are known to have existed historically can be incorporated in the simulation which, contrary to what one might think, is not restricted to systematic and general mechanisms and rules but can also take into consideration in its calculations contingent factors and causes. On the other hand, the collapse of the empire at the end of the VII century for internal causes might be predicted by the simulation by incorporating in the simulation a model of the organization of the Assyrian empire, and in particular of the relationship between its size and costs. But, independently of how one might obtain a better match between the simulation results and the actual historical phenomena in this particular case, the general lesson to be drawn from the simulation is that mismatches are always possible and that they may be useful for modifying the model and for better understanding the actual explanatory power and limitations of the ideas in terms of which we try to account for historical phenomena. Furthermore, a mismatch between the simulation results and the historical data in our possession can be useful if the simulation results can induce us to look for new, additional, data.

3 The expansion of farming in Europe

We now turn to the simulation of the expansion of farming in Europe starting from West Anatolia 9000 years ago and the possibly associated process of differentiation of European languages.

The entire territory of Europe is divided up into a grid of square cells of around 70 square kilometers.[4] (Adjustments are made for the spherical shape of the Earth.) Each cell is assigned four properties that determine the potential farming productivity of the cell: (1) extension and height of mountains; (2) river runoff (annual average); (3) rainfall (annual average); (4) nature of terrain with specific reference to its suitability for farming. These four properties are put together to determine a single index of the Carrying Capacity of the cell, i.e., of the number of farming people that can live in the cell. Each cell is also assigned a demographic index measuring the actual number of farming people currently living in the cell. At the beginning of the farming expansion process in the IX millennium before present only one cell in South West Anatolia has a value of 400 (people) for this index. All the other cells have a zero index. This means that farmers only live in the Anatolian cell and there are initially no farmers in Europe.

The simulation runs as follows. Each cell containing farmers 'looks at' its eight neighboring cells to find out whether these cells are available for occupation. A cell is available for occupation unless it is already occupied by other farmers or the cell is entirely unfit for farming (e.g., high mountains or desert). For each cell the number of neighboring cells that are available for occupation is determined and if this number is 4 or more, the population of the cell undergoes a demographic growth of 3.5%. If the number is 2 or 3, the growth is 2.5%; if it is 1 or 0, there is no growth. Updating the population of farmers living in all cells completes a cycle, and then a new cycle starts. A cycle represents one year since it reflects the demographic growth rate.

When the number of farmers living in a cell reaches 45% of the cell's Carrying Capacity, a migration occurs: a portion of the cell's inhabitants (25%) moves to one of the empty neighboring cells selecting the cell with the highest Carrying Capacity. Cells that represent sea cannot be occupied but they can be penetrated by the migration movement. Three conditions govern sea crossing: (1) a randomly selected neighboring sea cell is penetrated if none of the neighboring land cells is available for occupation; (2) once a population has penetrated a sea cell it automatically continues to move in each cycle from sea cell to sea cell in a straight line until it reaches a land cell; (3) if a land cell is not reached within a distance of 20 sea cells (around 150 km) from the beginning of the crossing, the population dies out. Condition (3) reflects the level of navigational technology and skills reached at the time.

Figures 1–8 show the expansion process at different times expressed in years since the beginning of the process in the IX millennium. Grey shades represent density of occupation by farmers (white = no occupation; black = maximum density). The Middle East area should be disregarded since it is probable that a different expansion process also tied to the Neolithic farming revolution had taken place in that area prior to the European expansion process originating in Anatolia which is the object of the present model.

Figure 1. Arrival to Greece through Rhodes at around 670 years: distance from origin (DFO) 640 km. Arrival to southern coast of Bulgaria after crossing the Bosphorus at around 700 years: DFO 700 km.

Figure 2. Arrival to Odessa along the Black Sea coast at 770 years: DFO 750 km. Arrival to Italy (Otranto, Apulia) at about 1000 years: DFO 1100 km.

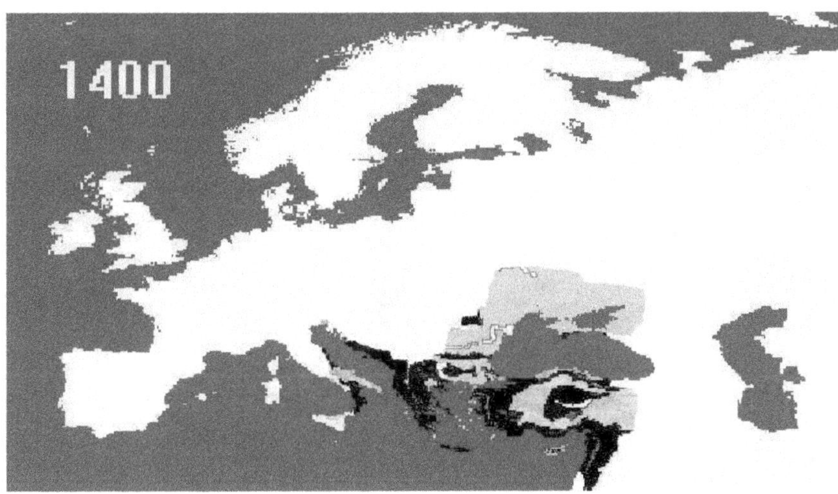

Figure 3. Arrival to Ancona (Adriatic coast) at 1400 years: DFO 1550 km.

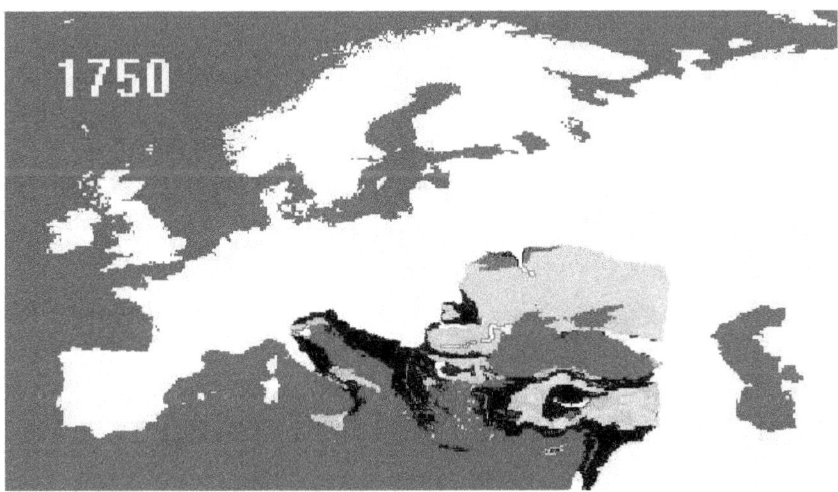

Figure 4. Arrival to Provence via Corsica and Sardinia at about 2200 years: DFO 2200 km.

Figure 5. Arrival to England at 3730 years: DFO 3600 km.

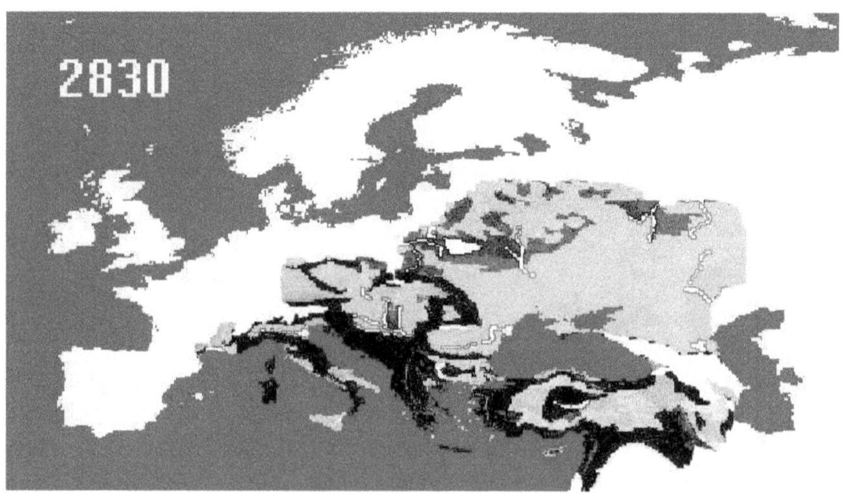

Figure 6. Arrival to Baltic at 2950 years: DFO 2650 km.

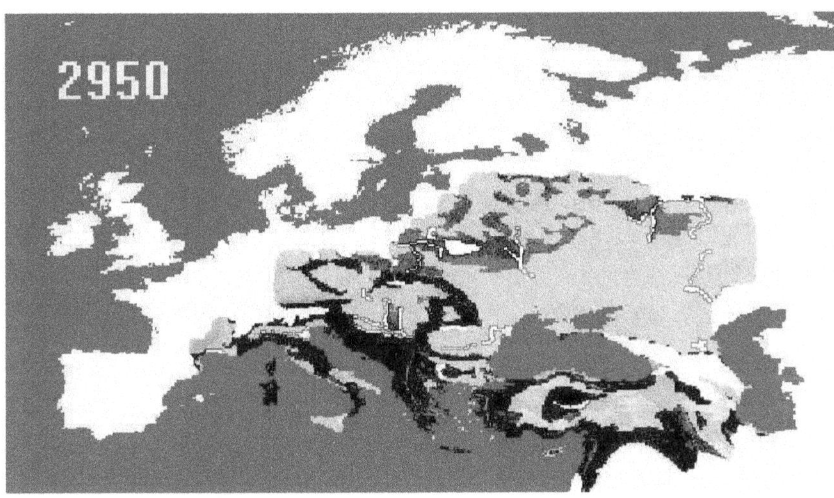

Figure 7. Arrival to Armenia at 1750 years: DFO 1650 km.

Figure 8. Arrival to Iran at 2830: DFO 2650 km.

Figure captions indicate the time taken by farmers to reach selected locations in Europe and the distance of these locations from point of origin (this distance may include sea crossings not exceeding 20 cells). An interesting result emerging from these data is that the expansion process turns out to be based on an average rate of advancement of around 1 km per year (somewhat more in the advancement along the Adriatic coasts and somewhat less towards the Baltic coast and the Easters territories). This is in agreement with the model of Ammerman and Cavalli-Sforza[5] and Renfrew[6] (see also[7]) and with archaeological evidence of Neolithic settlements on the terrain.) However, it is important that while in Ammerman and Cavalli-Sforza's and Renfrew's model the rate of advancement of 1 km/year is assumed as such and fitted into the model, in our simulation it results spontaneously from the demographic growth rate, the nature of the terrain, and the expansion rules postulated by the simulation. Ammerman and Cavalli-Sforza derive the expansion velocity from the archaeological evidence and in order to include this value in their model they assume that at each 25-year generation interval the population moves 18 km on. In contrast, the simulation simply assumes the demographic growth rates, which at a micro-scale level may be different in different cells, feeds them into a representation of the real terrain encountered at the micro-scale level, and generates as a result (in a by no means obvious way since it is a result of literally millions of local interactions) a macro-scale expansion velocity averaging 1 km/year.

This result seems to give independent support to Ammerman and Cavalli-Sforza's and Renfrew's model. By including in the simulation only the demographic growth rates and by making the mechanisms and effects of population growth and expansion process solely dependent on the properties of the occupied and immediately surrounding terrain at the very fine scale of 70 sq. km units, the simulation succeeds rather well in reproducing the real behavior of Neolithic farmers in the specific environment constituted by the terrain mapped in the simulation. The fact that this behavior reconstructed at such a micro scale produces through millions of local interactions macro-patterns that are in agreement with the observable evidence militates in favor of these local interactions having actually taken place.

A methodologically interesting aspect of the model concerns the level of navigational technology and skill as reflected in the maximum distance that could be navigated without touching land. In the model that we have described a distance of 20 sea cells, that is, around 150 km, is assumed. If we vary this value and assume a somewhat higher level of navigational technology/skill, say, 30 sea cells, i.e., around 225 km, the same overall results are obtained but with some quantitative and qualitative changes. For example, with only 20 sea cells of navigational autonomy the Black Sea is circumnavigated but not traversed from South to North. With a higher level of navigational autonomy of 30 sea cells the Black Sea is both circumnavigated and traversed. Another difference is that with a higher level of navigational technology/skill the West Mediterranean regions are reached earlier and, in Italy, the expansion along the Tyrrhenian coast plays a more important role even if the expansion along the Adriatic coast remains prominent. It may not be clear if these differences militate in favor of the higher level of navigational technology/skill in the period considered, or if the lower level assumed previously gives more historically accurate results. What is important is the light these different results shed on simulations as a research method. First, one can clearly see that simulations tend to generate a very rich and differentiated set of results that can be compared with different types of empirical and historical evidence, in our case archaeological evidence on expansion of farming but also on level of navigational technology/skill (which, incidentally, may have varied during the period considered, with the possibility to incorporate these variations in the simulation). Second, simulations clearly show how different factors, in our case level of navigational technology/skill and geographical factors, may interact with each other in complex ways that may be difficult to capture by simple reasoning. An assumed level of navigational technology/skill may give good results for how Italy was colonized by farmers but bad results for how the regions around the Black Sea were colonized. This represents a challenge to formulate explicit and self-consistent models for interpreting the past.

4 Origins and differentiation of European languages

Because the simulation reproduces the expansion process cell-by-cell and year-by year, for each cell it is possible to know when it was first occupied (number of years since the beginning of the expansion process) and to trace the entire path followed by farmers from the point of origin of the process to the particular cell. We can use this information to construct trees of expansion paths with a common 'root' in Anatolia and branches in the various regions of Europe. If we assume that the expanding people had a culture or a language that they carried with themselves and that became progressively differentiated because of internal changes and the lack of interactions with people living in distant cells, we can interpret these branching trees as reflecting different degrees of cultural/linguistic similarity among people living in different regions in Europe. Cultural/linguistic differentiation sets in as a function of the temporal length of separation of different groups from a single community originally having a shared culture and a common language. By choosing any two cells in Europe, tracking their paths of provenance, and computing the time elapsed since the separation of these paths, we can determine the degree of cultural/linguistic differentiation between the two cells.

We have done this for a number of 'critical' cells (geographical locations in Europe). Figure 9 shows the various paths of provenance of these cells, which obviously collectively take the form of a branching tree rooted in the Anatolian point of origin of the expansion process.

Figure 9. Branching tree of expansion paths with root in the point of origin of the expansion process.

What is the meaning of this tree? We can interpret the tree in linguistic terms and use it to assess the validity of one of the two main hypotheses that have been advanced to explain the similarities among most of the languages currently (and in the past) spoken in Europe. According to this hypothesis,[6] almost all the European languages spoken in Europe derive from a common Proto-Language which was spoken by farmers living in Southwest Anatolia 9000 years ago. The demic expansion of these farmers produced the different languages spoken in Europe, with the similarity tree of these languages derivable from the tree of expansion paths of Figure 9. (Another direction of expansion of these farmers was towards West Asia and this direction of expansion produced the Indo-Iranian branch of the Indo-European family, but this is outside the scope of our simulation.)

Let us try to read in these terms the branching pattern of Figure 9 in relation to its time depth. This can be done by comparing the branching pattern with the different states of advancement shown in Figures 1–8.

There are four initial branches that start directly from the root. They go off approximately towards the four directions North-West, North-East, South-East, and South-West. After 700 years (see Figure 1) – a period of time long enough to determine significant linguistic differences – the South-West branch has touched Greece having gone through Rhodes, the South-East branch is pointing towards the Caucasus after having gone through Cyprus, the North-East branch traverses the central part of Anatolia, the North-West branch has reached the Bosphorus strait, crossed it, and touched what today is Bulgaria.

For these first four main population branchings we can posit four major linguistic groups. However, in order to gain some insight into their correspondence with the Indo-European language family we have to consider their further development.

The first branch, the South-West one, divides into two: one goes north to settle Greece and the internal part of southern Balkans, the second tours around the Greek peninsula to land in Italy (Otranto). Here it divides up into two again, one group going up along the Adriatic Sea and the other one along the Tyrrhenian Sea. This last will eventually settle France, Spain, and England. It is not difficult to identify a Greco-Italo-Celtic language group, with Greek becoming separated from Italo-Celtic at an early stage (well before the end of the first millennium; cf. Figure 2), and Celtic branching off towards the end of the second millennium (date of arrival to Provence is at 2200; cf. Figure 4).

The second branch, the South-East branch, crosses the whole of Anatolia in the direction of Armenia, which is reached in around 1750 years (cf. Figure 7). Then it goes on towards the southern shore of the Caspian Sea, into Iran (reached after another 1000 years; cf. Figure 8), further proceeding towards Afghanistan. Although the simulation geographically stops there, one can easily foresee a further advance towards Pakistan and Northern India. In Indo-European terms, this branch corresponds to the Armeno-Aryan group, with Armenian branching off and leaving an Indo-Iranian group, and a subsequent branching of the Iranian languages spoken in Iran and Afghanistan from the languages of Northern India.

The third, North-East, branch occupies the whole of Central Anatolia and the southern shore of the Black sea but it does not proceed anywhere else: it essentially dies within Anatolia. We can identify it with what is known to be a separate family of (all extinct) languages within Indo-European: the Anatolian languages.

The fourth, North-West, branch, after crossing the Bosphorus departs north both from Bulgaria and from Odessa. It should be noticed that those two departure points are practically simultaneous (700 and 750 years), so that no linguistic distinction can be implied, and that the colonization proceeds through a thick ray-like pattern of contiguous branches of which we have traced only a few. Therefore, linguistic differentiation is here better seen as a function of time elapsed rather than geographic separation. This branch expands through the whole Slavic area and reaches the Baltic area after approximately 2200 years (cf. Figure 6). It, therefore, corresponds to the Balto-Slavic language group.

In sum, the simulation correctly predicts the existence of four major linguistic groups within the Indo-European family and, furthermore, it correctly predicts their internal constituency: Anatolian, Aryan-Armenic (with the Aryan later articulated into Indo-Iranian), Greco-Italo-Celtic (with Greek splitting off long before Italo-Celtic), Balto-Slavic. This degree of fitness between groupings of expanding farmers generated by the simulation and internal comparative linguistic analysis, two completely unrelated sets of data, seems to us, again, interesting evidence in favor of the hypothesized expansion process.

Two pieces of evidence stand instead in apparent contrast. They both concern Germanic. In traditional comparative analysis Germanic is classed with the Balto-Slavic group. Our simulation tells a different story. In Figure 9, we can clearly see an autonomous branch that occupies present-day Germany filling the entire space between the Celtic group to the west and the Slavic to the east. This branch originates, however, at approximately 1500 year, from the eastern Italic branch north of the Gulf of Trieste, corresponding to today Southern Austria. The Germanic group would thus be more closely related to the Italic. We have no explanation for this. However, it is worth noting that Cavalli-Sforza et al. [8] obtained the same close relation between Germanic and Italic by using both the UPGMA and the NJ reconstruction methods (see Cavalli-Sforza,[9] Figure 15).

The second anomaly is related to the first in that it also involves Germanic. As it can be seen in Figure 9, the whole Scandinavian area is colonized by people coming from the Balto-Slavic group. Instead, Scandinavian languages are traditionally classed as a branch of Germanic.

On the other hand, one nonobvious phenomenon receives a clear-cut explanation from the simulation. The great North European band of territory extending from the Atlantic coast of France to the Ural Mountains does not present any significant orographic barrier and hence no natural obstacle to the regular and continuous spreading of population from east to west or vice versa.[10] Yet both today and in early times it has always appeared as fractionated into three linguistic groups (albeit with variable borders): Celtic (French), Germanic, Slavic. The early Neolithic settlement, as determined by the purely demographic expansion and the nature of the terrain, if one accepts its origin in Anatolia, produces exactly this result. The three groups are sharply separated by the very dynamics of the expansion process. The central branching, the Germanic, starts its northern ascension from southern Austria at 1500 years from origin and proceeds for a long time completely separated to the east from the Slavic group coming up from Bulgaria and the Black Sea: the two will touch each other, determining a reciprocal border to their expansion, only 800–900 year later, at around 2300–2400 years from origin. The same thing happens for the separation between Germanic and Celtic. The Celtic line of expansion begins its ascension around 2200 and will reach and touch the Germanic line of expansion to the east only more than a thousand years later, thus determining the second fracture line in the Northern European plain.

Worth of note is also the situation that the simulation describes for Italy. From Figure 9 we can clearly see that the Neolithic settling of Italy is entirely operated (with the exception of a very thin Tyrrhenian coastal strip) by people coming from the Adriatic and crossing the Apennines mountains in successive parallel waves from south to north. This type of movement is widely attested, at least for later epochs, although perhaps the Tyrrhenian expansion may have been more important if we assume a higher level of navigational technology/ skill (see above). These same populations also cross the Adriatic Sea and expand into the Balkans. Today this territory is of late Slavic occupation. Not so in ancient times when it was occupied by so-called Illyrian populations, whose languages are all extinct: the simulation predicts their close relation to the Italic languages.

Finally, the whole process of Italian peninsular colonization, taking place from south (Apulia) to north (Po Plain) and from east to west, takes about 1000 year. If we place the origin of expansion in Anatolia at 6500 year BC, Italian Neolithic settlement happened between 5500 and 4500 BC along the specified path: available archaeological evidence is in substantial agreement with this prediction.

The remarkable correspondence between, on one side, the branching tree of expansion paths generated by our simulation, with the associated time depths at different geographical locations, and on the other side, the similarity tree of European languages gives some support to one of the two main hypotheses concerning the origins of European languages: the Proto-Indo-European language was spoken in Anatolia 9000 years ago and it expanded and differentiated in the subsequent millennia in Europe along with the diffusion of farming. This hypothesis appears to be rather well supported by the evidence [11] [12] and is consistent with other evidence which links language differentiation with diffusion of farming in other parts of the Earth [13]. The alternative hypothesis, more popular among historical linguists and based on glottochronological analyses and time depth considerations, is that Proto-Indo-European was instead spoken by nomadic people living north of the Black and Caspian Seas 5000–6000 years ago [14] [15]. This alternative hypothesis assumes that these nomadic peoples or, more probably, their culture/language expanded in Europe in a west-bound direction and that the similarity structure of European languages is the result of this expansion. We cannot test this alternative hypothesis with the current model because the cell parameters and the expansion rules used in our model are appropriate for earlier times and for another kind of expansion (farming). However, it should in principle be possible to modify our model by selecting different cell properties and different expansion rules for the cellular automata that are more appropriate for a later expansion of a different nature. In this way one could determine whether the resulting tree of expansion lines matches the similarity tree of European languages equally well as the current version of the model which is inspired by the hypothesis of a more ancient Anatolian origin associated with farming.

5 Demic or cultural?

The model that we have described presupposes a demic interpretation of the arrival of farming in Europe. Farmers actually moved from Anatolia and their descendants (i.e., their genes) progressively occupied the entire Europe. This interpretation may explain the genetic gradient which has been found with point of origin in the Near East and gradual decrements as one moves North and West in Europe [16]. However, the model can be modified to incorporate a cultural rather than demic interpretation of the expansion of farming in Europe. The model as we have described it ignores the Mesolithic people already living in Europe and adopting a hunting and gathering subsistence strategy. However, more recent analyses of mitochondrial and Y chromosome DNA suggest that the demic component of farming diffusion in Europe, i.e., the replacement of Mesolithic hunters/gatherers by Neolithic farmers, may have been less strong than assumed by the demic expansion model [17 18 19]. Our model can be interpreted as assuming not that Mesolithic people were physically (genetically) canceled by the expanding farmers but that they adopted farming by cultural/technological assimilation to the successful farmers living in neighboring cells. In this cultural interpretation of the model farming, not farmers, expanded in previously non farming cells, with a greater probability for farming to be adopted by cells which were more suitable for farming.

We have run this cultural version of the model with results that are generally similar to those of the demic version. In particular, the tree of expansion paths matches the similarity structure of European languages equally well as the tree obtained with the demic model. This seems to indicate that geographical factors linked to suitability for farming of different regions of Europe and the point of origin of the process in Anatolia may be the critical factors that determine both the branching tree of expansions paths and the similarity structure of European languages. These factors play a role in both the demic and the cultural versions of the model.

One difference between the two models is that with the cultural model farming invades the whole of Europe in hundreds, not thousands, of cycles of the cellar automaton. But the cellular automaton should be temporally re-calibrated if the expansion is interpreted as cultural. In the demic model the expansion of farming is linked to demographic growth which can be very fast and can lead to migration of farmers in one year. Cultural adoption of farming may be much slower and one cycle of the cellular automata may correspond not to one year but to, say, 10 years. With these adjustments, there is correspondence between these two models even from this point of view.

Of course, one might also assume, and test, a mixed demic and cultural model, with the early expansion of farming in the geographical regions near to Anatolia mainly due to demic factors and later diffusion in the rest of Europe mainly due to cultural factors. In any case an important consequence of considering the cultural interpretation of the model is that additional historical data, not included in the present version of the model, can be integrated in the model such as demographic and geographical distribution data on Mesolithic people already living in Europe, including the changes in these data during the period considered [17 18 19].

6 Further developments of the model

The current version of the model assumes that languages or cultures with a common origin become more and more different with the increasing length of time elapsed since separation. But the phenomenon of progressive divergence which is simply 'assumed' in the current version of the model can be actually 'observed' by modifying the model.

The current model assumes that progressive differentiation is a function of time since separation in that internal changes accumulate in a culture or in a language and, provided there are no interactions among cells that may lead to unidirectional or reciprocal assimilation, these changes lead to progressive divergence with time. In the case of language this may result in the appearance first of different dialects and then of different languages. But imagine we explicitly model culture or language as a string of bits, with each bit indicating the presence (1) or absence (0) of a cultural or linguistic trait. The initial Anatolian cell is assigned a randomly generated bitstring that represents the culture or the language spoken by the original farmers in Anatolia 9000 years ago and expansion is modeled as copying the bitstring of an expanding cell in the cell which is being occupied. Intrinsic changes in culture/language are modeled as random changes in bitstrings that can occur with a given probability. This allows us to actually observe (in the simulation) the progressive differentiation that occurs as a function of the time elapsed from separation from a common cell, i.e., from a shared culture/language. Random changes in bitstrings accumulate and lead to progressive divergence.

The new model, which explicitly, although very schematically, represents cultures/languages, makes it possible to observe two important phenomena which it was impossible to simulate with the preceding version. First, the new model can simulate culture/language contact and cultural/linguistic influence or assimilation, which is another mechanism for cultural/linguistic change in addition to internal changes. The model can implement a variety of cultural or linguistic assimilation rules that can all be tested to identify the rule that gives the best approximation to historical data. One assimilation rule is that in each cycle the bitstring of every cell is modified by making, with a given probability, the value of one or more of the bits of the cell's bitstring identical to the value of the corresponding bit of the majority of neighboring cells that contain a bitstring (i.e., of already occupied neighboring cells). This implements the notion of 'frequency bias' proposed by Boyd and Richerson in their model of cultural change [20]: cultural/linguistic change is towards the most frequent value of a given trait. Another assimilation rule assumes that the value of each bit in a cell's bitstring is made identical, again with a given probability, to the value of the corresponding bit of one of the neighboring cells, either randomly selected or selected on the basis of the already existing similarity between the two cells – with existing similarity favoring further assimilation. (This last rule was proposed by Axelrod [21].)

It has already been shown, using abstract cellular automata in which there is no geography, i.e., no natural obstacles to interaction among cells, that starting from randomly assigned bitstrings and using a variety of assimilation rules, assimilation between neighboring cells does not lead to complete homogeneity, with all the cells eventually containing the same bitstring [21, 22]. On the contrary, stable boundaries tend to emerge between internally homogeneous neighboring regions comprising many cells (cultural or linguistic communities) and these boundaries keep the bitstrings of different regions different. If one uses Axelrod's assimilation rule which postulates assimilation with a single neighboring cell based on already existing similarity, this results from the fact that strong existing dissimilarity prevents assimilation. If one uses the majority assimilation rule, stable boundaries emerge because greater internal pressures not to change on a cell currently belonging to a given community tend to win over external pressures to change emanating from other neighboring communities. This is true even if the bitstrings of all the cells of the cellular automaton originate from a single cell possessing a single bitstring, as in our model, and are the result of a process of expansion accompanied by the random internal changes in each cell's bitstring that we have already discussed [22]. Furthermore, if one adds to the model an abstract geography of 'mountains' separating different groups of cells, the eventual number of different cultural/linguistic regions turns out to be even greater [22].

A second important phenomenon that can be observed with the new version of the model is the actual geographical extent of internally homogeneous cultural/linguistic regions/communities. The preceding version allowed us to identify the date of arrival to isolated cells in Europe and the path followed to reach each cell, and this made it possible to measure similarity between cells.

However, the preceding model tells us nothing about the geographical limits of multi-cell areas possessing the same culture or language. Explicitly representing cultures/languages as bitstrings allows us to determine which neighboring cells have the same culture/language, and therefore the geographical boundaries of internally homogeneous regions, and to observe how the number of different cultures/languages increases in Europe starting from the single culture/language of the original Anatolian cell.

Preliminary experiments show that the number of different cultures/ languages in Europe does not increase very much in the first 1000 cycles (first 1000 years after the beginning of the process, in the demic expansion model), increases moderately up until around cycle 3000, and has a more rapid increase after cycle 3000. However, if we allow the simulation to continue well beyond the completion of the farming diffusion process in the whole of Europe until cycle 8000, the number of different cultural/linguistic regions becomes stable. Predictably, the results tend to be sensitive not only to the type of assimilation rule which is adopted, but also to the length of the bitstring representing language/culture, with longer bitstrings producing more different cultural/linguistic regions, and to the rate of random mutations representing internal changes in cultures/languages, with higher rates again resulting in larger number of different regions. Furthermore, all these results are based on a notion of cultural/linguistic homogeneity which requires that all the cells in a cultural/linguistic region possess exactly the same bitstring. Weaker notions of cultural/linguistic homogeneity may require only a sufficient degree of similarity among cells belonging to the same region. Notice that a precise, quantitative notion of similarity/distance between two bitstrings can be used: the number of bits which have a different value in the two bitstrings (Hamming distance). This may allow us to identify sub-regions (dialects or sub-cultures) inside a region and gradients which can make boundaries between neighboring regions fuzzy rather than clear cut.

A further development of the model is to define in terms of the model a notion of 'ethnicity' and to make the probability of assimilation between the bitstrings of neighboring cells dependent on the degree of co-ethnicity of the cells. Two or more cells are considered as belonging to the same 'ethnos' if the they have a recent common ancestor cell, i.e., if the time since separation from a common ancestor cell is not too great. Two neighboring cells can belong to the same 'ethnos' but they can also belong to different 'ethnos' if they result from two spatially diverging expansion paths which for some reason have re-converged. Cultural/linguistic assimilation between two cells can reflect their co-ethnicity if the probability of assimilation between the two cells is a negative function of time elapsed since the time the two cells had a common ancestor cell.

7 Conclusion

We have simulated using a cellular automaton a demic model of the expansion of farming in Europe which began 9000 years ago in Anatolia and the correlated process of expansion and differentiation of European languages. The model is able to generate the yearly expansion rate of 1 km which appears to be supported by the archaeological evidence on the basis of local geographical data and the assumption of reasonable demographic expansion rates due to adoption of farming. Furthermore, by modeling the actual geographical paths followed by farmers in their expansion in Europe and their time of arrival to various geographical locations, the simulation generates a tree of progressive linguistic differentiation which matches rather well the similarity tree of European languages posited by linguists.

It is quite probable that the demic model of agricultural/linguistic expansion in Europe will have to take into consideration various expansion and migration processes which took place in Europe both before and after the Neolithic expansion and that it will have to consider in more detail the actual processes of demic substitution vs. technological/cultural expansion and of language change. However, the simulation reported in this paper appears to give some support to the hypothesis that links the expansion of farming to the differentiation of European languages and in any case it seems to capture important aspects of what took place in Europe during the Neolithic.

However, the goal of the present chapter was not to support a particular hypothesis concerning the origin and expansion of farming in Europe or the origin and differentiation of European languages. Our goal was to illustrate with some concrete examples the potential of computer simulations as a new way to express scientific theories and models in the social and historical sciences.

Simulations make it inevitable to express theories and models in explicit, detailed, quantitative terms, which is rarely the case for theories and models in the social and historical sciences. For example, in our simulation model we had to specify, in explicit, precise, quantitative terms, the critical factors that can account for the historical phenomena of farming expansion and linguistic differentiation: geographical maps, level of navigational technology and skills, demographical growth rates, types of cultural/linguistic assimilation rules, etc.

Furthermore, simulations generate a rich variety of results that represent the empirical predictions derived from the theory or model expressed in the simulation, and this gives a rich and detailed empirical content to theories which normally lack such a content and guarantees that specific empirical predictions actually derive from a theory/model. Our simulation generates results on time taken to reach particular regions in Europe, on paths followed to reach these regions, etc., and these predictions are guaranteed to actually derive from the assumptions of the model incorporated in the simulation.

Finally, simulations are virtual experimental laboratories in which the researcher can manipulate the conditions, variables, and value of parameters which influence the results that are obtained. In our simulation we can manipulate such conditions and parameter values as the geographical map underlying the simulation, the level of navigational technology/skill, the assimilation rules, the probability of internal changes in culture/languages, etc. This allows the researcher in the social and historical sciences to do experiments – a very powerful tool in the natural sciences – with phenomena that are too big, too complex, or are simply no more existent to be brought into the physical laboratory.

References

1 Von Neumann, J. (1966) Theory of self-reproducing automata. *Urbana*, Ill., University of Illinois Press.
2 Wolfram, S. (2002) *A New Kind of Science*. Wolfram Media.
3 Parisi, D. (1998) A cellular automata model of the expansion of the Assyrian empire. In Bandini, S., Serra, R. and Liverani, F.S. (eds) *Cellular Automata: Research towards Industry*. London, Springer.
4 Antinucci, F., Cecconi, F., Natale, F. and Parisi, D. (2002) *Simulating the Indo-European Expansion through a Cellular Automata*. Institute of Cognitive Sciences and Technologies, National Research Council, Rome.
5 Ammerman, A.J. and Cavalli-Sforza, L.L. (1984) *Neolithic Transition and the Genetics of Population in Europe*. Princeton, Princeton University Press.
6 Renfrew, C. (1987) Archaeology and language. *The Puzzle of Indo-European Origins*. London, Cape, J.
7 Semino, O., Passarino, G., Brega, A., Fellous, M. and Santachiara-Benerecetti, A. S. (1996) A view of the Neolithic demic diffusion in Europe through two Y chromosome-specific markers. *American Journal of Human Genetics*, 59, 964–968.
8 Cavalli-Sforza, L.L., Minch, E. and Mountain, J. (1992) Coevolution of genes and language revisited. *Proceedings of the National Academy of Science*, 89, 5620–5624.
9 Cavalli-Sforza, L.L. (2001) *Genes, Peoples, and Languages*. Los Angeles, University of California Press.
10 Diamond, J. (1997) Guns, germs, and steel. *The Fate of Human Societies*. New York. Norton.
11 Barbujani, G. and Bertorelle, G. (2001) Genetics and the population history of Europe. *Proceedings of the National Association of Sciences*, 98, 22–25.
12 Bellwood, R. (2001) Early agriculturalist population diasporas? Farming, languages, and genes. *Annual Review of Anthropology*, 30, 181–207.
13 Diamond and Bellwood.

14 Gimbutas, L. (1970) Proto-Indo-European culture: the Kurgan culture during the fifth, fourth and third millennia B.C. In G. Cardona, Hoenigswald, H.M. and Senn, A. (eds) *Indo-European and Indo-Europeans*. Philadephia, University of Pennsylvania Press, 155–197.
15 Gimbutas, M. (1980) The Kurgan wave migration (c. 3400–3200 B.C.) into Europe and the following transformation of culture. *Journal of Near Eastern Studies*, 8, 273–315.
16 Cavalli-Sforza, L.L., Menozzi, P. and Piazza, A. (1994) *The History and Geography of Human Genes*. Princeton, Princeton University Press.
17 Semino, O., Passarono, G., Oefner, P.J., Lin, A.A., Arbuzova, S., Beckman, L.E., De Benedictis, G., Francalacci, P., Kouvatsi, A., Limborska, S., Marcikiae, M., Mika, A., Mika, B., Primorac, D., Santachiara-Benerecetti, A.S., Cavalli-Sforza, L.L. and Underhill, P.A. (2000) The genetic legacy of Paleolithic Homo Sapiens in extant Europeans: a Y chromosome perspective, *Science*, 290, 1155–1159.
18 Torroni, A., Bandelt, H.J., D'Urbano, L., Lahermo, P., Moral, P., Sellitto, D., Rengo, C., Forster, P., Savontaus, M.L., Bonne-Tamir, B. and Scozzari, R. (1998) MtDNA analysis reveals a major late Paleolithic population expansion from Southwestern to Northeastern Europe, *American Journal of Human Genetics*, 62, 1137–1152.
19 Torroni, A., Bandelt, H.J., Macaulay, V., Richards, M., Cruciani, F., Rengo, C., Martinez-Cabrera, V., Villems, R., Kivisild, T., Metspalu, E., Parik, J., Tolk, H.V., Tambets, K., Forster, P., Karger, B., Francalacci, P., Rudan, P., Janicijevic, B., Rickards, O., Savontaus, M.L., Huoponen, K., Laitinen, V., Koivumaki, S., Sykes, B., Hickey, E., Novelletto, A., Moral, P., Sellitto, D., Coppa, A., Al-Zaheri, N., Santachiara-Benerecetti, A.S., Semino, P. and Scozzari, R. (2001) A signal, from human mtDNA, of post-glacial recolonization in Europe. *American Journal of Human Genetics*, 69, 844–852.
20 Boyd, R. and Richerson, P.J. (1985) *Culture and the Evolutionary Process*. Chicago, Chicago University Press .
21 Axelrod, R. (1997) The dissemination of culture: a model with local convergence and global polarization. *Journal of Conflict Resolution*, 41, 203–226.
22 Parisi, D., Cecconi, F. and Natale, F. (2003) Cultural change in spatial environments: the role of cultural assimilation and of internal changes in cultures. *Journal of Conflict Resolution*, 47, 163–179.

10 Colin Renfrew's hypothesis on the Near-Eastern origin of the original Indo-European people: an evaluation

Jean-Paul Demoule
University of Paris I

When it appeared in 1987[1], the book of the British archaeologist Colin Renfrew, *Archaeology & Language. The Puzzle of Indo-European Origins*, did not come out of nowhere, contrary to what its significant media impact might lead one to believe. To the contrary, it was situated within a continuous scientific tradition that goes back to the very origins of the Indo-European question. In reality, it only brings up to date a traditional hypothesis that had been allowed to fall into oblivion due to the quite recent impact of Marija Gimbutas' proposals concerning steppic invasions. These proposals had themselves reopened the debate on the original homeland, which had somewhat quietened down apart from a few exceptions (of which Bosch-Gimpera) since 1945. Renfrew's thesis is simple, and besides, its development only occupies at most a tenth of the three hundred pages of the work, that is devoted essentially to a quite pedagogical exposition of all the historiographical and methodological problems posed by the 'Indo-European enigma': the Neolithic farmers coming from the Near-East who colonized Europe from the end of the VIIth millennium were Indo-Europeans, whose original homeland can thus be situated in Turkey.

The reaffirmation of this ancient hypothesis was nevertheless in part a paradox with respect to the intellectual background of Colin Renfrew. In the period after the war, British archaeologists had positioned themselves rather against the diffusionist tradition of German archaeology. From the 1960s onwards — and due also to radiocarbon datings — they tended to insist on the autonomy of European development. Thus dolmens and menhirs were traditionally considered to be faraway consequences of the Egyptian pyramids. In his intellectual testament, Childe recalled ironically that a large part of his work had been carried out under 'the unifying theme of the irradiation of European barbarism by Oriental civilization'[2]. Radiocarbon dating now shows that these megalithic monuments predate the renowned pyramids by around three millennia, a fact which provided Renfrew with the title of one of his books ('The Radiocarbon Revolution', 1973) that echoed the 'Neolithic revolution' of Childe, derived from the Near-East. He also pleaded in favor of an 'independent invention' of metallurgy in Europe, having no link with the Middle East, whereas in the same period, other Anglo-Saxon archaeologists even claimed that the European Neolithic had been invented in situ, without any Near-Eastern influence. More generally, Anglo-Saxon archaeology between 1960 and 1970, having rapidly proclaimed itself as 'the new Archaeology', was characterized by the particular attention that it gave to the study of the environment and prehistoric ecology, to adaptive processes in situ, of ancient societies, whilst giving precedence to evolution rather than to diffusion as well as to the necessity for a rigorous reasoning and proof apparatus. Colin Renfrew himself had organized the publication of several collective works on methodology and theory that insisted on the necessity in archaeology of constructing more complex explanatory models.

It is for these reasons that it might appear as extremely surprising that one of the leading figures of that particular form of archaeology could suddenly show such a great interest in one of the most traditional, if not outdated, problems of German archaeology, around which all diffusionist and migrationist debates turned. Nevertheless, precisely because Colin Renfrew was a well-respected archaeologist, his book was immediately highly successful and was translated into several languages, including Japanese (amongst books translated from English it was the bestseller in Japan during the year of its publication). It was the subject of numerous interventions in media, and several journals published far-reaching debates on its claims, such as Antiquity in Great Britain, Current Anthropology in the USA, or even (at a more modest French level) the journal Topoï of University Lyon II[3]. In works destined for a general readership, the claim of the Near-Eastern origin of Indo-Europeans became quite rapidly presented as obvious and generally accepted[4]. A short time later, Colin Renfrew was knighted by Queen Elizabeth II. The only other British archaeologist to have received this honor before him was John Lubbock in 1900, the creator of the terms 'Neolithic' and 'Palaeolithic', and an ardent defender of diffusionism in his own time.

It is known that the original homeland must comply with two conditions: a) to be able to prove its 'Indo-Europeaness'; b) it must be the epicenter of a migratory phenomenon. Colin Renfrew acquits himself of these two tasks with elegance, by retaining the only major migratory movement that was almost unanimously accepted amongst European prehistorians, thus dispensing himself with the first condition. In the present case there is therefore little to be debated concerning the reality of the migration of Neolithic farmers; rather the question can be raised as to what allows this historical fact to be associated with Indo-Europeans. Indeed, several points raise problems that are worth being taken up in detail:

a) Indo-European languages are little represented in the supposed homeland;

b) the resemblances between Indo-European languages are not organized in a way that follows the axis of the Neolithic colonization of Europe;

c) the wave of colonization of Neolithic Europe, supposedly Indo-European, has allowed non-Indo-European languages to subsist;

d) the so-called 'common vocabulary' of the reconstructed Proto-Indo-European language contains no term that evokes Mediterranean flora and fauna;

e) finally, Neolithic societies, as they are revealed by archaeology to be simple and egalitarian, possess none of the characteristics that are frequently used by comparative studies bearing on myths, vocabulary and institutions, that suggest a warlike and highly hierarchical Proto-Indo-European society.

1 The linguistic situation

Indeed, as for the first point, it is highly surprising that the proposed original homeland should be a zone where there might have been very few Indo-European languages in historical times. In the Near East, Semitic languages were mostly spoken (Arcadian, Aramean, Hebrew, Phoenician, Arabic, etc.) as well as languages that were neither Indo-European nor Semitic: Sumerian and Elamitic in Mesopotamia, Hattian and Hurrian in Asia Minor. The only certified Indo-European languages are those of Turkey: Hittite, Luvian and Palaite in the second millennium, and, no doubt related, Lycian, Lydian and Phrygian in the first millennium before the present era. Recognizing this difficulty, Renfrew therefore proposes to limit the original homeland of Indo-European languages only to Turkey. But Turkey is not a primary site of Neolithisation. As we mentioned above, the original zone of the domestication of animals and plants comprises essentially modern day Syria, Israel, Palestine and occidental Iraq[5]. Besides, this is what genetic DNA analyses of cereals and animals confirm. It was only later on, from the end of the eighth millennium that the constantly growing Neolithic populations spread out in different directions, and in particular towards Turkey. The site of Catal Hüyük, in the southwest of this country, is justly famous in this respect. It is thus completely improbable that Neolithic farmers, who appeared and developed in a geographical zone where, in historical times, the only attested languages are Semitic ones, could have transformed themselves, by spreading out into Turkey, into speakers of Indo-European languages.

There might be three possible ripostes. The first one, that Renfrew does not even attempt, would be to assume that the extension of the Neolithic from Syria and Iraq might be only a phenomenon of borrowing, without movement of populations. But it is the totality of the material culture of the original zone that can be found in Turkey where previously, the Mesolithic peoples were evanescent.

The second possible riposte, which Renfrew does not think of using in the original version of his work, but that he subsequently puts forward[6], would make the Indo-European languages of Turkey (Hittite, Palaite, Luvian, etc., cf. supra) the direct descendants of the original language. To be logical, they should be the closest to them. Now precisely, the position of Hittite in the genealogical tree of Indo-European languages is problematic. In effect, this language was the last to have been discovered, in the 1920s, whilst comparative grammar had already been completely created. Once it was deciphered by Hrozny, this came to disturb the tranquil confidence of Antoine Meillet, thirty years earlier, who, in the first edition of his *Introduction à l'Etude Comparative des Langues Indo-Européennes* (1903), estimated that comparative grammar had reached a 'term that could not be surpassed', and that no new findings could be expected[7]. The famous linguist was for a time reticent to Hrozny's discoveries[8], and thenceforth minimized their importance. Nevertheless, the position of Hittite remains today a subject of debate. For some, it is such a specific language that it must be classified apart; following the work of Emil Forrer then that of Sturtevant during the 1920s, it has even been proposed that the englobing term 'Indo-Hittite' should be created, to designate an even wider family of languages, whose two branches would be on the one hand, the 'classical' Indo-European languages, and on the other, Hittite and other less well known Anatolian languages. For others, to the contrary, Hittite might have gone through a process of degradation. Finally, for even others, Hittite might be a sort of pidgin, a contact language between a strong non-European language substrate (in particular, Hatti) and an invaders' Indo-European language, with strong influences of Mesopotamian languages[9]. In summary, Hittite, the most ancient known Indo-European language, poses major classificatory difficulties that are far from having been resolved. In all cases, it is therefore difficult to see in it the direct descendent from the original language, spoken in the supposed original homeland.

This was nevertheless precisely what was attempted. In effect, in parallel to the work of Renfrew, in 1988, the linguist Aaron Dolgoposky, one of the proponents of the nostratic theory[10], had taken up the Indo-Hittite hypothesis, whilst insisting of the possibility of linguistic contacts between Indo-European languages, the languages of the southern Caucasus (Kartvelian, of which Georgian is the most well known), and Semitic languages. These contacts were supposedly proven by a certain number of neighboring words, either borrowed from one linguistic group by another, or else going back to a common ancestor (this is the nostratic hypothesis). In all cases, the most plausible geographical zone for such contacts would be Turkey, which thus motivates placing there the original Indo-European birthplace. In all cases, the approach was not new. Such possible contacts between proto-Indo-European and Semitic had been pointed out since the 19th century, including in particular similarities concerning the number seven, words for bull, star, sun, wine, goat, salt, etc., adding up to between around twenty and forty close roots, according to researchers. This is why, as we mentioned earlier, several linguists who interested themselves in the localization of the original homeland, beyond any form of archaeological argumentation, have regularly proposed a near Middle-East homeland, this being assumed to be a possible zone of contact between these two linguistic families. Thus, without going back to Sayce, Hodge had assumed in 1981 an Egyptian original homeland, whereas Gamkrelidze and Ivanov, drawing on possible contacts with Caucasian languages, as had done Dolgoposky, at the same period had fixed the homeland in these high mountains[11].

However, while having being put forward during the same years, the respective hypotheses of Renfrew and of Dolgoposky seemed to come together via independent routes, this being a fact that did not fail to be pointed out. Nevertheless, such an encounter only holds up if: the general hypothesis of Renfrew is demonstrated (which is precisely what is being discussed here); if the 'Indo-Hittite' hypothesis, and its specific variant that would make Anatolian languages separated the earliest from the Indo-European genealogical tree, was also validated (which is far from being the case, as we have seen); and finally, if the phenomena of linguistic contact proposed by Dolgopolsky could be interpreted and datable from the Neolithic. Whilst Dolgopolsky, in his article of 1988, seems to assume rather that it is a matter of borrowing, one can accept the hypothesis of a common and even earlier origin, which brings us to the third possible riposte.

In effect, the third riposte to this weak representation of Indo-European languages in the hypothetical homeland consists in grouping together the entire set of languages of the Near Middle East into a single linguistic family. This is what Renfrew elaborated a short time after the publication of his book, at the time of the spectacular emergence of the work of American geneticists and linguists, who claimed to have reconstructed a global genealogical tree of all the world's languages and, simultaneously, all of the genes of the world. According to this 'big tree' hypothesis, modern human beings appeared around 100 000 years ago in East Africa (which is also known as the African Eve scenario) in the form of a quite restricted group speaking an original language. This group is supposed to have subsequently spread out over the whole planet, replacing the ancient homo erectus everywhere and dispersing its genes, whilst on the other hand, in each region, successive linguistic evolutions led to the creation of the present day 6000 languages, all descending from the same ancestor. The analysis of present day human genes, as with current languages, effectively would allow a global genealogical tree to be reconstructed, where each genetic family coincides strikingly with a linguistic family[12].

It is within the framework of this general model that Renfrew couches a specific hypothesis: the majority of linguistic diffusion could be linked to the diffusion of agriculture, generally by migration, during the most recent millennia. More precisely, the hunter-gatherers of the Natoufian culture, within which progressively emerged agriculture and stockbreeding around 9000 years before our era, would have been speakers of a particular language, corresponding not only to Indo-European languages, but also to several other linguistic families, of which Semitic languages. When, following their strong demographic growth, itself being due to a better nutritional system, the proto-farmers went out from their birthplace, spreading out little by little in different directions, the mother languages of different principal linguistic families might have been formed by schizogenesis. Thus, the Indo-European language would have been created from the moment when the farmers came to inhabit Turkey, the ancestor of all Semitic languages would have been undoubtedly formed in situ, the ancestor of the 'Elamo-Dravidian' group would have been formed in Mesopotamia, from where certain farmers would have continued their route up to the south of India. In this way, the few similarities between Indo-European languages and other linguistic groups would be explained, that have been brought to light for more than a century. But above all, on an obviously even more speculative level, would thus be resolved the paradox of making the Indo-European people originate from an essentially Semitic linguistic zone.

This much is well known, together with the wide popularity that the 'big tree' model currently enjoys, together with its numerous weaknesses. Firstly, the approach contented itself with bringing together the genetic tree and the linguistic tree, and in showing how their branches coincided. Such branches were not themselves precisely dated in time, other than by the approximate techniques of the 'molecular clock' and by the much more contentious glottochronological approach[13]. Correspondences with particular historical events were therefore not established. Renfrew's approach thus came to provide such an historical incarnation: not only in the Near East, but also over a major part of the planet, the expansion of the main linguistic families might coincide with the expansion of farmer-breeders to the detriment of hunter-gatherers, whose demography was much weaker. No one denies that during the last ten millennia, farmer-breeders have progressively eliminated societies of hunter-gatherers from the planet, by assimilation or destruction. It is generally accepted that the Near Eastern epicenter is responsible for the Neolithisation of all of western Asia, of a large part of North Africa and of the totality of Europe. But can one make this general historical phenomenon fit with linguistic facts?

Such an affirmation depends on at least two strong hypotheses:

a) that one can reconstruct a genealogical tree for the set of linguistic groups involved in this process.

b) that one can reconstruct the migratory pathway of speakers of each of these linguistic groups, whilst relating in space and time, from the Near-Eastern epicenter, a chain of archaeological cultures leading up to societies whose languages are identified, in the manner that Renfrew had proposed initially for only the Indo-European group.

The first question is only a specific and local case of the great general tree. The idea that Indo-European languages might only be particular cases goes back, if not to the Tower of Babel, at least to Franz Bopp, the founder of comparative grammar, who tried out comparisons well beyond the Indo-European group, and even up to Oceania. Possible relationships between Indo-European, Semitic, Finno-Ugrian (Hungarian, Finnish, Estonian, Lappish, Mordvian, Yukaghir, etc.), or even Caucasian and Dravidian languages from Southern India, were regularly proposed during the 19th century. This was what had led Alfredo Trombetti to propose in 1905 a tree of all the languages of the world[14]. At the same time, Meillet pointed out, without giving details, 'striking concordances' between these different families of languages. Whilst calling for restraint, he did not exclude the possibility of constructing an even vaster tree, but with some limits: 'one glimpses only that all the languages of the 'white' race have relationships between them'[15]. In fact, the primitive language that was supposed to be at the origin of the languages of Europe, Western Asia and North Africa was baptized 'nostratic' ('our' language, in opposition to others'). After Holger Pedersen in the 1920s[16], such research fell somewhat into oblivion, until it started up again in the 1960s with the soviet linguist Vladimir Illic-Svityc, who even took on the task of creating a dictionary of nostratic[17]. After his premature death, his school of thought pursued his work; the fall of the soviet block, in favoring East-West contacts, soon came to give this research a wider and much more numerous audience, this being marked by numerous joint publications[18]. The nostratic tendency was soon to be rejoined by and mutually influenced by the universalistic endeavors of Joseph Greenberg and Merritt Ruhlen.

Nonetheless, regarding the precise question posed here, it must be recognized that the situation of these commonalities is rather confused. In fact, in Meillet's period, proximities were sketched out between Indo-European, Semitic languages (Hebrew, Arabic, Akkadian, Arameian, Phoenician, etc.), Hamitic languages (linked to the precedent: Egyptian, Coptic, Ethiopian languages, etc.), languages of the Caucasus, Finno-Ugrian or Ouralian languages and Altaic languages (Turkish, Mongolian, Tunguz and similar languages, that can sometimes be grouped together with Finno-Ugrian languages, in an unique 'Ouralo-Altaic' group). Vladimir Illic-Svityc groups the set of these languages together in his own nostratic. He nevertheless makes a distinction amongst Caucasian languages between those from the south (Kartvelian), that belong to nostratic, and those from the north that are foreign to it; and he adds the Dravidian language group to it. On the other hand, the classification of Greenberg and Ruhlen is quite different: they in fact define a vast 'Eurasiatic', that includes the Indo-European groups, the Ouralo-Altaic group (to which they add Corean, Japanese and Ainou), Eskimo and Aleutian languages, and the Siberian languages of Tchouktches and Kamchatka. This 'Eurasiatic' is in turn grouped together in an even wider set, called 'Eurasian-Amerindian', covering most of Eurasia, the Americas and North Africa, and including, besides 'Eurasiatic', four other groups: 'Amerind' (corresponding to most Amerindian languages), the Dravidian group, Kartvelian of the southern Caucasus, and 'Afro-Asiatic', to which correspond approximately the Hamito-Semitic group of languages. The only languages that are classified separately are those of Sub-Saharan Africa, of South-West Asia and South-East Oceania, as well as a 'Dene-Caucasian' group, including Chinese, Tibetan, Basque, Burushaski (a little spoken isolated language of the north of Pakistan), Ienissean Siberian, North Caucasian languages, certain North-American languages, or even Sumerian[19].

There is thus no concurrence between the two classifications, even if 'Eurasian-American', given its planetary importance, includes both of them. Certainly, Merrit Ruhlen treats the defenders of nostratic with a great deal of consideration[20]; it is true that the philological erudition of the Russian linguists is considerable, and that their attempts to establish connections are much more detailed than the limited and succinct comparisons in which he invites the reader to participate. At first sight, the greater seniority of the nostratic tradition could seem to give credence to the Greenbergian tree. On closer examination, the differences between the two systems weaken each of them. Since the bases of each are the same, the difficulties that each face are also the same: they correspond to methods for establishing similarities that do not depend on incontestable and testable linguistic bases[21]. As is the case for any genealogical linguistic research, but with much more evanescent data, it is a question of firstly looking for resemblances between words, then interpreting them (a common source? subsequent borrowings? chance?). It is not without interest to point out yet again the uncertainties of such a method, just as much as the circular interdisciplinary effect with the big genetic tree.

But it is above all the historical explanation of this possible linguistic diffusion that poses problem –this is the second (external) point that was raised by the nostratic hypothesis, apart from its internal coherency. From the point of view of Greenberg and Ruhlen, from its African birthplace, humanity might have firstly been separated between carriers of Sub-Saharan languages, remaining where they were, and all others, who were destined to populate the rest of the planet. The first to leave would have been carriers of languages which would become those of South-East Asia, Oceania and Australia, then the 'Dene-Caucasian' group, which would have occupied most of Eurasia. But a final group is suppose to have separated in turn — the 'Eurasian-American' group — whose expansion might have been even greater, since it might have populated the Americas, North Africa, and above all, with its 'Eurasiatic' sub-group, Eurasia and, in the latter region, to the detriment of the previous group, which, with the exception of the Sino-Tibetan group, would have found itself confined to insular regions (Caucasus, Basque, Burushaski, Ienissean, etc.). This 'Eurasiatic' sub-group, according to Ruhlen, 'probably itself originates in the Near-East'[22]. Unfortunately, he has no argument in favor of this (for example, in a possible common vocabulary which would have described an environment of the Near-Eastern kind).

In using in turn the Greenbergian language tree, Renfrew has added a supplementary historical argument: the diffusion of most of the major linguistic families might correspond to that of agriculture. This can nevertheless not be the case with the 'Eurasian-American' macro-family of Greenberg-Ruhlen, since it includes the 'Amerind' group, to which is owed the first colonization of America, from the Bering Straits, but which was carried out by Paleolithic hunter-gatherers; agriculture would only appear much later, in Meso-America, and in the Andean zone. But neither can this be the case at the lower level of the 'Eurasiatic' group, since it also includes well-known hunter-gatherer societies in ancient times, such as the speakers of the Tchouktch-Kamchatka, Eskimo-Aleutian and Ouralian languages, and at least a part of Altaic languages (above all if one allows the addition of Japanese and Ainou in this group). Neither the dispersion of the 'Eurasian-American' nor 'Eurasiatic' groups can therefore coincide with that of agriculture from the Near-Eastern epicenter; if such migrations had existed, they are thus anterior to agriculture. It is thus necessary to assume the existence of successive migratory phases, beginning with hunter-gatherers, then farmers. But each of them co-exists with different branchings of the Greenberg-Ruhlen classification, as with the interior of nostratic. In this case, everything becomes possible, which is more convenient, but nothing is therefore verifiable.

In fact, one could restrict oneself to conserving, within nostratic, only the languages associated to notoriously agricultural societies, at historically known periods –and this is more or less what Renfrew does. The Near-Eastern linguistic homeland postulated by Ruhlen, would thus be the agricultural homeland recognized by archaeology, and from it would have separated respectively bearers of Semitic languages (remaining where they were or having left towards North Africa), the Dravidian group (having left for India after having left Elamite in Mesopotamia), the Indo-European group having gone towards Anatolia, and the South-Caucasian group, having left towards the mountains of the same name. Yet on one hand, such reasoning is strictly circular, from a methodological point of view: since there was diffusion of agriculture, there must have been linguistic diffusion and thus a common source to the different agricultural civilizations of western Eurasia; since the affinities between several linguistic families allow a common source to be postulated, there must necessarily have been a general expansion of populations from the original homeland. Here we return, one notch higher, to the problems posed by the equation: Indo-European expansion = Neolithic colonization of Europe.

But besides, several classificatory problems are raised, even if one accepts the demonstrated affinities. On one hand, the expansion of the vast group of Finno-Ugrian (or Ouralian) and Altaic languages from this given common homeland is not explained archaeologically (Renfrew dates it, without explanation, from after the diffusion of agriculture[23]); but for the nostratic theory, these languages are as close to Indo-European languages as they are to Semitic ones, and are even closer for Greenberg's theory. Moreover, Renfrew's model assumes that proto-Indo-European would have separated from proto-Semitic at the time of the extension of the Neolithic to Turkey, that is to say towards 7500 BC, since European proto-Indo-European would have been separated from that of Turkey (i.e. the ancestor of languages that are termed Anatolian, such as Hittite) at the moment when the Neolithic reached the Balkanic peninsula, i.e. towards 6500 BC. According to any linguistic logic, one should expect relatively strong linguistic relationships between Hittite and Semitic languages. This is not the case, to the extent that, as we have discussed, for Greenberg and Ruhlen, Semitic languages (conceived within their 'Afro-Asiatic' group) are further from Indo-European languages than Japanese or Eskimo ...

Thus, in summary, the first question raised by Renfrew's hypothesis, that is, the weak presence of Indo-European languages in the common homeland, does not receive a satisfactory response. One could even add that the initially supposed, and subsequently defended, affinities between Indo-European languages and other linguistic groups, of which Semitic languages, pose more problems than they resolve, since the proximities that should be expected can not be found. The structure of possible proximities, in this case internal ones, is the subject of a second line of questioning.

2 Linguistic relationships

Indeed, if Indo-European languages were diffused at the same time as the Neolithic colonization of Europe, it would be legitimate to expect that one could find a gradient of resemblances between successively close languages from the southeast towards the northeast[24]. Thus Greek and Albanian (and other less well-known ancient Balkanic languages) should be very close to each other, and also close to on the one hand, Anatolian languages (situated in the assumed 'cradle') and on the other hand, Italic languages (the Neolithic spread itself out from both Central Europe, going up the Danube valley, and following the Mediterranean coast). Then, the group of Celtic languages, localized in the first millennium before our era between Bohemia and the Parisian basin, should make a bridge between the precedent languages, implanted on the Mediterranean, and the Germanic languages of Northern Europe. The two latter groups should entertain special relationships with Baltic and Slavic languages, situated in the North East. Indo-Iranian languages, placed even further to the east, should therefore have special relationships with Slavic languages, as in the case of Tokharian, the easternmost of the Indo-European languages. Finally, Armenian, situated in the Caucasus, should be quite close to Anatolian languages, and notably Hittite. Since this should be a phenomenon of progressive diffusion from a given origin point, the genealogical tree of European languages should be organized according to such a diffusion.

Now this is not the case. We know that there is no current consensus amongst linguists concerning the precise organization of the genealogical tree of the set of Indo-European languages. Even the erstwhile traditional classification between 'centum' languages to the west and 'satem' languages to the east has been abandoned, all the more so given that Tokharian, being the easternmost, is a 'centum' language. And amongst the currently competing trees, none of them suggest the proximities suggested above. Only the classification sketched out by Kroeber a long time ago[25] — but which did not have a genealogical structure — expressed geographical affinities. One could retort that known Indo-European languages only go back to (in the case of the oldest) 1500 years before our era (Hittite, Mycenian, Sanskrit), and much less for most of them, whereas the arrival of the Neolithic in Europe took place around 6500–6300 BC: during the intervening five thousand years, many transformations could have occurred, either internally, in the subsequent evolution of each language, or else externally, given that their current geographical positions as they are known in historical times no longer reflect their initial situation at the moment of the colonization of Europe as a result of probable successive migrations. Thus it has often been assumed that the historical Greeks had only reached Greece during the Bronze Age; the situation of modern day Slaves dates from the beginning of the Middle Ages; as is well known, Romance languages originate from the expansion of the Roman Empire; Celtic languages, after a wide expansion in the last centuries before our era, have seen their territory strongly reduced by Germanic and Romance languages. Nonetheless, admitting that successive migrations have befuddled original geographico-genealogical relations between Indo-European languages up to the point of rendering them unreadable comes down to saying that one cannot say anything on this subject.

Just about the same thing goes with respect to the possibility of reconstructing the internal evolution of each family of Indo-European languages during all these unknown millennia. Some such attempts have been made. For Dolgoposky[26], once the Indo-Europeans had arrived in the Balkanic peninsula from their Anatolian homeland, a new linguistic fragmentation would have occurred, from which would have spread out ulterior migrations. By way of proof: the proportionally higher number of Indo-European languages in the Balkans, with respect to the rest of Europe, which would make this region a stepping stone for Indo-European dispersion. Nevertheless, if one excludes the languages which came late into the Balkanic peninsula (meridional Slavic languages, Rumanian and related Valak dialects), together with those whose Balkanic origin is controversial (Armenian), most of these ancient Balkanic languages are little known (Illyrian, Thracian, Dacian, Ancient Macedonian, or even 'Pelasgic'), and the knowledge of their existence is only due to the presence on their frontiers of literate civilizations; further to the north, they would have left no trace.

Likewise, Colin Renfrew has attempted to take on an old hypothesis, relating to 'Old-European' ('Alteuropäisch'), and originating in the German linguist Hans Krahe[27]. This term had nothing to do with the 'alteuropäisch' of the German archaeologist Max Ebert, who had designated the Neolithic cultures of the Balkans under this term[28]. On the basis of the study of a certain number of names for places and waterways across several regions of Europe, these being reputedly conservative words, Krahe had made the hypothesis of an archaic linguistic layer, being both Indo-European in its roots yet not connectable to a precise given language. For example, the same names for rivers, such as 'Alba' or 'Ara' can be found from England across through Germany. He had thus considered them to be the language of the original Indo-Europeans, once they had come to Europe. Such studies of toponyms and hydronyms are besides amongst the great classics of research on vanished languages, whether they are presumed to be Indo-European or pre-Indo-European, and have given rise to innumerable and mostly unverifiable speculations[29]. They have been particularly developed by linguists of Balkanic countries, on one hand, because they have available certain linguistic sources, thanks to Latin and Greek texts mentioning names of places, peoples or people from 'barbaric' countries; but also because, in these new nations that have been divided up and 'Balkanised' according to the whims of Western powers, the reconstruction of a distant past, at whatever cost, whether imaginary or not, was essentially at stake, if not a national cause. Even if these linguistic fossils are precious -faute de mieux- it would be perilous to see in them the slightest demonstration in favor of Renfrew's thesis, or, for that matter, of any other.

Two other British archaeologists, Andrew and Susan Sherratt[30], in a discussion of Colin Renfrew's thesis, have wished to add their contribution to it, in assuming that from the Anatolian homeland, Indo-European languages dispersed themselves throughout Europe in the form of a 'koïnê' (the name given to the dispersion of Greek during the Hellenistic period following the conquests of Alexander and far reaching commercial contacts), which pushes back yet further the frontiers of unverifiability. It was nevertheless a closely related hypothesis that Renfrew took up around a dozen years later. Adding nuances to his initial model, he assumed that such a 'koïnê' — or 'Sprachbund', according to a term derived from areal linguistics, explicitly borrowed from Trubetzkoy — could have been created in the Balkanic peninsula, thanks to prolonged cultural contacts during all of the Neolithic and Chalcolithic periods[31]. Whilst the Neolithic colonization of Western-Mediterranean Europe could have given birth to Italic languages, and the initial colonization of temperate Europe by the 'Culture of Linear Ceramic' (or LBK) could have achieved the same effect for Celtic and Germanic languages, the rest of Indo-European languages would have originated from such a Balkanic 'Sprachbund'. As for Tokharian, it is assumed to be the distant residue of the initial colonization of the Pontic steppes. Such a Balkanic 'Sprachbund' would account for the relatedness of the Indo-European languages termed 'satem', the others being grouped in the 'kentum' languages. Without mentioning the pertinence of this ancient division, which is often considered obsolete, it is clear that this new hypothesis, being even more speculative than Renfrew's genealogical tree, partly inspired by that of the linguist Adrados[32], is just as criticisable as many others: for example, it does not account for the numerous affinities between Baltic and Germanic languages. It also assumes as given that the Neolithisation of the steppes was carried out from the Balkans (this is one of the pillars of his critique of the 'steppic' theory). The demonstration of continuities in the archaeological material culture, between the Balkanic Chalcolithic Sprachbund and the different historically attested Indo-European languages, as well as those derived from them, is not carried out either.

In summary, there is no satisfactory reply to the second objection posed to Renfrew's model, i.e. that of the geographico-genealogical structure assumed by the model.

3 The non-Indo-European languages of ancient Europe

The third objection is the existence of non-Indo-European languages in the heart of the Eurasiatic space that was occupied by the wave of Neolithic colonization originating in the Near East. These non-Indo-European languages have diverse statuses and histories. The late arrival of certain of them is in fact historically documented: the Hungarians in the 9th century of our era in the Carpathian basin; the proto-Bulgarians, speakers of an Altaic language, in Bulgaria during the 7th century; the Ottoman Turks in the Balkanic peninsula from the 13th century onwards. Others have occupied the northern margins of Europe, certainly from ancient times. This is the case of Finno-Ugrian or 'Uralian' languages: Lappish (or Saami), Finnish, Estonian, Tcheremiss, etc., and it is from their group that Hungarians were separated. The current geographical placing of these languages constitutes in a certain manner a northern limit to the extension of Indo-European languages of Europe. Likewise, the interpenetration of different linguistic groups of Asia does not pose specific problems. However, without counting the numerous languages of the Caucasus, there exists one modern language –Basque- and several ancient languages that are not considered to be Indo-European, and which find themselves enclaved in the middle of the Indo-European group.

Amongst these ancient languages, the oldest is that which is notated by 'Linear A' writing in Crete, in the 2nd millennium before our era, that of the first Cretan palaces. It has not yet been decoded but is normally distinguished from the Indo-European group. In the 1st millennium before our era, Etruscan of northern Italy is in the same situation, despite a few relatively unconvincing attempts to establish its proximity with Indo-European[33]. At the same period, the languages of the Iberian peninsula are just as little known, and were transcribed into alphabets of Mediterranean inspiration at the moment when forms of civilization based on the state and urban life appeared in the south and in the east of the peninsula; they are also considered to be non-Indo-European[34]. Finally,

Pict, known by names of places and people, together with a few inscriptions from the medieval period, is considered to be a non-Indo-European language spoken in Scotland before the arrival of the Celts[35].

In response to the existence of these linguistic enclaves, Colin Renfrew replies that either they are languages that are prior to Neolithic colonization, that have resisted against it, or else they are languages that were installed subsequently – an alternative that corresponds to commonsense. The first hypothesis has been developed even further in the planetary model of Greenberg and Ruhlen[36], even if they do not deal with the case of rare languages (Linear A, Pict, Etruscan, Iberian). We should recall that Basque belongs to the vast 'Dene-Caucasian' assemblage, that includes amongst others the languages of the northern Caucasus, the infinitely small Burushaski language of Pakistan, the vast Sino-Tibetan group, Ienissean, and the Na-Dene languages of North America. This assemblage is supposed to correspond to a first wave of expansion, from the Near-Eastern homeland, across all of Eurasia. The expansion that followed it, called 'Eurasian-American', is assumed to have pushed the previous one into its currently reduced form, with the obvious difficulties already mentioned of distinguishing what is due to agriculture in the Renfrew variant.

This hypothesis is nevertheless contradicted, if one looks concretely at archaeological evidence, by the regular and methodical progression of the Neolithic colonization that archaeologists can follow almost step by step, from the southeast towards the north west of the European continent. It is know that three zones of ancient Neolithisation can in fact be identified in Europe: that of the Balkans, from around 6300 BC, characterized by very homogeneous painted ceramics throughout the whole of the peninsula; that of the Mediterranean coast, from around 5700 BC, also associated with homogeneous material culture, of which pottery decorated with points and sea shells; finally, from the Balkanic zone, that of all of temperate Europe, from around 5300 BC, associated with engraved pottery motifs called 'Linear Ceramic' or LBK, that would soon extend to the shores of the Black Sea to those of the Atlantic Ocean and the southern Alps, up to the north of the Baltic. At the beginning of the 5th millennium, the whole of the continent was neolithised, apart from the fringes, following this continuous process.

Apart from these fringes (the Baltic and Black Sea coasts), nothing allows us to distinguish isolated areas where neolithisation would have resulted from a process of adoption or borrowing of the Neolithic mode of production by local populations of hunter-gatherers. Neither the north of Italy, nor the Iberian peninsula (if one excludes independentist claims by some Basque archaeologists) in particular, have divergent behavior. As for Great Britain, once architecture and stockbreeding appeared there, towards the end of the 5th millennium, it was with a material and symbolic culture (monumental funereal architecture, major ceremonial circles) that is in all respects comparable to that of the continent at the same period. Symmetrically, in the zones where phenomena of cultural integration have been pointed out, around the Baltic and to the north of the Black Sea, no known non-Indo-European language exists. As for the second hypothesis, i.e. the subsequent arrival of non-Indo-European speakers, in the regions concerned, it is not supported by any archaeological evidence whatsoever either.

There is obviously a third hypothesis, which would have the merit of economy: all of these non-Indo-European languages, being in general badly understood and not decoded, might in fact be Indo-European. The obscurity of documented evidence allows such an hypothesis to be at least put forward, all the more so since just about everything has been attempted by way of decoding and there exists at least one linguist who has taken the risk (and others who have refuted such an attempt). This is quite well the case for Etruscan, for Cretan Linear A, and even for 'Tartessian', one of the Iberian languages[37]. Renfrew evokes this Indo-European hypothesis in passing, for Etruscan and Tartessian, whereas he attempted to put it to the test himself on the problem of Minoan[38].

Thus, in summary with respect to this difficulty relating to the presence of non-Indo-European isolated linguistic areas, there is no convincing evidence either: in other terms, the model works except when it does not work. It is not verifiable.

4 Linguistic palaeontology and comparative mythology

The two latter difficulties that have been raised have been countered in advance by Colin Renfrew. It is a matter of linguistic paleontology and, more generally, of the comparative study of myths, institutions and vocabulary, concerning which Renfrew recognizes none of its claimed results. Indeed, up to the present day, any attempt to find the original homeland had attempted to establish concurrences between data from 'common vocabulary' with a geographical zone and a specific archaeological culture. The localization of the homeland in a Mediterranean and relatively southern homeland (Turkey, and more generally the Near East), in a traditional approach, could have been based on the possible existence of environmental data (fauna, flora, countryside, etc.) that are specific to this region. Now, as has been remarked for a long time, not a single word from the common vocabulary evokes the Mediterranean zone. To the contrary, the Greek word for the sea ('thalassa') has a notoriously non-Indo-European etymology. Given that Renfrew has previously denounced 'the lure of the protolexicon'[39], this objection could hardly pose problems for him.

The same thing goes for the words of the common vocabulary that, symmetrically, suggest a warlike and hierarchical society, possessing the horse and chariot. Renfrew reminds the reader that things are not so clear as that. The supposedly common terms for designating the chariot are relatively rare (Sanskrit 'ratha', chariot, Latin 'rota'); most of its constituents (apart from the yoke, the hub, the draught pole) differ from one language to another, and part of the common technical terms relating to chariots could be derived from common metaphors for designating them[40]. As for the horse, as the linguist Robert Coleman has remarked, different roots exist according to the language in question; besides, nothing proves that the animal thus designated would have been from the outset a domesticated horse, since residual wild horses seemed to have been present in different regions of Europe and the Near East[41]. Thus, we are faced here with a preconceived idea of an original people of conquering horsemen which — in a circular manner, drawing on a certain amount of uncertain data relating to the horse and chariot — locates the steppes as the original birthplace, given that this was the primary place where this animal was domesticated.

In a similar way, Colin Renfrew deals with the work of Georges Dumézil and of Émile Benveniste only in a dozen of pages: the structures that have been brought to light simply bear on the general character of any warlike hierarchical society, as was the case of those whose vocabulary and mythology have been studied. More concretely, if one can compare the words for designating the king — the words 'rajah' of India, 'rex' of Rome and 'rix' of Celtic languages (present in 'Vercingetorix') — nothing proves that the common root would not have originally had a much more vague meaning; it could have subsequently evolved, but only in some languages, in order to designate the royal function when it appeared, in a way that was paralleled in several European societies. Renfrew also takes onboard the criticisms of the anthropologist Jack Goody with respect to the vocabulary of kinship that Benveniste interpreted as being patriarchal[42].

The criticisms that were put forward with respect to Georges Dumézil are the usual ones, according to which the so-called tripartite structure of some Indo-European mythologies, with their three-fold division between priest-kings, warriors and workers, could be found in any hierarchical society whatsoever, whether it be based on chieftains or on the state. Besides, he quotes Japanese mythology, that was compared with Indo-European mythologies in bygone days by two Japanese disciples of Dumézil, Atsuhito Yoshida and T. Obayashi[43]. Nevertheless, Colin Renfrew did not deal head on with Georges Dumézil's results, and in this respect he could be said to have been somewhat offhand. He restricts himself to referring the reader to two general summaries of the work of Dumézil, of which one, published in the principal journal of the so-called 'New Right' or Nouvelle Droite (in fact Extreme Right), is due to an author working within this tendency, Jean-Claude Rivière[44]. Discussing the Indo-Europeanness of the structural correspondences brought forth by Dumézil, as we have previously attempted[45], and denying all reality of these correspondences in the name of the universality of ideologies, as Renfrew does, does not at all correspond to the same approach.

Nevertheless, Colin Renfrew is not completely at ease, and admits in fine the validity of work on vocabulary: 'I do not doubt that a sensitive analysis and interpretation of the shared early vocabulary, insofar as it can be constructed, of very much the kind undertaken by Benveniste, can answer some of the relevant questions'[46].

5 In conclusion

In the final analysis, a reading of Colin Renfrew's book leaves the reader with the feeling of a paradox. The writer wanted, in his own way, to provide a solution to a problem that has haunted western humanities for at least two centuries. Resolving it was therefore tempting, and the solution provided was not particularly new. But in order to do this, Renfrew, whilst conserving the question in its traditional formulation (finding the Urheimat, in the place where the Urvolk spoke the Ursprache), freed himself from most of the commonly accepted constraints, and in particular from the data of vocabulary and mythology. All of a sudden, given that it is so little constrained, his hypothesis is not verifiable –or it is not 'falsifiable' in the vocabulary of the philosophy of sciences favored by the New Archaeology in the 1970' among them Colin Renfrew; i.e. there exists no means of proving that it is possibly false. In the best of cases, on could say 'why not?'; but equally well, 'why?'. Besides, as we have seen, a whole set of evidence would seem to weigh against the Near Eastern hypothesis. One could thus regret that the critical enthusiasm of Colin Renfrew had not led him to attack the very heart of the model, in other words that of the idea of a centrifugal diffusion from an unique point of origin. This is precisely to what his previous anti-diffusionist work, paying close attention to validation, could have led him[47].

From this point of view, one of their most recent articles on the question[48] shows some regrets concerning the simplified and diffusionist nature of his hypothesis. In effect, he attempts to introduce two elements of complexity. The first is a concession to Anglo-Saxon archaeology, which is traditionally reticent with respect to diffusionism. In contradiction to what is obviously the case, in effect, in the diffusion of agriculture, some archaeologists have minimized the importance of movements of peoples, in order to emphasize simple phenomena of contact and borrowing[49]. However, one can follow closely this migratory movement step by step from Anatolia up to north Western Europe, in the totality of material culture. Besides, the manifest demographic disproportionateness between small groups of indigenous hunter-gatherers and the colonizing population could only lead to the absorption of the former by the latter, even if this phenomenon took place more slowly in marginal zones. In adopting an hypothesis of Marek Zvelebil[50], Colin Renfrew thus concedes that in the northern margins of Europe, hunter-gatherers could have borrowed the language from farmers at the same time that they borrowed their agriculture, even if, in the absence of proofs, this remains in at the level of intuition: 'I now feel that the position as stated by Zvelebil [...] was broadly correct'[51].

The second element of complexity, mentioned above, is the introduction of a dose of convergence within the heart of a model based on pure divergence. Renfrew borrows from Trubetzkoy the notion of 'Sprachbund', in other words, of 'linguistic area', or again of a geographical zone of prolonged linguistic contacts, where phenomena of resemblance can be attributed at the least to encounters, contacts and borrowings, just as much to a common origin. This is what allowed Trubetzkoy to propose, in 1938, a counter-model to the habitual genealogical tree[52]. This hypothetical 'Sprachbund' attempts to respond to one of the objections raised above: the linear diffusion model of the Neolithic colonization corresponds to none of the (often contradictory) trees proposed by linguists, in order to account for affinities between the different Indo-European languages. One would thus be confronted with linguistic diffusion in two successive phases: the first would have accompanied the original diffusion of agriculture, and from the second, the Balkanic 'Sprachbund', would have resulted local interactions during the two millennia of the Late Neolithic and the Chalcolithic (between 5.000 and 3.000 BC, approximately). Here again the question is not that of 'why not?', since in this domain very many hypotheses are admissible, but rather, from the moment that one aims to be situated within the scope of demonstration, that of 'why?'. This is the reason why Renfrew multiplies rhetorical precautions throughout his exposition[53].

Nevertheless, the considerable impact in the academic world and among the broader public of Colin Renfrew's hypothesis, and its association with the defenders of the 'big tree', together with its genes, have made it into the currently dominant theory in Anglo-Saxon media. From 1993 onwards, the edition of the Time Atlas of World History considered it to be universally accepted, up to the point where the archaeologist James Mallory, a defender of the steppic hypothesis, considered his own cause to be provisionally lost, at least on the media front[54].

In reality, amongst strict Indo-Europeanists, whether they are linguists or archaeologists, at least amongst those who believe it to be possible to locate the original birthplace, notwithstanding different scientific traditions that are specific to each country, the steppic theory has the support of the majority.

Notes

1 Renfrew 1987; French translation: 1990.

2 Childe 1958, p. 70.

3 *Antiquity*, 62, 1988; *Current Anthropology*, 29, 3, 1988; *Topoï*, vol. 2, 1992.

4 Cf. Mallory in Mallory and Adams 1997, p. 307, who quotes in particular the *Time Atlas of World History* of 1993.

5 Heun et al. 1997.

6 Renfrew 1999.

7 Meillet 1903, p. 410–411; this should be compared with the 1937 edition, p. 479–480.

8 Meillet 1921, p. 99, note 1.

9 On this discussion, cf. Neu and Meid 1979 notably the contributions of W. P. Schmid and of W. Meid, Adrados 1982 and 1990, Justus 1992, K.-H. Schmidt 1992, Oettinger 1986, Forrer 1921, Sturtevant 1929 and 1962, Wagner 1985, Schlerath 1987, Voegelin and Voegelin 1973, Finkelberg 1997, Polomé 1980.

10 Dolgoposky 1988.

11 Sayce 1927, Hodge 1981, Ivanov and Gamkrelidze 1984.

12 Ruhlen 1997 and this volume, Cavalli-Sforza et al. 1988 and this volume, Pellegrini 1995; *contra*: Campbell, this volume.

13 On glottochronoly, cf. Swadesh 1972.

14 Trombetti 1905.

15 Meillet 1937, p. 38–39.

16 Pedersen 1903, 1931.

17 Illic-Svitych 1971–1984.

18 For the Nostratic, cf. e.g. Bomhard 1984, Shevoroshkin 1989a, 1989b.

19 For the place of Sumerian, cf. Bengston 1991; note besides that other linguists such as Diakonoff, place the North American Na-Dene languages in 'nostratic'.

20 For example, Ruhlen 1994, p. 185–188.

21 cf. Bateman et al. 1990, Campbell this volume.

22 Ruhlen 1994, p. 191.

23 Renfrew 1992, p. 457–459.

24 Renfrew 1987, p. 159–161.

25 Kroeber and Chrétien 1937, Kroeber 1960 ; cf. more recently Gray and Atkinson 2002, Atkinson et al. 2005.

26 Dolgopolsky 1988.

27 Krahe 1954, 1957; W. Schmid 1968, 1987; Renfrew 1990 p.194–198, 290; for a bibliography on the discussion: Sergent 1995, p. 139–140.

28 Ebert 1921.

29 Cf. aussi Georgiev 1961, 1973 also cited by Renfrew and, more generally, Sergent 1995, p. 96–105, 138–147.

30 Sherratt and Sherratt 1988.

31 Renfrew 1999.

32 Adrados 1987, 1990.

33 Cf. Sergent 1995, p. 149–150, Adrados 1989.

34 On these languages in general, see: Untermann 1961, 1975; Tovar 1961, 1987; Anderson 1980; Villar 1990; Neumann and Untermann 1980.

35 Jackson 1955.

36 Ruhlen 1994, p. 191.

37 For Etruscan, cf. Adrados 1989 and Sergent 1995, p. 49–50; for Linear A, e.g. Owens 1999; for Tartessian, Villar 1990, Tovar 1961, Sergent 1995, p. 147–148.

38 Renfrew 1998.

39 Renfrew 1990, p. 100–109.

40 Renfrew 1987, p. 86; Renfrew 1989, p. 845; Coleman 1988; Specht 1944.

41 Renfrew 1989 p. 845; Coleman 1988; Uerpmann 1990; Boessneck and von den Driesch 1976.

42 Goody 1959; Renfrew 1987, p. 80, 258.

43 Renfrew 1987, p. 257; Yoshida 1977, 1981; this difficulty was mentioned for the first time in Demoule 1980, p. 113.

44 Rivière 1973, Litleton 1973. Colin Renfrew, who had certainly not fully understood its meaning, allowed his name to be put on the editorial board of the journal *Nouvelle École*.

45 Cf. Demoule 1980, 1991.

46 Renfrew 1987, p. 262.

47 This is no doubt why he believes himself obliged to caricature — symmetrically and secondarily — my own approach: 'This reveals the extent to which the position of the French archaeologist Jean-Paul Demoule appears to be

unacceptable to the scientific community, when he asserts that the Indo-European linguistic group has no real existence, and that the observed similarities are derisory, insignificant and fortuitous' Renfrew 1987, p. 42.

48 Renfrew 1999.

49 E.g. Dennell 1983, Zvelebil 1986, Zvelebil et al. 1997.

50 Zvelebil and Zvelebil 1990a, 1990b.

51 Renfrew 1999, p. 259.

52 Trubetzkoy 1939.

53 For example, p. 275: seven occurrences of 'perhaps' in 18 lines, not counting conditionals.

54 Mallory 1997, p. 307.

References

Adrados, F.R. (1982) The archaic structure of Hittite: the crux of the problem, *Journal of Indo-European Studies*, 10, 1–2, p. 1–35.

Adrados, F. R. (1987) Ideas on the typology of Proto-Indo-European, *Journal of Indo-European Studies*, 15, 1–2, p. 97–119.

Adrados, F. R. (1989) Etruscan as an IE Anatolian but not Hittite language, *Journal of Indo-European Studies*, 17, p. 363–383.

Adrados, F. R. (1990) The new image of Indoeuropean, the history of a revolution, *Indogermanische Forschungen*, 97, p. 5–28.

Anderson, J.M. (1980) Languages of ancient Spain and Portugal, *Italic and Romance, Linguistic Studies in Honor of Ernst Pulgram*, Izzo, H.J. ed, Amsterdam, Benjamins, p. 247–256.

Atkinson, Q. D., Nicholls, G., Welch, D. and Gray, R. D. (2005) From words to dates: water into wine, matemagic or phylogenic inference?, *Transactions of the Philological Society*, 1032, p. 193–219.

Bateman, R., Goddard, I., O'Grady, R., Funk, V.A., Mooi, R., Kress, W.J. and Cannell, P. (1990) *The Feasibility of Reconciling Human Phylogeny and Linguistic History, Current Anthropology* 31, p. 1–24, 177–183, 315–316.

Bengston, J. D. (1991) *Notes on Sino-Caucasian, in Dene-sino-causasian languages*, Shevoroshkin V. ed., Brockmeyer, Bochum, p. 67–129.

Boessneck, J. and von den Driesch, A. (1976) Pferde im 4./3. Jahrtausend v. Chr. in Ostanatolien, *Saügenkundlichen Mitteilungen*, 24, 2, p. 81–87.

Bomhard, A. R. (1984) *Toward Proto-Nostratic*, Amsterdam, Benjamins.

Cavalli-Sforza, L.L., Piazza A., Menozzi, P. and Mountain, J. (1988) Reconstruction of human evolution: bringing together genetic, archaeological and linguistic data, *Proceedings of National Academy of Sciences,* 85, p. 6002–6006.

Childe, V.G. (1958) Retrospect, *Antiquity*, 32, p. 69–74.

Coleman, R. (1988) Review, in: A CA * book review: archaeology and language. The puzzle of Indo-European origins, by Colin Renfrew, *Current Anthropology*, 29, 3, p. 449–453.
Demoule, J.-P. (1980) Les Indo-européens ont-ils existé?, *L'Histoire*, n°28, Novembre, p. 108–120.
Demoule, J.-P. (1991) Réalité des Indo-européens: les apories du modèle arborescent, *Revue d'Histoire des Religions*, CCVIII, 2, p. 169–202.
Dennell, R. (1983) *European Economic Prehistory: A New Approach*, London, Academic Press.
Dolgopolsky, A. (1988) The Indo-European homeland and lexical contacts of Proto-Indo-European with other languages, *Mediterranean Language Review*, 3, p. 7–31.
Ebert, M. (1921) *Südrussland in Altertum, Kurt Schroeder*, Bücherei der Kultur und Geschichte, 12, Bonn and Leipzig.
Finkelberg, M. (1997) Anatolian languages and Indo-European migrations to Greece, *Classical World*, 91, p. 3–20.
Forrer, E. (1921) Ausbeute aus den Boghazköi-Inschriften, *Mitteilungen der Deutschen Orient-Gesellschaft zu Berlin*, 61, p. 20–39.
Gamkrelidze, T.V. and Ivanov, V.V. (1984) *Indoevropejskij jazik i Indoevropejcy. Rekonstrukcija i istoriko-tipologiceskij analiz prajazyka i protokul'tury*, Editions de l'Université d'Etat, Tbilissi, 2 vol.
Georgiev, Vl. (1961) *La Toponymie Ancienne de la Péninsule Balkanique et la Thèse Méditerranéenne*, Sofia, Académie bulgare des sciences.
Georgiev, Vl. (1973) *The arrival of the Greeks in Greece: the linguistic evidence, Bronze Age migrations the Aegean: Archaeological and linguistic problems in Greek prehistory*, Crossland, R.A. and Birchall, A. eds, London, Duckworth, p. 243–254.
Goody, J. (1959) Indo-European Society, *Past and Present*, 16, p. 88–92.
Gray, R. D. and Atkinson, Q. D. (2003) Language-tree divergence times support the Anatolian theory of Indo-European origin, *Nature*, 426 6965, p. 435–439.
Heun, M., Schäfer-Pregl, R., Klawan, D., Castagna, R., Accerbi, M., Borghi, B. and Salamini, F. (1997) Site of Einkorn wheat domestication identified by DNA fingerprinting, *Science*, 278, p. 1312–1314.
Hodge, C.T. (1981) Indo-Europeans in the Near East, *Anthropological Linguistics*, 23, p. 227–244.
Illic-Svitych, Vl. (1971–1984) *Opyt sravnenija nostraticeskih jazykov semitoxamitskij, kartvel'skij, indoevropejskij, ural'skij, dravidijskij, altajskij.* Sravnitel'nyj slovar', Nauka, Moskva, 3 vol.
Jackson, K. H. (1955) The Pictish language, *The Problem of the Picts*, Wainwright, F. T. et al. eds, Nelson, Edinburgh, p. 129–166.
Justus, C.F. (1992) The impact of non-Indo-European languages on Anatolian, *Reconstructing Languages and Cultures*, Polomé, E.C. and Winter, W. eds, Mouton de Gruyter, Berlin and New York, p. 443–467.

Krahe, H. (1954) *Sprache und Vorzeit, europäische Vorgeschichte nach dem Zeugnis der Sprache,* Quelle and Mayer, Heidelberg.

Krahe, H. (1957) Indogermanisch und Alteuropäisch, *Saeculum*, 8, 1, p. 1–16; cf. also in Scherer, A. ed., Die Urheimat der Indogermanen, Wissenschaftliche Buchgesellschaft, Darmstadt, (1968), p. 426–454.

Kroeber, A.L. (1960) Statistics, Indo-european, and taxonomy, *Language*, 36, p. 1–21.

Kroeber, A.L. and Chrétien, C.D. (1937) Quantitative classification of Indo-european languages, *Language*, 13, p. 83–103.

Littleton, C.S. (1973) *The New Comparative Mythology*, Berkeley, University of California Press.

Mallory, J. P. and Adams, D. Q. eds (1997) *The Encyclopedia of Indo-European Culture*, London and Chicago, Fitzroy Dearborn.

Meillet, A. (1903) *Introduction à l'étude comparative des langues indo-européennes*, Paris, 8th edition.

Meillet, A. (1921) *Linguistique historique et linguistique générale*, I, Paris, Klincksiek.

Neu, E. and Meid, W. eds (1979) *Hethitisch und Indogermanisch. Vergleichende Studien zur historischen Grammatik und zur dialektgeographischen Stellung der indogermanischen Sprachgruppe Altkleinasiens*, Innsbrucker Beiträge zur Sprachwissenschaft, Innsbruck

Neumann, G. and Untermann, J. (1980) *Die Sprache im römischen Reich der Kaiserzeit*, Köln-Bonn.

Oettinger, N. (1986) *'Indo-Hittite'-Hypothese und Wortbildung*, Innsbrucker Beiträge zur Sprachbildung, Innsbruck.

Owens, G. (1999) The structure of the Minoan language, *Journal of Indo-European Language*, 27, 1–2, p. 15–55.

Pedersen, H. (1903) Türkische Lautgesetze, *Zeitschrift der Deutschen Morgenländischen Gesellschaft* 57, 535–561.

Pedersen, H. (1931) The discovery of language, *Linguistic Science in the Nineteenth Century*, Bloomington.

Pellegrini, B. (1995) *L'Eve imaginaire*, Payot 1995.

Polomé, E. (1980) Creolization processes and diachronic linguistics, *Theoretical orientations in creole studies*, Valdman, A. and Highfield, A. eds, New York, Academic Press, p. 185–202.

Renfrew, C. (1987) *Archaeology and Language. The Puzzle of Indo-European Origins*, London, Jonathan Cape.

Renfrew, C. (1989) They ride horses, don't they? Mallory on the Indo-Europeans, *Antiquity*, 63, p. 843–847.

Renfrew, C. (1992) Archaeology, genetics and linguistic diversity, *Man N.S.*, 27, p. 445–478

Renfrew, C. (1998) Word of Minos: the Minoan contribution to Mycenaean Greek and the linguistic geography of the bronze age Aegean, *Cambridge Archaeological Journal*, 8, p. 239–264.

Renfrew, C. (1999) Time depth, convergence theory, and innovation in Proto-Indo-European, 'Old Europe' as a PIE linguistic area, *Journal of Indo-European Studies*, 27, 3–4, p. 257–293.

Rivière, J.-Cl. (1973) Pour une lecture de Dumézil, *Nouvelle École*, 21–22, p. 14–79.

Ruhlen, M. (1994) *The Origin of Language: Tracing the Evolution of the Mother Tongue*, John Wiley and Sons.

Sayce, A.H. (1927) The Aryan problem. Fifty years later, *Antiquity*, 1, p. 204–214.

Schlerath, B. (1987) On the reality and status of a reconstructed language, *Journal of Indo-European Studies*,15, 1–2, p. 41–46

Schmid, W.P. (1968) *Alteuropäisch und Indogermanisch, Akademie der Wissenschaften und Literatur Mainz, Abhandlungen der Geistes- und Sozialwissenschaftlichen Klasse*, Steiner, Wiesbaden.

Schmid, W.P. (1987) 'Indo-European' – 'Old European' On the reexamination of two linguistic terms, in Proto-Indo-European, the archaeology of a linguistic problem, *Studies in Honor of Marija Gimbutas, Skomal, N.S. and Polomé, E.C.* eds, Washington, D.C., Institute for the Study of Man, p. 322–338.

Schmidt, K.-H. (1992) Contributions from new data to the reconstruction of the proto-language, *Reconstructing Languages and Cultures*, Polomé, E.C. and Winter, W. eds, Mouton de Gruyter, Berlin and New York, p. 35–62.

Sergent, B. (1995) *Les Indo-Européens. Histoire, langue, mythes*, Payot, Paris.

Sherratt, A. and Sherratt, S. (1988) Agricultural transition and Indo-European dispersals, *Antiquity*, 62, p. 584–595.

Shevoroshkin, V., ed. (1989)a Reconstructing languages and cultures. *Abstracts and Materials from the First International Interdisciplinary Symposium on Language and Prehistory,* Ann Arbor, 8–12 Nov. 1988, Brockmeyer, Bochum.

Shevoroshkin, V., ed. (1989)b *Explorations in Languages Macro-families*, Brockmeyer, Bochum.

Specht, F. (1944) *Der Ursprung der Indogermanischen Deklination*, Vandenhoek and Ruprecht, Göttingen.

Sturtevant, E.H. (1929) The relationship of Hittite to Indo-European, *Transactions and Proceedings of the American Philology Association*, 60, p. 25–37.

Sturtevant, E.H. (1962) The Indo-Hittite hypothesis, *Language*, 38, p. 105–110

Swadesh, M. (1972) *The Origin and Diversification of Language*, London, Routledge.

Tovar, A. (1961) *The Ancient Languages of Spain and Portugal*, New York, Vanni.

Tovar, A. (1987) Lenguas y pueblos de la antigua Hispania, *Actas del IV Coloquio sobre las lenguas y culturas paleohispanicas*, Vitoria, p. 15–34.

Trombetti, A. (1905) *L'unità d'origine del linguaggio*, Bologna, Libreria Treves di Luigi Beltrami.

Trubetzkoy, N.S. (1939) Gedanken über das Indogermanenproblem, *Acta Linguistica*, I, p. 81–89; see also in Scherer A. ed., *Die Urheimat der Indogermanen, Wissenschaftliche Buchgesellschaft*, Darmstadt, 1968, p. 214–223.

Uerpmann, H.-P. (1990) *Die Domestikation des Pferdes im Chalkolithikum West- und Mitteleuropas,* Madrider Mitteilungen, 31, p. 109–153.

Untermann, J. (1961*) Sprachräume und Sprachbewegungen in vorrömischen Hispanien*, Harrassowitz, Wiesbaden.

Untermann, J. (1975) *Monumenta Linguarum Hispanicarum, I, Die Münzenlegenden*, Harrassowitz, Wiesbaden.

Untermann, J. (1997) *Monumenta Linguarum Hispanicarum, IV: Die tartessischen, keltiberischen und lusitanischen Inschriften*, Wiesbaden, Reichert.

Villar, F. (1990) Indo-Européens et pré-IndoEuropéens dans la péninsule ibérique, *When Words Collide: The Indo-Europeans and the Pre-Indo-Europeans*, Markey, T.L. and Greppin, J.A.C. eds., Karoma Publishers, Ann Arbor, p. 363–394.

Voegelin, C.F. and Voegelin, F.M. (1973) Recent classifications of genetics relationships, *Annual Review of Anthropology*, 2, p. 139–151.

Wagner, H. (1985) Das Hethitische vom Standpunkte der typologischen Geographie, Pisa, Giardini, *Testi Linguistici* 7.

Yoshida, A. (1977) Mythes japonais et idéologie tripartite des Indo-Européens, *Diogène*, 98, p. 101–124

Yoshida, A. (1981) Dumézil et les études comparatives des mythes japonais, *Pour un Temps*, Georges Dumézil, Bonnet J. et al. eds, Centre Georges Pompidou, Paris, p. 319–324.

Zvelebil, M., Dennell, R. and Domanska, L. eds (1997) *Harvesting the Sea, Farming the Forest, the Emergence of Neolithic Societies in the Baltic Region*, Sheffield, Sheffield Academic Press.

Zvelebil, M. ed. (1986) *Hunters in Transition*, Cambridge University Press, Cambridge.

Zvelebil, M. and Zvelebil, K.V. (1990a) Indo-European origins and the agricultural transition in *Europe, Journal of European Archaeology*, 3, p. 33–70.

Zvelebil, M. and Zvelebil, K. V. (1990b) Agricultural transition, 'Indo-European origins', and the spread of farming, *When Words Collide: The Indo-Europeans and the Pre-Indo-Europeans*, Markey T.L. and Greppin J.A.C. eds., Ann Arbor, Karoma Publishers, p. 237–266.

11 New perspectives on the origin of languages

Merritt Ruhlen
Stanford University

We don't often ask ourselves where languages come from because they just seem to be there: French in France, English in England, Chinese in China, Japanese in Japan, and so forth. Yet if we go back only a few thousand years none of these languages were spoken in their respective countries and indeed none of these languages existed anywhere in the world. Where did they all come from?

In some cases the answer is clear and well-known. We all learn in school that French has evolved from the Latin language that was spoken in Rome two thousand years ago. This language was spread with the Roman conquest of Europe and, following the dissolution of the Roman empire, the regional dialects of Latin gradually evolved into the modern Romance languages: Sardinian, Rumanian, Italian, French, Provençal, Catalan, Spanish, and Portuguese. A language family, such as the Romance family, is a group of languages that have all evolved from a single earlier language, in this case Latin.

But while the Romance family illustrates well the concept of a language family, it is also highly unusual in that the ancestral language—Latin—was a written language that has left us copious records. The usual situation, however, is that the ancestral language was not a written language and the only evidence we have are its modern descendants. Yet even without written attestation of the ancestral language, it is not difficult to distinguish language families, as can be seen in Table 1. Here similarities among certain languages in the word for 'hand' allow us to readily identify not only the Romance family (Rumanian, Italian, French, Spanish), but also the Slavic family (Serbo-Croatian, Polish, Russian) and the Germanic family (English, Danish, German). Irish and Japanese stand apart from these three families. There are, however, no written records of the languages ancestral to the Germanic or Slavic languages, so these two languages—which must have existed no less than Latin—are called Proto-Germanic and Proto-Slavic, respectively.

Table 1: Words for 'hand'

Language	'hand'
Irish	lāmh
Serbo-Croatian	ruka
Polish	rẽka
Russian	ruka
English	hænd
Danish	hānd
German	hant
Rumanian	mɨnə
Italian	mano
French	mæ̃
Spanish	mano
Japanese	te

If we were to examine words other than 'hand', we would find many additional instances where each of these three families is characterized by different looking roots, just as in the case of 'hand'. But we would also find from time to time roots that seemed to be shared by these three families, that is, the same root is found in all three families. What is the meaning of such roots? In fact, similarities among language families such as Romance, Germanic, and Slavic have the same meaning as similarities among languages in any one family—they imply that these three families are branches of an even more ancient family. In other words a language which existed long before Latin, Proto-Germanic, or Proto-Slavic differentiated first into these three languages and they in turn then diversified into the modern languages of each family. This larger, more ancient, family was first recognized by the English jurist Sir William Jones in 1786 and during the nineteenth century it became known as the Indo-European family. What led Jones to this conclusion was the fact that Latin, Greek, Sanskrit, Celtic, and Gothic (the oldest written Germanic language) showed 'a stronger affinity, both in the roots of verbs and in the forms of grammar, than could possibly have been produced by accident; so strong indeed, that no philologer could examine them all … without believing them to have sprung from some common source, which, perhaps, no longer exists.' Table 2 gives an example of a root and inflectional endings ('forms of grammar', as Jones called them) that characterize the Indo-European family. Map 1 shows the distribution of the Indo-European family, and its constituent branches, as it is currently understood. It should not be lost sight that what was revolutionary about Jones's hypothesis was not just that he had identified the Indo-European family for the first time, but rather that he had proposed an evolutionary explanation for linguistic diversity, and he had done so 73 years before Charles Darwin offered a similar explanation for biological diversity.

Table 2: An Indo-European paradigm

	Sanskrit	Classical Greek	Latin	Old Slavic	Gothic
I carry	bhár-āmi	phér-o	fer-ō	ber-ǫ	bair-a
You carry	bhár-asi	phér-eis	fer-s	ber-eši	bair-is
He carries	bhár-ati	phér-ei	fer-t	ber-etŭ	bair-iθ
We carry	bhár-āmas	phér-omen	fer-imus	ber-emŭ	bair-am
You carry	bhár-atha	phér-ete	fer-tis	ber-ete	bair-iθ
They carry	bhár-anti	phér-ousi	fer-unt	ber-ǫtŭ	bair-and

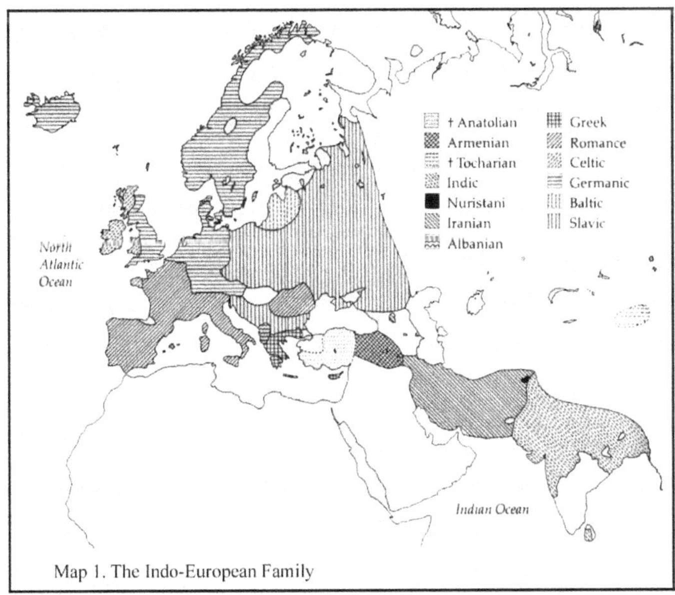

Map 1: The Indo-European family

1 Eurasiatic

During the nineteenth century many other language families, comparable to Romance, Germanic, or Indo-European, were discovered around the world. It became clear that simply by comparing basic vocabulary one could identify language families anywhere in the world and by the end of the nineteenth century several hundred such families had been recognized. Now if the comparison of languages leads quickly to families like Romance, and comparison of families like Romance, Slavic, and Germanic leads to more ancient families like Indo-European, the next step in the comparative method must surely be to compare Indo-European with other comparable language families to see whether these families in turn share certain common roots that would indicate an even more ancient language. Such comparisons were in fact carried out in the nineteenth century, and similarities between Indo-European and certain other language families were noted. At the beginning of the twentieth century, however, a reaction set in against the comparison of Indo-European with other families—and indeed against the comparison of any such families—and alleged similarities between Indo-European and other families were dismissed in one manner or another. This supposed splendid isolation of Indo-European became the central dogma of twentieth century historical linguistics and effectively prevented linguistic taxonomy from progressing beyond the obvious—for Indo-European is indeed a very obvious family.

The main rationale behind the supposed isolation of Indo-European—and hundreds of other such families—was quite simple: Language changes so fast that after around 6,000 years (coincidentally the assumed age of Indo-European!) all trace of linguistic connections has been eroded beyond recognition, so that even if Indo-European were historically related to some other family, there would simply be no evidence left to show it. We are thus doomed, according to this view, to discovering hundreds of obvious families of shallow time depths, but we will never be able to discover earlier groupings or to unravel human prehistory before around 4,000 BC. If one considers that Latin *aqua* has been reduced to a single vowel, [o], in French *eau*, the argument that language evolves so fast as to quickly erode all trace of former relationships seems plausible. However, when we consider French's closest relatives, Italian *acqua* and Spanish *agua*, we see that everything has not changed everywhere and therefore the information has not really been lost. It has just been obscured in French. In fact there are numerous examples of words in reconstructed proto-languages that have come down virtually intact into at least some modern languages. One such example is modern Rumanian *nepot* 'nephew', which derives from Proto-Indo-European **nepōt*. Now if the three consonants and two vowels in this word have persisted unchanged for six millennia, on what grounds can one maintain that everything has changed after this amount of time?

And it also seems strange that the comparative method, which leads so easily and so quickly from French to Latin to Indo-European, should all of a sudden become impotent at some particular point in time. And that the family in terms of which the comparative method in linguistics was discovered—Indo-European—should turn out to represent the limits of that method also seems strange. But the question of whether Indo-European really is isolated from all other families is an empirical question which cannot be decided by a priori rationalizations, and in fact several scholars pointed to Indo-European's closest relatives at the start of the twentieth century—at the same time the topic was being effectively banished from discussion. The Danish linguist Holger Pedersen proposed in 1905 that Indo-European was but a branch of an even more ancient family that he named Nostratic and which included—in addition to Indo-European—Semitic, Finno-Ugric, Samoyed, Yukaghir, Altaic, and Eskimo-Aleut. It is generally believed today that Semitic (or rather Afro-Asiatic, of which Semitic is one branch) is more distantly related to the rest of the Nostratic family, and the American linguist Joseph Greenberg calls this slightly smaller family Eurasiatic, a term which I will use since it is taxonomically more precise than Nostratic. For Greenberg the Eurasiatic family includes Indo-European, Uralic, Altaic, Korean-Japanese-Ainu, Gilyak, Chukchi-Kamchatkan, and Eskimo-Aleut (see Map 2).

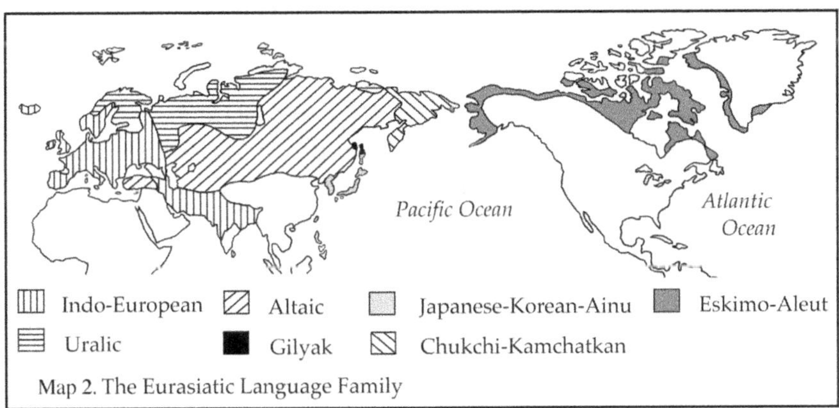

Map 2: The Eurasiatic family

Pedersen pointed to a number of lexical and grammatical items found in these Eurasiatic families, but apparently not elsewhere. One of the most persuasive bits of evidence is the first- and second-person pronouns ('I' and 'you'). These pronouns are known to be among the semantically most stable items in language, often retained unchanged over long periods of time. Now in the

Eurasiatic families enumerated above the first-person pronoun is characteristically based on M and the second-person pronoun on T, just as in French *moi* and *toi*. The Indo-European pattern of M/T 'I/you', which is found in virtually every Indo-European language, was of course always explained as due to common origin in the Proto-Indo-European language, but when scholars such as Pedersen pointed out that this same pattern was shared by other families, a similar explanation of common origin was rejected by Indo-Europeanists. The Italian linguist Alfredo Trombetti protested in 1905 against this cavalier use of different explanations to explain the same facts as follows: 'It is clear that in and of itself the comparison of Finno-Ugric [Uralic] *me* 'I', *te* 'you' with Indo-European *me*- and *te*- [with the same meaning] is worth just as much as any comparison one might make between the corresponding pronominal forms in the Indo-European languages. The only difference is that the common origin of the Indo-European languages is accepted, while the connection between Indo-European and Finno-Ugric is denied.'

How did the Indo-Europeanists explain the presence of the M/T pattern in other families, if not by common origin? According to the French comparatist Antoine Meillet, 'les pronoms doivent être des mots courts, nettement constitués avec des éléments phonétiques aisés à prononcer, et en général sans groupes de consonnes. Il en résulte que les pronoms se ressemblent plus ou moins partout, sans que ceci implique une communauté d'origine.' The problem with this explanation is that it is just not true. If one looks only at the language families of northern Eurasia and northern North America (Eskimo- Aleut) one is indeed struck by the prevalence of the M/T pattern, but throughout most of the Americas one finds an entirely different pronominal pattern, N/M, as we shall see below. And when one turns to Africa, or Australia, one finds pronominal systems completely distinct from these M/T and N/M patterns. There is no reason why pronouns should not be subject to the fundamental property of human language—the arbitrary sound/meaning relationship expressed by Ferdinand de Saussure as 'l'arbitraire du signe'—and they are not.

By themselves the M/T pronouns are a strong indicator of the validity of the Eurasiatic family, and other traits, such as the K/T 'dual/plural' endings, confirm this initial conclusion. But, in fact, the first-person pronoun itself provides additional, and almost conclusive, evidence for the correctness of Eurasiatic. In almost every Indo-European language the subject and object forms of the first-person pronoun are different: French *je/me*, English *I/me*, Russian *ya/menya*, etc. This same state of affairs can thus be projected back to Proto-Indo-European, for which the reconstructed forms are **eghom*/**me* (the * indicates a hypothetical reconstructed form, rather than an actual attested one). The use of two different roots in a single grammatical paradigm is know as suppletion in linguistics; one form suppletes, or replaces, another. This suppletive formation in the first-person pronoun has always been considered a defining characteristic of the Indo-European family, for the use of two different roots in one grammatical paradigm is not likely to have been independently invented by two different families.

Greenberg has shown, however, that this suppletive formation, far from being an innovation defining Indo-European, is also found elsewhere in the Eurasiatic family. The clearest evidence occurs in the Chukchi-Kamchatkan family at the other end of Eurasia (see Map 2), where we find Chukchi *-eɣəm* 'I' and Kamchadal *kim* 'I', *ma* 'me'. (There is only a slight difference in these forms from those posited for Indo-European since *g, ɣ*, and *k* are very similar consonants which are pronounced at the same position in the back of the mouth and differ only in that the vocal cords vibrate for *g* and *ɣ*, but not for *k*, and there is complete blockage of the airstream for *k* and *g*, but not for *ɣ*.) The Chukchi-Kamchatkan family has in fact extended this pattern to the second-person pronoun, as in Chukchi *-eɣət* 'you'.

While Indo-Europeanists have never been able to explain the origin of **eghom*, Greenberg has proposed that it was originally a periphrastic phrase consisting of three parts: **e-gho-m* 'this-is-me'. The first element, *e-*, is a widespread demonstrative pronoun in Eurasiatic, and the final element is simply first-person M (as the extension to the second person in Chukchi, with T in place of M, shows). The middle element, a verb meaning 'to be', has left additional traces in the Eurasiatic family, beyond those in Indo-European and Chukchi-Kamchatkan. The Uralic family presents several clear examples. In Hungarian, for instance, we find the first- and second-person object pronouns *engemet* 'I' and *tégedet* 'you'. It is clear that these are to be analyzed into three parts, *en-gem-et* and *té-ged-et*, in which the first part is simply the Hungarian pronouns 'I' and 'you', and the final part, the (optional) accusative ending. But the middle portions, -gem- and -ged-, are virtually identical with the Chukchi independent pronouns *ɣəm* 'I' and *ɣët* 'you' (*t* and *d* are both dental consonants, the former voiceless, the latter, voiced, just as in *k* and *g*). Elsewhere in Uralic we find Kamassian *igäm* 'I am', with exactly the meaning posited by Greenberg, and Vogul *am-kkem* 'I alone' (literally, 'I-it is me'). Finally, we find in the Eskimo-Aleut branch of Eurasiatic a Proto-Eskimo verb suffix that one might reconstruct as **-mkət* 'I … you'. Clearly the initial *-m* is the first-person pronoun and the second part, *-kət*, is the same element as Chukchi *ɣət* 'you' and the middle portion of Hungarian *té-ged-et* 'you'.

2 Language in the Americas

The effect of the myth that Indo-European had no known relatives, and that the comparative method was restricted to very shallow time depths of 6,000 years or so, was that there would also be numerous other such families scattered around the world, the relationships among which we would never be able to discover. Nowhere was this proliferation of small obvious families carried to such extremes as in the New World, where specialists decided that there were at least 200 independent families without known connections. And yet there is virtually no trace of human occupation in the Americas before around 13,000 years ago (the few supposedly earlier dates are disputed). How then did the Americas, in only twice the age of Indo-European, manage to give rise to such an exuberance of linguistic diversity?

The answer given by Greenberg in his book *Language in the Americas* (1987) was that it didn't. Greenberg concluded that there were in fact only three major groups in the Americas: Eskimo-Aleut, Na-Dene, and Amerind. The first two groups had already been recognized a century ago, so Greenberg's innovation was to group all other Native American languages into a single Amerind group (see Map 3). In support of the Amerind family Greenberg pointed out several dozen shared grammatical features and several hundred shared words. As with Eurasiatic, one of the strongest pieces of evidence is a distinctive pronominal pattern, but in the case of Amerind it is N/M 'I/you', not the ubiquitous Eurasiatic M/T. Furthermore, Greenberg was hardly the first to recognize the widespread N/M pronominal pattern in the Americas. As early as 1905 Alfredo Trombetti, whose recognition of the Eurasiatic M/T pattern we noted above, published in that same book an appendix laying out the evidence for the pervasive N/M pattern in the Americas. Clearly for Trombetti pronouns 'ne se ressemblaient pas plus ou moins partout'. And Trombetti was not the only one to notice all of the first-person N's and second-person M's scattered through the Americas. The American linguist Edward Sapir, who had discovered the Na-Dene family in 1915, wrote in a personal letter in 1917 that 'the curiously widespread American second singular meets us here once more' and only a year later wrote: 'Getting down to brass tacks, how in the Hell are you going to explain general American *n-* 'I' except genetically? It's disturbing, I know, but (more) non-committal conservatism is only dodging, after all, isn't it? Great simplifications are in store for us.' There is no indication that Sapir was aware of Trombetti's appendix, but in fact almost anyone who examined many Native American languages in the twentieth century saw the same N/M pattern. It was only the specialists, esconced in their comfortable niches, who failed to see the forest for the trees.

In addition to the distinctive Amerind pronominal pattern, Greenberg and I have discovered an Amerind lexical item that is equally persuasive for the validity of Amerind. Throughout the Americas, in both North and South, one constantly finds words for children in which the first consonant is T and the second N, forms such as *tina*, *tana*, and *tuna*. The meaning seems to include almost any kind of child: 'son, brother, daughter, sister, child, sibling, baby', etc. However, after collecting and analyzing several hundred such forms from different Amerind languages, it became apparent that originally the sex of the child was indicated by the first vowel in the word so that the hundreds of extant Amerind forms, in dozens of different languages, had all evolved from an original Amerind system that we might reconstruct as **t'ina/*t'ana/*t'una* 'son, brother/child, sibling/daughter, sister'. The fact that traces of this complex system are found throughout both North and South America would fit nicely with the archaeological evidence indicating that both continents were colonized very quickly, within a millennium, beginning around 13,000 years ago. North American examples of the original Amerind pattern include Nootka *t'an'a* 'child', Cayuse *-t'in* 'brother', and Central Sierra Miwok *-tūne* 'daughter'; South American examples are Aymara *tayna* 'first-born child', Tiquie *ten* 'son', and Tiquie *ton* 'daughter'. Tiquie is one of the few languages to preserve two forms of the original Amerind system. No contemporary language preserves all three.

3 Global etymologies

It is clear from the preceding discussion that the power of the comparative method in linguistics was vastly underestimated during the past century, with contradictory evidence either ignored or swept under the rug. As we have seen, however, the past decade has witnessed significant inroads on what had been established dogma and the picture that is emerging of the world's linguistic diversity is one of about a dozen large families, comparable to Eurasiatic and Amerind, as shown in Map 3. Russian scholars would add Kartvelian and Dravidian (which are small obvious families) to the Eurasiatic group to form a larger group that they call Nostratic. Greenberg, however, considers them related to Eurasiatic, but not part of the Eurasiatic family proper. Dene-Caucasian, which includes Basque, Caucasian, Burushaski, Sino-Tibetan, Yeniseian, and Na-Dene, also represents a family that has been essentially worked out in the past decade and I have elsewhere recently devoted an article to the origin of, and evidence for, this unusual family.

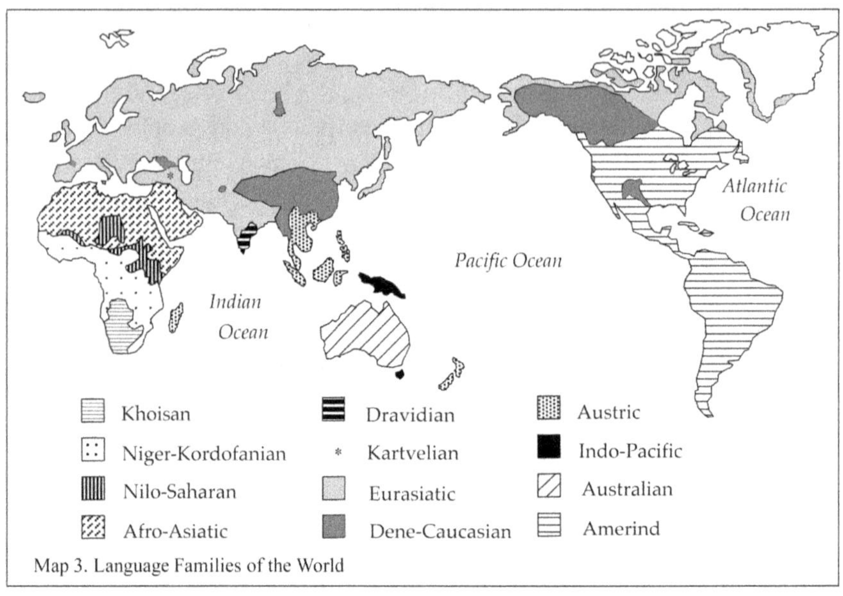

Map 3: The world's linguistic families

But what if we now compare these dozen or so large families with one another. Could they themselves share certain common roots that might indicate a single common origin for all extant languages? Such an idea is not new and is indeed often associated with the name of Trombetti. In fact, in the same book in which Trombetti pointed out the existence of the M/T pronominal pattern in Eurasia, and the N/M pattern in the Americas, *L'Unità d'origine del linguaggio* (1905), he also argued that all the world's languages were ultimately related and the evidence he adduced for this hypothesis was not inconsequential. In Europe, Trombetti's name became anathema. After all, if even Indo-European—on which hundreds of scholars had worked for over a century—had no known relatives, then the attempt to connect all known languages in a single family must be preposterous. In the United States, however, Edward Sapir was decidedly less negative in his appraisal of Trombetti's radical hypothesis, writing to the American anthropologist Alfred Kroeber in 1924: 'There is much excellent material and good sense in Trombetti in spite of his being a frenzied monogenist. I am not so sure that his standpoint is less sound than the usual 'conservative' one.'

Around a decade ago the time seemed ripe for a new attack on an overall comparison of the world's linguistic families. A great deal of work had been done since the days of Trombetti and, thanks largely to the work of Greenberg, the classification of African, New Guinea, and American Indian languages had been worked out in some detail. In 1987 John Bengtson and I began to compare all of the world's linguistic families with one another to determine whether they did, or did not, share common roots. This is, after all, an empirical question, though it was not treated as such during the twentieth century. In 1994 we published an article containing evidence for 27 roots that are found in language families from Africa to the Americas and which we believe can only be explained satisfactorily by the hypothesis that all extant languages share a common origin. The evidence for those 27 roots is also given in the appendix to my recent book, *L'origine des langues*.

Two of the roots that Bengtson and I found to be the most widespread are illustrated in Tables 3 and 4, with an example or two from each family in which they are found. The general form of these two roots is TIK 'finger', 'one' and PAL 'two'; both are found in at least a dozen families that traditional linguists consider historically unrelated. Now common origin is not the only possible explanation for linguistic similarities. There are three others: (1) borrowing, (2) chance, (3) onomatopoeia. Which of these four possibilities is most likely to be responsible for the similarities found in Tables 3 and 4? Let us begin by eliminating onomatopoeia, since no one has ever suggested that there is any intrinsic connection between the sounds TIK and PAL, and the meanings 'finger' and 'two', respectively. We may also eliminate borrowing as an explanation since it is not possible for languages on different continents to borrow words from one another (except in recent times, as 'television', 'tobacco' and 'alcohol' indicate). So the explanation for TIK and PAL, and the 25 other roots that Bengtson and I pointed out (and which represent but a small portion of the overall evidence), is either common origin or accidental resemblance.

But is it really likely that a dozen different families would have independently chosen the same sounds to represent the same meaning? A language with an average number of consonants and vowels would have a thousand or more CVC (consonant-vowel-consonant) sequences to encode any meaning. What is the likelihood that a dozen different families would all choose the same sequence for these two meanings? Bengtson and I believe it is very small, and certainly very much less likely than the hypothesis that these similar forms are related by common origin, no less than the Romance words for 'hand' in Table 1. Many linguists, when confronted with such evidence, exclaim 'How can such similar words from the four corners of the earth possibly be related?' We think this is the wrong question. The proper question is 'How can they possibly not?'

LANGUAGE FAMILY	LANGUAGE	FORM	MEANING
NIGER-CONGO	Gur Fulup	dike sik	'1' 'finger'
NILO-SAHARAN	Maba	tek	'1'
AFRO-ASIATIC	Proto-Afro-Asiatic Nefusa	*tak tukoḍ	'1' 'finger'
INDO-EUROPEAN	Proto-Indo-European Latin	*deik- dig-itus	'to point' 'finger'
URALIC	Zyrian	õtik	'1'
ALTAIC	Turkish Ainu Japanese	tek tek te	'only' 'hand' 'hand'
YENISEIAN	Proto-Yeniseian	*tok	'finger'
SINO-TIBETAN	Old Chinese Proto-Tibetan-Burman	*tek *tyik	'1' '1'
INDO-PACIFIC	Proto-Karonan	*dik	'one'
MIAO-YAO	Proto-Miao-Yao	*ntoʔ	'finger'
ESKIMO-ALEUT	Aleut Eskimo	tik-laq tik-iq	'middle finger' 'index finger'
NA-DENE	Eyak	tikhi	'1'
AMERIND	Proto-Hokan Mangue Upano Kukura	*dɨk'i tike tˢikitik tikua	'finger' '1' '1' 'finger'

Table 3: (Left) TIK 'finger', 'one'

LANGUAGE FAMILY	LANGUAGE	FORM	MEANING
NIGER-CONGO	Nimbari	bala	'2'
NILO-SAHARAN	Kunama	bāre	'2'
AFRO-ASIATIC	Proto-Central Chadic	*-bwVr	'2'
INDO-EUROPEAN	Proto-Indo-European	*pol	'half'
URALIC	Proto-Uralic	*pälä	'half'
DRAVIDIAN	Proto-Dravidian	*pāl	'part'
AUSTROASIATIC	Proto-Austroasiatic	*ʔ(m)bar	'2'
INDO-PACIFIC	Tasmanian	boula	'2'
AUSTRALIAN	Proto-Australian	*bula	'2'
MIAO-YAO	Proto-Miao-Yao	*(a)war	'2'
AUSTRONESIAN	Proto-Austronesian	*kə(m)bal	'twin'
AMERIND	Wintun Huave Colorado Proto-Nambikwara Quechua	palo- apool palu *p'āl(-in) pula	'2' 'snap in 2' '2' '2' 'both'

Table 4: (Above) PAL 'two'

4 Human origins

What if, contrary to current dogma, Bengtson and I are correct and the forms in Tables 3 and 4 are historically connected, thus implying a single origin for all contemporary languages. How might one place these findings in the broader context of human prehistory? If all current languages do indeed derive from one earlier language, when did this language exist? And where? And why did it alone leave ancestors in the modern world?

These are in fact the questions that currently confront not only historical linguists, but also archaeologists, geneticists, molecular biologists, anthropologists, historians, and indeed anyone interested in the origin of modern humans. Language is, unfortunately, a very poor indicator of time depth, and whether Amerind, for example, is 10,000, or 30,000 years old would be impossible to determine on strictly linguistic grounds. But the archaeological record indicates no human presence in the Americas before around 13,000 years ago, so the later date is presently supported by the archaeological evidence.

Might there not be, therefore, an indication in the archaeological record of the time and place of the transition to fully modern human language? Or, in other words, to fully modern humans, from which all current members of our species derive. But what would such a transition look like, if it was there? In fact, what it looked like, and when and where it took place, has been well known to archaeologists for some time. It coincides essentially with the transition from the Middle Stone Age to the Later Stone Age, which occurred roughly 50,000–40,000 years ago. The difference in the artifacts of the two periods is illustrated in Figure 1. Yet this transition from one tool type to another only hints at what must have been a profound change in human evolution.

In discussing human origins it is important to be precise about what we mean. Who qualifies as a 'modern human' and why? Anatomically-modern people—that is, people whose skeletons are indistinguishable from our own—first appear in the archaeological record, in Africa, around 195,000 years ago. But while these people may have looked like us, they didn't behave like us at all. In fact, for the next 150,000 years or so they behaved just like Neanderthals, with both a similar life style and tool kit and even living in the Middle East side by side with them. Suddenly, around 50,000 years ago, appear people, again first in Africa, who are called behaviorally-modern humans. They not only looked like us, they acted like us. Whereas the tools of the Middle Stone Age were produced in an almost identical fashion—as if stamped out by machine—and their form would often persist unchanged over enormous territories for tens, or even hundreds, of thousands of years, suddenly around 50,000 years ago the forms of the artifacts begin to change rapidly, not only in time but in space. Tools from neighboring populations

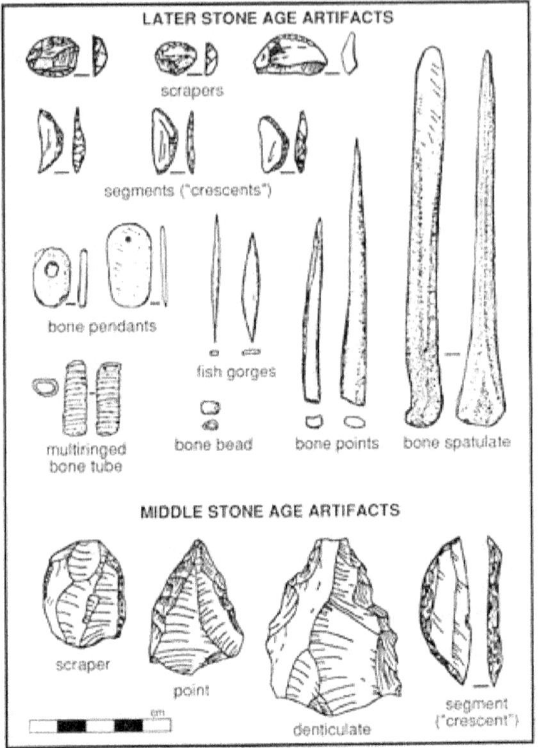

Figure 1: Differences between Middle Stone Age artifacts and Later Stone Age artifacts (from Klein, 1992)

begin to look quite different from one another and even in a single locality the tool kit can evolve rapidly. One might say that style appears in the human record at this moment for the first time. Some of the tools appear to have been made a certain way for purely stylistic reasons, without any functional motivation. And, finally, tools are at this time first fashioned from bone, ivory, and antler, materials not previously used even by anatomically-modern humans.

The startling changes in the tools at this time are, however, but one manifestation of the appearance of behaviorally-modern humans. Other recoverable evidence—graves, fireplaces, house ruins—are, like the tools, typically far more elaborate after the appearance of behaviorally-modern humans than before. We also find at this same time the first appearance of art, both in Australia and Europe. And finally it is at about this time (or perhaps somewhat earlier) that people began to leave Africa, perhaps in several waves, and to colonize the rest of the world, apparently replacing earlier forms of non-modern Homo sapiens such as the Neanderthals. In sum, it is only 40,000 years ago or so that cultural adaptation replaces biological evolution as the primary mechanism for adaptation to the environment and the rapidity of this cultural adaptation, particularly since the invention of agriculture around 10,000 years ago, we see around us every day.

It is hard to imagine these profound changes in human behavior taking place without a fully-developed human language playing a crucial role. Indeed the difficulty of distinguishing language and culture is familiar to anthropologists since each language essentially encodes a particular culture. And surely the appearance of a fully-modern language, such as those which now exist throughout the world, would have been of enormous adaptive value, since language is not a tool for a specific purpose, but is rather an all-purpose tool capable of solving an enormous array of problems. Exactly what kind of linguistic transition might have occurred at this time to change a more rudimentary linguistic capability into a full fledged modern human language is not known. The development of syntax, the ability to process sounds with amazing speed, a neurological change in the structure of the brain, and other hypotheses have been suggested as possible linguistic explanations for the changes in human behavior that are evident in the archaeological record. For the moment, however, these are all speculation, without any real empirical support.

In recent years there has been mounting evidence, both from the archaeological record and the study of human genetics, that all modern humans share a recent common ancestor in Africa within the last 200,000 years, and perhaps even within the last 60,000 years or so. Traces of an expansion out of Africa at about this time are found in the archaeological record and such an expansion is also indicated by the genetic evidence, including both Mitochondrial DNA and gene frequency studies. Such an expansion out of Africa would have taken with it, not only the genes of the people involved, but also their language. We believe that traces of this first fully-modern language can still be perceived in the world's contemporary languages and the two examples in Tables 3 and 4 are but a small portion of this evidence. If this hypothesis proves to be correct, then human language may turn out not only to support the 'Out of Africa' hypothesis, but to explain it as well.

References

Greenberg, J. H. (1987) *Language in the Americas*, Stanford: Stanford University Press.

Greenberg, J. H. (2000) *Indo-European and Its Closest Relatives, Vol. 1: Grammar,* Stanford: Stanford University Press.

Greenberg, J. H. and Ruhlen, M. (1997) L'origine linguistique des Amérindiens, *Pour la Science*, Dossier (October), pp. 84–89.

Klein, R.G. (1992) The archaeology of modern human origins. *Evolutionary Anthropology* 1.1 p10

Ruhlen, M. (1987) *A Guide to the World's Languages, Vol. 1: Classification*, Stanford: Stanford University Press..

Ruhlen, M. (1994) *On the Origin of Languages*, Stanford: Stanford University Press.

Ruhlen, M. (1997) *L'origine des langues*, Paris: Belin.

Ruhlen, M. (1997) Une nouvelle famille de langues: le déné-caucasien, *Pour la Science, Dossier* (October), pp. 68–73.

12 Linguistic history and computational cladistics

Don Ringe
University of Pennsylvania

Tandy Warnow
University of Texas

1 Principles

Attempting to reconstruct the origin and diversification of human lineages or of human languages is a matter of hypothesizing events within our undocumented prehistory. There are only two ways to do that: we can speculate, suggesting what must have happened on the basis of 'common sense', or we can find ways to extrapolate from the observable present into the unobservable past, using some appropriate version of the 'uniformitarian principle' (UP), as paleontologists and historical geologists do. As applied to linguistics, the UP can be stated as follows:

a) since the impoverishment of the historical record underdetermines analysis, all interpretations of the historical record must conform to the findings of scientific study of languages still spoken; and

b) since prehistory offers us no data at all, all extrapolations into prehistory must conform to the observed historical behavior of languages and the findings of scientific study of languages still spoken.

To paraphrase Labov's well-known principle, we use the present to explain the past, and the documented past to explain prehistory.

For more than a century mainstream linguists have refused to speculate and have insisted on using the UP; that was one of the most important innovations of the so-called 'Neogrammarian revolution' of the 1870s, which first began to put linguistics on a scientific footing. We see no reason to reconsider that decision. Accordingly this paper will be an attempt to work out the consequences of the UP for linguistic cladistics in a computational framework. Some of what we will say is presupposed in Ringe, Warnow and Taylor 2002. It will be seen that our point of view is compatible with that of Ross 1997, though we are interested in partly different aspects of the problem.

2 Application of principles in detail

To begin with, work which extrapolates into prehistory must conform to what is already known about language change from the historical record. For instance, it has been known for almost a century and a half that 'sound changes' —the spontaneous changes in pronunciation that occur in all languages over time—are almost completely regular; that they give rise to regular 'sound correspondences' between the words of related languages; that 'cognates'—that is, words which related languages have inherited from a common ancestor—can be recognized only by the presence of regular sound correspondences, and that the attempt to recognize cognates without exploiting regular sound correspondences leads to numerous errors in every case in which the facts can be checked against the historical record. It is also clear from the collective experience of historical linguists that, although cognation judgments are necessarily probabilistic, they can be practically certain; for instance, a pair of words from two languages which translate one another and whose sounds correspond one-to-one in patterns each of which reappears hundreds of times in a comparison of the lexica of those two languages is practically certain to be a cognate pair. And, although one might not guess it from the contentious scholarly literature, cognations as certain as that *are the norm* in mainstream historical linguistics: they are what scientific linguists ordinarily work with in attempting to find out other things about the historical relations between languages. Any research in historical linguistics which rejects those robust findings, such as the work of Greenberg and Ruhlen, is antiscientific and should be rejected. Our work is based on unproblematic cognation judgments between languages of an unproblematically related family; that is, we are starting from what is *known for certain.*

But while it is necessary to make our hypotheses conform to what has been known about linguistic history for more than a century, it clearly isn't sufficient. Even the best linguistic records of the past are comparatively poor data; we simply cannot learn from them anything like what we can learn from interviewing a representative sample of a community of native speakers. Therefore, not only must we make our inferences about prehistory conform to what is known about how languages change over time, we must also interpret the documents of the past and the hypothesized behavior of prehistoric humans in terms of what can be learned from observations of current linguistic behavior. That too is an application of the UP. It is especially important because over the past forty years or so we have learned an enormous amount about how linguistic changes spread through speech communities, what happens (and what does not happen) in language contact situations, how language acquisition proceeds, and so on. To demonstrate how important that is, we here give a brief description of how languages perpetuate themselves and change in terms of what has been learned in recent decades.

3 The cycle of language replication and its consequences

A language replicates itself one speaker at a time, normally by the process of native language acquisition (NLA) by children; the perpetuation of the language and the perpetuation of its speech community are literally the same thing. Since that is the usual situation, we define linguistic descent as follows:

> Language Y at a given time is descended from language X of an earlier time if and only if X developed into Y by means of an unbroken sequence of instances of NLA.

(Of course in principle this has nothing to do with biological descent; children do learn languages natively from people other than their parents.) Anything other than what has just been described is by definition something other than linguistic descent. Whether we can determine which languages are descended from which others is a separate empirical question (to which we will return below).

NLA is developmentally driven and tightly constrained; its more important features can be summarized as follows. Children begin to acquire native languages as soon as their development permits; conversely, NLA is normally impossible after the onset of puberty. Children raised in multilingual environments do not learn 'mixed' languages; they acquire more or less perfectly all the languages which they use regularly and become natively multilingual (Fantini 1985, Meisel 1989). A language's system of inflectional morphology is normally learned by age four, and all the rest of the 'basic' grammar—inflectional irregularities, the contrastive system of sounds, basic syntax, and so on—are fully in place by about age seven under normal circumstances (Slobin (ed.) 1985, 1992). Acquisition of complex syntactic structures and some patterns of word derivation takes a few years more. By contrast, the only thing that adults are normally able to acquire *perfectly* is further vocabulary;

their native patterns of contrastive sounds, inflectional morphology, and syntax which were laid down in early childhood strongly resist modification later in life (cf. e.g. Labov 1994:518–26). A direct consequence is that the *successful* importation of basic linguistic structures into one's native dialect from significantly different dialects or languages is normally beyond the capability of adults, for essentially the same reason that the native acquisition of foreign languages is beyond the capability of adults. On the other hand, adults routinely import their native linguistic structures into languages that they have learned imperfectly in adulthood (Rayfield 1970:103–7, Prince and Pintzuk 2000); that phenomenon is, so to speak, the other side of the same coin.

It should now be clear how we recognize cases of direct linguistic descent: since descent is an unbroken chain of NLA, and since basic language structures are acquired well only in NLA, basic linguistic structure is the best guide to linguistic ancestry. That is why Antoine Meillet was right to assert, nearly eighty years ago, that a language's inflectional morphology reveals its descent most clearly (Meillet 1925:22–33).

We know that parts of speech communities lose contact over time, and that their (originally identical) dialects gradually become more and more unlike each other because they are no longer sharing linguistic changes. Taken together with what has been said above, that makes the use of a tree model of linguistic evolution obviously appropriate. Moreover, if there were no further relevant phenomena, linguistic evolutionary trees should be clean in the following sense. If loanwords and easily repeatable innovations are excluded from consideration, every remaining historical development should occur at a unique position in the evolutionary tree, dividing it without residue into two non-overlapping portions each of which forms a connected subset of the nodes of the tree. In the technical language of cladistics, such an innovation separates two *states* of a *character* (a parameter in terms of which languages can be compared). All characters should be *compatible* with the true evolutionary tree; that is, each state of every character should be assignable to a connected subset of the nodes of the tree.

This is worth emphasizing, since the tree (or *Stammbaum*) model has been out of fashion in historical linguistics for a long time. Yet evolutionary trees seem to be virtually forced on us by the structure of language replication as discovered by modern work on language acquisition. That is actually not surprising: the fact that linguistic evolutionary trees with which a great majority of characters are compatible can be constructed shows that the model has some validity (cf. Ringe, Warnow and Taylor 2002:111–2).

However, a closer look reveals that, while evolutionary trees do in fact capture fundamental aspects of language diversification for exactly the reasons outlined above, the real situation is not so simple (cf. especially Ross 1997). Though we do not need to reject the tree model, we do need to look beyond it.

4 Complications

Everything said above is solidly grounded in scientific observation, but for the nonspecialist interested in language history the discussion raises more questions than it answers. To begin with, structural changes are known to spread through speech communities by a kind of borrowing; if the borrowing of structure is so difficult, how do innovations spread at all? Part of the explanation is that they spread via speakers still in late childhood, who are still able to learn new structures natively; but there are two other important aspects of the problem as well. In all well-studied cases innovations are spreading by borrowing between closely related dialects whose structures are already very similar anyway; and it stands to reason that the more closely congruent the structures, the easier structural borrowing will be. That point needs to be emphasized because it is often not understood: contact between closely related dialects is *not at all* the same as contact between significantly different speech forms, and the consequences of those two types of contact are very different. But it is also true that the borrowing of structural innovations is often imperfect, so that the innovations actually change as they spread. Obvious examples are the spread of raised diphthongs in the English of Martha's Vineyard to new speakers and new phonological environments simultaneously (as described in Labov's pioneering study of 1963) and the spread of tensed and raised /æ:/ in an irregular pattern in the English of north eastern U.S. cities (as described by Labov, Yaeger, and Steiner 1972).

What are the consequences of all this for linguistic history and linguistic cladistics? The consequences for historical linguistics in general are not as great as might be expected, because of a major methodological constraint: the structural patterns which are the 'signature' of the spread of innovations through a speech community can be indistinguishable, at a distance of only a few generations, from patterns that arise in other ways. For instance, the inconsistent spread of a sound change will normally give rise to a handful of lexical irregularities in the phonological pattern of a language; but such irregularities can also arise by lexical analogy, by paradigm leveling, and perhaps in various other ways, and we can't always reconstruct how they arose. Those of us who conduct research on languages of the past deal with this problem by accepting a slight relaxation of theoretically optimal precision; for instance, we accept a sound change as fully regular even if there are a few unexplained lexical exceptions (say, one or two percent of the examples), and we treat as single lines of descent linguistic entities which we know must have been a little more complex than that, namely groups of closely related dialects in constant contact. As Malcolm Ross puts it, the evolutionary tree model 'is isomorphic enough with a wide-angle view of linguistic prehistory' (Ross 1997:213), though tree diagrams 'are unavoidably unsubtle' (ibid. p. 215).

For cladistics this is not problematic, either theoretically or practically, in most cases. There is no theoretical problem because closely related and mutually intelligible dialects do belong to the same language (by definition), and a language (so defined) is a real social entity with a history that can be traced. There is no practical problem in most cases because the data of the past are hardly ever good enough to allow us to distinguish subdialects from one another anyway. However, at the nodes of a tree at which languages diverge from one another a real problem does arise, because as two dialects begin to diverge they can continue to borrow linguistic material from one another (with steadily decreasing success as they become more and more different), and the 'clean speciations' which the tree model posits are in most cases idealizations which we must be careful not to take literally. Grammatical borrowing from closely related dialects also causes problems in some exceptional types of linguistic development. We will revisit that phenomenon later.

Larger-scale problems will also have occurred to the perceptive reader. Most obviously, there are foreign elements in every language; how did they get there, if children learn multiple languages without confusion and if adults are unable to adopt foreign structures into their native languages? For the most part the answer is simple: most foreign elements in every language are just vocabulary items—the kind of linguistic material that adults can learn with ease—and the borrowing of words from foreign languages by adults is both commonplace and irrelevant to linguistic descent. It is true that adults don't usually borrow items of basic vocabulary; but once a word has been borrowed in any meaning, and has become part of the native lexicon, its meaning can gradually shift over time until it works its way into the language's basic vocabulary. In our previous work we have reacted to this fact in the obvious way: we have attempted to identify all loanwords and exclude them from the input data, since instead of contributing to our attempts to recover linguistic ancestry they actually distort the picture.

But there are also phenomena in the historical record of language which look very much like the borrowing of foreign structures into native languages, a development which we provisionally regard as impossible because it has not actually been observed to occur. There are at least four quite different classes of such phenomena, which we will address in detail.

5 Nontrivial contact phenomena

The class of cases that has generated the largest literature by far are creole languages in the strict sense of the term. According to the classic definition, a creole is a pidgin which has been learned natively by children at some point (after which it behaves like any other native language). A pidgin, in turn, is a makeshift language cobbled together for the purposes of trade or other urgently necessary communication by people who do not share any language. Recent work has suggested that this scenario is oversimplified (see e.g. Sankoff 1977, 1996, Mufwene 2001); but to the extent that it is correct, the evolution of pidgins and creoles can be modeled straightforwardly as follows. According to the definition of 'descent' which we employ, a pidgin has no ancestors, and the only ancestor of a creole is a pidgin; thus every pidgin (with the creoles to which it has given rise, if any) constitutes a completely new family of languages. Because it is completely clear how to model the genesis of creoles cladistically (if the classic definition is correct), this class of phenomena is not a problem, though it is theoretically interesting and important because it represents a limiting case. On the other hand, to the extent that the genesis of creoles is more complex, they probably belong to the fourth class of contact phenomena described below.

Equally extreme and interesting, but much less well studied, is a tiny class of languages of which Michif, spoken by the Métis of western Canada, is perhaps the only unarguable example. Unlike almost all other human languages, Michif has a robustly mixed morphosyntax: its verb phrases are Cree (an Algonkian language), while its noun phrases are French. As Peter Bakker emphasizes in his recent book on the language (Bakker 1997), Michif cannot be a creole, since there has been no significant simplification of its morphology; in fact the differences between the French and Cree parts of Michif and the corresponding parts of the languages from which they have apparently been borrowed are trivial, so that speakers of Michif appear to speak a mixture of 'good' French and 'good' Cree in spite of the fact that none of them can speak either French or Cree. Unfortunately the genesis of Michif is now about two centuries in the past, so we have no opportunity to study how such languages arise. Bakker's suggestion that Michif was the conscious creation of a Métis community who were natively bilingual in French and Cree, and that its original purpose was to reinforce Métis identity and exclude outsiders, is interesting but remains unproven. But whether or not Bakker is right, the mixed morphosyntax of Michif argues strongly that it must be a language with two different linguistic ancestors; in an evolutionary tree it would have to occupy a node at which two lines of descent converged over time. Again, this is a clear and unproblematic type of case, though an extremely rare type. The only other probable example known is Mednyj Aleut, of which the morphosyntax is partly Aleut and partly Russian; unfortunately the language is not well researched. (Bakker suggests that various other 'mixed' languages may have had similar origins (Bakker 1997:195–202), but since all his other examples exhibit the morphosyntax of one preexisting language but a lexicon largely taken from another, they can have arisen by a different and less unusual process to be discussed below).

A third class of phenomena is typified by the French dialect of Prince Edward Island (PEI), one of the maritime provinces of Canada. We choose that example because, surprisingly, it is the only instance of this class of languages which has been adequately studied; we follow the analysis of Ruth King's remarkable book. What is usually said is that the francophones of PEI, who are more or less bilingual in English, have borrowed into their native language not only English words but also English syntax, thus corrupting it. King shows in detail that any such claim is unsustainable. It *is* true that contact with English has had some sort of structural effect on the dialect; and it might seem that borrowing of syntax is involved if one merely looks at a few examples, for instance:

(1) Où ce-qu' elle vient de? 'Where does she come from?'

(2) Quoi ce-qu' ils parlont about? 'What are they talking about?'
(King 2000:136)

But it turns out that some examples which are completely unproblematic in PEI French are at least very odd in English. For instance,

(3) Quoi ce-que tu as parlé hier à Jean de? (ibid. p. 146)

translates into English literally as

?*'What did you speak yesterday to John about?'

which many speakers of English find prosodically peculiar. It is also the case that colloquial French—not only the PEI dialect—does allow prepositions without surface objects, though not in the same syntactic constructions; for instance, Zribi-Hertz notes that one can say

(4) Cette valise, je voyage toujours avec. 'This suitcase I always travel with.'
(Zribi-Hertz 1984, quoted by King 2000:137)

Some of those examples, too, are ungrammatical if translated word-for-word into English; for instance,

(5) la fille que je connais très bien le gars qui sort avec (King 2000:137)

is perfectly acceptable, at least in Québec, whereas its English translation

*the girl that I know very well the guy who goes out with

is clearly unacceptable, and in fact hard to parse. What are we to make of this pattern of facts? King argues persuasively that, although PEI French has borrowed plenty of English prepositions and verb-and-particle combinations, and although that has obviously facilitated some unusual syntactic developments in the dialect, it is not a matter of borrowing English syntax. Rather, the borrowing of English words has led to a reanalysis and extension of already existing French structures, leading to a result which is different from other dialects of French, but also from any variety of English. You can call that grammatical borrowing if you like, but the fact remains that in the first instance it is lexical items that have been borrowed, and although the foreign structures associated with the foreign words have had some impact on the language's grammar, they have not simply been borrowed whole.

The importance of King's book is not, of course, that it has saved the reputation of a maligned dialect of a major language, but that it automatically casts doubt on *every* claim of direct borrowing of morphosyntax that has not been investigated in similar detail. After all, this was supposed to be one of the *best* cases of grammatical borrowing: anyone would have said, after a superficial examination of the evidence, that PEI French had obviously borrowed English preposition-stranding; but the real situation turns out to be less simple and not at all straightforward. What surprises await us in other supposedly obvious cases—for instance, the famous case of language convergence in Kupwar village in Maharashtra, for which (as King points out, pp. 44–6) we have only an anecdotal description of the social situation and a few pages of parallel examples—that is to say, *no* data that a sociolinguist would be bound to respect?

It is perfectly clear how a linguistic cladist should react to these facts: cases like PEI French are only marginally different from the completely unremarkable cases of lexical borrowing that we see everywhere we look, and they have no impact at all on linguistic descent as we have defined it; in other words, the tree model still holds. Moreover, it seems very likely that most cases of supposed structural borrowing will turn out to be similarly unproblematic.

Not all cases are unproblematic, though: the fourth and final class of odd-looking contact phenomena is a serious problem for the tree model of language evolution. It can be described as follows. A whole community of adults learns a language nonnatively, and therefore imperfectly, usually because they are a minority group residing in a country whose dominant language is not their own. Their imperfect dialect of the dominant language normally dies with them, because their children learn the language natively from native-speaker children. However, there are social circumstances in which that is not possible, so that the children of the minority group are obliged to learn natively the defective dialect of their parents, into which their parents have naturally imported some of the grammar of their native language. The result is a native dialect of the dominant language which has not arisen by an unbroken chain of instances of NLA, and that is, by definition, a problem for the evolutionary tree model.

This kind of development is rare enough that we have no studies of it in progress, but we are fairly certain that it occurs, because there are some phenomena of the historical record that cannot be explained in any other way. Three cases in particular deserve brief discussion. The dialects of Greek formerly spoken in enclaves in Asia Minor (described in Dawkins 1916) were peculiar in a number of ways, of which the most telling was that they replaced the inherited interdental fricatives, which are quite common in other dialects of Greek, with other consonants in an inconsistent pattern. The dialect of Semendere was typical: one generally found /x/ for /θ/ (thus /xerízu/ θερίζω 'I reap', /xjoró/ θεωρῶ 'I look at', /káxumi/ κάθομαι 'I sit', aorist passive suffix /-xa/ for -θα), but a few words instead exhibited /t/ (/tíra/ θύρα 'door'), /f/ (/klofára/ κλωθάρα 'spindle'), or /z/ (/angáz/ ἀγκι̃θι 'thorn'). While it is perfectly possible that the local dialect of Greek underwent a regular sound change /θ/ > /x/, it is literally inconceivable that native speakers of Greek are responsible for the other, more haphazard replacements of /θ/. Can anyone imagine native speakers failing to learn common sounds of their *native* language and consequently replacing them with other sounds? On the other hand, that is exactly what adult second-language learners do. That occurred to Dawkins in his article of 1910:

> This avoidance of the dental spirants is explained locally by the fact that these sounds do not exist in Turkish and that therefore Turkish speakers have a difficulty in pronouncing them. Also the variety of substitutions *ch, t, d, r, z* looks like the results of failures in different directions to pronounce the different sounds. It would seem from these considerations that Greek, although now losing ground, was at one time talked at least to some extent both by Italians [in the Terra d'Otranto, where a similar phenomenon is observed] and Turks. (Dawkins 1910:270)

In his book of 1916 Dawkins abandoned that explanation without discussion, presumably because he felt that he was 'getting ahead of the data'; yet in the first footnote to the book he quoted a remarkable letter of 1437:

> 'Notandum est, quod in multis partibus Turcie reperiuntur clerici, episcopi et arciepiscopi, qui portant vestimenta infidelium et locuntur linguam ipsorum et nihil aliud sciunt in greco proferre nisi missam cantare et evangelium et epistolas. Alias autem orationes dicunt in lingua Turcorum.' (Dawkins 1916:1 fn. 1)

> 'It should be noted that in many parts of Turkey are found priests, bishops and archbishops who wear the garments of the infidels and speak *their* language and don't know how to say anything in Greek, other than chanting the liturgy and the gospel and epistles. Other prayers, though, they say in the language of the Turks.' (Ringe's translation)

It perfectly clear from this document that at some point the Greek village clergy of Anatolia had become, at least in part, native speakers of Turkish! This is that rarest of rarities in historical linguistics—a sociolinguistic smoking gun—and it renders a reconstruction of the history of those dialects easy. The village clergy were the leaders, and whatever they spoke was necessarily the prestige dialect; moreover, since Greek Orthodox parish priests marry and their sons tend to become priests, the clerical class was semi-hereditary, and its dialect would continue to have a 'home base' generation after generation. But at some point the clerical families became native speakers of Turkish and not of Greek (as the letter says explicitly). Still, they had to communicate with their congregations, so they learned Greek imperfectly—and because their faulty Greek was the prestige dialect, it eventually won the sociolinguistic contest for dominance in at least some villages.

The second case is that of Ma'a, an unusual language of East Africa with Bantu (specifically, kiPare) inflectional morphology but a very mixed lexicon, over half the vocabulary being Cushitic (see Thomason and Kaufman 1988:223–8, Ehret apud Thomason 1983:216–7, Ehret 1980:105–13, 385–9). However, even the Cushitic vocabulary has been Bantuized; for instance, word-final consonants have been lost, which is what one would expect if a Cushitic language were learned nonnatively by speakers of a Bantu language (Thomason 1983:201–5, 213–4, 218). On the other hand, there are occasional Cushitic features in the productive Bantu inflectional system (ibid. pp. 205–13), including variable omission of noun-class prefixes on singular nouns and omission of object prefixes when there is an overt noun phrase object, which might suggest the imperfect acquisition of Bantu grammar by speakers of a Cushitic language. What Ma'a oral history has to say about this is interesting. They were immigrants in the South Pare area, presumably speaking a Cushitic language, but they found that their traditions and language were being lost as the younger generation learned kiPare. A large group of Ma'a therefore migrated again to preserve their cultural identity, and sure enough, those clans that did not migrate wound up speaking kiPare. Those that did migrate clearly believed that they had 'saved' their language, but the outcome suggests that they left the migration until too late: by then the younger generation were native speakers of kiPare—possibly an imperfectly learned kiPare—but not of Old Ma'a, with the result that they could learn *well* only the vocabulary of the latter language.

What is most interesting about these two cases is how different the outcomes are. We might consider modeling the case of Ma'a like that of Michif, with converging lines of development from two different evolutionary trees; but the outcome is not really similar, since the *grammar* of Ma'a is solidly Bantu while that of Michif is mixed. And Asia Minor Greek is different again: both the grammar and the vocabulary of those dialects are largely Greek, the Turkish influence appearing most notably in a few of the rarer verb endings and in a pattern of sound substitutions that must originally have been mispronunciations. So we have a range of different cases that we need to model, and it is not yet clear how to do so accurately.

The third case raises even more serious problems. As so often in historical linguistics, the problem language is English. Kroch, Taylor, and Ringe (2000) have argued that at least one Middle English dialect from the north or northeast of England was descended from the imperfect English learned by Norse-speaking adults and subsequently learned natively by their children. But the strange dialect of English that resulted from that process was mutually intelligible to its neighbor dialects, which eventually borrowed a considerable number of Norse elements from it and passed them on to other dialects of English, including the ancestor of standard Modern English; the most obvious (and notorious) Scandinavianism in our language is the 3rd person plural pronoun *they,* which is unarguably Norse in origin (Morse-Gagné, 2003). Does it follow that English as a whole has an interrupted ancestry? No, because in southern England there has surely been an unbroken chain of instances of NLA from well before King Alfred's day right down to the present. So it turns out that the borrowing of grammatical material from closely related dialects, which we cited as a problem for other reasons above, also interacts with imperfect language learning to create even more complex modeling problems.

It is not clear how common cases like the three discussed here are, but it does appear that they are not rare; if many creoles have similar origins (cf. the references at the beginning of this section), cases of the persistence of nonnatively learned grammars may actually be much more common than has been suspected. Thus the contention of Thomason and Kaufman (1988) that historical linguists need to pay more attention to contact phenomena is fully justified, whether or not one accepts their analysis of particular cases.

6 Future research

Now that we have laid out the problems we should say what we propose to do about them. Basically the difficulties are of two types:

1) Although 'classic' pidgins and creoles, and languages with genuinely mixed grammars like Michif, can be integrated into the evolutionary tree model of language descent without conceptual difficulties, native dialects which are descended from nonnative dialects are a conceptual problem, because there has been a discontinuity in transmission which is nevertheless not so great that converging lines of development or a completely new language family are appropriate models.

2) The borrowing of grammatical material between closely related dialects renders an evolutionary tree not fully adequate as a model of descent, especially

    a) at nodes in the tree where languages diverge, and

    b) when it interacts with (1).

    We have not yet figured out how to model (1). However, (2) is mathematically equivalent to a problem that we are already addressing, namely:

3) If the divergence of closely related languages has not yet resulted in any regular sound changes diagnostic of either line of descent, borrowing of vocabulary between the languages can be undetectable by philological means.

In the case of (3), the result is that no evolutionary tree will be compatible with all the data; in addition to the vertical edges that represent linguistic descent, we must posit lateral edges at specific points in time between specific languages to account for the undetectable borrowings, thus transforming the tree into a network. This is algorithmically nontrivial, since the problem, like the problem of finding evolutionary trees consistent with all the data, is NP-hard.[1] Obviously the same device is needed to model grammatical borrowing between closely related but diverging dialects, which can likewise be undetectable. Once such a network has been found for a particular dataset, it will be a matter of linguistic interpretation whether it is more likely to reflect undetectable lexical borrowing or undetectable grammatical borrowing; we are currently pursuing work on that problem (Nakhleh, Ringe and Warnow, 2005). When we have a better idea what patterns of linguistic development correspond to particular network patterns, it will be time to tackle problem (1).

Notes

1 The problem of finding evolutionary trees with which all characters are compatible is called the Perfect Phylogeny (PP) problem; on its NP-hardness see Bodlaender et al. 2000. Polynomial-time solutions of the PP problem are obtainable if one of the input parameters can be bounded (cf. Agarwala and Fernández-Baca 1994, Kannan and Warnow 1997). On NP-hardness in general see Garey and Johnson 1979.

References

Agarwala, R. and Fernández-Baca, D. (1994) A polynomial-time algorithm for the perfect phylogeny problem when the number of character states is fixed, *SIAM Journal on Computing* 23: 1216–24.

Bakker, P. (1997) *A Language of Our Own.* Oxford: Oxford U. Press.

Bodlaender, H. L., Fellows, M. R., Hallett, M. T., Wareham, H. T. and Warnow, T. (2000) The hardness of perfect phylogeny, feasible register assignment, and other problems on thin colored graphs, *Theoretical Computer Science* 244: 167–88.

Dawkins, R. M. (1910) Modern Greek in Asia Minor, *Journal of Hellenic Studies* 30: 109–32, 267–91.

Dawkins, R. M. (1916) *Modern Greek in Asia Minor.* Cambridge: Cambridge University Press.

Ehret, C. (1980) *The Historical Reconstruction of Southern Cushitic Phonology and Vocabulary.* Berlin: Reimer.

Fantini, A. E. (1985) *Language Acquisition of a Bilingual Child.* San Diego: College Hill Press.

Garey, M. and Johnson, D. S. (1979) *Computers and Intractability: A Guide to the Theory of NP-Completeness.* New York: Freeman and Co.

Gumperz, J. J. and Wilson, R. (1971) Convergence and creolization, in D. Hymes (ed.), *Pidginization and Creolization of Languages.* Cambridge: Cambridge University Press, 151–67.

Kannan, S. and Warnow, T. (1997) A fast algorithm for the computation and enumeration of perfect phylogenies when the number of character states is fixed, *SIAM Journal on Computing* 26: 1749–63.

King, R. (2000) *The Lexical Basis of Grammatical Borrowing.* Amsterdam: Benjamins.

Kroch, A., Taylor, A. and Ringe, D. (2000) The Middle English verb- second constraint: a case study in language contact and language change, in Herring, S. C., van Reenen, P. and Schøsler, L. (eds), *Textual Parameters in Older Languages.* Amsterdam: Benjamins, 353–91.

Labov, W. (1963) The social motivation of a sound change, *Word* 19: 273–309.

Labov, W. (1994) *Principles of Linguistic Change. Volume 1: Internal Factors.* Oxford: Blackwell.

Labov, W., Yaeger, M. and Steiner, R. (1972) *A Quantitative Study of Sound Change in Progress.* Philadelphia: U.S. Regional Survey.

Meillet, A. (1925) *La Méthode Comparative en Linguistique Historique.* Oslo: Aschehoug.

Meisel, J. M. (1989) Early differentiation of languages in bilingual children, in Hyltenstam, K. and Obler, L. K. (eds), *Bilingualism Across the Lifespan.* Cambridge: Cambridge University Press, 13–40.

Morse-Gagné, E. (2003) *Viking Pronouns in England: Charting the Course of THEY, THEIR, and THEM.* Dissertation, University of Pennsylvania.

Mufwene, S. (2001) *The Ecology of Language Evolution.* Cambridge: Cambridge University Press.

Nakhleh, L., Ringe, D. and Warnow, T. (2005) Perfect phylogenetic networks: a new methodology for reconstructing the evolutionary history of natural languages, *Language* 81: 382–420.

Prince, E. F. and Pintzuk, S. (2000) Bilingual code-switching and the open / closed class distinction, *University of Pennsylvania Working Papers in Linguistics* 6 (3): 237–57.

Rayfield, J. R. (1970) *The Languages of a Bilingual Community.* The Hague: Mouton.

Ringe, D., Warnow, T. and Taylor, A. (2002) Indo-European and computational cladistics, *Transactions of the Philological Society* 100: 59–129.

Ross, M. D. (1997) Social networks and kinds of speech-community event, in Blench, R. and Spriggs, M. (eds), *Archaeology and Language I: Theoretical and Methodological Orientations.* London: Routledge, 209–61.

Sankoff, G. (1977) Creolization and syntactic change in New Guinea Tok Pisin, in Sanches, M. and Blount, R. (eds), *Sociocultural Dimensions of Language Change,* New York: Academic Press, 119–30.

Sankoff, G. (1996) The oceanic substrate in Melanesian pidgin/creole revisited: a tribute to Roger Keesing, *Pacific Linguistics* C-133: 421–50.

Slobin, D. I. (ed.) (1985) *The Crosslinguistic Study of Language Acquisition. Volume 1: The Data.* Hillsdale (NJ): Lawrence Erlbaum.

Slobin, D. I. (1992) *Volume 3.* Hillsdale (NJ): Lawrence Erlbaum.

Thomason, S. G. (1983) Genetic relationship and the case of Ma'a (Mbugu), *Studies in African Linguistics* 14: 195–231.

Thomason, S. G. and Kaufman, T. (1988) *Language Contact, Creolization, and Genetic Linguistics.* Berkeley: University of California Press.

Zribi-Hertz, A. (1984) Prépositions orphelines et pronoms nuls, *Recherches Linguistiques* 12: 46–91.

13 What do creoles and pidgins tell us about the evolution of language?

Salikoko S. Mufwene
University of Chicago

1 Introduction

Bickerton (1990) and Givón (1998) claim that the development of creoles and pidgins can provide us with insights about how language has evolved in mankind. This extrapolation has been encouraged by the position that creoles have typically been developed by children from erstwhile pidgins, transforming them from protolanguages (with just embryonic grammars) to full-fledged languages (endowed with complex syntactic systems).[1] Underlying this position is the unarticulated assumption that systems evolve from simpler to more complex structures. It has mattered very little that over the past few millennia the inflectional systems of many Indo-European languages have likewise evolved from rich to poor ones, and their syntactic structures into increasingly analytical ones in which the position of syntactic constituents is critical to determining their functions. This is as true of the gradual development of the Romance languages from Latin as of English from Old English.

I argue that what little the development of creoles and pidgins tells us about the evolution of language in mankind is definitely not what has been claimed in the literature. It has to do with competition and selection during the evolution, with how gradual the process was, and with how communal norms arise. The histories of the development of creoles and pidgins in, respectively, the European plantation and trade colonies of the 17th to 19th centuries present nothing that comes close to replicating the evolutionary conditions that led to the emergence of modern language. Nor are there any conceivable parallels between, on the one hand, the early hominids' brains and minds that produced the protolanguages posited by Bickerton (1990, 2000) and Givón (1998) and, on the other, those of both the modern adults who produced (incipient) pidgins and the modern children who produce child language, even if one subscribes to the ontogeny-recapitulates-phylogeny thesis.

Givón (1998) certainly makes some correct observations regarding gradualness in the evolution of language, the coevolution of language and the cognitive infrastructure necessary to carry it, and the centrality or primacy of some aspects of language. These are precisely some of the hypotheses defended by Li (2002) and Slobin (2002), to which I also subscribe. Relying largely on my own longitudinal study of my daughter's child language (Mufwene 1999), I capitalize both on Tomasello's (2002) 'cut and paste' model of language acquisition, which suggests that learners develop the grammars of their idiolects incrementally, and on Slobin's observation that the order in which child language develops is largely also influenced by the kinds of primary linguistic data to which the learners have been exposed. My arguments regarding creoles corroborate Slobin's other observation that where a full-fledged language is already in usage, children (at child language stage) are not the innovators of the new forms and structures that spread in the language of a population. However, I also agree with DeGraff (1999a, 1999b, 2002) that they contribute to the development of creoles qua communal systems by selecting some of the adults' innovations (often associated with substrate influence), just like any other features that become part of their idiolects, and will thus make them available to future learners. (See also Mufwene, 2004.)

2 Why creoles have not developed from pidgins[2]

Most of the arguments summarized below are intended to provide a notional, not so speculative, background to the discussions in the following sections. Space limitations dictate that I not repeat here demonstrations that are elaborated in Chaudenson (2001) and Mufwene (2001).

It is surprising that the pidgin-to-creole developmental scenario has hardly been disputed for almost a whole century, from Schuchardt (1914), Jespersen (1922), and Bloomfield (1933) to the present day. A simple look at the geographical distribution of our heuristic prototypes of creoles and pidgins — those lexified by European languages — suggests already that the alleged ancestor-to-descendant connection is tenuous. Most pidgins are concentrated on the Atlantic coast of the African mainland and on Pacific islands, whereas most creoles are concentrated on Atlantic and Indian Ocean islands (including places such as Cape Verde and São Tomé) and on the Atlantic coast of the Americas.

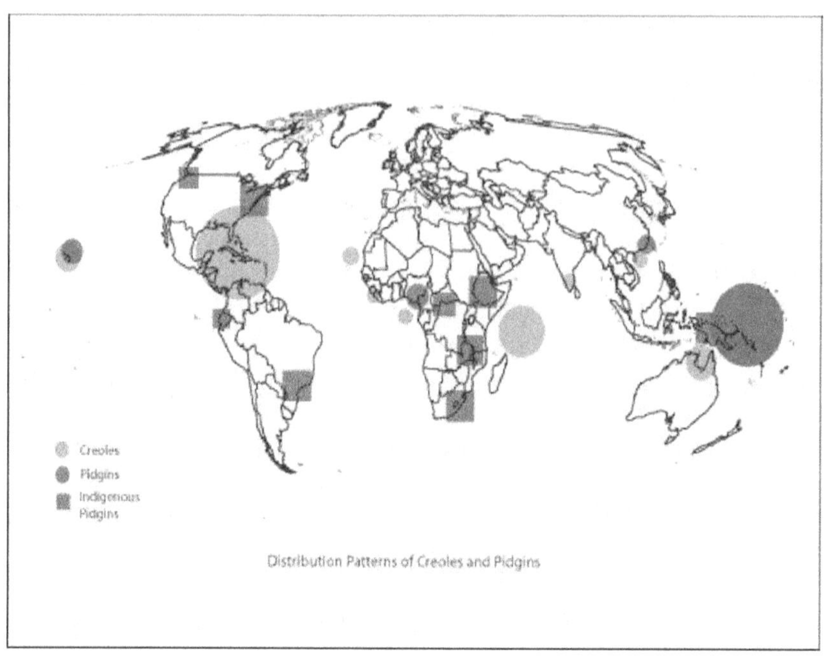

Map 1: Complementary geographical distribution of creoles and pidgins, adapted from Mufwene (2005)

The European colonization of the coast of Africa and of the Pacific islands started on the trade model,[3] characterized initially by egalitarian and sporadic contacts with the Natives, whose exposure to the European trade languages was limited. Rather than anything have to do inherently with adult L2-learning, the sporadicness of the contacts is the primary reason why incipient pidgins having been characterized as 'broken'. It is worth pointing out that the initial contacts of Europeans and the Natives depended on a handful of non-European interpreters, who spoke non-pidgin varieties Mufwene (2005). As the contacts increased, more and more non-Europeans who had no training and no access to interpreters would attempt to speak the trade language. As the number of such speakers grew, the structures of the trade languages became more divergent from the relevant European vernaculars and apparently more 'broken'.[4] The direction of the divergence is similar to that of the basilectalization process associated with the emergence of creoles, as shown below.

On the other hand, as the pidgins' communicative functions increased (such as in the cities that emerged from erstwhile trade factories), these 'contact varieties' became structurally more complex, and regularity of use gave them more stability. These additional characteristics changed them into what is known as *expanded pidgins*, like Tok Pisin and Nigerian Pidgin English, which for some speakers function also as vernaculars, rather than as lingua francas only. History suggests that children had no privileged role to play in this structural expansion (see, e.g., Mühlhäusler 1997), though they certainly helped vernacularize the varieties. The fact that some pidgins in Africa and the Pacific would develop later into vernaculars identified as *expanded pidgins* bears no consequence on Chaudenson's and my position on the development of creoles, as becomes obvious below.

Creoles have typically developed in plantation settlement colonies, in which non-Europeans formed the majority of their respective populations (Chaudenson 2001, Mufwene 2001). Although some non-plantation settlement colonies, such as those of North America and Australia, also developed with European majorities that were non-native speakers of English or French (which count among the languages that produced 'classic creoles and pidgins'), their new non-standard vernaculars have not been identified as creoles. This is a distinction that has to do more with a social bias in genetic linguistics than with actual differences in the structural processes by which new creole and non-creole varieties of European languages have evolved outside Europe (Mufwene 2001). I submit that what the relevant colonial histories show is that contact has generally played a central role in recent language speciation and most likely also in earlier stages of language evolution of the past 10,000 years or so.

In any case, creoles developed in those settings where interactions between Europeans and non-Europeans were regular during the initial, homestead phase of the colonies. Communication in almost all cultural domains was then (intended) in the European language, since, on average, non-native speakers did not have anybody else to speak their own ethnic languages with. If one were the only non-European in a homestead relatively isolated from others, there was nobody else to speak his/her language with. If there was another one in the homestead or in a neighboring one, he or she probably did not speak the same language. If they had a common language, they probably did not interact regularly enough to maintain and pass it on to children they could have had in different sexual relations. Or the children did not find the command of such non-European languages particularly advantageous to their daily lives. The earliest varieties commonly spoken and appropriated by non-Europeans were approximations of the European colonial languages forged in part by non-native European indentured servants. All locally-born children from European and non-European parents who grew up in the same homestead and spent their days together while their parents were at work spoke alike, regardless of how their parents spoke the local vernacular (Chaudenson 1992, 2001). The experience of such children would not have been different from that of Black middle-class kids growing up in integrated neighborhoods in American cities today, whose linguistic features typically reflect those of the larger community rather those of their parents, especially if these are immigrants.

Among the non-Europeans, the local European language gradually evolved into a different variety during the plantation phase, after the population majorities consisted not only of non-Europeans but also of non-native speakers, thanks to rapid population turnovers and increases made possible by importations rather than by birth. Although segregation played a role in fostering the divergence of speech varieties of Europeans and non-Europeans, the increasing demographic dominance of non-native speakers among non-Europeans communicating primarily among themselves in the new vernacular also favored a greater role of non-European substrate influence.[5]

Bickerton (1988) agrees with part of the above position, as he admits that creoles did not develop from erstwhile pidgins and that their basilects developed later than their mesolects. The intimate living conditions shared by Europeans and non-Europeans alike during the homestead phase of settlement colonies made no allowance for the development of pidgins as structurally reduced language varieties associated with sporadic contacts. As we rethink the colonial history of the New World in particular, it appears that the Europeans colonized it in two concurrent ways. All along the Atlantic coast and on its barrier islands — including the Caribbean, Bermuda, and the Bahamas — they developed settlement colonies on land which they gradually took away from the Native Americans. At the same time, the Europeans also developed trade relations with the Natives, before they eventually drove them westwards and into reservations and eventually absorbed large proportions of the survivors of this invasion into new, European-styled socio-economic systems, especially since the 19th century. Pidgins in the Americas developed from those originally sporadic trade contacts between Europeans and non-Europeans. We just must address the enigma of why 'classic pidgins' in Africa and the Pacific developed from European languages but their counterparts in the Americas did from indigenous ones, for instance, Chinookan for Chinook Jargon, Delaware for Delaware Jargon, Choctaw for Mobilian Jargon, and Tupi for Lengua Geral.[6]

Structural similarities between expanded pidgins and creoles reflect the fact that they were developed largely by linguistic adults interacting regularly among themselves, using materials from typologically related European and/or substrate languages to meet diverse and complex communicative needs, and thus needing complex grammatical structures. Substrate influence seems to have been greater in colonies that Chaudenson (1979–2001) identifies as endogenous and where there was relatively more ethnolinguistic homogeneity in the substrate population (Sankoff & Brown 1976, Sankoff 1984, Mufwene 1986, Keesing 1988, Singler 1988). It was less significant in exogenous colonies (i.e., those where both Europeans and non-Europeans had relocated, such as in the New World and in the Indian Ocean) and obviously where the pattern of population growth from the homestead to the plantation societies fostered gradual divergence from the relevant European language, contrary to the allegedly catastrophic kind of restructuring that has often been claimed (notably by Bickerton 1981, 1094, 1999).

The above observations are among the assumptions underlying my discussion below about whether or not the development of creoles and pidgins can inform our speculations about how language evolved in mankind. In sum, creoles did not evolve from erstwhile pidgins. Creoles developed independently from pidgins, the former in plantation settlement colonies and the latter in trade colonies. Both developed gradually, from closer approximations of the initial targets to varieties more and more different from them. They are creations no more of children exclusively than they are of adult L2-learners exclusively. Actually, substrate influence in creoles would be difficult to account for if the role of adult non-native speakers as carriers of xenolectal features were not factored in our hypotheses. The role of children in the development of creoles involved selecting some of those substrate features into their idiolects and making them available to future learners.

3 Why creoles were not made by children

Kegl and McWhorter (1997), Kegl et al. (1999) and Goldin-Meadow (2002) argue convincingly that children could develop elaborate sign languages. The fact that, in the case of Nicaraguan Sign Language (NSL), the new system is largely a systematization of materials that were already available to the children in their community (Sengha & Coppola 2001, Kegl et al. 1999, Morford 2002) reduces nothing in the important role that children played in elaborating a long-lasting communicative system. In this respect, they can very well be compared to our hominid ancestors at various stages of the evolution of mankind, who would develop a more elaborate and systematic communicative means from what had been used by the earlier generation of hominids. Goldin-Meadow's evidence can even be used to argue that systematicity did not develop because speakers/signers had to communicate with each other but because they had to be individually consistent (Mufwene 1989). Among the relevant questions at the population level are the following two: How do communal norms develop? Does the development of communal norms entail the elimination of inter-individual variation? The available evidence from child language and creoles militates for a negative answer to the second question. MacWhinney (2002:254) even observes that 'we should not be surprised to find large individual differences in the neuronal basis of higher-level dynamic control of language.'

In any case, the evidence from home sign language and NSL are not comparable to those of the development of creoles or pidgins. More interesting about incipient pidgins is the fact that they represent simplifications, reductive developments of some sort, from full-fledged languages. Evolutionarily, they have evolved in the opposite direction of protolanguage, which started from non-linguistic means of communication.[7] At best, what they teach us about the evolution of language is that not all structural components of modern linguistic systems are as deeply entrenched. Those morphosyntactic components that survive the 'breakdown,' so to speak, that produces incipient pidgins may be the most deeply entrenched in the architecture of language. The same is true of these incipient varieties' heavy dependence on the pragmatic context for the interpretation of utterances, as highlighted by the language disorder cases discussed by MacWhinney (2002). The development of more complex structures would thus have streamlined the interpretation of utterances and reduced dependence on non-linguistic context.

MacWhinney (2002:250–251) also argues that the ability to use articulate sounds to communicate linguistically developed between 200,000 and 50,000 years ago, and thus brought the increased brain size in hominids to its full communicative potential, such as to develop a larger lexicon and, later on, to combine words into larger strings.[8] Interestingly, the phonemic systems of incipient pidgins reflect mostly interference from languages previously spoken by the speakers. They don't reveal the kind of 'breakdown' evidenced by the morphosyntactic components, which dispenses with some lexical and grammatical categories. Thus incipient pidgins support the hypothesis that the ability to produce phonemic sounds is one of the most deeply entrenched components of spoken languages.

Regarding creoles, we must recall that it has all along been misguided to define creoles as nativized pidgins. Neither the geographical distribution of creoles and pidgins nor the respective socio-economic histories of the territories where creoles developed support this position. Assuming that contact has played a central role in the evolution of, say, Indo-European languages outside and within Europe, creoles developed by the same normal restructuring processes, although the role of language contact must have been made more obvious by the non-European composition of the populations appropriating the European languages (Mufwene 2001). Below, I adduce structural arguments against the position that creoles were made by children, although, in communities where adult L2-speakers and children use the same vernaculars, children produce utterances that apparently vary less in their structures from one speaker to another (p.c., Givón, 11 June 2001). Senghas and Coppola (2001) show that the signers exposed to NSL as children (below 10 years of age) sign more systematically, uniformly, and fluently than adults.

Children did indeed play a non-negligible role in the development of these new vernaculars, but it was not that of creating a grammar where their parents would presumably have failed. It is not true that incipient pidgins have no grammars, although these are internally variable.[9] Rather than creating new grammars for the overall community, children participated in the development of creoles (not from erstwhile pidgins) by selecting particular features (including xenolectal ones) and helping them prevail over other alternatives and thus possibly reducing the extent of variation as a new norm emerges (DeGraff 1999a, 1999b, 2002). Creole children did this in the same way children everywhere normally contribute to both changes and stabilization of their target language.[10]

First language (L1) development is a protracted process and reaches maturity after the speaker passes the critical period, i.e., by the time the speaker may be considered linguistically adult. Structures of English creoles are not identical with those of English child language, despite some similarities between them. For instance, English-speaking children do not produce the kinds of serial verb constructions attested in Saramaccan, for example, where a serial *give* conveys a dative function. Nor do they distinguish between the kinds of aspectual nuances attested in Gullah and Guyanese Creole, in which the preverbal marker *don(e)* (from non-standard/colloquial English PERFECT verb *done* 'finish' rather than from the standard English past participle of *do*) conveys a different PERFECT meaning from the post verbal marker *don*, at least to those who use both constructions. While *me done talk* [mi dʌn/dɔn tɔ:k/ta:k] simply means 'I have spoken', *me talk done* means more than that in these creoles, viz., 'I have said all I had to say and don't intend to talk again'.

Aside from the PROGRESSIVE construction with preverbal *de*, as in *mi de taak* 'I am talking', Guyanese Creole also has a more specific, composite construction with preverbal *de a*, as in *mi de a taak* 'I am busy talking'. These are sophisticated grammatical distinctions which do not seem to have been inovated by English-speaking children. No parallel contrasts have been documented in English child language. Also, almost all Atlantic creoles have Predicate-Clefting, as in *duh* [də] *talk he duh talk*, illustrated here from Gullah and meaning 'he is/was really talking'. This can also be heard in nominalizations such as *you shoulda hear da* [də] *talk he duh talk* 'you should have heard how he was talking.' Like regular cleft constructions in English, this is definitely linguistic competence beyond child language, at least by age 3, the period that seems to have concerned Bickerton (1990).

If children innovated these structures in creoles, then they must have innovated them when they became linguistically adults, and we must wonder why their adult parents would have waited for them (the children) to innovate for the community when they (the parents) could have done so themselves.

The answer can of course be similar to that provided by Judy Kegl and her associates about the role of children in the development of NSL, on which I comment above. However, the fact that only English creole-speaking children, but not their Anglophone counterparts, acquire these distinctions by the end of the critical period is a reflection of the influence that adult speech exerts on child language development. It also shows that, by the principle of least effort, creole children, like children everywhere, develop their idiolects from the PLD available to them from adult speech, even if this happens horizontally through the mediation of other children. We could also extrapolate that where the PLD lead to variable systems, children will also make allowance for variation in their idiolects. This extrapolation explains why the variation mischaracterized as '*(post-)creole* continuum' was not eradicated by children who participated in the development of creoles, not any more than any variation, or speech continuum, in any other language community would have been eliminated by children.[11]

Thus, we should not confuse variation in the structures produced by adult L2-speakers with the suggested inability on their part to develop a grammar or to innovate in the direction of a new full-fledged vernacular.[12] Although several of their innovations must have not made their way into today's creoles, this is the normal case with innovations, which occur daily, in any speech community. The vast majority of them bear no impact on the communal language of a population. There is no compelling evidence for the conjecture that creoles owe to creations by children the structures that distinguish them from the European languages from which they have evolved. The case is even less convincing where the innovations can be related to features of substrate languages. The language bioprogram hypothesis (LBH) precludes children from transferring elements of substrate languages into the emergent creoles, because they had no prior knowledge of a language before the one they are misguidedly claimed to have created for their communities.

The fact that not all creoles have the particular constructions discussed here also suggests that, in the first place, there is no particular, uniform creole grammar that is replicated from one creole to another. It also shows clearly how futile it is to invoke children as the primary or exclusive makers of creoles — at least not at the child language stage — because these vernaculars contain some structures that have not been attested in child-language versions of the relevant European languages.

Most of the arguments for claiming that creoles were developed by children have had to do with the poverty, or absence, of inflections in these vernaculars. First, as argued by Slobin (2002), whether or not child language lacks inflections depends on what the target language is and how significant the role of inflections is in it. DeGraff (2001) also shows that creoles are not as much deprived of inflections as has been claimed. In the very least, the old myth is not true of Haitian Creole.

What all these observations point to is that like language development among children, the development of creoles is subject to structural and ethnographic factors in the relevant linguistic communities. My own study of my daughter's child language (Mufwene 1999) suggests that the kinds of over-generalizations of regular morphological rules (such as *goed* for *went* and *falled* for *fell*) that occur when English-speaking children are 3 to 4 years old are transitional. At a younger age, my daughter had *fell* in contrast with *falling* and *went* in contrast with *going*, though there was no evidence that the pairs were grammatically related. While acquiring negation before age 3, my daughter also produced *didn fell, didn took, didn saw*, and *didn woke*, instead of *didn't fall, didn't take, didn't see*, and *didn't wake*, and she abandoned these deviations as soon as she became aware that adults around her do not typically use these past tense forms with *didn't*. Note, however, that the origins of the forms and constructions themselves are in adult speech, consistent with the Tomasello (2002) 'cut and paste' model of L1-learning assumed here.

From a developmental perspective, children are more conformist and imitative than has been suggested, or claimed, in some child language literature, although they do indeed construct gradually the grammars of their idiolects by inference from the PLD that are accessible to them. They abandon their deviations quickly to conform to adult norms, including variation within those norms, as is evident from language communities anywhere, creole and non-creole alike. Given the way plantation settlement societies developed, we have no evidence for assuming that, linguistically and socially, slave children behaved differently from other children and did not just learn the vernaculars around them, as emergent as these were. Creole children must have contributed to the normalization through the selections they made from the feature pool of variants, thus determining (albeit non-deliberately, through the population-level distribution of their individual selections) how much xenolectal element would become part of the systems these vernaculars now have. The children never were the majority, nor did they form sub-communities of their own that were isolated from adult communities. There is no particular non-structural, ethnographic reason why they would have imposed norms of their own over those of the adults about them. They mostly perpetuated variants of the vernaculars that were already normalized or normalizing around them. We must recall that creole children were not in situations similar to those of Nicaraguan deaf children, because there always was a full-fledged language of the same modality around them, regardless of the extent of population-level variation in it.

According to Mufwene (2001), children actually slowed down the divergence process during the development of creoles. This is because during the most prosperous period of the plantation colonies (i.e., the 18th century in the Atlantic and Indian Ocean colonies, and the 19th century in the Pacific), their populations grew more by importations than by birth. While the children 'acquired' natively the local vernaculars that they heard around them and targeted, adult non-native speakers continued to restructure them, influencing them with their xenolectal features. There is still a lot to be learned about the dynamics of competition and selection among structural features of the European and substrate languages in the plantation settlement colonies (Mufwene 2001, 2002).

Still, we must remember that in this respect the difference between plantation societies and other communities is only a matter of degree. Variation is everywhere. Nowhere else have children been led by the circumstances to create a new language which would replace their parents' variable system. Slobin (2002) is correct again in holding adults as the primary innovators that should matter in language change and the development of creoles. Children play an undeniable role in helping determine which of those innovations become part of the communal language and which of the extant variants become recessive and may eventually die out of the ever-evolving language. So far we have no reason for assuming that the development of creoles is not the outcome of normal language change and diversification (Mufwene 2001). Thus, there is no empirical support for the LBH or the way Bickerton (1981) hypothesized Universal Grammar (UG) to work in the development of creoles, crediting children almost exclusively with the emergence of their grammars.

4 Do creoles tell us something about the evolution of language in mankind?

Bickerton's (1990) arguments that creoles and child language can give us insights about how language evolved in mankind are partly based on the assumption that ontogeny recapitulates phylogeny. They are also based on his hypothesis that creoles were made by children from erstwhile pidgins. As explained above, his position both lacks the support it would need from the socio-economic histories of creole-speaking societies and the logical justification that would make it even plausible.[13] I focus here on the ontogeny-recapitulates-phylogeny aspect of Bickerton's arguments and derive my support largely from Givón (1998), Li (2002), and MacWhinney (2002).

We must start with the fact that creoles' grammars show no evidence of having started from scratch or of having developed according to unmarked parametric settings of UG (cf. Bickerton 1981–1999). If these vernaculars had been produced by children, independent of the PLD available in their alleged grammar-less pidgin ancestors or, more realistically, independent of the data available in the colonial varieties of the European languages from which they have evolved, their grammars would not vary at all from one creole to another.[14] Creoles' grammars do indeed vary, reflecting the extent of inheritance from the European language and/or that of substrate influence.

Contrary to what has been suggested at least by the earliest versions of Bickerton's LBH (1981, 1984), speakers do not develop grammars of their language varieties independent of the acquisition of their vocabularies. As suggested by Bolinger (1973), grammars are largely generalizations over the behaviors of individual lexical items. As a matter of fact, I submit that they are more projections on the part of the linguist, in their attempt to account for how we communicate (as we infer the existence of systems consisting of units and of combinatory rules) than they exist of necessity. (See also Le Page & Tabouret-Keller 1985:332.)

The connection between, on the one hand, creoles and, on the other, the relevant European and substrate languages is unmistakable once one compares them not so much with the standard varieties of European languages but with the non-standard vernaculars actually spoken by the European yeomen and indentured servants with whom the non-European labor interacted regularly. Alternately, creoles' structures should be compared with those of the other vernaculars that have evolved from the koinés spoken by the proletarian European settlers, the typical founder populations of European colonies, with whom non-Europeans lived fairly intimately during the homestead phases.

One is hard-pressed to find in creoles any grammatical features that have not been selected from the non-standard varieties of the relevant European vernaculars or in their substrate languages. There is in non-standard English evidence of most of the features associated with English creoles, for instance, nominal plural with *them*, copula absence, periphrastic marking of tense-aspect (viz., unstressed habitual *do* [də] and *does* [dəz], stressed remote phase *been* [bɪn] — though this occurs typically with a contracted *have* — continuative *do/duh* [də], perfect *done*, invariant relativization with *what* or a null complementizer, and reported speech introduced by *say*.)And there is similar evidence in Romance creoles (Chaudenson 1992, 2001). Even serial verb constructions have partial models in the relevant European languages. (See, for instance, Pullum 1990 regarding how they work in English.)

The key to understanding why creoles are different from their non-creole kin that evolved from similar colonial varieties of European languages is that language acquisition is a reconstruction process, which is sensitive to the variants in competition in the pool of features available to individual learners. The contact ecology of the appropriation of the European languages varied from one colony to another and from one period to another, which accounts also for why each creole is somewhat different from others that developed from what has been identified, for convenience sake, as more or less the same language. Moreover, linguistic features often get modified during the acquisition process, especially during L2 acquisition, as every learner analyses the PLD from which they develop their idiolects on their own, without particular explicit training. In the case of the development of creoles, congruence between structural features of the relevant European and substrate languages has been a critical factor, as clearly articulated recently in Corne (1999), Chaudenson (2001), Mufwene (2001), and DeGraff (2002). Thus, as also argued by Chaudenson (1992, 2001) and Mufwene (2001), creoles have developed by gradual restructuring away from structures of the earliest colonial koinés of the relevant European languages in the direction of their basilects, which are actually the latest to have evolved. (See also Bickerton 1988.) None of this evolutionary process is remotely suggestive of how language evolved in mankind, originally from prelinguistic means of communication to protolanguage, concurrently with changes in the structure of human brain (Li 2002, MacWhinney 2002).

The relation of the development of creoles to language acquisition deserves some elaboration. We must first of all dismiss the myth that creoles have diverged from the relevant varieties of European languages because there was a break in the transmission of the latter to non-European groups on the plantations (e.g., Polomé 1983, Thomason & Kaufman 1988). Not even the lexicon of creoles would have been inherited so predominantly from the relevant European languages (at least 90% on average) if there had been a break in the transmission of the latter. And one could not possibly imagine a group acquiring the vocabulary of a language, even under the conditions of sporadic contacts that produced pidgins, without getting some of the grammar associated with it.[15]

Admitting substrate influence does not entail ignoring numerous basic structural similarities (not due to any universals) which obtain between creoles and the relevant European languages from which they developed. The following randomly cited features will suffice to illustrate my point: 1) the phonologies of creoles largely reflect how the colonial varieties of the relevant European languages were spoken (e.g., the palatalized pronunciation of *cat* as [k^{y}at] and *pear* as [p^{y}ɛ] in Jamaican Creole); 2) the extensive use of adjectives and their prenominal use in English creoles;[16] 3) English creoles have definite articles where most substrate languages use a distal demonstrative;[17] 4) the postposed 'determiner' *la* in Haitian Creole does not lack affinity with a similar morpheme which has similar morphosyntax, semantics, and pragmatics in non-standard colloquial French varieties; and 5) the fact that only (Atlantic) English creoles use a form evolved from the verb *say* as a complementizer must have something to do with the fact that colloquial and non-standard English has more uses of *say* to report speech quotatively than French (Mufwene 1996) etc. An important question here that has typically been overlooked in the literature on the development of creoles is: Does 'substrate influence' mean the same thing as 'source of a structural feature?'

Language acquisition is of course imperfect, but, as noted by Lass (1997), imperfect replication is a normal condition in language transmission. Otherwise, there would be no language change in the first place, regardless of whether it is internally or externally motivated. Even in ethnographic ecologies where no contact of significantly different dialects or separate languages is involved, a language or dialect is usually appropriated by other speakers with minor modifications. Most of these coincide with variants already available in the communal language or dialect. However, sometimes others creep in, and/or the dynamics of the coexistence of variants in the population of speakers may change in such ways that some of the variants become stronger and may even drive others out. Such accretions of modifications are what linguists later identify as language change.

It is also useful to underscore the fact that 'language transmission' and 'language acquisition' are convenient misnomers for processes that are much more complex (DeGraff 1999a, 1999b, 2001, 2002; Mufwene (2001, 2004). Speakers of a language provide only the PLD to the learners. Nobody ever transmits an integrated linguistic system to other speakers, and no speaker ever passively inherits such a ready-made idiolect from previous speakers. Acquisition as a reconstruction process advances piecemeal, with the language learner developing competence in the target language only gradually. There is indeed some language-building activity on the part of the learner, though it is not clear how the construction proceeds, i.e., whether or not the learner is focusing on developing a system or just trying to communicate successfully.

In the case of a child, misperception or inaccurate analogy with something previously learned may account for deviations. In the case of an adult learner, aside from these particular reasons, previously established linguistic habits (i.e., xenolectal influence) also account for such deviations. One thing is certain, the learner tries to speak like those speakers of the language that he/she targets, but he/she is not targeting a grammar or system in the way that a linguist would do by collecting a body of data, analyzing them, and producing an analysis of the system that can be inferred. McCawley's (1976) observation that a child should not be thought of as a mini-linguist can be generalized to say that a naturalistic language learner is not a linguist, especially since he/she approaches his/her communicative challenges bit by bit, without waiting until enough data have been collected. The process of generalizing from previously learned cases appear to be analogical.

Tomasello (2002) provides just the right kind of language development framework to account for this natural phenomenon of deviation or divergence from the target. His approach makes it possible for us to realize that the difference between deviations in L1 development and deviations in L2 development lies not in how these deviations happen but in the additional causes for the deviations in L2 development. Naturally the additional causes increase the potential for deviations and produce in part what is known as non-native accent. Otherwise, we see in both cases a confirmation of Meillet's (1929) and Hagège's (1993) observation that language 'acquisition' involves both inheritance from the target and recreation by the learner. The recreations involve innovations by the learner, regardless of whether they are made possible by analogies perceived in the target language itself or are caused by knowledge of another language. It is irrelevant whether at the communal level such innovations produce new features or mere deviations from the target communal language. When they do, we say that a language has evolved into another state, such as from Old to Middle English, or from English to creoles. As creoles appear to be normal outcomes of language appropriation by new populations under contact conditions in which substrate influence applies, Bickerton's (1990, 2000) claim that they can inform us about how language has evolved in mankind is not justified. If they do, it must be in respect to gradualness, competition and selection among variants, and the development of norms in populations of speakers. I return to these determinative factors of evolution below.

5 What creoles tell us about the evolution of language

We can now return to Givón's (1998) thesis that the evolution of language in mankind is an adaptive process. In child language, the development of creoles, and other cases of language change, semantic and morphosyntactic innovations are especially exaptive, responding to (new) communicative needs of speakers beyond functions they have fulfilled in the target or earlier stages of the relevant language (Mufwene 2001). One thing that is especially noteworthy about creoles is that, despite their divergence from their non-creole kin, they have preserved both several features of the relevant European languages and complexities similar to those attested in several other languages spoken by modern humans.

If creoles had really developed from erstwhile pidgins, progressing from simpler to more complex grammatical structures, their development would share with the evolution of language as hypothesized by Givón the fact that every later stage exapted materials in the earlier stage. The closest analog to this evolution would be home sign language starting in part from the gestures used by their speaking parents and innovating on their own, gradually developing a communicative system with rudimentary grammar. However, this observation remains guarded, because Goldin-Meadow (2002) does not discuss whether such home sign language had developed into adult language. She does not discuss it as a population-level process similar to the NSL case, in which one can observe the development of a communal norm.

One particular characteristic that all the above cases of language development and evolution share is that they are all gradual processes. Givón (1998:105) submits that 'human language (...) arose from the co-evolution of cognitive, neurological, communicative and socio-cultural patterns of pre-human *hominids.*' Complementing this, Li (2002) and MacWhinney hypothesize that (proto) language evolved from gestural means of communication (about 6 million years ago) to vocalizations and eventually to phonetic linguistic systems (between 200,000 and 50,000 years ago), concurrently with the emergence of the specific physiological and mental infrastructures required to support the complex-thought-processing capacity required to manipulate modern human languages. L1 development, from child to adult grammar, is also correlated with cognitive maturation/sophistication. The development of creoles and pidgins is similar only in being gradual processes.

Note that the problem pointed out by Slobin (2002) and Li (2002) remains, viz., that human infants today are born both with a brain infrastructure and in language ecologies that already distinguish them from our hominid ancestors. Therefore the ontogeny-recapitulates-phylogeny assumption does not apply at all. Modern children are typically born to social environments in which full-fledged languages are being spoken. The order in which they develop competence in their native languages, starting with basic and simple structures, reflect the maturation of their cognitive capacities. Although language 'acquisition' is a reconstruction process, modern children cannot be credited with inventing a language in the same way that our hominid ancestors gradually invented language. If it is true that an individual's genotype determines his/her biological life trajectory, then, by the natural selection process that favored the modern human over other hominid alternatives, modern infants are born prewired to 'acquire' the modern languages of the communities to which they are born. In this respect creole children are <u>not</u> different from other children.

The development of creoles and pidgins as communal languages also suggests another rarely discussed parallelism with the evolution of language in mankind as a population process, viz., inter-individual variation and the competition and selection that follow from it in the emergence of communal norms. We must remember that communal languages are only extrapolations from idiolects and language acquisition is an individual-based process (Mufwene 2001). Inter-individual variation is a consequence of the fact that no explicit teaching is involved in naturalistic language transmission and humans are not equally gifted in learning social skills. Current speakers only provide the PLD from which the learners can construct their idiolectal systems, which need not be identical with each other, though they are similar. As remarked by Chomsky (2000:100), 'We need not assume shared pronunciations or meanings to account for [successful communication], any more than we assume shared shapes to account for people who look alike.'

We must, however, ask why inter-idiolectal differences among the members of a language or dialect community are not as great as they could be. Part of the answer lies in the Cartesian assumption that UG, also identified as the biological endowment for language, is the same for all modern humans. According to Chomsky (2000:30), 'The only (virtually) 'shared structure' among humans is generally the initial state of the language faculty' (i.e., UG). Consistent with the fact that language development is gradual and protracted over years, another part of the explanation lies in the mutual accommodations that speakers make to each other, bringing their systems closer to each other, at least in respect to the structures of the utterances they produce. These mutual accommodations are part of what Mufwene (2001) characterizes as competition and selection, which operate in the feature pool to which all speakers make contributions. Like in evolutionary biology, *competition* is a convenient misnomer for the coexistence of variants associated with the same, or similar, functions in a system, in which they are not equally weighted. *Selection* refers to the advantage conferred to some of the variants that either prevail alone or are simply preferred (in more contexts) over other alternatives. In settings where several languages and/or dialects are spoken, competition and selection apply also to the different varieties (dialects and/or languages) in contact. We can say that they compete for speakers. It can reasonably be surmised that these principles, which are obvious in language acquisition and language change, must have also applied in the evolution of language in mankind. (Influences across languages are possible because languages are not selected wholesale with their features integrated, but rather because speakers develop their competences piecemeal, selecting features incrementally, often regardless of their sources.)

Notwithstanding the fact that ecology rolls the dice to resolve competition, even in maintaining variation, we can imagine that spoken language was generally favored over signed language for precisely some of the reasons articulated by Givón (1998:89), such as the following: 1) 'freeing the hands and the body

(...) so that communication may now proceed simultaneously with manual activities, and can in fact support them'; and 2) 'transcending the visual field' so that 'auditory-oral communication may proceed in the dark, in thick bush, over physical barriers that prevent eye contact.'[18]

Structural differences and typological variation among the world's languages are a reminder of the variation that must have obtained locally and across distances in the evolution from gestural to linguistic communication in mankind. It is not far-fetched to speculate that competition and selection must have played an important role in reducing the range of wave frequencies used by humans in their phonetic inventories. They must also have played a role in leading members of individual communities to agree on the number of the specific phonemes they use, on the range of variation in the production of these phonemes, and on the way they combine them into longer meaningful utterances (words and sentences). Thus, they can tell which variants have normally been generated by their communal language and which ones have not.

Given the ways in which incipient pidgins dispense with much of the structural systems of the languages from which they evolved, we can surmise that they preserve the components of language architecture that are the most robust and perhaps the most deeply entrenched.[19] For instance, they remain languages because they remain discrete and combinatorial spoken systems (relying on limited phonetic inventories), make use of lexical items, and preserve the symbolic referential function of language.[20] Not having a complex grammar accounts for why pidgins are said to rely heavily on pragmatic context for rich semantic interpretation, which seems to support Givón's (1998:92) hypothesis that grammar has provided 'speeded-up, more automated language processing,' making full-fledged languages less dependent on pragmatic context.

From the point of view of child language, one can argue that modern human infants are already preprogrammed for symbolic communication, in the spirit of Chomsky's UG (though details remain to be worked out) and that learning a native language entails starting with those aspects of communication that are phylogenetically the most deeply entrenched as determined in part by the state of the infant's cognitive capacity. However, we must remember that, unlike our hominid ancestors, modern children do not normally develop their own separate communal languages from particular gestural means of communication nor embryonic languages, and independent of what the adults who nurture them do to communicate. Thus the above observations do not lead to the traditional conclusion that ontogeny recapitulates phylogeny. There is certainly nothing in the development of creoles and pidgins that comes close to supporting such a claim.

It is also noteworthy that the structural heterogeneity of creoles that has aptly been characterized in the literature as a continuum largely reflects the fact that those who developed them were not engaged in the process as a team. Rather, each one of them was personally trying to communicate and in the process developed their own individual idiolect, though they exerted mutual influences on each other — which accounts for the family resemblance that obtains among the idiolects of a communal language. The divergence of creoles from the relevant European languages is simply a selective accumulation of divergences that took place convergently in the idiolects of speakers, just what happens in any case of language evolution. We can surmise that our hominid ancestors who developed protolanguage(s) did not proceed like a team either, as much as members of every community must have wanted to communicate successfully with each other and converged their systems through mutual accommodations.[21] There must have been variation at all stages of language evolution, which fostered competition and selection, hence continuous evolution. Thus, at every stage of the evolution of mankind, speakers modified the language they learned from the preceding 'generation of speakers' (regardless of age group), children and adults all engaged in the process.

Acknowledgments

I am grateful to Michel DeGraff, Alison Irvine, and Bertram Malle for feedback on earlier versions of this essay. All the remaining shortcomings are my sole responsibility.

Notes

1 The order of the terms *creoles* and *pidgins* is deliberately reversed in the title of this chapter and in the whole discussion to reflect the contention that creoles have not evolved from pidgin ancestors (Alleyne 1971; Chaudenson 1992, 2001; Mufwene 1997, 2001). There is no compelling evidence in support of such an evolutionary trajectory, at least not among creoles of the New World and the Indian Ocean. What is suggested by the socio-economic histories of the territories where these language varieties have developed is an interesting geographical division of labor, which situates pidgins typically in former trade colonies and creoles in plantation settlement colonies (Mufwene 2001). More on this below.

2 Bickerton's notion of pidgins that bears on the present discussion is that they are grammar-less, which justifies comparing them to the protolinguistic ancestor of modern human languages. Among his central arguments is the

inter-individual variation observable in them. There is yet no evidence that the idiolects they consist of are not internally systematic. Neither can we overlook the inter-idiolectal variation that obtains in any language or dialect community (Paul 1891). I will assume in the rest of this paper that Bickerton must have had incipient pidgins in mind.

3 In Mufwene (2001, Chapter 1), I distinguish three different colonization styles since the 16th century, which account partly for the different linguistic developments discussed in the main text. Only the third colonization style needs to be mentioned here, the *exploitation colonies*, which developed in the 19th century from trade colonies of Africa, Asia, and Pacific islands. Europeans came to them on short-term contracts, to work for companies headquartered in their metropoles or to administer them. European languages were (re-) introduced through the school system to form an elite class of indigenous colonial auxiliaries. In using them as lingua francas, the latter developed varieties identified as *indigenized*, for instance, Nigerian English (different from Nigerian Pidgin English) and African French, which are based on scholastic, rather than non-standard or colloquial, models. The controlled, rather than naturalistic, mode of transmission associated with their emergence makes them rather irrelevant to the present discussion.

4 Bolton (2000, 2002) provides very informative accounts of the development of Chinese Pidgin English that is in agreement with the position submitted here.

5 The reader should remember that non-plantation settlement colonies had similar beginnings, with small homesteads, although they depended more on European indentured than on African slave labor. As the colonies grew larger and admitted immigrants from European nations other than the mother country, dialect and language contact played an increasingly more significant role in the evolution of colonial vernaculars, especially as the populations became less segregated by nation of origin.

6 Note that according to Keesing (1988), the birth place of Melanesian pidgins is not the plantations on which they have flourished. Rather, it is the whaling and trade ships on which some of the first plantation laborers had worked and spoken a proto-Melanesian Pidgin. This would account for structural similarities among Melanesian English pidgins, especially in those respects that distinguish them as a group from Atlantic creoles. However, Baker (1993) argues that a truer proto-Melanesian Pidgin would have evolved earlier in Australia, especially in Queensland, where several Melanesians had worked too. Moreover, Australia controlled much of that fishing and trade fleet in that part of the Pacific.

7 This is more or less in the spirit of Comrie (2000) and Kihm (2002), who observe that the makers of protolanguage did not have an antecedent (proto)language to derive materials from, although there must have been an earlier means

of communication that would have paved the way for the evolution of the earliest linguistic systems. Jackendoff (2002) speculates that communication before protolanguage must have consisted of one-'word' signs, as among non-human primates. This still makes the case of creoles and pidgins, which developed from fully developed languages, quite different.

8 Jackendoff (2002) comes close to this idea as he argues against 'syntactocentrism' in favor of 'parallel architecture' of phonology, syntax, and semantics. The evolutionary order he suggests on page 238 seems intuitively less plausible than MacWhinney's (2002) alternative, according to which syntax must have developed later than the aptitude to articulate sounds beyond vocalization (which made it possible to produce larger vocabularies) and the referential ability to use vocal symbols earlier than phonetic communication. For MacWhinney, the ability to form more words made it possible to convey more complex thoughts, which called for more complex syntax.

9 Insofar as the notion of 'idiolect' is metalinguistically significant, each one has a grammar to the extent that it is systematic, regardless of whether or not its system is identical with those of other idiolects in the relevant communal language or dialect. Like biological species, communal languages and dialects (as constructs of convenience) are internally variable (Mufwene 2001). Such variation can of course be more conspicuous in some varieties, such as incipient pidgins, than in others.

10 This fact does not of course preclude current children from producing innovations that can spread within their language communities once they are past the child-language stage.

11 For arguments against the decreolization hypothesis see Mufwene (1994).

12 Please note that pidgins have typically evolved in settings where their creators had their own vernaculars to speak outside their contacts with the populations they did not share a language with. This factor explains why expanded pidgins developed only in contact settings where speakers could not continue using their ancestral vernaculars with the other members of their new communities. Thus, creoles developed directly as vernaculars, because the members of the contact communities had no other language in common.

13 The Hawaiian plantations, which have figured prominently in Bickerton's hypothesis on the development of creoles, did not develop on the model of those of the Atlantic and Indian Oceans. To begin with, they started later (after the abolition of the slave trade and slavery), in the mid-19th century, and as a peripheral American settlement/exploitation colony. If they had a homestead phase at all, it must have been a (very) short one. In addition, the indentured laborers were not mixed, at least not as much as on the plantations of the Atlantic and Indian Oceans. They were brought successively from China,

Japan, Korea, and, later, the Philippines, at intervals of more or less twenty years (Masuda 1995) and kept in separate work camps (Masuda, p.c., March 2002). Unlike the other plantation settlement colonies, the Hawaiian setting was definitely propitious to the development of a pidgin as a reduced means of communication, because every ethnic group lived separately and used its own ethnic vernacular for in-group communication. Thus, a pidgin was needed for inter-group communication. The creole developed not on the plantations but in the city (Roberts 1998), where a more pervasive form of contact took place. It is not obvious from Roberts that the features that make Hawaiian Creole distinctive from English or other English creoles from local English were innovated by children rather than by adults. Complicating the scenario is also the fact that Pidgin Hawaiian had been spoken on the islands before the plantations started and it seems to have contributed to the development of both Hawaiian Pidgin and Creole Englishes.

14 This is where Bickerton's (1989) 'lexical learning hypothesis' still falls short of an adequate account, as he suggests that children would be inventing on their own the grammatical properties of the lexical items they nonetheless took from their parents.

15 Independent of history, Bickerton's assumption that creoles' grammars largely reflect UG with their parameters set in their unmarked options is more biased by typological markedness than by anything else. This is itself a function of a probability factor that need not be part of UG! The Cartesian conception of UG suggests that all parametric options are equivalent and only particular linguistic systems would make some variants more, or less, marked than others. Thus makers of creoles are likely to have selected options that were less marked in the structural and ethnographic contact ecologies of their developments, not necessarily in UG (Mufwene 1991, 2001).

16 We must bear in mind here the fact that the category 'Adjective' is hardly part of the grammars of many substrate languages.

17 It is not evident that usage of the quantifier 'one' in the stead of the indefinite article is exclusive substrate influence.

18 In evolutionary terms, sign language (not to be confused with communication by gestures) has indeed not been eliminated; it has remained statistically an alternative to spoken language.

19 Wimsatt (forthcoming) argues that the structures that are phylogenetically the most deeply entrenched are also the most resistant to change in biological and cultural systems, including research paradigms. See also Wimsatt (2000).

20 See Deacon (1997) for similar ideas about features that distinguish the earliest forms of human languages from communication systems in other animal species, especially the significance of symbolism.

21 This communal behavior is undoubtedly cooperative but it differs from that of a team. In the latter case, the goal of the activity, the roles of the participants, and the rules of cooperation are explicitly articulated. The participants are often required to behave altruistically in the interest of the team. With successful communication as the goal, linguistic behavior is not altruistic.

References

Alleyne, M. C. (1980) *Comparative Afro-American.* Ann Arbor: Karoma.

Baker, P. (1993) Australian influence in Melanesian Pidgin English. *Te Reo* 36.3–67.

Bickerton, D. (1981) *Roots of Language.* Ann Arbor: Karoma.

Bickerton, D. (1984) The language bioprogram hypothesis. *Behavioral and Brain Sciences* 7.173–221.

Bickerton, D. (1988) Creole languages and the bioprogram. *Linguistics: The Cambridge Survey. Volume 2: Linguistic theory: Extensions and Implications*, Newmeyer, F. J., ed., 268–284. Cambridge: Cambridge University Press.

Bickerton, D. (1989) The lexical learning hypothesis and the pidgin-creole cycle. *Wheels within Wheels: Papers of the Duisburg Symposium on Pidgin and Creole Languages*, Pütz, M. and Dirven, R., eds, 11–31. Frankfurt am Main: Lang, V. P.

Bickerton, D. (1990) *Language and Species.* Chicago: University of Chicago Press.

Bickerton, D. (1999) How to acquire language without positive evidence: What acquisitionists can learn from creoles, DeGraff, M., ed., 49–74.

Bickerton, D. (2000) How protolanguage became language. *The Evolutionary Emergence of Language: Social Function and Origins of Linguistic Form*, Knight, C., Studdert-Kennedy, M., and Hurford, J. R., eds, 264–284. Cambridge: Cambridge University Press.

Bloomfield, L. (1933) *Language.* New York: Holt, Rinehart and Winston.

Bolinger, D. (1973) Getting the *words* in. *Lexicography in English*, McDavid, R. Jr. and Duckert, A., eds, 8–13. New York: New York Academy of Science.

Bolton, K. (2000) Language and hybridization: Pidgin tales from the China coast. *Interventions*, 5.35–52.

Bolton, K. (2002) Chinese Englishes: From Canton jargon to global English. *World Englishes,* 21.181–199.

Chaudenson, R. (1979) *Les créoles français.* Paris: Nathan.

Chaudenson, R. (1992) *Des îles, des hommes, des langues: essais sur la créolisation linguistique et culturelle.* Paris: L'Harmattan.

Chaudenson, R. (2001) *Creolization of Language and Culture.* London: Routledge.

Chomsky, N. (1986) *Knowledge of Language.* New York: Praeger.

Chomsky, N. (2000) *New Horizons in the Study of Language and Mind.* Cambridge: Cambridge University Press.

Comrie, B. (2000) From potential to realization: An episode in the origin of language. *Linguistics* 38.989–1004.

Corne, C. (1999) *From French to Creole: The Development of New Vernaculars in the French Colonial World.* London: University of Westminster Press.

Deacon, T. W. (1997) *The Symbolic Species: The Co-Evolution of Language and the Brain.* New York: W. W. Norton & Co.

DeGraff, M. (1999a) Creolization, language change, and language acquisition: A Prolegomenon. DeGraff, M., ed., 1–46.

DeGraff, M. (1999b) Creolization, language change and language acquisition: An epilogue, DeGraff, M., ed., 473–543.

DeGraff, M., ed. (1999) *Language Creation and Language Change: Creolization, Diachrony, and Development.* Cambridge, MA: MIT Press.

DeGraff, M. (2001) On the origin of creoles: A Cartesian critique of 'neo'-Darwinian linguistics. *Linguistic Typology* 5.213–310.

DeGraff, M. (2002) On creole genesis and language acquisition: Some methodological and theoretical preliminaries. Unpublished manuscript.

Givón, T. (1998) On the co-evolution of language, mind, and brain. *Evolution of Communication* 2.45–116.

Givón, T. and Malle, B. F. eds. (2002) *The Evolution of Language out of Pre-Language.* Amsterdam: John Benjamins.

Goldin-Meadow, S. (2002) Getting a handle on language creation. Givón,T. and Malle, B. F., eds, 343–374.

Hagège, C. (1993) *The Language Builder: An Essay on the Human Signature in Linguistic Morphogenesis.* Amsterdam: John Benjamins.

Hagège, C. (2001) Creoles and the notion of simplicity in human languages. *Linguistic Typology* 5:167–175.

Jackendoff, R. (2002) *Foundations of Language: Brain, Meaning, Grammar, Evolution.* Oxford: Oxford University Press.

Jespersen, O. (1922) *Language: Its Nature, Development and Origin.* London: Allen & Unwin.

Keesing, R. M. (1988) *Melanesian Pidgin and the Oceanic Substrate.* Stanford: Stanford University Press.

Kegl, J. and McWhorter, J. (1997) Perspectives on an emerging language. *Proceedings of the Twenty-Eighth Annual Child Language Research Forum*, Clark, E., ed., 15–38. Stanford, CA: Center for the Study of Language and Information.

Kegl, J., Senghas, A. and Coppola, M. (1999) Creation through contact: Sign language emergence and sign language change in Nicaragua. DeGraff, M., ed., 179–237.

Kihm, A. (2002) Langues créoles et origine du langage: état de la question. *Langages* 146.59–69.

Lass, R. (1997) *Historical Linguistics and Language Change*. Cambridge: Cambridge University Press.

Le Page, R. B. and Tabouret-Keller, A. (1985) *Acts of Identity: Creole-Based approaches to Language and Identity*. Cambridge: Cambridge University Press.

Li, C. N. (to appear) On the evolutionary origin of language. *Mirror Neurons and the Evolution of Brain and Language*, Stamenov, M. and Gallese, V., eds. Amsterdam: John Benjamins.

MacWhinney, B. (2002) The gradual emergence of language. Givón, T. and Malle, B. F. eds, 233–263.

Masuda, H. (1995) TSR formation as a discourse substratum in Hawaii. *Journal of Pidgin and Creole Languages*, 10.253–288.

McCawley, J. D. (1976) Some ideas not to live by. *Die Neueren Sprachen* 75.151–165.

Meillet, A. (1929) Le développement des langues. *Continu et Discontinu*, 119ff. Paris: Bloud & Gay. Reprinted in Meillet 1951:71–83.

Mufwene, S. S. (1991) Language genesis and human evolution. (Review article on Bickerton 1990.) *Diachronica* 8.239–254.

Mufwene, S. S. (1994) On decreolization: The case of Gullah. *Language and the Social Construction of Identity in Creole Situations*, Morgan, M., ed., 63–99. Los Angeles: Center for Afro-American Studies.

Mufwene, S. S. (1997) Jargons, pidgins, creoles, and koinés: What are they? *The Structure and Status of Pidgins and Creoles*, Spears, A. and Winford, D., eds, 35–70. Amsterdam: John Benjamins.

Mufwene, S. S. (1999) The language bioprogram hypothesis: Hints from Tazie. DeGraff, M., ed., 95–127.

Mufwene, S. S. (2000) Creolization is a social, not a structural, process. *Degrees of Restructuring in Creole Languages*, Neumann-Holzschuh, I. and Schneider, E., eds, 65–84. Amsterdam: John Benjamins.

Mufwene, S. S. (2001) *The Ecology of Language Evolution*. Cambridge: Cambridge University Press.

Mufwene, S. S. (2002) Competition and selection in language acquisition. *Selection* 3.45–56.

Mufwene, S. S. (2004) Multilingualism in linguistic history: Creolization and indigenization. *Handbook of Bilingualism*, Bhattia, T. and Blackwell, W. R. eds. pp. 460-488. Malden, MA: Blackwell.

Mufwene, S. S. (2005) Créoles, écologie sociale, évolution linguistique. Paris: L'Harmattan.

Mühlhäusler, P. (1997) *Pidgin and Creole Linguistics*, expanded and revised edition. London: University of Westminster Press.

Paul, H. (1891) *Principles of the History of Language*. London: Longmans, Green and Co.

Polomé, E. (1983) Creolization and language change. *The Social Context of Creolization*, Woolford, E. and Washabaugh, W., eds, 126–136. Ann Arbor: Karoma.

Pullum, G. K. (1990) Constraints on intransitive quasi-serial verb constructions in modern colloquial English. *When Verbs Collide: Papers from the 1990 Ohio State Mini-Conference on Serial Verbs*, Joseph, B. D. and Zwicky, A., eds, 218–239. Department of Linguistics, Ohio State University.

Roberts, S. J. (1998) The role of diffusion in the genesis of Hawaiian Creole. *Language*, 74.1–39.

Sankoff, G. (1984) Substrate and universals in the Tok Pisin verb phrase. *Meaning, Form, and Use in Context: Linguistic Applications*, Schiffrin, D., ed., 104–119. Washington, DC: Georgetown University Press.

Sankoff, G. and Brown, P. (1976) The origins of syntax in discourse: A case study of Tok Pisin relatives. *Language* 52.631–66.

Schuchardt, H. (1914) *Die Sprache der Saramakkaneger in Surinam.* Amsterdam: Johannes Müller.

Senghas, A. and Coppola, M. (2001) Children creating language: How Nicaraguan Sign Language acquired a spatial grammar. *Psychological Science* 12.323–328.

Singler, J. V. (1988) The homogeneity of the substrate as a factor in pidgin/creole genesis. *Language* 64.27–51.

Slobin, D. I. (2002) Language evolution, acquisition, diachrony: Probing the parallels. T. Givón and Malle, B. F., eds, 375–392.

Thomason, S. G. and Kaufman, T. (1988) *Language Contact, Creolization, and Genetic Linguistics*. Berkeley: University of California Press.

Tomasello, M. (2002) The emergence of grammar in early child language. Givón, T. and Malle, B. F., eds, 309–328.

Wimsatt, W. C. (2000) Generativity, entrenchment, evolution, and innateness.*Biology meets Psychology: Constraints, Connections, Conjectures*, Hardcastle, V., ed., 139–179. Cambridge, MA: MIT Press.

14 Does history begin before Sumer?

Serge Cleuziou
Université Paris 1

History begins at Sumer. These four words, written more than fifty years ago by the great philologist Samuel Noah Kramer as the title of his most famous book (1956), are a successful example of the kinds of lapidary sentences which historians use to reduce complex issues in order to convey a message. Every undergraduate in ancient studies knows them and most archaeologists would not hesitate to attribute to the Sumerians the roots of historical civilizations of the Middle East, including the earliest known written documents (ca. 3400 years BC), various administrative techniques, urbanism and the Early State. Under the term Sumerians, archaeologists and philologists include people who spoke a language called Sumerian according to the name *Shumeru* by which the inhabitants of the southern Mesopotamian plain were later called in the texts written in Akkadian, a Semitic language[1]. These same archaeologists do not hesitate to recognize Sumerian cities, a Sumerian art and a Sumerian culture, defined through spectacular finds at Telloh, Uruk or Ur since the late 19th century. The Sumerian language itself was deciphered by that time, Thureau Dangin's edition of *Les inscriptions de Sumer et d'Akkad* (1905) being considered as the real breakthrough, although the first comprehensive grammar was only published in 1923 by Arno Poebel. This paper is a short essay by an archaeologist, not a specialist of ancient languages, written with the aim of reflecting on what could have been the 'linguistic landscape' at the dawn of writing, when historically known languages and people emerged through written documents, by adding to previous linguistic studies some information taken from the present state of the art in archaeology. It does not pretend to describe the linguistic state of the oriental world at this time. This would be completely unrealistic, simply because archaeology alone does not carry information concerning language.

One clearly hesitates to address such issues in the scientific milieu, since they appear at best too speculative and are often linked to old 'unscientific' ways of dealing with the past. Whoever feels this attitude comfortable may also have difficulties when, wandering on the web, he discovers by chance a sentence such as: 'The Hurrians, *who once accounted for much of the Sumerian society* (…) are viewed by modern-day historians as the earliest precursors of the Nakhs (Chechens, Ingushis and Tsova-Tushins)'[2]. Beyond rejecting such statements in the backyard of non-scientific or pre-scientific ranting, we can try evaluating how recent advances in archaeology can shed some light on the matter. Are we forever constrained by the pessimistic statement of Leroi-Gourhan (1945, p. 345) according to whom: 'la linguistique et l'anthropologie [physique] qui donnent dans leurs aspects comparatifs de belles séries continues, de robustes ensembles, dès qu'elles se surimposent a un cadre d'histoire, avec des dates, des lieux et des noms de peuples, deviennent hasardeuses et discontinues'[3]? In what follows, we will not try to link any precise event with language, but will consider some very general 'cultural spreads', that Leroi-Gourhan himself has sometimes denominated 'plates', according to a distant analogy with plate tectonics. Since most specialists will recognize that various language groups such as Sumerian, Akkadian, Hattic and Elamite were present in the area by the end of the 4th millennium BC, let us start with this situation.

1 Sumerians in the Garden of Eden: newcomers or earlier inhabitants?

In 1675, Athanasius Kircher proposed to locate the Garden of Eden in Mesopotamia (Spar 2003), a proposal later refined by Mgr. Huet, Archbishop of Avranches in Normandy who in 1698 located it south of the confluent of the Tigris and Euphrates, in the present day marshes of southern Iraq[4]. Both of them ignored the existence of the Sumerians, who were only discovered dwelling in that same place two centuries later, and are still at the centre of archaeological and linguistic studies. Needless to say, they also ignored the actual geography of the region.

Since the first decipherable texts, Mesopotamia is at the junction of various languages, namely Semitic to the west and 'Asianic' to the east and north. The term 'Asianic' covers a wide variety of languages such as Hattic, Hurrian, Vanic, Sumerian and Elamite, the latter often being considered as having affinities with Dravidian languages. 'Asianic' languages are all of an agglutinative type, but cannot be considered as belonging to a single linguistic group like those classified as Semitic or Indo-European. It is to be noted here that although many speculations on the penetration of Indo-European languages and people were proposed, scholars focusing on these issues have ignored until now Colin Renfrew's hypothesis, locating the origins of the colonization of Europe by Indo-European speaking people in the highlands of Anatolia (Michalowski 2006, p. 162). This area is considered to have been settled by Hattic or Hurrian speakers at the dawn of history, and later replaced or 'infiltrated' by Indo-European ones. It is only with Hittite (or more precisely Neshite) that around 2000 BC Indo European languages appear on the Middle-Eastern scene.

Sumerian as a spoken language disappears at the beginning of the second millennium BC or even earlier, being replaced all over the country by Semitic languages such as Akkadian and its main offsprings, Babylonian and Assyrian. Having vanished without descendant, it could not be deciphered through linguistic affinities with a later known spoken language, but rather thanks to the bilingual lists and texts in Sumerian and Akkadian compiled by scribes, notably during the Old Babylonian period (ca. 1800–1600 BC). Its grammar has been rebuilt by philologists who still discuss many of its aspects and also its vocalization. Akkadian is reputed to have borrowed many words from Sumerian, and Sumerian some words from Akkadian, but we do not know how long the two languages coexisted in daily life. It should be clear that Sumerian is known 'solely through the medium of writing' (Michalowski 2006). We read it 'backwards, from the better known and better understood early second-millennium texts (*ibid.*). 'Our' Sumerian is a language, or more precisely a written form of a language, that may have been much different from any actual form of spoken Sumerian, and we may assume that it had different forms throughout time and space. We know nothing of the way Sumerian and Akkadian interacted as spoken languages[5]. The fading away of Sumerian is also the first (admittedly poorly) documented case of the disappearance of a language although, as a written one, it remained in use for over two millennia. Sumerian was still written on clay tablets when the army of Alexander the Great conquered Uruk, the place where the first known documents appear around 3400 BC, and the last known tablet is dated of 74/75 AD; but most authors agree that Sumerian was not spoken anymore after 2000 BC. Some even advocate a much earlier extinction, already by the mid-third millennium BC (Cooper 1973, p. 242) whilst others suggest that pockets of Sumerian language remained until the 16th century BC in the South (Lieberman 1977; Woods 2006).

Over 4000 archaic clay tablets were excavated in the southern Mesopotamian city of Uruk, possibly the largest city of its time, mainly found discarded as debris in architectural fillings of the Eanna area, the elite or 'ceremonial centre' of the town. Only a handful was found in a context related to their use, in the destruction layer of a large building called 'Red Temple' by the excavators and attributed by them to level IVb that can be dated around 3400 BC. Other tablets have been found in other sites such as Larsa and Umma in southern Mesopotamia, or Jemdat Nasr and Tell Uqair in central Mesopotamia, to quote only sites with a significant amount (several dozens) of finds. These documents are mainly administrative accounts listing commodities and their number, volume or weight, but also lexical lists. The signs that represent things but also actions or ideas quickly took (or already had) a phonetic value suggesting that these early cuneiform tablets are a transcription of Sumerian language. There are about one thousand Sumerian words that are transcribed by a cuneiform sign or a logogram, and much more expressed by a compound of separate signs. The work of decipherment is still going on (Nissen, et al. 1993), but most specialists agree that the first language ever written was Sumerian. A recent and comprehensive study of the origins of cuneiform writing can be found in *Écrire à Sumer* by Jean-Jacques Glassner (2000), whom I follow on most points. Whether the much higher number of tablets found at Uruk is a result of the large area excavated or of the centrality of the city remains a matter of discussion, but there seems to be a general agreement that the earliest known writing in the World was developed (created? invented?) by the Sumerians and that this invention took place in Southern Mesopotamia, probably at Uruk.

Many authors also considered, following an idea already expressed in 1869 by Jules Oppert[6], that Sumerians entered lower Mesopotamia from elsewhere, at a time that would correspond to the 5th or 4th millennium BC in recent chronologies. The idea has many implications and needs to be discussed. The name of many rivers, including the Tigris and Euphrates, and of many places, including those of Sumerian cities such as Lagash, Shuruppak or Adab, has no convincing Sumerian etymology and the same can be said of various Sumerian words, notably some of those dealing with handicrafts, agriculture or the making of beer (Landsberger 1943). When did Sumerians settle in Mesopotamia and where did they come from?

The answer to the first part of the question was sought in transformations of archaeological data, mainly pottery. Sir Leonard Woolley, who excavated the city of Ur in the 1920s, advocated the change from painted to non-painted pottery in the late levels of the 'Ubaid cemetery' at Ur, and the same could be found in the deep sounding excavated few years later by the German expedition at Uruk, which revealed the same change. This would have dated the event at some time around 4000 BC according to the chronology accepted nowadays. One should however notice that a similar change took place at the same time in other places that are not recognized as peopled by Sumerians, such as Tepe Gawra in northern Mesopotamia. André Parrot and many archaeologists in the 1950s and 1960s favored a later date, by the Jemdat Nasr period (3100–2900 BC), which they considered as that of the invention of writing (therefore still granted to the Sumerians). By doing so, they considered as non-Sumerian, 'Semite or Subarean' according to Parrot, the large monuments excavated by the Germans at Uruk, thus conceding that 'en Mésopotamie les Sumériens se trouvèrent devant une civilisation déjà très élaborée et solidement installée. Leur dynamisme leur permit de s'imposer sans discussion'[7]. Eventually, Julius Jordan[8], who dug the deep sounding at Uruk, advocated a much later arrival, around 2900 BC, associating the Sumerians to a particular type of mud bricks, plano-convex in section and obliquely arranged in alternate courses forming a herringbone pattern. These were supposed to imitate the original material used by the Sumerians, stone, in a new environment where stone was absent. Jordan's proposal also takes into account major transformations in architecture and pottery between the Jemdet Nasr period (that most authors consider as a simple last stage of the Uruk period) and the following Early Dynastic period (2900–2350 BC) during which the plano-convex mud bricks were in use, before they were abandoned during the Akkadian period, the first Semitic empire. By doing so, he obviously attributed the archaic tablets of Uruk to non-Sumerians. The presence of Sumerian terms had not been recognized at that time, and the first intelligible texts written in Sumerian, at Ur or Farah (Shuruppak), are dated one or two centuries after 2900 BC.

Two possibilities were favored concerning the origin of Sumerians. In 1920, Michael Rostovtzeff proposed the identification as Sumerian of a hoard of precious vessels and tools found in 1844 near Asterabad (presently Gorgan) in northeastern Iran, probably on the archaeological site of Tureng Tepe. He elaborated on similarities between these objects and those found at Telloh or Susa in Southern Mesopotamia and concluded that 'It arises anew the question of the roots whence sprung the cultures of Elam and Mesopotamia' (Rostovtzeff 1920, p. 382), recommending that excavations should be carried out in this area. Oppert himself saw a Turanian origin for Sumerian, as with the views of Sir Leonard Woolley. Jordan had a similar analysis when considering a mountainous origin for the users of the plano-convex mud bricks. This was still the opinion of André Parrot in the 1960s when he wrote 'Ils venaient d'ailleurs, de l'Est très vraisemblablement, probablement de l'Iran'[9]. Most sumerologists however favour another origin to the south, in the area of the Persian Gulf: 'Si, comme c'est mon cas, on fait confiance à un vieux mythe local, celui dit des Sept Sages, ils doivent être arrivés dans la Mésopotamie du Sud … par la mer … en remontant peut-être le rivage iranien du Golfe persique'[10] (Bottero 1996, p. 24). Some mundane facts, such as the reputation of Sumerians as fish eaters, are considered, while others are of a more elevated nature. There seems to be a close tie between Sumer and the land of Dilmun (commonly identified with the island of Bahrain) the pure and holy land of Sumerian myths where the God Enki placed Ziusudra, the Noah of the Sumerian version of the Flood or where the legendary king Gilgamesh went to recover the flower of immortality. The Garden of Eden of Kircher and Huet with one restriction however, the virginal and pristine paradise on Earth of the Sumerian myths was not habited by humans!

Such views have been abandoned by most archaeologists advocating continuity in population: ‘la civilisation sumérienne est le résultat de la lente évolution, sur place, de communautés qui occupaient ce pays difficile depuis des millénaires. A un certain moment de cette évolution elles se sont dotées d’un outil, l’écriture, qui leur permit de noter une langue qu’elles pratiquaient depuis longtemps sans l’écrire … [le peuple sumérien] s’est formé bien antérieurement et sur place … La cristallisation des éléments qui composent cette civilisation n’avait besoin d’aucun apport étranger pour se produire et peut s’expliquer, dans une large mesure, sans recours à de mythiques invasions’[11] (Huot 1989, p. 58). This is also the view expressed by Michalowski (2006, p. 175) according to whom ‘Sumerian was not the language of overland or maritime marauders’ or by Glassner (2000, p. 68): ‘il convient probablement d’abandonner l’hypothèse … qui n’est qu’un pur produit de l’esprit, d’une invasion de chefs de bandes sumériens qui se seraient imposés comme princes dans certaines bourgades’[12]. The rejection of the migration hypotheses is mainly the result of a new paradigm that arose in the 1960s, when the development of urbanism and a pristine state became the main topic of archaeological research. The abandon of painted decoration on pottery became interpreted as a result of the ‘industrialization’ of its production and not as a change in population. A fading away of painted decoration that became less frequent and less complex was already noted during the 5th millennium BC and interpreted as indicating the lowering importance of pottery as a support of symbolic values, due to ongoing changes in society. Continuities in architecture are also advocated between the plans of some large buildings of the mid-5th millennium BC, interpreted as ‘temples’ or ‘meeting halls’, and the large ones of Eanna IV at Uruk, like the ‘Red Temple’ where the first dated written tablets were found, also interpreted as ‘temples’ or ‘meeting halls’.

It is not my intention to revive the Sumerian migration. Sumerian is interpreted by Michalowski (2006, p. 174) as ‘the last remnant of a broad linguistic continuum that existed in areas of Western Asia before the Semitic extensions’. Bottero (1996, p. 27) added to his own views that ‘on their arrival in the country, the Sumerians seemed to have cut off all links with their previous habitat’, and considered that the disappearance of Sumerian was linked to the absence of a kin-population background, and to some extent, to the broad linguistic continuum of Michalowski. It should here be mentioned that recent geomorphological studies have shed new light on the geography of southern Mesopotamia during late prehistory and early history, which can change Bottero’s perspective. The Persian Gulf was empty at the peak of the last Ice Age around 20 000 years ago, when the general level of the oceans was around 120 m below the present, whilst the bottom of the Gulf did not exceed 80 metres (Pirazzoli 1991). A large marshy area extended like a prolongation of the Mesopotamian plain until the Strait of Hormuz, between the deserts of Arabia and the mountains of Iran. Waters rose quickly and started invading it around 12 000 BC, reaching their present level by 5000 BC (Lambeck 1996). This means that at the time of the earliest known painted pottery in Southern Mesopotamia at Tell el-'Oueili near Larsa, around 6500 BC, the sea was 15 to 20 meters lower and the mouths of the rivers were some 500 km to the South. Rainfall was higher upstream, there was more water in the rivers, and large marshy areas and freshwater lakes made a permanently changing landscape, which was gradually invaded by the sea. Here was probably the landscape that is represented, with its reed made huts and boats, on the earliest cylinder seals around 3600 BC at Uruk. The waters were raising at a pace of over 10 meters a millennium, over one meter a century. During the 4th and 3rd millennia BC, the sea level was some two meters higher than nowadays and the southernmost Sumerian cities, Eridu, Ur, Girsu (Telloh) or Lagash were near or even on the edge of the sea, as is known from cuneiform texts. It is only after 2000 BC that, following a lowering of waters to their present level (or slightly below), the marshes and mudflats of present-day southern Iraq were built up (Sanlaville 1989). Such changes could be felt in a man's time life, feeding memories and myths. 'I consider it as a basic error to assume that the memory of Sumerian myths, or any other kind of cuneiform text, reaches back to the Ubaid period' wrote the assyriologist Bent Alster (1983, 69 note 47). Are we so sure?

The progress of archaeological research in the Persian Gulf now contradicts Bottero's statements in another way. Mesopotamian and Mesopotamian-like potteries of Uruk type (4th millennium BC) have been found in the Land of Dilmun of cuneiform texts, on the coastal Island of Tarut and in the al-Hasa oasis in the interior, near Dhahran in Saudi Arabia. They are considered as attesting the existence of important seafaring relations at that time. They were preceded by the presence of Ubaid painted potteries during the 6th and 5th millennium BC all along the Arabian coast down to the Strait of Hormuz. Their presence has raised a heated discussion between specialists of Mesopotamia, that considered these sites as fishing stations of Sumerians or their predecessors in the Gulf (Oates, et al. 1977) and some specialists of Eastern Arabia that advocated an Arabian origin of the painted Ubaid pottery and its holders (Masry 1974). Both positions are probably excessive and do not take into account an important fact: the Persian Gulf is a lost province of late prehistory, and most of the coastal sites, but also those that were on the edge of rivers, lakes and marshes, are below the mudflats of present Southern Iraq and the waters of the

Gulf. Was this the 'Lost paradise' of Kircher and Huet, the home of Bottero's kin-populations?

Prehistoric languages leave no trace, but we may speculate on technologies. I would like to quote an interesting example. During the 3rd millennium BC, the Sumerians built and used a particular type of boat, made of a reed hull caulked with bitumen, which they called *Magan* boats after the name they gave to the Oman peninsula in the cuneiform texts (Cleuziou and Tosi 1994). Slabs of the bitumen caulking of seagoing boats have been found on 3rd millennium sites in Oman but also on two Ubaid sites of the Gulf, at as-Sabiyah near Kuwait and Ayn as-Sayh near Dhahran, both dated of the last centuries of the 6th millennium BC while in Northern Mesopotamia, similar pieces of the bitumen caulking of river-going boats have been found at Hacinebi on the left bank of the Euphrates, dated from the 4th millennium BC. Reeds and bitumen, which are available all over the area, are also the materials of Ziusudra's boat in the Mesopotamian flood legend, or those of the boat built by Gilgamesh to reach Dilmun. From this viewpoint at least, Mesopotamia and the nowadays flooded Persian Gulf formed a technological province, like those which André Leroi-Gourhan tried to define in the last chapters of his major work on *Évolution et technique* (Leroi-Gourhan 1945), accepting language as part of the definition of these groups, although he acknowledges a large degree of flexibility. These considerations do not solve however the 'Sumerian problem': if they once peopled part of the present days Persian Gulf, the Sumerians would, as in Mesopotamia, have been in contact with Semitic speaking people, that are supposed to have been long since dwelling in Arabia. When we know some names of individuals in the Gulf, by the end of the 3rd millennium BC, they all are of a Semitic or Elamite origin (Glassner 2002).

2 Some methodological aspects

How far back can we go from known cultural assemblages to languages, and how can we do it? The association between language, culture and 'race' expressed through physical anthropology, was a major topic of human sciences for more than a century, since the mid-19th century. The pessimistic comment of Leroi-Gourhan about insuperable discrepancies between linguistic and anthropological series on one hand, and discontinuities in historical, historical and geographical records on the other hand, abruptly and successfully terminated any new attempt in France. The disrepute of a direct association between these elements became such, after the horrors committed in the name of an ideology that had incorporated these views in its visions of populations history[13], that few young prehistorians influenced by his teaching would risk a step along the forbidden path, even if some still naïvely did it more or less consciously. As is often the case, the baby was thrown out with the bath water and the bath water was extremely turbid. Most prehistorians turned to the meticulous description of technical aspects of ancient societies, firmly rooted on material data, at best trying to integrate it into larger technical systems in order to follow part of the program traced by Leroi-Gourhan. Instead of seeking more sophisticated ways to study relations between ethnic affiliation, language and cultural identity, most specialists came to consider it as a definitely irrelevant problem, unworthy of serious science. Contrary to the old manuals (and Nazi manuals among them) there would never be a Germanic or Slavic pottery assemblage – and this is wise. Our secondary school textbooks could still refer to invasions of the Western Roman Empire by Alains, Alamans, Sarmats, Vandals, Visigoths and other Ostrogoths; local studies could still refer to toponyms such as Allaine or Allones for Alains, Allemagne for Alamans, Sermaise or Sermoise for Sarmats. Early medieval studies refer to villages settled by Faramans, i.e. men from far away (Poly 1984); nobody would dare to trace even a material culture, particular settlement types or particular burials related to these same people, and especially not to particular skeletons.

The study of flint tools in prehistory and pottery in late prehistory is the basic way to establish cultural assemblages that are supposed to represent past societies and their evolution. Pottery appeared in the Middle East at some time around 7000–6800 BC and its use generalized so fast that it is very difficult if not impossible to determine where the invention took place. An important characteristic of pottery in our perspective is that all over the ancient Orient, it became for almost three millennia until ca. 4000 BC, the support for painted decorative patterns of obvious symbolic value. Their variation is our main tool for defining assemblages, often forgetting that clothes, baskets and wall paintings, which are never or only rarely preserved, would provide a much richer assemblage. Stylistic differentiation among pottery shapes, even if they are mainly utilitarian, the use of different clays or fabrication processes can be used to distinguish assemblages and add to their relevance, considering that selection of clays, methods of fabrication and firing, together with types of temper added to the clay are a not only a matter of local availability of materials but also of technical choices made by the producers. Considering these arguments, archaeologists allow themselves to interpret these assemblages as 'cultures' that are to some extent part of the identification of groups of people, even if they well aware, or say they are well aware, that pots should not be confused with people. A basic problem behind such assemblages is that although we have sophisticated means to establish and compare them, we still do not know how they come to being, i.e. why potteries change. Of course partial explanations have been suggested, such as adaptation to new tasks, new environments, improvements of efficiency, but when we come to what is usually considered as 'style', and the relations between style and society, we seem condemned to silence or unfounded speculation. Ethno-archaeological studies have been an attempt to cover that gap, and since the pioneer work of James Deetz on Arikara Indians in California (1965), individual behavior and circulation of pottery makers in the group or among groups, or competition among specialized producers have been considered to explain diffusion of particular decorative patterns. The role of decorative patterns in the border areas has been enhanced by Ian Hodder (1982), and studies have since been going on in many parts of the World (among many others Dietler and Herbich 1994; Van der Leeuw 1993). But since it was a question of archaeological cases, results have been rather disappointing. At least can we see that many causes and timescales are at work. Anne-Marie and Pierre Pétrequin for instance, working on Jura Neolithic pottery, have pointed out rapid successive changes, that would necessitate a chronological control unavailable in present Middle Eastern archaeological studies during the Late Prehistory (Pétrequin 1993).

The hidden corpses never disappeared however and came back in from the cold in the last two decades of the 20th century with Russian scientists that had gone through Soviet times with migrationists ideas inherited from Kossina's schemes, accompanied shortly afterwards by bloody ethnic turmoil in Balkan countries. 'After many years in archaeological exile, ethnicity has recently resurfaced', wrote recently an American archaeologist (Pearce 1999, p. 35). In the meantime, genetics seemed to provide new and accurate ways to link physical individuals to cultural groups (Ammermann and Cavalli-Sforza 1984) and the 'New Synthesis' proposed to work again on a larger relation between physical individuals, culture and language. We are anew invited to work on what had been long ago criticized by Leroi-Gourhan (1945, p. 323): 'Lorsqu'on parle de migration des Mongols, on voit à la fois un type anthropologique, une langue, des mythes et des objets. Sans poser que ce point de vue soit toujours erroné, on peut dire que la majorité des cas étudiés ne se prête pas à de telles vues'[14].

Pearce's statement was written about the situation of Northern Mesopotamia towards the mid-4th millennium BC, a situation relevant to the main topic of this paper that will be addressed later. Ethnicity, and beyond it language, were as a matter of fact never absent from archaeological interpretations in the Middle East. In the 1960s many archaeologists were still trying to trace through pottery assemblages the coming of Persian speaking populations in Iran, tentatively identifying them with several varieties of pottery. The idea was not new. At the beginning of the 20th century, the American geologist and archaeologist Raphael Pumpelly was already looking for the Indo-Europeans when he excavated a prehistoric mound at Anau near Ashgabat (formerly Askhabad), the capital of Turkmenistan. This was also the aim of a new wave of excavators who worked in the early 1930's on several mounds in the Gorgan plain south-east of the Caspian Sea at Tureng Tepe (Wulsin 1932) and Shah Tepe (Arne 1945), or on the Iranian plateau at Tepe Hissar (Schmidt 1937). In 1931, the famous physician and physical anthropologist Sir Arthur Keith wrote a strange sentence in relation to the newly found royal graves at Ur in the *Illustrated London News*, (p. 1000): 'There was the original home of the inventors or pioneers of our modern civilization. From the Iranian uplands, our pioneers descended on the neighboring river lands of India and Arabia, probably using native labor to execute their great schemes'. He was obviously confusing the Sumerians with the Indo-Europeans, and we should therefore make a small detour with the Indo-Europeans.

The three mounds mentioned above yield a particular type of burnished grey wares and all three excavators express their concern with migration of Indo-Iranian tribes[15], to whom they attributed these potteries. The new excavations led by Jean Deshayes at Tureng Tepe in the 1960s were aimed again at that same question and he did not hesitate to reach some unbalanced conclusions: 'It was the Gorgan plain which was the first region occupied by the Iranian peoples, whose history can now be traced back to the last centuries of the 4th millennium B.C.' (Deshayes 1968, p. 38). Around the same time, Timothy Cuyler Young (1965; 1967) considered that the Iranian people were already settled in the Zagros Mountains of Western Iran by the 10th century BC, elaborating from continuities in architecture and pottery with the Achaemenid period when the use of an Indo-European language (Old Persian) is well attested from written documents. Advocating again from continuity in the evolution of pottery shapes and decoration between this assemblage and that of several cemeteries at the piedmont of the Elburz Mountains near Tehran (Khurvin, Qeytaryeh) and between those and the Burnished grey wares of Tepe Hissar and the Gorgan plain to the East, he proposed that such was the route followed by the Persian speaking settlers of the Zagros. This came in opposition to older theories favored in the late 19th to early 20th century, which located the origins of these same people westwards, in Transcaucasia. It is interesting here to note that whilst research on linguistic groups located in this region had continued after the closing down of the Iron curtain, relations between archaeologies on both sides of it were almost inexistent: work of Soviet archaeologists in Georgia, Armenia and Azerbaijan was ignored by western scholars, who were themselves unable to excavate in the area south of it. The eastern hypothesis became fashionable in spite of the many problems it raised. The Gurgan plain appeared to have been almost depopulated at the beginning of the 2nd millennium BC, since the only excavated sites present a long gap in occupation before later layers (Islamic at Shah Tepe, middle Iron Age at Tureng Tepe), whilst south of the Elburz Tepe Hissar was abandoned and never resettled. This was attributed to newcomers pushing in front of them the previous populations. But if the 'Burnished Grey Ware people' who left the region were already Indo-Europeans, who were the newcomers? The possible destruction of the main monument linked to Burnished Grey Ware at Tureng Tepe overcame the doubts of Deshayes, who first hesitated in favour of an ecological cause like dryness or soil salinisation: 'il est alors probable que cette civilisation de la plaine de Gorgan ... est tombée victime des raids de ces nomades qui n'ont cessé d'inquiéter jusqu'à nos jours les populations sédentaires ... N'étaient-ce pas déjà ces Indo-européens qui bientôt après devaient faire leur apparition en de nombreux secteurs du monde oriental?'[16] (Deshayes 1975, p. 530). This echoed the opinion expressed thirty years before by Arne for the abandonment of Shah Tepe: 'one is most inclined to assume an invasion by nomads who forced the older population to move elsewhere ... they may have been the Turks ... It is also conceivable that a nomadizing 'Indo-European' or 'proto-Mediterranean' people penetrated the region and destroyed the civilization of kinfolk that had settled there' (Arne 1945, p. 329–30). The fact that a previously unknown coarse ware appeared in the very late layers at Tureng Tepe seemed to strengthen the hypothesis, as archaeologists in these areas used to attribute such a coarse ware to nomads. With the temporary closing down of Iran to western archaeological research, but also with the rise of new paradigms, such as environmental studies or process-oriented archaeology, the debate temporarily came to an end, although this was not to be for long. Towards the east, the discovery of many objects dated at the end of the 3rd and the beginning of the 2nd millennium BC and also found in south-eastern Iran, Afghanistan and Baluchistan reopened the question of influences or migration of southern central Asia people southwards, now in connection with the end of the Indus civilization. Indo-Europeans could also have been involved (Lamberg-Karlovsky 2002; Mallory 1997). But this is another story: let us go back westwards in Mesopotamia.

3 The early roots of Sumerian's archaeology

When they published the materials of the prehistoric levels found in a sounding below the mass of mud bricks of a later Sumerian temple, the excavators of Eridu chose to emphasize continuity in painted pottery rather than discontinuity (Safar and Lloyd 1950). They were convinced that for the first time they could present a complete sequence of buildings and potteries covering the whole prehistoric occupation of Southern Iraq. They interpreted the architectural remains as a succession of temples from the earliest building, a small rectangular room found in level XVI, to the latest one, a large building on a terrace identified as a 3rd millennium temple dedicated to the water god Ea, close to the sea at that time. Painted pottery was therefore classified under four periods (Ubaid 1 to 4) that was to shape our understanding of the late prehistory of Southern Mesopotamia until the present. The excavators did not however establish cultural continuity between the bearers of painted pottery and the Sumerians, and the question of the arrival of new people at the end of Ubaid 4 remained open.

The role of cultural labels is in itself significant. Pottery styles were labelled Hassuna and Samarra in the north, contemporaneous with the earlier part of the Ubaid sequence (Ubaid 0 and 1) in the south[17]. Neither Hassuna nor Samarra are real type-sites, being only the first place these styles were recognized by archaeologists. Hassuna is a small site with a small sounding, the important ones being Tell Soto or Umm Dabbagiyah. Samarra pottery was found — to their great surprise — by German archaeologists excavating below the pavement of an Abbasid palace of this temporary capital city of the Arab world, the type-site being the fortified village of Tell es-Sawwan on the left bank of the Tigris river, south of that same city. But most archaeologists do not hesitate to see Hassuna and Samarra 'people' interacting with other cultures. Eastwards, a long sequence of painted potteries is also known from the Iranian foothills of Khuzistan. Beyond obvious local aspects, all these cultures display several similarities such as dark-brown or black painting on buff ware, generally all over decoration outside the jars or inside the plates and bowls and dense decorative patterns in cruciform composition (bowls and plates) or horizontal registers (jars). Labels in the north were insisting on discontinuity whilst labels in the south induced continuity. Some researchers however were not fully convinced. It has for instance been argued that the period Ubaid 2, also known as Hajji Muhammad after the name of a small site near Eridu, was an intrusive pottery probably coming from Khuzistan, therefore hiding the transition between Ubaid 1 and Ubaid 3… No doubt that under different circumstances, discontinuity rather continuity would have been emphasized, and this would have led to a different story. To match with Michalowski's hypothesis, was Mesopotamia at that time peopled by speakers of the linguistic group to which Sumerian can be related? Or was this linguistic group already restricted to the Ubaid culture of the south?

By ca. 6000 BC, the painted wares of Samarra type in the north were replaced by a new type of painted ware, often decorated with polychrome patterns (black and reddish brown on a buff body), labeled Halaf pottery after the name of Tell Halaf in Northern Syria where it was first found. It is very distinctive, very well made, and some of the pots can be considered as real masterpieces. With some new representations such as stylized bucrania, the patterning and motives are reminiscent of those of Samarra in the north or Ubaid 2 in the south and so are the main shapes of the vases. There are however several changes in other aspects of material culture and notably the presence of round unicellular buildings accessible through an elongated room, together with rectangular multi-roomed buildings of the previous periods. These were called 'tholoi' by archaeologists educated with respect to Greek antiquity, a rather inappropriate term as it is used in naming graves in the Aegean world, whilst these buildings obviously had a domestic function. Such vaulted round architectures recall those of some villages of northern Syria today, but are generally speaking rare in the Middle East. They are however distinctive of the Neolithic cultures of Georgia and Armenia. Halaf sites, rooted on a mixed pastoral and agricultural economy, are found on a wide geographic area from the region of Baghdad to the Mediterranean coast around the Gulf of Cilicia, and deep in the Taurus Mountains to the shores of Lake Van. This led to interpreting the 'Halaf culture' as originating from the north, or at least having a strong northern component. For our purpose in this paper, we will retain the proposition that it extends over an area that is supposed to have covered the area of the Hattic, Vanic and Hurrian languages, but no archaeologist to our knowledge has proposed a conjunction between these languages and the 'Halafians'. The terms 'Halafians' and 'Ubaidians' are however widely used, obviously again referring to people.

The breath of history has continued. Almost a millennium later, Halaf potteries were replaced by the same Ubaid 3 potteries as in the South, forming a huge cultural area that extends all along the eastern branch of the Fertile Crescent, from the Persian Gulf to the Mediterranean, including eastwards the Khuzestan plain. This is almost unanimously considered by archaeologists as indicating an extension of the southern people to the north, although only a few would have run the risk of explaining the mechanisms of such an acculturation. Jean-Daniel Forest has suggested an interaction amongst populations, considering that marriage patterns may have been involved, brides transporting to new residence the techniques and decorative patterns, leading to a stylistic homogenization (Forest 1996). This is the kind of causality suggested forty years ago by James Hill (1968) for pottery change in the American Southwest, although applied here on a much larger scale. Forest's interesting attempt to interpret acculturation through population dynamics has however raised little interest until now. According to him, these population dynamics would explain why the 'Halafian' area entered the movement towards complexity after one millennium of cultural stagnation due to its segmentary structure. Whether adoption of new decorative patterns would also be associated with adoption of a new language is a totally different question that is not considered in the hypothesis.

Whatever had happened, we are left with a wide cultural area that would last for almost one millennium, with an internal evolution that was to lead from a village style of life to the appearance of the first cities around 4000 BC. This evolution is poorly documented, but when painted potteries disappeared, they were replaced by assemblages that clearly differ at both ends of the previous Ubaid 3–4 continuum. This includes 'chaff faced' wares of the 'Late Chalcolithic' assemblage in the Syro-Anatolian area, Uruk wares in the south, plus some particular local situations. All authors agree that this was a period of drastic and repeated changes, that are almost impossible to understand according to our present knowledge, but most will also admit that these evolutions had roots in the previous periods. As a matter of fact, it is interesting to note that no major movement of people was advocated in the explanation of this evolution. The abandon of painted wares is everywhere accepted as the result of a transition towards 'industrial' wares made in large workshops, with the help of new tools, among them the potter's wheel.[18] Not all areas however were considered to move at the same pace. On the contrary, the size of Uruk around 3500 BC (probably over 200 ha.), the monumental aspect of its architecture (some buildings are over 80 m long), the deep transformations in administrative techniques eventually ending in the development of writing led to consider that southern Mesopotamia, and most particularly Uruk, was quite ahead on the road to more economic and social complexity. But our data on this process is very poor, restricted to the deep sounding excavated in the late 1920's by Jordan at Uruk, whose interpretation is complex and controversial. It has recently been convincingly argued that the collection of pottery published from Uruk was selected according to criteria that would not allow tracing an evolutionary sequence, and is therefore unreliable in establishing the relative chronology of other sites (Nissen 2002, p. 3–5). The corresponding layers have not been investigated at Kish, the place were Kingship came on earth according to Sumerian chronicles or at Nippur, the sacred city, and excavations at Telloh in late 19th/early 20th century have destroyed forever what they were supposed to reveal. Notwithstanding such important restrictions, the primacy of Southern Mesopotamia has never been seriously disputed and remains an unquestionable dogma of Oriental archaeology. It is therefore no surprise that Sumerians, newly settled or present since times immemorial, are considered to be at the origin of all innovations.

4 Mesopotamia and the east: Elam and beyond

The archaeological sequence of Susa in Khuzestan has led to a strengthening of the dogma whilst things may have been different under different circumstances. The site has been excavated since 1884, yielding some of the most important linguistic and historical monuments of oriental archaeology, nowadays in the Louvre Museum, but a precise sequence could only be drawn in the 1970s, by partially excavating the last remnants of the 'acropolis' that appeared as a pinnacle left by the earlier excavators in the middle of an immense hole[19]. Susa is a privileged point of linguistic contacts between the Mesopotamian plain and the Iranian plateau. In historical times, it was one of the capitals of Elam whose language (Elamite) is reputed to be Dravidian-related and appears to have been the tongue of southern Iran (McAlpin 1981). Susa was for long supposed to have been the core of Elam, but is now interpreted as its westernmost capital in contact with the Mesopotamian plain, the other one being Anshan (present Tal-i Malyan) near Shiraz (Vallat 1980). This duality between mountains and plain was to be lasting in historical times, Susa being with Persepolis one of the capitals of the Achaemenid Empire. Its beginnings are however unclear. The city was founded at the end of the 5th millennium BC among a network of earlier villages. It was characterized by a large cemetery and, shortly later, by a huge mud brick terrace, some 80 meters long and 10 meters high, on the top of which were erected 'hall buildings' similar to those of Uruk. Chronologically, this period would correspond to the earliest phases of non-painted wares at Uruk, although it is characterized by very fine painted wares with sophisticated decorations that are also found on other sites of the area. It was sometimes suggested that in these early centuries of its long existence, Susa was mainly a ceremonial centre for the populations of the area. Relations with the plateau are unknown, although some similarities with the painted wares of Luristan and Fars can be noted. No suggestion can be made about language at that time, although Elamite seems a tacit assumption.

What is interesting in our perspective is that by ca. 3700 BC, painted pottery disappears and is replaced by a new assemblage almost similar to that of Uruk, so much that this is interpreted as a mark of the domination of Southern Mesopotamia on Susiana[20]. This is also the time when administrative techniques such as cylinder seal and sealings, clay hollow balls[21] and numerical tablets that are considered as forerunners of writing appear, found in a sequence of private houses and not in a ceremonial centre like at Uruk. The cylinder seals and their imprints on clay hollow balls and tablets are almost identical on both sites and also on other sites in Susiana such as Choga Mish. Susa is even the place where this process is best documented with the first known cylinder seal appearing in level 21, the first imprint of a seal in level 20, hollow clay balls with imprints of cylinder seals in level 18, together with the first numerical tablets with imprints of cylinder seals, the latter remaining alone in level 17 (Le Brun and Vallat 1978). Texts with numbers and signs similar to the archaic texts of Uruk, the first proper writing, have not been found at Susa. This can be interpreted either as an indication that writing invented at Uruk had not reached Susa yet, where numerical tablets only were still in use, or that the layers with the earliest archaic texts are absent at Susa. Although never clearly expressed, the first interpretation is usually accepted because it is well known that, as everybody agrees, writing was invented at Uruk ... There is unfortunately a hiatus between level 17 and the following level 16, and we may imagine that the time of this hiatus, which duration is unknown, can be that of the archaic tablets. We do not know how long the hiatus lasted, it may have been a matter of a few years or a few generations, but if Jean-Jacques Glassner's hypothesis according to which the elaboration of the first writing was made in a short time is correct, the time of the whole process is clearly beyond our chronological control (Glassner 2000, p. 65).

When the area was settled again, tablets with signs and numerals are present in levels 16 to 14, but these signs are wholly different from the archaic signs of Uruk. They merely appear to be pictograms indicating animals or alimentary products, but we do not know how to read them nor even if they transcribe any particular language. They have however been called 'proto-Elamite' entertaining the possibility that they transcribe Elamite language, being in some manner an indication that Susa had turned back to its own cultural trajectory after having received improvements from Sumerian Uruk[22]. Proto-Elamite tablets and cylinder seals have been found on the Iranian highlands at Tepe Sialk, Anshan (Tal-i Malyan), Tepe Yahya and as far away as Shahr-i Sokhta near the Afghan border. Whether diffusion of techniques, community of language or establishment of trading posts is involved is still a matter of discussion. This obviously strengthens the idea that Susa belongs to the community of languages of the Iranian plateau and beyond, but does not prove anything as signs could be read in different languages on such an immense cultural area. As already said, Elamite is sometimes considered to be related to Dravidian languages and some authors have expressed the idea that proto-Elamite signs may have been at the origins of Indus writing (Fairservis 1992). There is however too much time and too many kilometers between both areas to base such an hypothesis on firm ground; we do not even know if there was one or several languages noted by the non deciphered Indus Valley script nor if one or several of them were Dravidian. Elamite as a written language is only ascertained in the last centuries of the 3rd millennium BC.

Writing seems to have been abandoned among Elamites by 2900 BC, or at least we do not know of any use of writing in the Elamite world at the time cuneiform writing developed among Sumerian cities. The subsequent written documents from Susa were written in Akkadian and sometimes in the Sumerian language, when the country again entered into the Mesopotamian sphere of influence in the 24th century BC with the first unification of the whole country by Sargon of Akkad, who established a governor in his name at Susa. The first text certainly written in Elamite, using cuneiform signs according to a syllabic value is an alliance treaty between an unknown Elamite official and Naram Sin, the grand son of Sargon. In the 21st century, Susa has recovered a complete independence from Mesopotamia and is anew linked with the Iranian highlands. The new master of the country, an Elamite named Kutik Inshushinak, maintained the use of Sumerian and Akkadian but introduced a new type of writing, called linear Elamite. It has until now thwarted any attempt at deciphering, but in many aspects it recalls the long since vanished proto-Elamite. There are few documents, two dozens, but they are scattered across a very large area, from Susa to the Zagros and Central Asia. Relations between Mesopotamia and countries eastwards were since long active and multi-facetted. King Shulgi of the 3rd dynasty of Ur married one of his daughters with a ruler of Mahrashi, probably located east of Elam; another diplomatic wedding with a ruler of Anshan in Elam followed twelve years later. Ambassadors of both countries are frequently received at the royal court (Steinkeller forth.) and the same Shulgi claims to have known Sumerian, Amorite, Elamite, Subarean (probably Hurrian at that time) and the language of Meluhha (the Indus), his mother tongue being probably Akkadian (Michalowski 2006, p. 176). The language of Mahrashi is unknown to us, but we may imagine that there were translators in official meetings and that Shulgi's daughters were taught it before their royal wedding[23]. Four documents recently found in the excavations of Konar Sandal in the Jiroft valley of southeastern Iran, a possible location for Marhashi, are written with characters similar to linear Elamite, although they apparently predate the inscriptions of Kutik Inshushinak. This needs confirmation, but may be an indication that writing continued on the Iranian plateau after the disappearance of proto-Elamite[24].

Some authors have advocated migrations of population from Southern Mesopotamia at the time Susa is under Uruk (or Sumerian) influence, on the basis of archaeological surveys and estimated populations according to the size of the sites (Wright and Johnson 1975). This is not impossible but remains very uncertain. A period of economical intensification, as with the mid-4th millennium BC, may also have been accompanied by a demographic transition, implying much higher birth rates for a rather short period of time, enough to create a considerable raise of a population without involving large migrations. Did the newcomers, if they ever existed, speak Sumerian? If Susiana was under Uruk influence, did its elites speak Sumerian, before returning to Elamite a few centuries later? These are so many questions that we cannot answer. We can hardly say that Susiana at that time was a multilingual area, as it was to be for three more millennia. It has been recently proposed that 'the earlier texts [at Uruk] may even preserve a hint that some form of Elamite was also in play' (Michalowski 2006, p. 168).

5 From colonies to Urukian wars and people from the north

In 1993, Guillermo Algaze proposed the most successfully developed version of a theory that was already expressed by several specialists (Algaze 1993), elaborating on the results of some twenty years of intensive archaeology in Northern Syria, notably the Djezireh plain between the foothills of the Taurus mountains and the left bank of the Euphrates river. The area had been rather neglected until then, but development programs in Syria and Turkey combined with the interest of these countries for archaeological research and the decrease or cessation of activities in Iraq and Iran made the middle Euphrates and its tributaries one of the best-investigated areas in the Middle East. According to Algaze's theory, the southern Mesopotamians expanded to the north and to the east by the mid-4th millennium BC in order to secure the catchments of foreign materials that were requested by the elites of the growing urban centers. The use of terms such as Uruk, Uruk expansion or even Urukeans rather than Sumer, Sumerian expansion or Sumerians is in itself interesting, as it clearly indicates that the 'Sumerian question' is no longer topical in archaeological studies; but we should here keep in mind that according to the commonly shared assumption, Uruk people were Sumerians ... This expansion is considered to have been demonstrated by the presence of buildings, potteries and administrative items similar or even identical to those found at the same period in lower Mesopotamia or in 'Sumerian' Susiana, as these monuments and objects are reputed to have first been used in the Sumerian lowlands: 'artifacts and indeed entire settlements which look as though they have been transported on a magic carpet from South Mesopotamia' (Postgate 2002, p. v). Sites have been classified according to the extent that 'southern' elements are present within the 'local' substratum, which is usually called Late Chalcolithic and characterized by buff 'chaff-faced' wares. It ranges from fully Uruk sites considered as 'colonies' to Uruk 'enclaves' on Late Chalcolithic sites, sites displaying Uruk influence in their material culture and non influenced ones, with rather different understanding of such configurations according to various authors. A summary of these approaches can be found in Rothman (2001), Postgate (2002) or Butterlin (2002). The question of veritable colonies has been raised from the discovery of the complete plan of a small city at Habuba Kabira on the right bank of the Euphrates in Syria (Strommenger 1980). It was built *ex-nihilo* and had a short duration (some two centuries) before being abandoned and never resettled. It had a double curtain wall with regularly spaced towers, several monumental city gates, a network of perpendicular streets and lanes, and an 'acropolis' with large tripartite buildings consisting of rectangular halls with lateral rooms. Although it is the first town plan known in the history of mankind, there has been no claim that Habuba Kabira is the place where urbanism was born, and this was certainly wise. The date of the foundation of Habuba Kabira itself remains disputed. Two clay hollow balls and ten numeral tablets were found there in private houses, as with the case of Susa. If we follow the scenario proposed for the beginning of writing at Susa, this would indicate a contemporaneity with level 18 of the acropolis where clay hollow balls and numeral tablets are present whilst only tablets remain in the following level 17 (Le Brun and Vallat 1978), and assuming that numeral tablets precede the development of proper writing, Habuba Kabira should be dated before period IV at Uruk, that is around 3600–3400 BC. Jean-Jacques Glassner (2000, p. 62–63), discussing the nature of numeral notations themselves, convincingly demonstrates that such tablets precede those of Uruk IV. Advocates of the Uruk expansion hypothesis however do not hesitate to consider that the use of numeral tablets only at Habuba Kabira or nearby Jebel Aruda (13 tablets found) is linked to the provincial status of the sites compared with the developments that were taking place in the centre and date it around 3400–3200 BC, a date that seems confirmed by radiocarbon. There are obvious risks of circular reasoning, but the diffusionist model is such that the latest date is now generally accepted.

The model of Uruk trading posts appearing as enclaves in local sites, ethnically and linguistically different, has been advocated to interpret the discovery of sealings and tablets both in Iran and northern Mesopotamia. This is for instance the case of Godin Tepe in the Kangavar valley of northern Luristan where a walled area that yield some Uruk-like pottery and 42 numeral tablets has been interpreted as the trade post of Uruk merchants originating from Susa (Weiss and Young 1975). The presence of a surrounding wall, the final destruction of the area by fire, suggested relations of dominance between the dwellers of the outpost and the surrounding local population. A different case has recently been raised with a series of contributions about the small site of Hacinebi published in *Paléorient* (1999). According to the excavators, the foreigners settled in the enclave traded peacefully with the local people, and various attempts made to study the relations between the two ethnical groups, on the basis of archaeological material, notably bringing out differences in lifestyle (food, pottery), lead to a rather unbalanced conclusion: 'Both Anatolians and Mesopotamians raised their own crops, slaughtered their own animals, made their own pottery, wove their own clothes, and stored their own goods' (Stein 2002, p. 153). 'There is absolutely no evidence to suggest that the Mesopotamians were politically, socially or economically dominant' (*ibid.*). It is however suggested elsewhere that the local elite was emulated by the foreigners, a factor supposed to explain acculturation throughout the whole northern Mesopotamia (Stein 1999, p. 12–13). We may suppose that such an apartheid can also be extended to language! But language is never mentioned and the term Sumerian never used, while it is admitted that 'ethnicity is not a biological phenomenon, but instead a social construct that is created and maintained through a variety of conscious or unconscious behaviors — such as the use of specific styles of material culture' (*ibid.* p. 21). Considering the classical definitions of ethnicity, the absence of any reference to language is surprising, and significant: ethnicity is back from exile, but not so much as to include speculations on language.

These views have recently been challenged by discoveries at Tell Hamoukar, some 200 km eastwards. By c. 3500 BC, the town was already engaged in a process of evolution towards complexity similar to what is supposed to have taken place in the south. To some extent the excavators recognized that although regionalized in various assemblages, the former Ubaidian *koiné* was moving at a similar pace, from a similar background. Administrative devices like hollow clay balls and cylinder seals were already in use, whilst tripartite buildings with central hall were used for feastings or redistribution of goods. Later on however, a battle raged in the same area, witnessed by hundreds of sling bullets, indicating that the site had undergone heavy 'bombardment' and eventually collapsed in an ensuing fire, this being the earliest evidence for large scale organized warfare according to the excavators. Dug into the destruction debris that covered the buildings excavated during the 2005 season were numerous large pits that contained a vast amount of Uruk pottery from the south. The settlement of the southerners was apparently less peaceful than advocated in the case of Hacinebi. In other words, social evolution towards complexity in the north may have been the accomplishment of local communities, but at some time Uruk people came to control the area, imposing their own material culture.

Movements of people never ceased in these border areas, and the last one that we would like to mention here came from the North. It is best documented by the excavations of Arslantepe in the Euphrates valley, north of the Turkish border. The site had gone through a phase of Uruk 'influence' or local evolution towards complexity, including the use of cylinder seals and hollow clay balls, and belongs to the same broad cultural complex as Hamoukar or Hacinebi. At some time around 3000 BC, the architecture and the pottery completely changed, houses being made of wooden frames and *pisé* instead of the previous mud bricks, while black or red burnished pottery with completely new shapes replaced the former 'Uruk like' and local 'chaff-faced ware' vessels. To this period belongs the rich burial of a warrior containing an array of copper weapons, swords, daggers and spears. All archaeologists agree to link these objects and in particular the pottery with those found in Transcaucasia, and notably with what is known as the Early Kura-Arax culture, which extended over parts of Georgia, Armenia, northern Turkey and Azerbaijan, even displaying relations with the Early Bronze Age sites of Kuban, north of the Caucasus Mountains. Such a cultural assemblage was to characterize the highlands of eastern Anatolia for the next centuries to come.

What conclusions can be drawn from these complex situations as far as languages are concerned? To start with the simplest, we should imagine that if Habuba Kabira or Jebel Aruda were colonies from the south, and if as suggested by some authors, these colonies had cultivation as their primary aim (Frangipane 1996, p. 213), the newcomers may have formed a 'Sumerian' speaking enclave in the area, whose local language(s) is/are unknown to us. We may also think that part of the colonists sent there were people displaced from other areas, why not Elamites? Further north, we may imagine that the Uruk people of trading posts like Hacinebi were Sumerians with their families, and such would have been part of the people who settled at Tell Hamoukar after the battle that took place around 3500 BC, if it ever happened.

In these areas, the local background displays a material culture called 'Late Chalcolithic', and is characterized by the 'chaff faced ware', which extended from the Gulf of Cilicia on the Mediterranean coast to the upper valley of the Tigris River. Some eight centuries later, in the archaic texts of Fara, northern Mesopotamia is named as the land of the Subareans (*Shubur*), and we may hypothesize that the northern piedmonts of Mesopotamia were the land of the Subareans (also called *Subartu*)[25]. Should we therefore suggest that the 'Chaff wares' which followed the abandon of the Ubaid painted potteries are linked to the Subareans, and that these Subareans were moving towards social complexity like the southerners? And as we can hypothesize that people of *Shubur* were not Sumerians, what was their language? Rubio (2006, note 106) mentions that 'although the majority of anthroponyms associated with Subartu are Hurrian, the label 'Subarean' (or 'Subartean') appears in some lexical lists along with words that are neither Akkadian nor Sumerian'. The earliest known written documents in the Syrian Djezireh have been found at Tell Beydar, ancient *Nabada*, and are dated around 2500 BC. They appear written in an archaic form of Akkadian and we may believe that local people at that time spoke an Old-Semitic language, but the situation could be much more complex. Phenomena of alloglottography have been suggested and we may read documents written in this area as Akkadian texts although 'we are very aware that they may have been dictated and read out in local languages that would have been very different' (Cooper 2006, p. 85 commenting on Rubio 2006)[26]. There is at least one more element. It is a tantalizing hypothesis that suggests that the appearance of a completely new material culture around 3000 BC at Arslantepe but also in the Amuq plain near the mouth of the Orontes river in the Mediterranean Sea or even southwards in Upper Galilea (the so-called Khirbet Kerak ware) is linked to a new people, and considering the links of this material culture with Transcaucasia and the historical importance later taken by the Hurrians in this area, this would suggest that these new people were the Hurrians. There is however no Hurrian name in the dozens of personal names recovered in the administrative documents of Beydar, that all appear to be of a Semitic origin.

Let us speculate about this situation. As already noted, the names of most Sumerian towns and Mesopotamian rivers have no Sumerian etymology, but the former present some formal analogy with the names of northern cities (Garelli 1969, p. 245), and one may wonder if those people of *Shubur* could have been linked in some way to the matter, reviving the old idea of André Parrot quoted at the beginning of this paper. Michalowski (2006, p. 161–163) has recently suggested a spread of Semitic languages in northern Syria and Mesopotamia, transforming Hattic (to the north) and Sumerian (to the south) into residual linguistic niches.[27] Was there once an area of contact between Hattic[28] and Sumerian? Were the people of the 'Late Chalcolithic cultures' of the Syro-Anatolian borderlands speaking Hattic related language, or already for part of them a Semitic one? These are so many questions without answers.

We raise these ideas in order to end with a final problem. By the 24th century BC, Hurrian names, which are absent a century earlier from Tell Beydar, appear in rather large number in the Akkadian texts recovered at Tell Chagar Bazar in the Djezireh and slightly later we know about *Atalshen*, *endan* of *Urkish*, from a bronze tablet written in Akkadian. *Atalshen* is a Hurrian name, *endan* is the royal Hurrian title and *Urkish* is identified with modern Tell Mozan immediately south of the Turkish border in the Djezireh, where recent excavations yield hundreds of clay sealings of another Hurrian king. Hurrian became a major linguistic group of the Syro-Anatolian borderlands in the 2nd millennium BC, notably with the empire of Mitanni that ruled from the Mediterranean Sea to Assyria between the 16th and the 13th centuries BC. The Taurus mountains under Hurrian control since the late 4th millennium BC are rich in minerals, particularly copper, and it is interesting to note that the

Sumerian words for copper and bronze have no Sumerian etymology (Edzard in Sollberger 1960, p. 313), whilst the Sumerian word for coppersmith, *ta/ ibira*, is usually considered as Hurrian in origin. This is in agreement with the idea that Sumerians tried to control in a way or another their supply in mineral resources from the north, and among them copper, and illustrates some form of direct or indirect contact on the occasion of historical events that we suspect, but cannot demonstrate that some centuries before, history began in Sumer.

6 Concluding remarks

Questioning language through archaeology is obviously, and by definition, an impossible task. What we attempted to do here was only to inquire as to how archaeology can contribute to the question, in addition to insights gained from textual and linguistic evidence. Archaeologists work with 'cultures' that are at best very general abstractions mostly constructed using mundane material data. They have been trained to distinguish cultures conceived as assemblages of items, amongst which pottery is the principal one, because it is obviously related to identity as far as shapes, decoration and fabric are concerned, and because these criteria may change rather quickly, allowing the creation of chronologically or spatially significant subgroups. On the other hand, they also became aware that pots, like languages, are not people, although they are to some extent related. The entire question therefore concerns this relation: on the basis of what type of data can we move from one domain to another? Are there preferential ways for doing it? Or is it forever an insuperable challenge?

Recent advances in analytical techniques have allowed archaeology to investigate various fields connected with identity, such as technological, residential or culinary habits (Stein 1999, for example). The reconstruction of Colin Renfrew, associating the diffusion of Indo-European languages with that of agriculture, is among such attempts; but we may also consider that most techniques may penetrate in many societies, being adapted or re-interpreted according to their 'milieu intérieur' (to keep Leroi Gourhan's terminology) and that such an adoption may or may not be associated with partial adoption of words from other tongues. In the context of philological reconstructions, mainly based on vocabulary lists (the bilingual Sumerian-Akkadian or Hittite-Hattic for instance), there has been a constant temptation to associate new languages or new people with the coming of new techniques. The fact that most of the agricultural terms and part of those linked to handicrafts used by Sumerians have no Sumerian etymology (i.e. no etymology in Sumerian as it has been rebuilt from lexical texts) has been used to support the idea that

Sumerians were an allochtonous population, and it is significant that this idea, apparently still commonly accepted 30 years ago, has almost disappeared from recent syntheses where Sumerians are considered as direct descendants of the 'Urukeans' of the 4th millennium BC (who themselves apparently wrote in Sumerian if we accept the presence of this language in the archaic texts of Uruk). A soft and silent approbation, almost never discussed, has replaced the former consensus on a foreign origin of Sumerians and their language, based on the same very vague assumptions. Another commonly used argument for changes in languages is the name of places, rivers, mountains and even towns. We have seen that philologists still accept that many of these are not Sumerian, and we have speculated on the idea of a possible northern origin, obviously giving rise to very weak conclusions: Subarean may have once existed, but we do not know anything about it. Was there any relation with a Proto-Hattic? At least these regions are now under dense archaeological investigations, and a better knowledge of their results may in the future be of interest if, to paraphrase a sentence of Pearce quoted above 'after many years in archaeological exile, ancient languages are resurfacing'. The proposal of Michalowski according to whom a 'Semitic spread' has once separated Sumerian from these northern languages may be an interesting hypothesis to be considered.

In a recent summary of French ancient studies (Rickal in Leclant 2005, p. 770) we can read the following: 'Au IVe millénaire av. J.-C., les Égyptiens disposaient vraisemblablement déjà d'un langage oral élaboré'[29]. Obviously nobody would oppose this, but it would certainly be difficult to go further[30]. We will never know what was the actual language of human communities before writing, as we continue to ignore most of it during the millennia that followed this invention. In a beautiful page of his classical book on Ancient Mesopotamia, L. Oppenheim (1964) evoked the populations of dropouts, land dispossessed peasants, debtors escaping creditors, deserters and fugitive slaves that populated vacuums between Early State territories: can we ever imagine their languages, and the contribution of these languages to those of the general population? Obviously not, but they existed. We have limited our comments to large and abstract entities, either cultural or technical, trying to link them to similarly wide linguistic entities that may themselves be mere abstractions, obvious oversimplifications. However, if our goal as archaeologists or as historians is to understand ancient societies, can we work whilst ignoring the importance of languages in the life of any society? Don't we risk in so doing to open an easy path to uncontrolled speculation based on common sense, and therefore to the most deeply felt prejudices that we would like to denounce? This paper would have reached its goal if it could be a step in a dialogue, if not a synthesis, between culture (as rebuilt by archaeologists) and languages (as rebuilt by philologists). Considering the complexities of history already by the 4th millennium BC in the Ancient Orient and the state of the art on physical anthropology in these regions, there may be a long way to go until genetics can add to the picture.

Notes

1 The Sumerian term is KI.EN-GI, the native country, EME-GI being the Sumerian language.

2 I found it on http://www.chechnyafree.ru/index, an internet site obviously sponsored by the Government of the Russian federation. My italics.

3 '... once linguistics and [physical] anthropology, which provide good continuous series and robust ensembles in their comparative aspects, are superimposed on an historical framework, with dates, places and names of peoples, they become hazardous and discontinuous.'

4 I found a reproduction of Huet's map in *La creation de l'homme et les premiers âges de l'humanité* by Henri du Cleuziou, Marpon and Flammarion, Paris 1887, fig. 77. It has since been reproduced by Huot (1989, p. 59).

5 The relations between Semitic and Sumerian have been widely studied, and we will not refer to them here. For recent literature see Rubio (2006), Cooper (1999, 2006), Woods (2006) or Michalowski (2006).

6 Jules Oppert (1825–1905) was, with Edward Hincks and Henry Rawlinson, one of the decipherers of cuneiform writing. He suggested as soon as 1854 that a non Semitic language coexisted with Assyrian and Babylonian in the Cuneiform documents. He is also the author of a Sanskrit grammar.

7 '... in Mesopotamia, the Sumerians found themselves faced with a civilisation that was already well elaborated and solidly integrated. Their dynamism allowed them to impose themselves without discussion.'

8 Apart from being the director of Uruk excavations, director of the Baghdad Museum (1931–1934) and then advisor to the first Iraqi director (1934–1939), Julius Jordan, played a key role in the Nazi-led insurrection against the Iraqi government in 1941.

9 'They came from elsewhere, most probably from the east, probably from Iran'. Here and above, we quote André Parrot (1901–1980) from his article 'Sumer' in the *Encyclopaedia Universalis*, 1985 edition, vol. 17, p. 399–403, but the article itself was already present in the earlier versions. It can still be found unchanged in the electronic version of 2006.

10 'If, as is my own case, one trusts an old local myth, that of the Seven Wise Men, they must have arrived in southern Mesopotamia ... from the sea ... perhaps by coming up the Iranian coastline of the Persian Gulf'.

11 'the Sumerian civilisation is the result of a slow evolution *in situ*, of communities that occupied this difficult country since millennia. At a certain moment of this evolution, these communities endowed themselves with a tool, writing, which allowed them to note down a language that they had practiced for a long time without having written it. ... [the Sumerian people] had formed itself well before and *in situ* ... The crystallisation of the elements that composed this civilisation had not needed any foreign contributions in order to produce itself, and can be explained to a great extent without recourse to mythical invasions.'

12 '... it would probably be appropriate to abandon the hypothesis ... which is nothing more than a pure product of imagination, of an invasion of Sumerian chieftains who would have imposed themselves as princes in certain small villages'.

13 In a beautiful paper entitled 'Silence in the Darkness', the Austrian ethnographer Walter Dostal shows how the views of the Nazi theoreticians were widely shared amongst the social and physical anthropologists of that time, particularly in archaeology where the teaching of Gustav Kossina was dominant.

14 'When one speaks of the migration of Mongols, one sees at the same time an anthropological type, a language, myths and objects. Without claiming that this point of view should be always erroneous, one can say that the majority of cases that have been studied do not lend themselves to such views.'

15 In reference to the previous note, it is interesting to note that T.J. Arne is rather careful in his conclusions whilst Sven Hedin (1865–1952), a famous traveler and director of the Archaeological expedition to the North Western provinces of China, that sponsored the excavations, was a committed Nazi during WWII. He was made *doctor honoris causa* of the Ludwig-Maximilian University of Munich in 1943. Ernst Schäffer who led the famous SS Schäffer to Tibet in 1938–1939 had created a *Sven Hedin Institut für Innerasienforschung* which became one of the most important ones of the SS Ahnenerbe. American excavations, and most specially Tepe Hissar, were launched by Ernst Herzfeld, director of the Persian Expedition of the Oriental Institute of Chicago, that had been until 1931 professor of oriental archaeology in Berlin University. He certainly did not share Hedin's admiration for the Nazis, but basic ideas on ancient societies were not that different.

16 'it is thus probable that this civilisation of the plain of Gorgan ... was prey to raids from these nomads, who have never ceased to worry sedentary populations up to the present day ... Was it not already these Indo-Europeans who soon afterwards would appear in numerous sectors of the oriental world?'

17 The presence of a zero may be surprising, but the earlier levels found at Tell el-'Oueili in the 1980s clearly predate the Ubaid 1 levels of Eridu. There may even be a hiatus between both.

18 Its use has often been advocated in cases where recent technical studies have demonstrated that it was not involved, a strong indication that social and economic change rather than ethnic change was considered as an explanation of pottery change.

19 Jacques de Morgan was an engineer trained at the École des Mines in Paris and he explicitly employed a mining technique with tunnels, open trenches, and pits. The pinnacle shaped 'témoin de Morgan' is all that remains of thousands and thousands of cubic metres of archaeological soils and mud bricks. Ironically, it appears as the physical opposite of the deep sounding at Uruk. They together constitute the main, and admittedly very poor, chronological data on which to ground our reconstruction of the origins of State and writing in two of the most important sites.

20 But according to the reservations expressed by Nissen, it would be risky to decide to which level of the Uruk 'sequence' the carefully documented sequence established by Alain Le Brun can be compared.

21 These very distinctive items of 4th millennium BC Mesopotamian cultures, also named 'bullae', are 2–3 inches in diameter. They contain small objects named tokens that are considered as representing quantities of various commodities, and bear outside the imprints of cylinder seals. A common interpretation is that they travelled with the commodities represented by the tokens, thus allowing control at reception. In the scenario proposed by Le Brun and Vallat (1978), these tokens were later represented on the bullae themselves (Susa level 18). With a 'standardization' of these numeral representations, the inside tokens became useless, and the bullae were abandoned for tablets only bearing numerals and seal imprints (level 17).

22 Recent work on Susa material has however brought to light at least one numeral tablet and one fragment with obvious proto-Elamite signs in level 17, suggesting a possibly different scenario.

23 We do not know of any Mahrashi interpreter, but from that same period comes the famous seal of Shu-Ilishu (an Akkadian name), translator of Melluha language (the Indus valley), presently in the Louvre Museum.

24 An undated inscription of four proto-Elamite like signs has been found at Shahdad, a large almost unexcavated site on the edge of the Lut desert, north of the modern city of Bam.

25 This is now the title of a series of books devoted to these areas: *Subartu*.

26 According to Rubio (2005, p. 41), partial or total alloglottography was not particularly unusual in the ancient Near East and apparently Sumerian texts were actually read in Semitic already by 2400 BC.

27 Some authors (Bauer 1998 quoted by Michalowski 2005, p. 161) have tried to reconstruct 'proto-Tigridian' or 'proto-Euphratean' tongues that served as a substrate for Sumerian, inferring them from lexical elements deemed as 'non Sumerian', and among them names of places and rivers.

28 Hattic is our modern denomination for the land of Hatti, after which the Indo-European speaking Hittites named their country. We know it from bilingual texts or Hattic texts written in cuneiform during the Hittite rule. Some authors have also discussed the possibility of a pre-Hattian population (Kavtaradze 2004, p. 553). Our use of the term Hattic is therefore maybe an oversimplification.

29 'In the IVth millenium before Jesus Christ, the Egyptians already probably disposed of an elaborated spoken language'.

30 Some researchers privately entertain the possibility that sounds once made or pronounced in enclosed spaces, such as caves, may have been 'recorded' by various material traps and may one day be recovered. A French Nobel Prize winner in Physics (Georges Charpak) once suggested that throwing pottery on the fast wheel may have recorded sounds in micro grooves preserved in clay. To some extent the 'archive of paradise' containing the first writing and the first languages of the first nation in the world imagined in the 18th century BC by Johannes Gottfried Herder (Olender 1989) may come back one day as a result of high tech studies. But this is obviously not on the agenda for the next decades …

References

Algaze, G. (1993) *The Uruk World System, the Dynamics of Expansion of the Early Mesopotamian Civilization.* Chicago, Chicago University Press.

Alster, B. (1983) Dilmun, Bahrain and the alleged paradise in Sumerian myth and literature. New studies in the archaeology and early history of Bahraïn, edited by Potts, D. T., pp. 39–74. *Berliner Beiträge zum Vorderen Orient 2.* Berlin, Riemer, D.

Ammermann, A. J. and Cavalli-Sforza, L. L. (1984) *The Neolithic Transition and the Genetics in Europe.* New Jersey, Princeton University Press.

Arne, T. J. (1945) Excavations at Shah Tepe, Iran. Reports from the Scientific Expedition to the North Western Provinces of China vol. 27. Stockholm.

Bottero, J. (1996) Religiosité et raison en Mésopotamie. *L'Orient Ancien et Nous*, edited by Bottero, J., Herrenschmidt, C. and Vernant, J.-P., pp. 17–91. Paris, Hachette.

Butterlin, P. (2002) *Les Temps Proto-Urbains de Mésopotamie, Contacts et Acculturation à l'époque d'Uruk au Moyen-Orient*. Paris, CNRS éditions.

Cleuziou, S. and Tosi, M. (1994) Black boats of Magan. Some thoughts on bronze-age water transport in Oman and beyond from the impressed bitumen slabs of Ra's al-Junayz. *South Asian Archaeology 1993*, edited by Parpola, A. and Koskikallio, P., pp. 745–761. vol. II, Suomalaisen Tiedakatemian Toimituksia ser B, tom 271. Helsinki, Suomalainen Tiedakatemia.

Cooper, J. S. (1973) Sumerian and Akkadian in Sumer and Akkad. *Orientalia* n.s. 42:239–246.

Cooper, J. S. (1999) Sumerian and semitic writing in most ancient Mesopotamia. *Languages and Cultures in Contact at the Crossroads of Civilizations in the Syro-Mesopotamian Realm*, edited by Van Lerberghe, K. and Voet, G., pp. 61–77, Orientalia Lovaniensia Analecta 96. Leuven, Peeters.

Cooper, J. S. (2006) Response for the first session: origins, function, adaptation, survival. *Margins of Writing, Origins of Cultures*, edited by Sanders, S. L., pp. 83–90. Oriental Institute Seminars 2. Chicago, The Oriental Institute.

Deshayes, J. (1968) Tureng Tepe et la plaine de Gorgan à l'âge du Bronze. *Archaeologia Viva* 1:35–41.

Deshayes, J. (1975) Les fouilles récentes de Tureng Tepe: la terrasse haute de la fin du IIIe millénaire. *Comptes Rendus de l'Académie des Inscriptions et Belles Lettres* novembre-décembre 1975:522–530.

Dietler, M. and Herbich, I. (1994) Habitus et reproduction sociale des techniques, l'intelligence du style en archéologie et en ethno-archéologie. *De la Préhistoire aux Missiles Balistiques. L'Intelligence Sociale des Techniques,* edited by Latour, B. and Lemonnier, P., pp. 187–201. Paris, La découverte.

Fairservis, W. A. (1992) *The Harappan Civilisation and its Writing: a Model for the Decipherment of the Indus Script*. Leyden, Brill, E. J.

Forest, J.-D. (1996) *Mésopotamie: la Naissance de l'Etat*. Paris, Editions Paris Méditerranée.

Frangipane, M. (1996) *La nascita dello stato nel Vicino Oriente.* Quadrante 85. Rome and Bari, Laterza.

Garelli, P. (1969) *Le Proche Orient asiatique, des origines aux peuples de la mer.* Nouvelle Clio, l'Histoire et ses Problèmes 2. Paris, Presses Universitaires de France.

Glassner, J.-J. (2000) *Cunéiforme,* L'univers Historique. Paris, Editions du Seuil.

Glassner, J.-J. (2002) Dilmun et Magan: le peuplement; l'organisation politique, la question des Amorrites et la place de l'écriture, le point de vue de l'assyriologue. *Essays in the Late Prehistory of the Arabian Peninsula,* edited by Cleuziou, S., Tosi, M. and Zarins, J. Rome, Serie Orientale Roma XCIII. IsIAO.

Hill, J. N. (1968) Broken K Pueblo: patterns of form and function. *New Perspectives in Archeology,* edited by Binford, S. R. and Binford, L. R., pp. 103–142. Chicago, Aldine.

Hodder, I. (1982) *Symbols in Action, Ethnoarchaeological Studies of Material Culture.* Cambridge, Cambridge University Press.

Huot, J.-L. (1989) *Les Sumériens*. Paris, Errance.

Kavtaradze, G. L. (2004) The chronology of the Caucasus during the Early Metal Age, observations from central Trans-Caucasus. *A View from the Highlands, Archaeological Studies in Honour of Charles Burney*, edited by Sagona, A., pp. 532–556, Ancient Near Eastern Studies. Leuwen, Peeters.

Kramer, S. N. (1956) *History begins at Sumer*. Philadelphia, University of Pennsylvania Press.

Lambeck, K. (1996) Shoreline reconstruction for the Persian Gulf since the last glacial maximum. *Earth and Planetary Science Letters* 142:43–57.

Lamberg-Karlovsky, C. C. (2002) Archaeology and language: the Indo-Iranians. *Current Anthropology* 43(1):63–88.

Landsberger, B. (1943) Die Sumerer. *Ankara Universitesi, Dil ve Tarih Geografia Fakültesi Dergisi* 1:97–102.

Le Brun, A. and Vallat, F. (1978) L'origine de l'écriture à Suse. *Cahiers de la DAFI*, vol. 8:11–59. Paris, Gueuthner.

Leclant, J. (dir.) (2005) *Dictionnaire de l'Antiquité*. Paris, Presses Universitaires de France.

Leroi-Gourhan, A. (1945*) Evolution et Techniques: Milieu et Techniques*. Paris, Albin Michel.

Lieberman, S. J. (1977) *The Sumerian Loanwords in Old Babylonian Akkadian 1: Prolegomena and Evidence*. Missoula, Scholar Press.

Mallory, J. P. (1997) BMAC. *Encyclopedia of Indo-European Culture*, edited by Adams, D. Q. and Mallory, J. P. Fitzroy-Dearborn. London and Chicago.

Masry, A. H. (1974) *Prehistory in Northeastern Arabia, the problem of inter-regional interaction.* Field Research Projects. Miami, Coconut Grove.

Michalowski, P. (1999) Sumer Dreams of Subartu: Politics and the Geographical Imagination Languages and Cultures in Contact, *At the Crossroads of Civilizations in the Syro-Mesopotamian Realm*, edited by Van Lerberghe, K. and Voet, G., pp. 305–315, Orientalia lovaniensa Analecta 96. Leuven, Peeters.

Michalowski, P. (2006) The lives of Sumerian language. Margins of writing, origins of cultures, edited by Sanders, S. L., pp. 159–184, *Oriental Institute Seminars 2*. Chicago, The Oriental Institute.

Nissen, H. J. (2002) Uruk: key site of the period and key site of the problem. *Artefacts of complexity. Tracking Uruk in the Near East*, edited by Postgate, J. N., pp. 1–16. Iraq Archaeological Reports 5. British School of Archaeology in Iraq, Warminster, Aris and Phillips.

Nissen, H. J., Damerow, P. and Englund, R. K. (1993) *Archaic Bookkeeping: Early Writing and Techniques of Economic Administration in the Ancient Near East*. Chicago, Chicago University Press.

Oates, J., Davidson, T., Kamilli, D. and McKerrel, H. (1977) Seafaring merchants of Ur? *Antiquity* 203:221–234.

Olender, M. (1988) *Les Langues du Paradis. Aryens et Sémites: un Couple Providentiel*. Paris, Gallimard-Le Seuil.

Oppenheim, A. L. (1964) *Ancient Mesopotamia: Portrait of a Dead Civilization*. Chicago, University of Chicago Press.

Pearce, J. (1999) Investigating ethnicity at Hacinebi: ceramic perspectives on style and behavior in 4th millennium Mesopotamian-Anatolian interaction. *Paléorient* 25(1):35–42.

Pétrequin, P. (1993) North wind, south wind. Neolithic technical choices in the Jura Mountains, 3700–2400 BC. *Technological Choices, Transformations in Material Cultures since the Neolithic*, edited by Lemonnier, P., pp. 36–76. London, Routledge.

Pirazzoli, P. A. (1991) *World Atlas of Holocene Sea-Level Changes*. Amsterdam, Elsevier.

Poly, J.-P. (1984) Guinefort et les Faramans des Dombes. Un exemple d'anthropologie médiévale. *Raison Présente* 69:103–128.

Postgate, J. N. (ed.) (2002) *Artefacts of Complexity. Tracking the Uruk in the Near East 5*. Iraq Archaeological Reports 5, British School of Archaeology in Iraq, Warminster, Aris and Phillips.

Rostovtzeff, M. I. (1920) The Sumerian Treasure of Asterabad. *Journal of Egyptian Archaeology* 6:4–27.

Rothman, M. S. (ed.) (2001) *Uruk Mesopotamia and its Neighbours*. School of American Research Press, Santa Fe.

Rubio, G. (2006) Writing in another tongue: alloglottgraphy in the Ancient Near East. *Margins of writing, origins of cultures*, edited by Sanders, S. L., pp. 67–82. Oriental Institute Seminars 2. Chicago, The Oriental Institute.

Safar, F. and Lloyd, S. (1950) Eridu: a preliminary report on the third season's excavations, 1948–1949, *Sumer* 6:27–38.

Sanlaville, P. (1989) Considérations sur l'évolution de la basse Mésopotamie au cours des derniers millénaires. *Paléorient* 15(2):1–28.

Schmidt, E. F. (1937) *Excavations at Tepe Hissar, Damghan*. Philadelphia, University of Pennsylvania Press.

Sollberger, E. (1960) Aspects du Contact Suméro-Akkadien. *Genava* n.s. 8:241–314.

Spar, I. (2003) The Mesopotamian legacy: origins of the genesis tradition. *Art of the First Cities. The Third Millennium B.C. from the Mediterrannean to the Indus*, edited by Aruz, J., pp. 485–494. New Haven and London, The Metropolitan Museum of Art, New York and Yale University Press.

Stein, G. J. (1999) Material culture and social identity: the evidence for a 4th millennium BC Mesopotamian Uruk colony at Hacinebi, Turkey. *Paléorient* 25(1):11–22.

Stein, G. J. (2002) The Uruk expansion in Anatolia: a Mesopotamian colony and its indigenous host community at Hacinebi, Turkey. *Artefacts of complexity. Tracking the Uruk in the Near East*, edited by Postgate, J. N., pp. 149–172. Iraq Archaeological Reports 5. British School of Archaeology in Iraq, Warminster, Aris and Phillips.

Strommenger, E. (1980) *Habuba Kabira, eine Stadt vor 5000 Jahren.* Mainz, Von Zabern, P.

Thureau Dangin, F. (1905) *Les Inscriptions de Sumer et d'Akkad.* Paris.

Vallat, F. (1980) Suse et l'Elam *Mémoires n° 1.* Paris, ERC.

Van der Leeuw, S. E. (1993) Variation, variability and explanation in pottery studies. *Ceramic Ethnoarchaeology*, edited by Longacre, W. A., pp. 11–39. Tucson, University of Arizona Press.

Weiss, H. and Young, T. C. (1975) The merchants of Susa: godin V and the plateau-lowlands relations in the late fourth millennium BC. *Iran XIII*: 1–17.

Woods, C. (2006) Bilingualism, scribal learning, and the death of Sumerian. *Margins of writing, origins of cultures*, pp. 91–120, edited by Sanders, S. L. Oriental Institute Seminars 2. Chicago, The Oriental Institute.

Wright, H. T. and Johnson, G. L. (1975) Population, exchange and early state formation in southern Iran. *American Anthropologist* 77:267–289.

Wulsin, F. R. (1932) *Excavations at Tureng Tepe near Asterabad.* Supplement to the Bulletin of the American Institute for Persian Art and Archaeology vol. 2 n° 1. Philadelphia.

Young, T. C. (1965) A comparative ceramic chronology for Western Iran. *Iran* 3:53–86.

Young, T. C. (1967) The Iranian migration into the Zagros. *Iran* 5:11–34.

Index of authors

Index of languages

Index of subjects

www.ingramcontent.com/pod-product-compliance
Lightning Source LLC
LaVergne TN
LVHW010443080826
844660LV00026B/1205

* 9 7 8 1 8 4 5 5 3 5 5 3 7 *